American Heroes
in a Media Age

THE HAMPTON PRESS COMMUNICATION SERIES

Mass Communications and Journalism
Lee Becker, supervisory editor

American Heroes in a Media Age
 Susan J. Drucker and Robert S. Cathcart (eds.)

Media, Sex and the Adolescent
 Bradley S. Greenberg, Jane D. Brown and Nancy Buerkel-Rothfuss

forthcoming

Magazine-Made America: The Cultural Transformation of the Post War Periodical
 David Abramson

American Heroes in a Media Age

edited by
Susan J. Drucker
Hofstra University

Robert S. Cathcart
Queens College

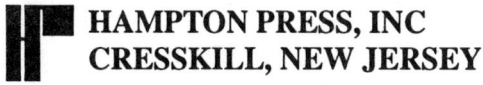
HAMPTON PRESS, INC
CRESSKILL, NEW JERSEY

Copyright © 1994 by Hampton Press, Inc.

All rights reserved. No part of this publication may be reproduced, stored in a retrieval system, or transmitted in any form or by any means, electronic, mechanical, photocopying, microfilming, recording, or otherwise, without permission of the publisher.

Printed in the United States of America

Library of Congress Cataloging-in-Publication Data

American heroes in a media age / edited by Susan J. Drucker, Robert S. Cathcart.
    p. cm. -- (Hampton Press communication series. Mass communications and journalism)
    Includes bibliographical references and indexes.
    ISBN 1-881303-19-5. -- ISBN 1-881303-20-9 (pbk.)
    1. Heroes--United States--History--20th century. 2. Popular culture--United States--History--20th century. 3. Celebrities--United States--History--20th century. I. Drucker, Susan J. II. Cathcart, Robert S. III. Series.
E169.04.A5183   1994
973--dc20   94-19788
                                                                                    CIP

Hampton Press, Inc.
23 Broadway
Cresskill, NJ 07626

Contents

1. The Hero as a Communication Phenomenon
   Susan Drucker and Robert S. Cathcart 1

HEROES, CELEBRITIES AND THE MEDIA

2. Heroes: A Communication Perspective
   Lance Strate 15

3. Are Heroes Always Men?
   Joan M. Fayer 24

4. From Hero to Celebrity: The Media Connection
   Robert S. Cathcart 36

5. The Wrinkle Theory: The Deconsecration of the Hero
   Gary Gumpert 47

6. The Life and Death of Media Friends: New Genres of Intimacy and Mourning
   Joshua Meyrowitz 62

7. The Mediated Sports Hero
   Susan J. Drucker 82

THE MAKING OF MODERN HEROES

8. The Making of a Journalistic Celebrity, 1963
   Barbie Zelizer 97

9. Autobiography, Cultural Mythology and the Modern Hero
   David Bryan McLennan 111

10. Iacocca: Chrysler's Mass-Mediated Hero (1979-1983)
    Risë J. Samra 134

CRITICAL THEORIES: PERSPECTIVES ON THE HERO/CELEBRITY

11. Phyllis Schlafly: Great Mother, Heroine, Villain
    Karin J. Billions — 149

12. Rhetorical Devices for Hero Making: Charles Lindbergh and John F. Kennedy
    Carol Wilkie Wallace — 168

13. From Celebrity Entrepreneur to Civic Hero: Donald Trump's Campaign of Self-Transformation
    Brenda Cooper, David Descutner, and Sandra Alspach — 188

14. Theorizing Postmodern Stars: George Michael and Madonna
    Florence Rogers and Michael Real — 203

THE CELEBRITY-HERO CONNECTION

15. From Wild Western Prodigy to the Ageless Wonder: The Mediated Evolution of Nolan Ryan
    Nick Trujillo and Leah R. Vande Berg — 221

16. Jimmy Swaggart as Hero: People of a Narrative Tradition
    Kathaleen Reid — 241

17. The Celebrity and the Fan: A Media Relationship
    Susan J. Drucker and Robert S. Cathcart — 260

18. Who are the Puerto Rican Heroes?: A Cross-Cultural Study
    Joseph Ferri, Joan M. Fayer, and Alma Simounet-Geigel — 270

19. Trying to Learn How to Walk Like the Heroes: Bruce Springsteen, Popular Music, and the Hero/Celebrity
    Thomas Gencarelli — 281

References — 299
Author Index — 323
Subject Index — 329

Preface

> We hear the lamentations
> Through time's corridor resounding;
> We can see revealed before us
> Heroes, martyrs, saints and scholars[1]

Heroes speak of who we were, who we are, and who we would be. The purpose of this volume is to make available to researchers, scholars, and students the findings of current research into the changing role of the hero in American culture. It advances the position that the nature of "hero" and its function in society is a communication phenomenon; thus, the scope and function of hero has been and is being altered by the rapid advance of electronic media.

There is a great deal of concern surrounding changing concepts of "hero" and what those changes portend for the future. A variety of scholars are presently working on this "problem" but to date this body of scholarship had not been brought together in a single focused volume.

This volume is intended for students of communication arts and sciences, popular culture, sociology, political science, journalism, and American literature. We do not provide merely an historical overview of past and present heroes nor is the attempt made to establish a unified theory of "hero." Rather, we have compiled and organized a body of research that develops a focus on the media/communication dimension of "hero" as opposed to an anthropological, historical, or literary approach.

Within these pages we have included explorations into historical developments and traditional definitions of hero along with the status of the traditional hero and theories about the "hero" phenomenon. We have examined its form as myth and ritual, narrative and its societal uses, and the role of communicative media in establishing and perpetuating heroes. Further diverse methodologies suitable for research into the hero phenomenon are provided as are case studies of recent and current American heroes, and the role of media in their rise and demise.

---

[1] Ancient Hebrew meditation, Kol Nidre services.

One popular theme concerning heroes is that of the hero who ventures forth, embarking on a great journey. For the editors, this volume is the end result of an 8-year excursion into thoughts, ideas, literature, interpersonal relationships, organizational challenges, and contract law. There are many to whom we wish to express our appreciation and acknowledge their contributions. The discussion and exchanges furnished by all participants in the original Speech Communication Association seminar held in 1989 were invaluable to this project. In particular, we wish to thank Tracy Shario, Carl Moore, and Roger Wallace for their insights and interest.

Heroes stir up many emotions and with the indulgence of her co-editor, Robert Cathcart, Susan Drucker would like to yield to those. The journey of this volume was launched in a large lecture hall at Queens College in which a favorite professor roused a shy student sitting quietly in the back of the room. That student, would like to thank her colleague, Robert Cathcart, for years of stimulating ideas, discussion, patience, and guidance. For sharing the flame, for scholarly inspiration, for the tour of the edge, for encouragement, support, and even computer expertise she is grateful to Gary Gumpert. During the years of journey to publication it becomes easy to fall into the trap of assuming that the supporters, the cheerleaders in one's life will be there at the finish line. For two cherished and sorely missed friends who are no longer here to buy a copy of this book, Mary Ellen Farrie Mabry and Michael Sadowsky, thank you for our time. To my parents, thank you for showing me that "real" heroes have staying power.

We are indebted to Barbara Bernstein of Hampton Press for her continued and unfaltering support of this project and its editors. Finally, we wish to express our gratitude to all of the contributors who have patiently and loyally joined us on this "heroic quest."

New York S.J.D.
September 1993 R.S.C.

☐☐☐☐☐ **1**

The Hero as a Communication Phenomenon

Susan J. Drucker
Hofstra University

Robert S. Cathcart
Queens College

☐ *At this point in American history it is difficult to escape noticing that there is a plethora of celebrities and a dearth of traditional heroes. Why this is and what it means is the focus of this book. The editors, in this introductory chapter, examine the changing role and place of the hero and how these changes relate to the communicative process of celebrification. They explain, briefly, the connection of the hero and the media of communication from orality to print to modern electronics. They survey some of the issues raised by contemporary critics who believe that the mass media create and destroy celebrities resulting in a permanent alteration of the positive relationship of hero to community. The introductory chapter concludes with an overview of the essays offered in this volume.*

> The very concept of man is bound up with that of the hero. (Brombert, 1969, p.11)
>
> Unhappy the land that needs a hero. (Brecht, 1938, p. 392)
>
> Every account of mythology—unless it reproduces its sources in the original text and in their fragmentary condition . . . must be an interpretation. And every interpretation is conditioned by the degree of receptivity of the contemporary presenter of the material. (Kerényi, 1960, pp. 8-9)
>
> More people know Johnny Carson's image than any other person in the history of the world. (Postman, TV interview, 1985)

Heroes transcend ordinary human qualities embodying the divine, the ideal, the quest, the courageous, the virtuous, the superior. All cultures have heroes, but the hero and the heroic varies from culture to culture and from time to time. What constitutes the heroic and who becomes the hero is a function of cultural priorities and values, and, most significantly, is related to the communication medium utilized for presenting and preserving information about heroes (Cawelti, 1985; Strate, 1985).

The necessity of the hero and the function of the hero has for many decades occupied a prominent place in the research and writings of cultural anthropologists, social psychologists, political scientists, and literary critics (Brombert, 1969; Campbell, 1968b; Carlyle, 1908; Fishwick, 1954, 1985; Wecter, 1941). The hero myth, in particular, has been studied as an important manifestation of the struggle to understand the world, to make order of crisis and chaos, and to bring understanding to the unexplained and unexplainable. Myth analyses have been central in standard works on the hero, such as Thomas Carlyle's *Sartor Resartus: On Heroes and Hero-Worship* (1908), Joseph Campbell's *The Hero With a Thousand Faces* (1968a), Lord Raglan's *The Hero* (1975), and Dorothy Norman's *The Hero: Myth/Image/Symbol* (1990). The hero myth, told and retold, created heroes and has become one of the great basic myths of western culture (Norman, 1990). These myths with their accompanying archetypes, according to mythologist Joseph Campbell (1968a), are significant in understanding "who we are and how we live our lives."

The hero myth, however, is transformed in the telling and retelling, according to the time and place, and, most importantly, by the means of conveying *the story*. The methods of hero creation alter with the changes in narration, "Since the ways in which myths of the heroes are presented change constantly, they provide both miraculous bridges between one era and another and unexpectedly clear markings that distinguish disparate epochs" (Norman, 1990, p. 4).

As Strate points out in Chapter 2, "It is through communication that we come to know our heroes, and consequently, different kinds of communication will result in different kinds of heroes" (p. 15). In today's world, analyzing the creation, form, and function of the hero necessitates an examination of the role of the technological media of communication in the social construction of mythology about heroes as well as the more standard myth analyses. Therefore, central to the studies in this volume is communication about heroes: How is a hero myth made, disseminated, by whom, to whom?

CHANGING NOTIONS OF THE HERO

Since ancient times people have agreed on the importance of heroes as role models for the young, as inspiration for the citizenry, and as containers of cultural myths (Fishwick, 1954; Rushing, 1985; Wecter, 1941). The word *hero* first appeared in print in Homer's *Iliad* (Curtius, 1963). It was a name given to each free man who had participated in the Trojan Wars and *about whom a story could be told* (Arendt, 1958). The development of the hero myth in Homer's *Iliad* and Virgil's *Aeneid* gave the hero a special distinction (Curtius, 1963, p. 42):

> The hero is distinguished by a superabundance of intellectual will and its concentration against instinct. It is this which constitutes his greatness of character. The specific virtue of the hero is self-control. But the hero's will does not rest here, it presses on into power, responsibility, daring.

Until well into the Middle Ages the hero was one who performed brave and noble deeds—in most cases an illustrious warrior. With the advent of print the hero became one who exhibited extraordinary bravery, firmness, or greatness of soul in connection with any pursuit, work, or enterprise (Ong, 1981; Strate, 1985). Of late, however, there has been a growing body of literature decrying the *loss* of "traditional" heroes; some of it claiming that much of the cynicism and alienation in American society is because "we don't have heroes any longer" (Boorstin, 1961). Arthur M. Schlesinger, Jr. decries the loss of the hero; "Today no one bestrides our narrow world like a colossus; we have no giants" (Campbell, 1968, p. 15). Campbell further asserts:

> It is not only that there is no hiding place for the gods from the searching telescope and microscope; there is no such society any more as the gods once supported. . . . The democratic ideal of the self-determining individual, the invention of the power-driven machine, and the development of the scientific method of research, have so transformed human life that the long-inherited timeless universe of symbols has collapsed. (cited in McGinniss, 1990, p. 27)

The search for heroes traditionally led to warriors and eventually to leaders, lovers, wisemen, artists, and authors. Modern heroes are still sought in war, but in the wake of the televised Vietnam War and the videogame war in the Persian Gulf with revelations concerning deaths by friendly fire and "jobs left undone," even General Schwarzkopf may have a difficult time maintaining hero status. Politics, too, offered candidates for "herodom." Currently, however, heroics in politics and leadership have receded in significance as the age of mastering the soundbite and of performing great deeds of glibness and apparent candor on the talk-show circuit have grown in popularity. The political hero, particularly on the order of "Presidential hero," is virtually impossible in the wake of post Watergate-Irangate media scrutiny and with a public that, in opinion polls, reveals a preference for image and personality over action and courage. Burns (1978) argues our present-day political leaders are not the equivalent of heroes:

> While emotional needs in hero and spectator may be deeply involved, no central purpose, no collective intent other than short-run psychic dependency and gratification unites performer and spectator. . . . Idolized heroes are not, then, authentic leaders because no true relationship exists between them and

the spectators—no relationship characterized by deeply held motives, shared goals, rational conflict, *and* lasting influence in the form of change. (p. 248, emphasis in original)

Now, when the national anthem is sung, it is not the politician but the sports figure waiting to take center field, court, or ice who is perceived as a likely hero. The concept of sports hero is arguably an illusion as sports figures today may be said to be performers acting in the process of mediated celebrification. Lacking heroes on earth, the search for the modern hero has taken us into orbit as early astronauts were billed as heroes on the order of the classical warrior or explorer type. As the names of the men who walked on the moon slip from the public's memory and the space program becomes a controversial budgetary item, this potential source of heroes has also dried up.

Today, we not only lack heroes, according to many social commentators, but we engage in the denigration of traditional heroes. Boorstin (1961) claims:

It matters little whether we see the hero exemplifying a universal falsehood or a universal truth. In either case we now stand outside ourselves. We see greatness as an illusion, or, if it does exist, we suspect we know its secret. We look with knowing disillusionment on our admiration for historical figures who used to embody greatness. (p. 51)

Ralph Waldo Emerson's aphorism that "every hero becomes a bore" seems to ring true. Noted author Joe McGinniss's (1990) personal memoir narrates his pursuit of heroes, a pursuit which led to the discovery of mere shadows of greatness. The resulting disillusionment is reflected in his comment: "The task of the searcher after heroes, then, or at least the task of him who would search after the vanished American hero—seemed primarily to be to go out and rummage through the debris of America's shattered illusions" (p. 28).

Some claim the search for national heroes has been altered by the 1970s and 1980s search for self. In *The Hero Within,* Pearson (1989) defines heroic archetypes "that exist in all of us." McGinniss (1990) concludes his search for heroes by observing:

Mostly, I think we have to get by for a while with private symbols. I do not think we can be as comfortable as we once were with hand-me-down illusions; with prefabricated myths. I think, as Campbell has suggested, that each of us who seeks dimension will have to construct his own mosaic; will have to build his own myth, slowly, painfully, piece by piece. (pp. 175-176)

With the demise of traditional heroes of deed and thought, fed by 20th-century Freudian turning inward and Nietzscheian pleasure seeking, we are now confronted with the fantasy world of entertainers, those ever present, ever glamorous, ever "on" figures—the celebrities. Can real heroes emerge from deeds of make believe? Peoples' search for modern heroes is confounded by interest in, and concern over, the plethora of celebrities who are as famous, if not more so, than traditional heroes. Has the hero been completely replaced by the celebrity, or can true heroes still emerge in this media world in which fantasy is continually merged with reality? If the former is the case, do celebrities serve the same functions as heroes? If the latter, how will we know the true heroes from the pseudo heroes? Put another way, the question arises: With fragmentation, heterogeneity, pluralism, and multiculturalism—the watchwords of the day—can the American community reach the requisite consensus on societal ideals and morals for bestowal of the title of hero? Communities require leaders as well as heroes, but what is the relationship of leader to hero? Are leaders different than heroes, or does a leader evolve into a hero? Journalist Bill Moyers posed this very question to Joseph Campbell in *The Power of Myth* (Campbell, 1988), but received no clear response. Burns (1978), however, suggests an alternative: the concept of *heroic leadership* that is distinguished by a relationship between leader and led in which belief in the leader is based on personage rather than experience or past performance (p. 244).

Many today are confused and made fearful by this hero/celebrity dilemma. This can be attributed to the fact that heroism is a social rather than a private impulse. Heroes represent agreed upon norms; the very word *hero* comes from the Greek meaning "embodiment of composite ideals" (McGinniss, 1990, p.16). It is expressed in a public form and raises the concept of community in a spiritual sense (Edwards, 1988). All communities need heroes; communities form around heroes. What is the relationship of community to the creation and perpetuation of heroes? What is the relationship between the hero and the creation and perpetuation of community? What is the relationship between the hero and the celebrity? What does the rise of celebrity tell us about community in today's mass media world? The following chapters address these questions from a variety of perspectives offering both old and new ways of finding answers.

THE HERO AND THE DEVELOPMENT OF COMMUNICATION TECHNOLOGIES

The heroes of any culture are inherently famous. Fame itself can be defined as a state that exists when a general public is acutely aware of a significant deed or deeds and their perpetrator. One of the truisms about being a hero is that information about her or him is widely disseminated. The hero, therefore, can be viewed as a communication phenomenon, that is, the study of the hero incurs the study of communication about heroes (Strate, 1985, p. 48).

Who are the heroes of a culture? How are they chosen, or created, and from where may they come? To begin with there are male heroes, female heroes, and heroines. In Western culture, heroes, representative of a culture's values, have typically been reflected in male actions of courage, command, and conquest in conflicts. The term *heroine*, according to Fayer in Chapter 18, is a distinct term reserved for accomplishment in the realm of feminine pursuits: the domain of the womanly, perhaps even the ladylike. However, the heroic principle may be found in, among others, kings and emperors, priests and saints, wisemen and fools, warriors and artists, and the Good Mother to name a few. How it is found and the form it takes depends on what roles and which concepts of self a society values along with the medium preferred for heroic communication.

Historically, public spaces were one medium through which face-to-face communication took place in a context (i.e., the town square, the street, the plaza, the park, the agora, the forum). Public places become important as media of communication used for transmission of the hero myth and for significant communal public rituals of hero creation and maintenance. Public places are required by hero worshippers as sites for retelling tales of great deeds, for enacting ceremonies of hero worship, and as a locale for public statues erected to honor the hero (for the lasting and literal placement of the hero on a pedestal) (Czarnowski, 1978; Rudofsky, 1969; Rykwert, 1978).

There exists considerable evidence that the dominant medium of communication of a culture affects the notion of the hero (Ong, 1981; Strate, 1985):

> When the dominant cultural medium is orality there is an emphasis on the immediate and concrete. The figures around whom knowledge is made to cluster, those about whom stories are told or sung, must be made into conspicuous personages—foci of common attention, individuals embodying open public concerns. (Ong, 1981, pp. 204-205)

It is the communication process, the means of disseminating and storing information, that makes heroes in an oral culture different from those in print and electronically dominated cultures. Oral culture is primarily concerned with the preservation of information over time. The ephemeralness of spoken discourse serves to limit the number of figures selected and sharpens the focus on those figures to be remembered. Heroes' actions in an oral culture are more readily remembered because they are portrayed as having marked influence on the outcome of events and are designed to serve as inspiration to those who feel they have little control over natural forces.

Strate, in Chapter 2, reveals that when orality was replaced by print as the dominant cultural medium the oral hero was supplanted by the print hero. The new "print" hero was characterized by ideas or mental capacity as well as events. Not only were authors and inventors considered heroes, but also political and military leaders were recognized for their cunning and strategy rather than strength and courage. The hero of the printed history books stood the test of time. If anything, he or she became even more a heroic figure as generations passed and people found more to admire in the protective and selective print information aura that developed. The heroic acts of the print-age hero can be read and reread and the written story can be revised and rewritten to meet the needs of new generations. Some heroes might be found to have feet of clay when academic historians rewrite events and scholarly biographers dig for personal secrets, but prior to the 20th century little of these revisionist texts reached the general public. As with oral cultures, print heroes were persons of the past. Their deeds became known only after the fact—in many cases only after they were dead. Whatever the individual did in daily life was forgotten or surpassed in the written story of the heroic event.

In our contemporary mass media culture the hero is invariably a contemporary figure. He or she is both made and unmade by the same agency—media attention. The mass media relentlessly search out those who satisfy the public's appetite for super status and just as relentlessly portray their human faults and failings. The traditional hero, Gumpert explains in Chapter 5, who suffered a fall did so because of a tragic flaw. The mass media hero who falls, suffers not from any tragic failing, but from a lack of media attention that places him or her back into the commonplace world. The celebrity's need for continued exposure and the attainment of fame has been well documented in Boorstin's *The Image: A Guide to Pseudo-Events in America* (1961), Braudy's *The Frenzy of Renown: Fame and its History* (1986), Monaco's *Celebrity: The Media as Image Makers* (1978), and Schickel's *Intimate Strangers: The Culture of Celebrity* (1985).

Boorstin (1961) suggests that the simplest way to distinguish between the traditional hero and the celebrity is to recognize that although the hero of the past was created by deeds and maintained by the oral and print record, it is the film/electronic media that create and maintain the celebrity of today (p. 65).

Paradoxically, in an electronic culture, the greater amount and more rapid dissemination of information has made even more numerous the number of famous persons, while at the same time making them less heroic. Boorstin (1961) contends that heroes in the old-fashioned mold (of print dominant cultures)—the Shakespeares, Napoleons, and Washingtons—are in smaller proportion than ever before due to the increased amount of information made available to the public (pp. 46-47). In a related study, Meyrowitz (1985) explains, in a chapter entitled "Lowering the Political Hero to Our Level,"

> The camera brings a rich range of expressive information to the audience; it highlights . . . mortality and mutes abstract and conceptual rhetoric. While verbal rhetoric can transcend humanity and reach for the divine, intimate expressive information often exposes human frailty. . . . Highly replicative media are demystifying leaders not only for their own time, but for history as well. But less replicative media allowed, at least, for greater idealization of leaders after they died. . . . Through new media, however, the idiosyncrasies . . . are preserved and passed down to the next generation. (pp. 272-275)

It is not just the tremendous amount of information that modern media bring us about individuals that has "deheroized" them, but also the plethora of scientific and economic information on all levels that leads us to question the efficacy of the traditional hero. Recent events such as Watergate have dramatized the peril of the "Great Leader." Widespread public knowledge of the influence of economic and social forces and the inability of single individuals to alter these forces have made the individual hero less important and imposing. The demise of the all-knowing, all-powerful hero is reflected in the popular fiction of Williams, Miller, Hemingway, and Faulkner and the movies of Spielberg, Allen, and Truffaut in which the central characters are likely to be not traditional heroes, but persons buffeted by circumstance. It can also be seen in our cynical search for dark heroes. As Gumpert (Chapter 5) notes, the fascination with a flawed and contaminated hero, and the strange appeal of the villain as hero, can be traced to both the influence of Aristotle's concept of the tragic flaw and the tendency of modern media to sensationalize the personal flaws of those in the limelight. Given the reality of the televisions, radios, newspapers, magazines, books, telephones, and so on, that fill our every waking moment with people and events, the singular hero fades into insignificance as great figures become diluted, become only one of scores of people we read about or see each day in the panorama of electronic events. Heroes may have stood the test of time, but celebrities quickly go to "fame heaven" (Gaither, 1991).

In the past, some individuals may have been able to achieve heroic status by setting out to accomplish valorous deeds, but today it is the media and the myth makers who construct the hero and the celebrity. Moore (1989) supports the position that World War I marked the end of an era when one could plan to construct oneself as a hero, leaving us with no renown heroes in the post-World War II era. A chronology of celebrity linked to the publicity industry (Gamson, 1992) supports the assertion that celebrity became systematized by the early 20th century. From developments in newspaper distribution, telegraphy, photography, through the early stages of sound recording, motion pictures, and ultimately television, celebrity creation evolved into a powerful, professionalized, ultimately visible industry. It is an industry that produces fame and even manufactures sincerity through behind-the-scenes real-life glimpses that take the fan beyond the image. The papparazzi become creators of art, and audience voyeuristic tendencies are fulfilled by the print and electronic media. Ultimately celebrities, the commodity produced by the publicity industry, come to serve as pseudo-heroes for American society and as major products for export (Wallace, 1989). We note, however, that not everyone agrees the only heroes we have today are pseudo-heroes (see Billions, Chapter 11; Trujillo & Vande Berg, Chapter 15; and Reid, Chapter 16).

Section I, "Heroes, Celebrities, and the Media," brings together six chapters concerned with the significant role of the technological media of communication, particularly contemporary mass media, in developing and altering the form and function of the hero in society. Each chapter selects a particular aspect of media communication and analyzes its affects on our perceptions of the hero. In Chapter 2 Strate, tracing the historical evolution of the hero through oral, print, and electronic cultures, explores how the nature and function of the hero in society is dependent on the dominant medium of communication. In the next chapter Fayer examines the changing conceptions of gender, relating these to the designations of heroines and heroes. Cathcart, in Chapter 3, provides an historical analysis of the symbiotic relationship between the hero and the media of communication utilized in constructing the image and fame of the hero. In the next chapter Gumpert goes on to trace the evolution and fall of the hero and the role of various media in either elevating or toppling the hero. Next, Meyrowitz describes the mediated interpersonal relationship shared with famous media friends (celebrities) and its effects on people's feelings about famous personalities. Drucker, in Chapter 7, reveals how the mass media, by concentrating on certain activities, in this case sports, are able to create psuedo-heroes.

Section II, "The Making of Modern Heroes," contains three chapters, each one devoted to a particular media form and its role in producing modern hero/celebrities. Chapter 8 relates how modern media storytellers (news commentators) are able to make themselves into celebrities because of their relationship to heroic events. Zelizer utilizes the Kennedy Assassination as a case study to show how reporters made themselves into heroic celebrities. McLennan provides another case study in Chapter 9 in which he examines Tom Hayden's use of written autobiography as a means of elevating himself to hero status. Finally, in Chapter 10, Samra provides a critical analysis of the role of TV advertising in the establishment of Lee Iacocca as a corporate hero.

Section III, "Critical Theories: Perspectives on the Hero/Celebrity," offers four chapters in which various critical theories are utilized to reveal the hero/celebrity-making process. Chapter 11 by Billions relies on Joseph Campbell's theory of the archetypal metaphor, in this case "The Great Mother" archetype, to explain how Phyllis Schlafly could be a true hero to many women and men, whereas she is an arch villainess to others. In Chapter 12 Wallace shows how the Quest theory can explain Lindberg's place as a hero, whereas Burke's Victimage theory explains Kennedy's role as a hero. Chapter 13 by Cooper, Descutner, and Alspach applies Bormann's Fantasy Theme theory to determine the success or failure of Donald Trump's attempt to elevate himself to the position of civic hero. The last chapter in this section looks at two popular media celebrities—George Michaels and Madonna—and uses postmodern theory to explain their role and its importance in American culture.

Section IV, "The Celebrity-Hero Connection," contains five chapters in which the authors claim that the celebrities they examine have also achieved status as heroes. Trujillo and VandeBerg argue in Chapter 15 that the professional baseball pitcher Nolan Ryan has transcended his celebrity status and is now a true hero to baseball fans and Texans in general. In Chapter 16 Reid explains how televangelist Jimmy Swaggert can be both a much maligned TV celebrity and a real hero to the penecostal sect that follows him. In Chapter 17 Drucker and Cathcart explore the nature of people's relationships with media celebrities and what those relationships mean to them. Chapter 18 examines who the heroes in Puerto Rico are and how the media unhindered by borders play a role in the selection of the heroes and celebrities of a culture. Ferri, Fayer, and Simounet Geigel find that Puerto Rico's mixed Hispanic and Anglo-American heritage has produced a unique mix of local and international heroes and celebrities due in part to the nature of the island community and in part to the effects of modern mass media. In the final chapter, Gencarelli examines the career of singer Bruce Springsteen and examines how he has become a folk hero as well as a popular singing star.

THE HERO/CELEBRITY PHENOMENON: IDEAS, ISSUES, AND PROBES

Taken together the chapters in this volume reveal a number of insights into the changing role of the hero in contemporary American society. First, it has become quite clear that the very notion of hero and the form that it takes is now, and has always been, related to the means of communicating about heroic actions and their perpetrators. An "unsung hero" is an oxymoron. Without the story and the storyteller there can be no fame, and without fame individual acts, no matter how courageous, become part of the passing parade. The studies reported here reveal that the means of telling the story and keeping it in the public eye determines what is heroic and who and what is to be celebrated. As media technology developed, the old God-like colossus of oral storytelling became more human and more humane as befitting a print culture that celebrated these attributes. With the rise of the more recent media technologies of photography, telegraphy, radio, film, and television, the form and function of the hero continued to change. As information became more instantaneous and able to reach millions of people at the same time, and as the mass media became more information voracious, fame became a matter of who could hold the spotlight. Those who could control media coverage became famous, not for heroic deeds, but because they represented what ordinary humans might become when they could gain media attention. Performance rather than heroic deeds is what is celebrated now. Thus, we have celebrities. Heroism is not dead, as these studies reveal, but it has been changed by the pace and the form of contemporary media. Contemporary heroes must also be celebrities. They must be able to present the performance and the image that the media demand. Not all celebrities are heroes, but today no person can be a hero without also being a celebrity.

Ultimately, if the societal selection of heroes is indeed indicative of the values and needs of that society, then the change from traditional hero to media celebrity may well be indicative of the power the dominant media of communication has over societal needs and values. This volume is about the changing nature and role of heroes and how these changes are manifested in the communicative process of celebrification. The succeeding essays deal with the issues of where heroes come from, how they are created and sustained, and are they gone or have they been created in a new form? Part and parcel of this concern is the dominating role of the mass media in creating, maintaining, and destroying our heroes/celebrities. There is an important connection between the changing form and function of the hero and the technological development of the media of communication. This connection has important implications for the study of public discourse and mass media as well as our understanding of heroes/celebrities.

The ideas, issues, and probes to be found in the following pages emerged from a seminar conducted in 1989 in San Francisco under the auspices of the Speech Communication Association. Many of the authors whose work appears in this volume were in attendance and presented early versions of their work. In addition, the editors are indebted to Carl Moore and Roger Wallace who made notable contributions to the seminar. The significance of this area as a research topic as well as appropriate research methodologies for study of this phenomenon were discussed. Participants presented and evaluated works in progress and committed themselves to producing a unified work devoted to the hero/celebrity phenomenon.

The following chapters offer diverse viewpoints about the status of the hero in contemporary society. In some the hero has disappeared, in others the hero has undergone a metamorphosis, a transformation, and in still others the hero has been replaced—supplanted by celebrity. Yet, all agree that the key to this phenomenon is understanding the role of the communication media in determining the form and function of the hero in any society. Presently the terms *hero* and *celebrity* are used as counterpoints by some and synonyms by others, revealing an uneasiness and uncertainty with regard to the concept of each and their relationship to one another. If indeed American heroes in a media age are called celebrities, what can be learned about the role of the contemporary hero, the character of communicative media, and society? We hope this volume suggests some intriguing answers and stimulates further questions.

Section I:
Heroes, Celebrities, and the Media

2

Heroes:
A Communication
Perspective

Lance Strate
Fordham University

❐ *The author develops one of the central themes of this volume: The nature and function of hero in any society is dependent upon the dominant medium of communication. Strate argues that there is no such thing as heroes, only communication about heroes. There can be no hero or heroism without a distributable narrative capable of constructing the heroic. One can refer to an "unsung hero," but never to a "sung" hero because it is in the presentational form of the narrative that heroism comes to be. The historical evolution of the hero and the nature of fame is traced from the oral hero to the print hero to the electronic hero. The author demonstrates how the kinds of heroes, their qualities, and characteristics in each historical period are determined by the dominant medium of communication at the time rather than by any a priori sets of acts and values.*

Every people and every era has its heroes. They are the anchors of human culture, the personification of values and beliefs. They serve as guides to the psyche, role models in the process of socialization, and sources of authority and legitimation. As Potok (1973) puts it, "Heroes are the inevitable concomitant of a system of value and thought that has been embraced by an aggregate of men" (p. 71). We may take this to mean that the hero is as universal to human societies as communication. This should come as no surprise, for insofar as we as human beings love to talk, our favorite subject matter is ourselves, including idealized versions of ourselves. It is through communication that we come to know our heroes, and consequently, different kinds of communication will result in different kinds of heroes. For example, different levels of communication would be associated with different types of heroes, such as the interpersonal hero, known through interpersonal communication (e.g., parents, teachers, clergy, and community leaders); the organizational hero, known through organizational communication (e.g., the company founder); and the culture hero, known through cultural or mass communication (e.g., mythic and legendary figures such as an Achilles or Odysseus; historical figures such as Caesar, Napoleon, Plato, Galileo, Shakespeare, Joan of Arc, etc.; and modern celebrities such as Sylvester Stallone, Michael Jackson, Madonna, David Letterman, etc.). This chapter focuses on the latter: heroes known and admired by an entire society.

Let me stress at this point that culture heroes are not actual human beings. The two are often confused, probably because so many culture heroes are based on real people. This, of course, is not a problem when dealing with fictional culture heroes such as Hamlet or Superman, but in this chapter I am more concerned with those heroes who are considered "real," including mythical heroes who are considered true by the society that worships them (Eliade, 1975). When the hero is based on a human being, there may be certain individuals who have personal relationships with that man or woman, but, as Napoleon once remarked: "No man is a hero to his valet." By this he meant that no one can be a culture hero through personal relationships. To those who know the man or woman behind the culture hero, that individual may serve as an interpersonal hero, but this would constitute an entirely different type of hero. There is also the possibility of a kind of schizophrenic relationship in which the intimate despises the real person, but admires what he or she stands for, that is, admires the culture hero. But, as a general rule, members of a society are separated from their culture heroes by time, space, and social class and therefore know their heroes only through stories, images, and other forms of information. In this sense, there are no such things as heroes, only communication about heroes. Without communication, there would be no hero.

We may speak of an "unsung hero," but the term is oxymoronic, implying injustice: The unknown hero may possess certain qualities deemed heroic, but can there be a hero without an admirer? Can there be a hero who is not a hero to someone? Similarly, terms such as *unsung hero*, *known hero*, or *famous hero* would be redundant. Fame itself is a communication phenomenon, the state that exists when information about a subject is widely disseminated among a group of people. Therefore, in order to fully understand the phenomenon of the hero, we need to ask questions about how that information is disseminated and about the means through which a society communicates about its heroes.

That the subject of our communication is influenced by the method of our communication is a point that has been made by theorists such as McLuhan (1964, 1969), Innis (1977), and Ong (1981, 1982a, 1982b), and more recently by Postman (1979, 1982, 1985), Meyrowitz (1985), and Gumpert (1987). For example, a painter who works with water colors will get a very different result from one who works with oil paints. A sculptor who molds clay will produce something significantly different from one who chisels stone. A musician who plays a piece on a violin will obtain a quite different effect from one who plays the same composition on a kazoo. In the same way, technological innovations such as writing, print, and electronic communication have changed the way in which we talk about heroes, tell stories about heroes, and experience heroes, and thus have altered our conceptions of the hero. Communication technologies also exert an indirect influence through their impact on the ways in which we think and organize ourselves. Clearly there are factors other than media that influence a particular culture's conception of the hero, but I would argue that the most significant characteristics of the hero are related to communication technologies. The most dramatic shifts in conceptions of the hero have been associated with innovations in communication such as the invention of writing and printing and the development of electronic media.

ORAL HEROES

The impact of written and printed communication on the concept of the hero can best be understood by considering nonliterate or oral cultures in which information can only be transmitted through speech and can only be stored in the human memory. Under such conditions, culture heroes are known through oral poetry and song and are used as mnemonic devices to aid in the retention of important information. Consequently, heroes in oral cultures must be memorable and therefore larger than life, superhuman or supernatural beings. Oral heroes are the heroes of myth and legend, heavy figures as Ong (1981) refers to them:

> The figures around whom knowledge is made to cluster, those about whom stories are told or sung, must be made into conspicuous personages, foci of common attention, individuals embodying open public concerns, as written laws would later be matters of open public concern. In other words, the figures around whom knowledge is made to cluster must be heroes, culturally "large" or "heavy" figures like Odysseus, or Achilles or Oedipus. Such figures are essential for oral culture in order to anchor the float of detail which literate cultures fix in script. These figures, moreover, cannot be too numerous or attention will be dissipated and focus blurred. The familiar practice sets in of attributing actions which historically were accomplished by various individuals to a limited number of major figures (Rome's complex early history is seen in the biography of Aeneas or as the story of Romulus and Remus); only with writing and print could the number of characters in a modern history book or in fiction such as Finnegans Wake be possible at all. Thus the epic hero, from one point of view, appears as an answer to the problem of knowledge storage and communication in oral-aural cultures (where indeed storage and communication are virtually the same thing). (pp. 204-205)

Limited capacity for the storage of information in turn limits the number of heroes possible in oral cultures so that they tend to be composite figures; the actions of many are attributed to one hero. Needing to be both economical and memorable, oral heroes tend to be predictable, characterized by clichés and formulas (e.g., clever Odysseus, brave Achilles, etc.). They also tend to be impersonal, generic, or type characters, as details relating to individual idiosyncrasies would tax the storage capacity of collective memory and are not essential for cultural survival. Moreover, to enhance memorability, the stories of oral heroes are dramatic and conflict-oriented, characterized by contests and combat. Thus, oral heroes are known for their actions; the myths and legends surrounding heroes such as Gilgamesh, Hercules, and Beowolf all emphasize acts or actions.

TYPOGRAPHIC HEROES

Joseph Campbell in *Hero With A Thousand Faces* (1949) attributes the disappearance of the mythic hero to such diverse factors as democracy, modern science, and the industrial revolution. Undoubtably, these developments have had an effect on the concept of the hero, but Campbell fails to acknowledge the significant relationship between the mythic hero and oral culture. A more satisfying explanation is provided by Eliade (1975):

> Through *culture*, a desacralized religious universe and a demythicized mythology formed and nourished Western civilization.... There is more here than a triumph of *logos* over *mythos*. The victory is that of the *book* over oral tradition, of the document—especially of the written document—over a living experience whose only means of expression were preliterary. (p. 157)

The introduction of writing, and later print, extended human memory and overcame its limitations. With the presence of a means to store information outside of collective memory, the heavy figures of myth and legend were no longer necessary, and greater numbers of lighter heroes were made possible. As oral poetry and song were replaced by written history, the hero was brought down to earth, and as more information could be stored about any given individual, heroes became more individualized. The heroes of literate cultures are realistic, mortal figures, objects not of worship, but of admiration. The introduction of the printing press extended these trends; according to Eisenstein (1980), typography "made it possible to supplement tales of great men teaching by example and the lives of saints and saintly kings, by biographies and autobiographies of ordinary people pursuing more variegated careers" (p. 229). Greater numbers of heroes and greater amounts of information were related to the emergence of more specialized types of heroes. As literacy undermined an older kind of hero, the mythic or legendary hero, it also introduced new types of hero. Thomas Carlyle, lecturing in 1840, demonstrated an awareness of this development:

> Hero-Gods, Prophets, Poets, Priests are forms of Heroism that belong to the

old ages, make their appearances at the remotest of times; some of them have ceased to be possible long since, and cannot any more show themselves in this world. The Hero as *Man of Letters* . . . is altogether a product of these new ages; and so long as the wondrous art of *Writing,* or of Ready-writing which we call *Printing,* subsists, he may be expected to continue, as one of the main forms of Heroism for all future ages. He is, in various respects, a very singular phenomenon. (1840/1940, p. 383)

Clearly, the author as hero could not exist without literacy, but writing and print made possible many other new types of heroes, such as scholars, scientists, inventors, artists, musicians, and so on. These new typographic heroes are known for their ideas, their intellectual and creative production. Action may still be present, but it is the mental, not the physical, that is emphasized. As much as the man of letters, the leader of men is also known for ideas, as a strategist, not as a warrior. Napoleon and Washington are celebrated not for fighting prowess, but for military and political achievements. Columbus, unlike Odysseus, is not remembered for the events of his quest, but for the idea behind his voyage. A further difference between oral and literate cultures is that in the latter, a clear distinction is made between fact and fiction, leading to a further distinction between fictional and nonfictional heroes, a distinction that does not exist in oral cultures.

ELECTRONIC HEROES

The concept of the hero changes as we move from oral to literate and typographic cultures and continues to change with the transition to an electronic culture in the 20th century. Daniel Boorstin (1978) was one of the first to discuss this more recent change:

> In the last half century the old heroic human mold has been broken. A new mold has been made. We have actually demanded that this mold be made, so that marketable human models—modern heroes—could be mass-produced, to satisfy the market, and without any hitches. The qualities which now commonly make a man or woman into a "nationally advertised" brand are in fact a new category of human emptiness. Our new mold is shaped not of the stuff of our familiar morality, nor even of the old familiar reality. (pp. 48-49)

Boorstin refers to these new heroes as celebrities and human pseudo-events and as measured by the standards of print culture, the electronic hero is no hero at all. The problem is that the standards themselves have changed. Our new standards are based on a reality mediated by the televised image.

Electronic telecommunications favors rapid dissemination of information over space and allows ever greater amounts of information to be transmitted throughout a culture. The result is even greater numbers of heroes who tend to be even lighter figures. Telecommunications also favors rapid turnover of information, the new and the up to date over the old and traditional. Thus, the electronic hero tends to be a contemporary, rising to stardom overnight and fading from view just as rapidly. In the words of Andy Warhol: "In the future everyone will be famous. For fifteen minutes." Or as David Bowie and John Lennon wrote: "Fame—what you get is no tomorrow." In the past, biographies and autobiographies were not written until after the subject was dead, or at least not until the end of the subject's career; now they appear at the first hint of widespread fame. By the time his or her career is over, the electronic hero may be long forgotten and the biography of little interest. Rapid turnover is the rule, but there are a growing number of exceptions: Those heroes from the past who were recorded on audiovisual media, thereby, retaining their immediacy. Thus individuals such as John F. Kennedy, Marilyn Monroe, and Elvis Presley continue to intrigue and enthrall; some long-dead celebrities including Charlie Chaplin, Laurel and Hardy, Humphrey Bogart, and Louis Armstrong have even appeared in television commercials.

The emphasis on novelty and the expanded volume of information that is transmitted mean that information about the hero will be disseminated whether it is important or not—generally it is not. Electronic communication trivializes heroes. We learn about their health and family problems, about the food they eat, the car they drive, the person they are sleeping with. Unlike the heavy figure of oral culture who is qualitatively greater than us, or the typographic hero characterized by significant achievement in a specialized sector, the light figure of electronic culture is ordinary, just like us. As Boorstin (1978) puts it, "the celebrity is a person who is known for his well-knownness" (p. 57). In other words, the electronic hero is famous simply for appearing on or in the media, not for any intrinsic qualities.

Inasmuch as this type of hero is not worthy of our worship, so it is that the hero worshipper or admirer is replaced by the fickle fan. The large number of heroes to choose from and their rapid turnover work against any loyalty the admirer might feel toward a hero, as does the interchangeability of celebrity and fan. The lack of distance between fan and hero results in an illusion of intimacy on the fan's part (Horton & Wohl, 1982) and at its most extreme gives way to the pathology of celebrity assassins such as Hinckley and Chapman, who gain a fame of their own through attacks on electronic heroes.

Known primarily for their media coverage, electronic heroes are characterized by their image. By image I refer to the audiovisual representation and replication of the hero. Although people have always had mental images of their heroes, the mental image is superseded by the mediated one. Of course, there are older types of visual arts, but emphasis on the image above all else begins with the invention of photography, progresses through the development of sound recording and the motion picture, and culminates in television and related technologies. On television, it is not actions and ideas that are emphasized, but appearance and personality. There is no room in television's schedule for the lengthy presentation and consideration of ideas. Ideas can occupy an individual for a lifetime; images can be presented and digested in a matter of seconds.

Even when ideas are presented on television, they are overshadowed by images, creating an image of ideas, divorced from any substance. Actions may be a component of the image, for television is a dramatic medium, but unlike the oral hero, the electronic hero's actions are not memorable. We are left only with an image of action, an image of the hero as a man or woman of action, whereas specific deeds are forgotten. Compare, for example, the often bizarre labors of Hercules to the hundreds of ultra-violent but otherwise unexceptional actions of Rambo. In short, electronic heroes are known for images, not actions or ideas. In an oral culture, the hero lives and dies by the sword. In a print culture, the pen is mightier than the sword. But in an electronic culture, the deciding factor is neither arms nor pen, but appearance and personality.

Moreover, just as the pen and printing press created new kinds of heroes, so does the electronic media. Often referred to as celebrities, many of our new heroes are entertainers: the television and movie star, the recording artist, and the disk jockey. Others are media professionals such as the newscaster, sportscaster, and fashion model. These new types of heroes have all but eclipsed the older forms. For example, in 1980, Scholastic Magazines surveyed its youthful readership, asking them to name their heroes; the top five responses were Steve Martin, Erik Estrada, Burt Reynolds, John Wayne, and Jerry Lewis ("Heroes," 1980). Less one-sided results were obtained in 1985 when *U.S. News and World Report* published the results of a Roper poll in which young adults between the ages of 18 and 24 were asked who their heroes were. The most popular choice was Clint Eastwood, followed by Eddie Murphy, Ronald Reagan was third, Jane Fonda fourth, and Sally Field and Steven Spielberg were tied for fifth place. Pope John Paul II was seventh, Mother Teresa eighth, and Michael Jackson and Tina Turner were tied for ninth place ("Heroes are back," 1985).

Today's college students generally list a television or rock star as their hero according to Birnbach (1984); in particular, students named Blake Carrington, the fictional, unprincipled tycoon played by John Forsythe on television's *Dynasty*. Novelist Bret Easton Ellis (1985) reports in *Rolling Stone* magazine that the heroes of college students include rock stars Bruce Springsteen and Madonna, movie star Sylvester Stallone, and television talk show-host David Letterman.

The change in the concept of the hero is one that defies age, however. For example, in Orange County, CA, an airport was named for a movie star: John Wayne Airport (the luggage tags read DUK). In 1985, 13 individuals were awarded the Medal of Freedom by Ronald Reagan, among them Frank Sinatra and Jimmy Stewart, as well as TV anchor Frank Reynolds and Jacques Cousteau, the star of numerous television documentaries ("Thirteen are named," 1985). Entertainers now routinely grace our postage stamps. Moreover, the U.S. Postal Service recently scored a publicity coup by allowing fans to vote on which picture of Elvis Presley they would want to appear on a commemorative stamp—the young or older Elvis. In short, the entertainer has become an authority figure. As Phelan (1977) puts it: "To produce a movie, get a star. To cure diseases, get a star. To sell soap, get a star. To save souls, get a star. To be heard, be a star" (p. 64).

Although the transition to an electronic culture has created new types of heroes, it also has undermined the older heroes of print culture. As images eclipse ideas, more traditional types of heroes are transformed into media professionals and entertainers. Thus, politicians appear on situation comedies, on *Saturday Night Live*, and in advertisements, and the 1992 Presidential campaign was conducted via daytime talk shows. At the same time, movie and TV stars become politicians, rising to the White House. Once, when I was teaching a course on political communication, a student came up to me to ask a question about Reagan and prefaced this question by saying, "I know you're a Democratic fan . . ." When politicians become entertainers, voters become fans. Similarly, whereas scientists like Newton and Einstein were known for their ideas, today the most famous scientist in America is Carl Sagan, who is best known for his appearances on the *Tonight Show* and his own TV series, *Cosmos*. Writers, such as Truman Capote, Norman Mailer, Jerzy Kosinski, and Kurt Vonnegut become television and movie actors. Musicians can no longer rely on their performance skills, they must produce video clips. Religious leaders obtain their own television programs and become talk- and variety-show hosts, and sometimes inadvertently, soap opera stars. Lee Iacocca adds appearing on television commercials to the job description for running a major corporation.

As entertainers become heroes, other types of heroes become more like entertainers. The specialized heroes characteristic of print culture disappear as occupations are transformed into roles to be played in front of the camera, roles that are easily discarded in favor of others. As John Lahr (1984) states: "Politicians become newscasters; newscasters become movie actors; movie actors become politicians. Celebrity turns every serious endeavor into a performance. Everything that rises in America must converge on a TV talk show" (p. 218).

On television, the distinction between fact and fiction becomes meaningless. The performance is the only reality. When characters are experienced only through the printed word, there are accepted procedures for determining whether they are fictional or real-life heroes. This is not the case when a fictional character is brought to life on television. Actors who play fictional roles appear to be as real, or unreal, as those who play themselves. They are both performers; both are performances. In many ways, the fictional character seems more real than the person who plays the part. For example, Archie Bunker and Captain Kirk become better known than Carroll O'Conner and William Shatner. The distinction between fictional and nonfictional heroes, a product of literacy, becomes increasingly irrelevant in an electronic culture, even among the well educated. Thus, Robert Young, the actor who played Marcus Welby, has been called on to address the American Medical Association, while an ad for an over-the-counter medication features an actor endorsing the product, saying "I'm not a doctor, but I play one on TV." Alan Alda has delivered commencement addresses at medical schools, and Raymond Burr at law schools, as has Judge Joseph Wapner of television's *The People's Court* (at least Wapner did once serve as a judge, albeit an undistinguished one).

CONCLUSION

Just as the oral hero was delegitimized as writing and print gained ascendance, so today the print hero is disappearing, replaced by the electronic hero. There is much that is disturbing about this development, and critics such as Boorstin (1978) are correct in reminding us that the older types of heroes provided us with inspirational models of human greatness in a way that electronic heroes are unable to. But even if we have lost more than we have gained, it can at least be said of today's heroes that they are more democratic in their ordinariness. As for the future, we can expect continued change in our concept of the hero as our media continue to evolve.

One technology in particular that has the potential to significantly alter the way in which we experience heroes is the computer. Even though computer programmers constitute a new kind of hero, the major impact will be in the development of computer simulated personalities. It is quite possible that in the near future media programmers may be able to substitute computer simulations of actors and entertainers for real persons and genuine performances. We may even be able to buy software that would allow us to interact with computer simulations of celebrities, further extending the sense of intimacy in fan-celebrity relationships and further blurring the line between fiction and nonfiction. This is already an actuality on a very primitive level: Some computer games feature real individuals or the characters they play in movies and on television (e.g., Bruce Lee).

Artificial intelligence programming and expert systems have already begun to record some of the thought processes of distinguished individuals in a variety of fields; further work may succeed in recreating some semblance of the individual's personality as well. Such procedures may "capture" contemporaries and store them indefinitely; others may simulate historical individuals such as Lincoln, Plato, and so on, and allow us to interact with them. Fictional personalities may also be developed; one such personality with an admittedly limited range has already appeared on the market: Racter. Nineteen eighty-three may only be the first of many years to follow in which *Time* magazine selects a "machine of the year" over a human being. Clearly, the relationship between communication technologies and conceptions of the hero requires continued surveillance.

Are Heroes Always Men?

Joan Fayer
University of Puerto Rico

☐ *Even a cursory examination of scholarly research, not to mention popular talk, will reveal that hero and heroism is typically recognized as a male domain. Although the word heroine has been around for some time, Fayer points out that male heroes and female heroines are not functional equivalents. In order to understand this gender bias the etymology of the words hero and heroine is explored, as is the role of gender in the conceptualization of that which is considered heroic. The author finds that the "female hero" has received little attention in the past and that sexist language in the present has done little to change the situation.*

Are heroes the sole domain of men? The need for heroes is not gender based, although the traits of the hero traditionally recognized seem to be. In Western culture, heroes representative of a culture's values have typically been reflected in actions of courage, command, and conquest in conflicts—typically a male domain. These characteristics are found in the definitions of heroes, and heroes are typically defined as men. Thus language not only plays a significant role in reflecting the values, perceptions, and stereotypes of the culture in which it is used, but it also serves to perpetuate stereotypes. The words for "the heroic"—hero and heroine—reflect a gender bias. There are male heroes and female heroines, but are they functional equivalents? Are there female heroes?

THE LANGUAGE AND GENDER

According to the linguistic relativity hypothesis developed by Whorf, language shapes both thought and behavior. In his studies of languages and cultures Whorf (cited in Carroll, 1956) found that language acts as a filter through which the world is perceived. He found:

In informal terms, that users of markedly different grammars are pointed by their grammars toward different types of observations and different evaluations of externally similar acts of observation, and hence are not equivalent as observers but must arrive at somewhat different views of the world. (p. 221)

Although the initial formulations of this hypothesis discussed overt or covert grammatical categories of language, lexical examples were also included, and most of the empirical investigations of the hypothesis have been done with lexicon. In his research Whorf found that workers in factories used caution around "full" drums of gasoline, but often threw lighted cigarettes around "empty" drums which contained gasoline vapor. These drums defined as "empty" were the source of fires. This faulty definition and the behavior caused by it has serious consequences.

Another way that words can cause limited or false perceptions of reality is by the use of sexist terminology. In a discussion of language and gender, Poynton (1989) notes that if a language utilizes sexist structures or lexicon, there will be sexist perceptions of events and people. These perceptions can reinforce what Bate (1988, p. 10) describes as the *gender filter,* which she defines as "unexamined assumptions and expectations about how members of each sex are likely to behave in various communication settings." This gender filter can operate at a lexical level. Key (1975, p. 39) states that "the labels and words which are used to refer to people and to describe others are based on deep-seated attitudes toward those particular people or groups of persons." Examples of this are the frequent references to women using animal metaphors such as chick, cow, dog, and so on, or referring to women as things to be eaten such as tomato, peach, cookie, and so on (Ashen & Ashen, 1983, p. 77). References to God as Father reinforce "the distinct impression that God is thought of in exclusively masculine terms" (Pagels, 1976, p. 293). Another type of linguistic sexism is the unequal pairing of such words as "man and wife," "master and mistress," and so on. To these could be added many examples of words that perpetuate male supremacy.

In order to eliminate sexism in language use, guidelines for nonsexist usage have been adopted by many journals, newspapers, and presses. One of the publications that attempts to free language of semantic bias is Miller and Swift's (1980), *The Handbook of Nonsexist Writing.* This book and others analyze the use of generic pronouns and nouns, the negative connotations of gender-marked terms, and the lack of adequate terms to describe the experiences of women as well as proposals for gender-neutral words. Sexist language is one of the ways that the subordinate position of women in society is reinforced.

Among the words discussed by Miller and Swift is *heroine,* which they feel has a condescending connotation. They state that "anyone who performs a heroic deed is a hero, regardless of their sex" (p. 112). The word heroine "today involves the same problem presented by other English words used specifically of females when no comparable masculine-gender term exists" (p. 112). Some words are gender-specific because they refer to people or activities that are intrinsically male or female. Words such as mother, father, and so on, are gender-specific. Other words such as mailman, manmade, and stewardess are sexist and are being replaced by gender-neutral terms. Words such as heroine are among the many examples of sexist terminology. Women can be heroes, but just how often is hero used for women? For too many people the word refers exclusively to men. The term *heroine* conjures up connotations of one who helps, assists, is prized, is victimized, "obeys, falls into line, takes second place" (Edwards, 1988). The actions of heroines represent cultural values associated with femininity. Other gender marked nouns such as poetess, aviatrix, and so on, are not currently used. Unfortunately, other words continue to make distinctions that serve to relegate the females to whom they are applied to inferior status.

The histories of the words hero and heroine provide some insights into the sexual biases of these words. *Hero* comes from the Greek word *heros* which in ancient times was the name given to men who possessed superhuman strength, were favored by gods, and who performed noble and great deeds. Its use in English is first cited in 1387. The original singular form was heros, and the modern hero is a back formation. The first definition given in *The Oxford English Dictionary* is "A name given (as in Homer) to men of superhuman strength, courage or ability, favoured by the gods; at a later time regarded as an intermediate between gods and men, and immortal" (1989, vol. VII, p. 171). In ancient mythology, a heroine/heroina was a female who was an intermediate between a goddess and a woman. Heroine was first used in English in 1664—almost 300 years after hero (p. 173). An earlier term, *heroess/heriosse*, cited from 1612 to 1715, has become obsolete (p. 172). The fact that there was no equivalent feminine term for hero for such a long period of time deserves comment. It no doubt says something of the role of women in English society during this period. Of course, the lack of any term in a language does not mean that concepts cannot be discussed. It is always possible to use existing words, descriptive phrases, and so on. Women could be described as great, brave, noble, saintly, and so on, and as people who performed great deeds. Although this is true, language usually supplies concise terms for things, people, actions, and ideas that are common or significant in the culture. The lack of the term *heroine* indicates at least a public lack of general recognition of the contribution of women and their deeds.

Gender making of nouns with feminine suffixes such as *-ess, -ette, -trix,* and *-ine* are now considered examples of linguistic sexism. Miller and Swift (1980, p. 109) state that:

> when French or Latin feminine-gender suffixes like -ess and -trix are attached to these words to designate women, even if the addition is intended as a courtesy, the basic form acquires a predominately masculine gender sense with the unavoidable implication that the feminine-gender form represents a substantial variation.

Some of these suffixes, such as *-trix* have fallen into disuse. The *-ine* suffix occurs in very few words and is no longer a productive suffix. It is still found in proper nouns such as Josephine and Ernestine, but as a feminine suffix it is only found in obscure nouns such as margravine, vicereine, and so forth. These nouns are so uncommon that their meanings are not even generally known. Baron (1986, p. 123) notes the few new coinages using the *-ine* suffix and cites freudine meaning "women friend," which was created by Richard Verstegan in 1605. More recent words with this suffix that have not survived include *actorine, actress; booberine*—a stupid or scatterbrained young women; *chorine*—chorus girl; *doctorine*—female doctor or medical student; *dudine* (also *dudene, dudette,* Mrs. Dude); *knitterine*—female knitter; *motorine*—female driver; *peacherine*—attractive female; *sailorine, soldierine*; and *starine*—female star. The *-ine* suffix is no longer used in new word creation.

Current dictionaries include both male and gender neutral definitions for hero. In *Webster's Third New International Dictionary* (1964) the first definition is gender-neutral, the second male, the third male, and the fourth gender-neutral. The term *hero* is not exclusively used for males, but *heroine* is just used for females. As noted above, recent guidelines for nonsexist language stress the elimination of needless gender terms. Gender neutral terms such as letter carrier, waitperson/server, flight attendant, and so on, are required in job descriptions. *Hero* should be a gender-neutral word that is used for both men and women. If *hero* continues to be the term for males and *heroine* for women, gender stereotypes will continue.

GENDER AND THE CONCEPT OF THE HEROIC

The relationship of men and women to society and heroism are rooted in assumptions of authority and ruling systems. Our civilization's typical heroic figures—biologically male and culturally masculine (Edwards, 1988, p. 48)—have long represented the prototype of heroism. With regard to female heroes, Edwards asserts that "insofar as she resembles the male hero, she questions the conventional associations of gender and behavior" (p. 48).

Gender and Myth

The word *hero* and the initial definitions of the term are Greek, and "The heroic concept was first framed in myths which were vehicles of religion and custom" (Fishwick, 1985, p. 60). In these Greek myths women were either excluded or assigned lesser roles. Of the 12 Greek Titans there was an equal division: 6 were male—Oceanus, Coeus, Crius, Hyperion, Iapetus, and Cronus—and 6 were female—Theia, Rhea, Themis, Mnemosyne, Phoebe, and Tethys. However, the female Titans, Phoebe and Theia, were only included in the general list and did not have individual entries in *Bulfinch's Mythology*

(Bulfinch, 1979). Two female Titans were described as wives of Titans and just two as having special characteristics or powers—Mnenosyne, the god of memory, and Themis, the god of justice and law.

The Titans were succeeded by the family of the Olympians; Zeus was the chief, followed by his brothers Poseidon and Hades. The other males were Ares, Apollo, Hermes, and Hepaestus. The females were Hera, wife of Zeus; Athena, god of wisdom, arts, and sciences; Aphrodite, god of beauty and love; Artemis, god of the moon and hunting as well as the protector of women; and Hestia, god of the hearth. Here, too, with the exception of Diana, the roles of the female gods centered around love, family, and intellectual pursuits. These Olympian gods were adopted by the Romans who did not have gods with distinctive personalities. "Greek and Roman mythology is quite generally supposed to show us the way the human race thought and felt untold ages ago" (Hamilton, 1953, p. 3). This was a world in which women had some roles, but it was nevertheless a male-dominated world. This formulation of heroes and heroic deeds has provided the western world with a paradigm that has changed little.

Gender and Religion

The predominance of males in religious systems continues today. One example of this is found in the liturgical calendar of the Roman Catholic Church. This calendar lists the feasts of saints and other celebrations of the church year. Not including days devoted to aspects of the life of Jesus, there are a total of 212 saint days designated. Of these 77% are for male saints and 34% for female. Of all the total female saint days, 29% are for the Virgin Mary (Foley, 1990).

Turpin (1990) in *Women in Church History* reinterprets Christian history by focusing on the lives of one woman in each century who made significant contributions. Summaries of these outstanding women began with Prisca, who preached the gospel with Paul in the first century, and concluded with Jean Donovan, a Maryknoll missionary killed in El Salvador. The others included were empresses, mystics, writers, saints, founders of religious orders, diplomats, reformers, and so on. Teresa of Avila's writings "on the mystical life are valued as gems of Spanish literature as well as treasuries of spirituality" (p. 135). Catherine of Siena, a 14th-century mystic who wrote *Divine Dialogue*, was a brilliant theologian. Clare of Assisi was the founder of the order of Poor Clares. Sixth-century Bridgit of Kildare founded the first convents in Ireland. The liberal arts and religious curriculum in the cathedral schools which were part of these convent communities attracted students from all over Europe. It was not until the 11th century that women religious had to "look to male authority for the last word" (p. 91). Before this time women founded and directed double monasteries with a convent for nuns and an abbey for monks (p. 91). Turpin presents an alternative view not only of church history which she found to be similar to secular history—male dominated.

Gender and Military Battle

"Western culture . . . has represented heroes typically as military leaders: commanding, conquering and above all, male" (Edwards, 1988, p. 48). Despite the fact that warriors have generally been considered to be male, there have been females who were exceptional warriors throughout history. Fraser (1988) in *The Warrior Queens* chronicles the lives and deeds of women rulers who have led their countries in battle. Her analysis which begins with Boadicea, the British queen who led the revolt against the Romans in the first century, is used as a prototype for all the other warrior queens. Included in the study are 20th-century women such as Margaret Thatcher, Golda Meir, and Indira Gandhi. In other centuries there are Elizabeth I, Isabella of Castile, 12th-century Tamara of Georgia, 17th-century Jinga in West Africa, 19th-century Rani of Jhansi, and so on. Fraser explores the paradox that:

> Whereas woman has on the whole, taking the rough with the smooth, the good epochs with the bad, been considered inferior to man throughout history, the arrival of a Warrior Queen, by whatever accident of fate, descent or sheer character, has been the signal for a remarkable outburst of excitement and even awe, sometimes accompanied by admiration and enthusiasm for her cause, beyond the ability of a mere male to arouse. (p. 6)

Fraser's study is important for several reasons. First, it brings attention to the women who were warriors, an archetype of hero that has been almost exclusively male. The female warriors span centuries and continents. Some of the reasons for the warfare were similar to those of males—liberation of the country, uniting of the empire, personal ambition—but some were different—motherhood, protection of children, moral authority.

> The most successful Warrior Queens have always been those who pre-empted the obvious disadvantage of their sex in this field by turning it into an apparent advantage; and biological motherhood is after all the one role which is totally closed to man. (p. 333)

Fraser concludes that the "study of Warrior Queen is that it represents the meeting point of visionary feminism and its direct opposite: war is an unnatural occupation for a woman" (p. 330).

Leadership has been recognized as an essential element of heroism (Moore, 1988); however, it is not the only quality needed to be a hero. Not all leaders, male or female, become heroes. It is true that not all heroes are leaders. When the word heroine is used it is usually for the victim who is saved. Her deeds are less active or more noble than those of the hero. Heroines follow, and heroes lead. But women have been leaders even in areas that have been male dominated, such as battle. To describe these female warriors as heroines is contradictory. To describe them as female heroes is not.

Gender and Definitions of Hero

The biased recognition of males and their achievements continues in general books about heroes and heroism. There is still a noticeable absence of women, and in those books in which women are included, they are not given equal analysis. In an 1840 series of lectures, Carlyle said that "the History of the World . . . was the Biography of Great Men" (1956, p. 21). Using this male-biased world view as the basis of the study, heroes are described as divinity, prophet, poet, priest, man of letters, and king. The examples of heroes in these categories are men.

Sabatini (1934) in *Heroic Lives* does include two women, Joan of Arc and Florence Nightingale, among the six biographies. These "heroines" are described as exceptions. Joan of Arc "takes up a task that properly belongs to the other sex" (p. 363). Nightingale, "a lady, delicately nurtured and carefully educated" (p. 363), became a nurse at a time when nurses were "slatterns notorious for drunkenness and unchastity" (p. 364). Sabatini finds that both were devoted to a cause, self-sacrificing, and capable of overcoming prejudice; each woman left behind her "an inspiration to posterity" (p. 363).

In a more recent book, *The Hero with a Thousand Faces*, Campbell (1949) defines a hero as "the man of self-achieved submission" (p. 16), but occasionally includes women as in the following description. "The hero, therefore, is the man or woman who has been able to battle past his personal and local limitations to the generally valid, normally human forms" (pp. 19-20). Included are Ariadne who enabled Theseus to get out of the labyrinth and Anna Karenina. Although a few women are included in Campbell's study, their deeds are not equal to those of men. Women are symbolized as prizes or victims—the "hegemony wrested from the enemy, the freedom won from the malice of the monster. . . the maiden of innumerable dragon slayings, the bride abducted from the jealous father, the virgin rescued from the unholy lover" (p. 342).

> She is the "'other portion" of the hero himself—for "each is both": if his stature is that of the world monarch she is the world, and if he is a warrior she is fame. She is the image of his destiny which he is to release from the prison of enveloping circumstance. But where he is ignorant of his destiny, or deluded by false considerations, no effort on his part will overcome the obstacles. (p. 342)

Although this analysis gives some recognition to women and their importance, it is far from equal treatment. Women are the "other portion," thus attempting to make some heroes and their deeds androgynous. This androgyny is explicit in the example of Tiresias, the blind seer, who is bisexual. Androgyny can be just another type of sexism when the feminine part is the less active, more "noble," more spiritual, and so on. Morgan (1989) notes that "what Campbell does not see is that even the token female hero is an imposter in a realm created and defined by male consciousness and reinforced by male power." F. Raglan (1975), using data primarily from mythology, describes 22 common features or incidents in the life of the hero. Once again, the heroes are male and the features and incidents "masculine." Women assume secondary roles. After passing a series of tests or winning victories in these myths,

> The hero marries the daughter, or widow, of his predecessor, and becomes king. It has often been assumed from this that the throne always went in the female line, and that the reigning queen or heiress could confer the title to her husband simply by marrying him. (p. 191)

Raglan disagrees stating that there were qualities for kingship that the hero had to have and that the king "established his title to the throne by his birth, his upbringing, and his victories" (p. 191). Thus it would seem that the importance of marrying a queen was not the only thing necessary to acquire the throne.

Women receive little recognition in Raglan's study. The Cinderella type of hero is briefly discussed. In this prototype "the future queen has to achieve her journey, her tests, and her victory" (p. 191). Cinderella may become the queen, but does she rule or does she just live happily ever after? Raglan provides no answers.

This male bias is also reflected in Wecter's *The Hero in America: A Chronicle of Hero-Worship* (1941) which begins with Captain John Smith and ends with Edison, Ford, Lindbergh, and Franklin Delano Roosevelt. One reason why women heroes are not heroic, according to Wecter (p. 476), is that they are not feminine and their deeds are imitations of those of men. "Women have had a curiously small share in the major hero-worship of America. . . . (Although women are among the most ardent hero-worshippers, as all mothers and some wives know, the cynical may suggest that no woman is ever a heroine to any other woman.)" He adds that there have been heroic American women. Some of them lacked symbolic appeal or "became heroic by imitation of the stronger sex" (p. 477). The main reason is that the great heroines of all time such as Joan of Arc and Queen Elizabeth I "were not, in the stricter sense, ladies . . . (and in America) the dominant ideal has been the perfect lady" (p. 477). It could be argued that Wecter, who wrote this in 1941, was just reflecting the opinions of that time, but just how much have they changed in the studies that followed?

Klapp (1962) divides heroes into types such as winners, splendid performers, heroes of social acceptability, and independent spirits. In discussing the examples of each type, he finds:

> There is about one specifically feminine for every three masculine hero types . . . Of course . . . there are important, specifically heroic roles such as beauty contest winner, prima donna, glamour girl, best dressed woman, Lady Bountiful and self-sacrificing nurses. Tradition also provides attractive models of heroic women: Ruth, Rachel, Cordelia, the Patient Griselda, Cinderella, Penelope, Antigone, Helen of Troy, Madame DuBarry, Cleopatra, and Queen Elizabeth. (p. 97)

He summarizes by saying that these examples are of two general types of women: "the faithful, submissive Penelope-mother-sufferer helper" and the "erotic queen (who may use her attraction as a means to power over men but does not strike out for herself)" (p. 97). In light of these examples, Klapp's conclusion "almost any kind of person can be famous in America" (p. 97) should be changed to "any type of *man*".

In 1976 McGinniss wrote about the vanished American hero. His theory was that "America no longer had national heroes as it once did because the traditional sources of heroes had dried up, . . . after a long period of erosion, they had ceased to be dominant in the 1960's" (p. 16). His definition of a hero taken from *The American Heritage Dictionary of the English Language* is that heroes are men. His search for heroes and the qualities of heroes, both recognized and unrecognized, included Daniel Berrigan, John Glenn, a test pilot, the most decorated soldier of the Vietnam War, Edward Kennedy, Eugene McCarthy, and so on. McGinniss confirmed his theory. However, a male author, using a male definition for heroes and interviewing only males, is not an unbiased methodology. In many ways this book is not much different from *The Hero in America* (Wecter, 1941) which was written 30 years earlier.

In *Seven Pillars of Popular Culture* Fishwick (1985) defines heroes as superior men (p. 3). "In classic times, heroes were god-men: in the Middle Ages, God's men: in the Renaissance, universal men: in the eighteenth century, gentlemen: in the nineteenth century, self-made men. Our century has seen the common man and the outsider become heroic" (p. 61). He restricts the term hero for men: women were *heroines*. Fishwick (p. 73) finds that "a new relationship between hero and heroine has not yet been widely understood or accepted. . . . In what sense are Janis Joplin, Joan Baez, Jackie Onassis and Geraldine Ferraro 'heroic'?" He notes that the process is still an enigmatic one in popular mass culture.

There were others writing at the same time as Fishwick who were reappraising history from nonsexist perspectives using nonsexist terminology. One of these new perspectives is found in feminist scholarship. As a result of this research, there is recognition of the roles women have played not only in the past, but also in the world today.

In *The Hero Within* (1989) and *Awakening the Heroes Within* (1991), Pearson develops an alternative analysis of archetypes to that of Campbell in *The Hero With a Thousand Faces* (1968a) which "assumed either that the hero was male or that male heroism and female heroism were essentially the same" (1989, p. xx). Her descriptions of personal heroic journeys were based on several traditions including archetypal psychology and feminist theory. She found:

> although on the archetypal level the patterns of male and female heroism were quite similar, they differed in detail, tone, and meaning from analogous stories about men. Moreover, the female hero's journey was more optimistic and equalitarian than her male counterpart. (1989, p. xx)

The dominant heroic archetype in history is that of the warrior, who takes a journey, defeats the enemy, and saves the woman in distress. Pearson notes, "In our culture, the heroic ideal of the Warrior has been reserved for men—usually only white men at that" (1989, p. 2). She adds that this is limiting not only for women, but also for men, because it is too strict a definition and does not permit development beyond this. However, "men consciously or unconsciously believe they cannot give up that definition of themselves without giving up their sense of superiority to others—especially to women" (p. 3).

CHANGE OF THE PARADIGM

There were female heroes in the past, but they were rarely included in written histories for various reasons. Browne (1987), in *Heroines of Popular Culture*, gives one explanation:

> Through the centuries men have treated women heroes as invisible. They have kept women stored away, like explosives in a warehouse, priding themselves on the treasures they possess, yet afraid to unleash that power lest it tend to overpower its possessor. (p. 1)

Browne asserts that women can fit the definition of hero given by Campbell, and that "women as well as men can be heroic" (p. 1). The essays in this collection begin with the emergence of heroic women in the 19th century and continue with female heroes in literature, art, soap operas, rock music, and aviation. In one of the essays, Oglesbee discusses the differences between male and female heroes, finding that the female hero "although threatening an established order, expands the essence of heroism and suggests a better order" (p. 160).

The definitions of female heroes are also explored in literary and feminist criticism as in Edwards's (1984) *Psyche as Hero*, which analyzes women as independent heroes. When women are not identified with conquest or male authority, the definition of hero is expanded. She notes that heroes reflect cultural values and that:

> The woman hero is an image of antithesis. Different from the male—her sex her sign—she threatens his authority and that of the system he sustains . . . the woman hero is an emblem of patriarchal instability and insecurity . . . she questions the conventional associations of gender and behavior. (pp. 4-6)

Women heroes have had a long history, and the story of Amor and Psyche in Greek mythology was used as the "classic example of the female heroic paradigm" (p. 10). If heroism is limited to physical deeds, military skills, and military deeds, women will tend to be excluded, even though there have been women who have excelled in these areas. "But if action is important for what it tells us about knowledge, then any action—fighting dragons, seeking grails, stealing fleece, reforming love—is potentially heroic. Heroism thus read and understood is a human necessity, capable of being represented by either sex" (p. 11).

Several factors have contributed to making female heroes invisible. History has usually been written by men and has emphasized the activities of men, and definitions of heroes have represented "male" characteristics. When women write history, the lives of women are given more attention. The heroic qualities of these women may be the same as men, but when they differ, female heroic qualities can enrich the current definitions of heroism.

Definitions of heroes reflect cultural value systems. Like language, these systems are always in a process of gradual change. One of the ways cultural values and the heroes that reflect them change is through culture contact. The study of Puerto Rican heroes in this volume describes the mixture of North American and Puerto Rican heroes that has resulted as these two cultures continue to be in contact. Another way that changes occur is by the different heroes selected by each generation within a culture. Because it was true that male heroes dominated in the past due to a male bias in history, it might be expected that younger generations today will select a more balanced list of male and female heroes.

However, several studies of the heroes selected by male and female adolescents found that this was not the case. Miller (1978), in a survey published in the *Ladies Home Journal,* concluded that teenagers selected males to be the people they felt would win the prize in the categories of art, science, sports, and so on. Male subjects selected just two women as runners-up, and females chose 15 women as runners-up. The preference of male heroes by both men and women was also found in the study of heroes in Puerto Rico.

Balswick and Ingoldsby (1982) asked over 1,000 high school students in Georgia—"Who are your heroes and heroines currently?—in the categories of music, acting, religion, literature, government, sports, comedy, family members, and friends. For all students, males were chosen more often than females in all categories. Balswick and Ingoldsby concluded that "the results are not surprising, given the differential rate of involvement of males and females in public professional roles in American society" and "both males and females are more aware of hero than heroine role models" (p. 248). This can explain the differences in public roles, but males ranked as high as females in the personal domain. Although women may be expected to spend more time in private roles, "we do not reward women—in this case symbolically—for their greater commitment" (p. 249).

The media also can explain why there are more male public heroes. Rickey (1991), in a recent article, "Too Male & Too Pale," discusses the reasons white males get the major roles in movies. One is that it is "commercially safer to make movies where boys and men enjoy adventures and where women wait to be rescued . . . heroines come with too much baggage to take off at the box office" (p. 14). Women are given roles in which they are victims to be rescued by men. This view is reinforced by an article in *Time* (November 11, 1992, p. 88) describing female heroes on television as "betrayed, battered, and bewildered." Women consist of 58% of the typical adult evening viewers, and an increasing number of prime-time programs have women in central roles; "but such attention comes at a daunting price: the rise of victimization drama" (p. 88). Women are given roles in which they are victims to be rescued by men. Another reason is that it seems to be easier for women to identify with male heroes than it is for males to identify with female heroes.

If the stereotype of the hero as a male is changing, it is changing very slowly. One of the ways this change can be accelerated is by the elimination of the term *heroine*. Today the word *poetess* is seen as deprecating, and *aviatrix* is no longer recognized by young people. Looking at the lives and deeds of female heroes can expand current definitions of heroism. If only masculine qualities are considered heroic, women will continue to be excluded. As the contributions of women in religion, art, literature, government, science, and other fields are being included in texts, films, criticism, and so on, public awareness of heroic women will increase.

Just why the identification and analysis of heroes is important can be answered in several ways. According to Fishwick (1985), "The hero is archetypal, a paradigm who bears the possibilities of life, courage, love—the commonplace which define our human lives" (p. 60). Klapp (1962) said that his studies of the types of heroes "tell us about American life and character.... The hundreds of American types show a striking variety of role models compared with simpler and more traditional societies" (p. 95). If this is true, the limited number of women in the discussion of heroes reflects the sexual bias and the lack of role models for women that is exemplified in Greek mythology, by Christian saints, and that is still evident in American culture today. However, it is time to change the male-biased paradigm.

Popular opinion often claims that heroes are no longer common, but this is not a new observation. Over 150 years ago Carlyle lamented the loss of great men. More recently Baker stated that "heroes are pretty well all washed in America these days," and Sam Shepard wrote that "all the heroes are dying like flies/they say it's a sign of the times" (cited in Stasio, 1990, p. 1). This may not be true. We may just be using the sexist words, male-biased definitions, and looking in the wrong places. A nonsexist search using nonsexist terminology may reveal different types of heroes and more heroes than ever imagined—many of them female.

4

From Hero to Celebrity: The Media Connection

Robert S. Cathcart
Queens College

☐ *This chapter takes the position that heroes, like celebrities, are inherently famous, and that the fame of both rests on the technological media which create and support the famous. The author examines the role of media technology, from ancient times to the present, pointing out how changes in media have always influenced what constituted fame and who was to become famous. He focuses on 19th- and 20th-century America revealing how American democratic egalitarianism, driven by American capitalism, was framed and narrated by photography, film, radio, and television producing a new form of hero—the celebrity. Celebrities are famous not because they occupy some transcendent space beyond mere mortals, but because they are extra-"ordinary" beings who reflect what all of us can become.*

The present-day rush to fame and notoriety appears to be a recent phenomenon brought about by our modern mass media. Some would claim that the motion picture, radio, and television have thrust upon us a plethora of celebrities so catching us up in their notoriety that there is no longer room for or even awareness of "real" heroes. Yet, a look into the history of Western civilization will quickly reveal that, since the time of the ancient Greeks and Romans, "image" and media technology have been linked in the production of heroes. It was Alexander The Great, the conquering hero of the Western world, the demigod of the Greeks, who cast his image (in stern profile with flowing locks) on a coin circulated in all the lands of his victorious armies. In this case it was the "information" carried by the technological medium of the silver and bronze coin that made his image known to all and reminded all of his heroic exploits.

Roman generals whose private armies crushed the enemies of Rome and filled her coffers were rewarded with seats in the Senate or advancement to Proconsuls in recognition of their heroic deeds. They were called *nobles*, the Latin word for "known." To be a hero was to be known, to be celebrated. In ancient Rome all noble houses displayed *imagines* (wax masks)—first idealized, later realistic—of ancestors who had held the chief offices in Rome. In this case, another technological medium—the wax mask—was used to keep the image of the hero before the public. Romans were enamored of the images of those who were known; so much so that every temple and garden was replete with bronze and marble statues of past and present heroes (nobles). Perhaps no civilization other than our modern electronic one has exceeded the Romans in their ability to fill cities with the images of their hero/celebrities.

Visibility (the image) and fame (notoriety) were connected long before the invention of photography and the moving picture—the mass media most commonly linked with the creation of celebrity. In 18th-century France, as well as ancient Rome, civic sculpture, the marble and plaster bust, appeared almost as regularly as engravings to celebrate the hero of the moment or of the neighborhood. In the early stages of the industrial revolution, Josiah Wedgewood (circa 1774) utilized assembly-line methods to create and mass produce portrait medallions of "illustrious moderns" to bring their images into the less prosperous homes of the evolving middle class. Plates, figurines, earthenware pitchers, flatware—a multitude of household objects—featured the faces of the new generation of great men. (Braudy, 1986, 452). In this case we find another technological medium adding to the spread of fame and notoriety, making heroes more widely known and more sought after.

The 18th-century industrial revolution brought mass production and distribution to the image—necessary ingredients of hero worship. It also introduced commercialism into the process of creating and communicating about heroes. With the increasing demands of a growing public (the rapidly expanding middle-class audience) for images of popular heroes, it became possible to build a business and make profits on the distribution of heroic images. Sculpting large statues for public display and painting heroic portraits required time and the talents of an individual artist. With industrial assembly lines and easily made moveable-type printing presses, images of the famous could be quickly and economically produced and placed in the homes of an admiring public. With this increase in the commercialization of images came the demand for more images (more heroes) to satisfy the public's appetite and the entrepreneur's pocketbook.

During the 19th century the march of industrialization and urbanization continued and with it came the new technologies of communication—the photograph, telegraph, telephone, and linotype press—that would inevitably change the concept of the hero and our ideas of the heroic. As Braudy (1986) points out:

> Photography [was] perfected enough [by mid-nineteenth century] for all the fashionable and aspiring of Europe and America to consider it an unpardonable lapse not to have their pictures taken. By the mid-nineteenth century we have already reached a point in the history of modern fame when the rapid growth of newspapers and magazines, the development of the railroad and the

telegraph, along with the rapid sophistication of photography begin the immense changes in the process of communication that still shape our attitudes toward the famous. (p. 450)

George Washington and the founding fathers had been the heroes of the Republic's history books and, not incidently, provided the images for the engravings that could be rapidly reproduced on hand printing presses and hung in public places. But, by mid-19th century, Abraham Lincoln and the Civil War generals were the heroes of the new media—the telegraph, the photograph, and the mass-produced (linotype) newspaper. Even before the Civil War, Lincoln's rapid rise to the presidency and to fame was due in large part to a new medium—telegraphy—that could instantaneously spread his latest words (e.g., the "House Divided" speech) from the Eastern Seaboard to the Illinois frontier and vice versa, and the penny press that could rhapsodize about his exploits as a frontiersman and country lawyer. It was, however, the photograph that made Lincoln a popular celebrity/hero during his lifetime. Lincoln was quick to grasp its political importance. Regular trips to Brady's new Washington, DC photography studio were part of his agenda, and the ensuing photographs did much to popularize him as a Union hero (Braudy, 1986). Brady was able to do the same for Ulysses Grant and other Civil War generals.

Photography would prove to be the ultimate medium of transmission of the image so essential to hero worship. It finalized what began with Alexander the Great and the engraving of his portrait on Greek coins. The photograph made it possible to capture every nuance of the visage of the hero and to inundate the public with hundreds of "realistic" images, thereby firmly establishing that this must truly be a person of notoriety. (Note that our coins and paper money still carry the portraits of our founding fathers and Civil War heroes.) Mass-produced newspapers, on the other hand, provided an equally essential ingredient in the recipe for the modern celebrity/hero—the journalist as storyteller for the hero.

Crucial therefore, to the dissemination of such fame were those new professionals on the American scene—the journalists—who simultaneously said that there were wonderful stories and people in the world, but that they were only really appreciated when written about in the pages of the daily newspaper. When big city dailies expanded after the Civil War, journalists almost immediately nominated themselves as intermediaries between their readers and those they wrote about, familiarizing the already famous and celebrating the previously anonymous, like so many Dantes deciding who should be allocated to hell, purgatory, or heaven. The newspapers and magazines, by their incessant highlighting of individuals and events to sell papers, and their tendency to translate every situation into terms of personal will and conflict, were instrumental in creating the signs by which modern fame would be recognized (Braudy, 1986, p. 508).

The newspaper journalists fulfilled the ancient role of storyteller in the oral culture, and at the same time, that of validator of events required by the print culture. More importantly, the journalist in meeting the commercial demands of selling more and more newspapers became the publicist who sought out an endless number of personages to fill the daily columns of newsprint. There simply were not enough acts of heroism to meet the voracious appetite of the daily newspapers. Wars, of course, were always good for a few heroes as was politics, but as war became more mechanized and less personal, and as politics became more egalitarian and more mundane, journalists had to search elsewhere for celebrity. What better place than the stage—the public performance?

Traditional heroes had always been "on stage" in that they produced a "performance" that was witnessed by those who spread the tale of heroism. Princes, knights, and nobles were constantly aware of their public performances and often staged heroic performances for the benefit of their subjects. America, lacking a monarchy and the aristocracy that provided the material of celebrity for continental journalists, had to create hero/celebrities from the ordinary citizenry. It was the "common man" of America who had to be made into a hero reflecting the democratic values of individualism and success. It was the journalists who sought out these "common" heroes and placed them on stage, both literally and figuratively. Buffalo Bill and Annie Oakley, John L. Sullivan and Ty Cobb, were brought on stage and their performances made notorious by myriads of journalists who kept the public informed of every word and deed.

> The journalists and other publicists of late nineteenth-century success were selling the public a fascinating blend of empathy and control: empathy with the successful; control through information about them and their world. Here, they said, were people whose integral sense of self, their "character," allowed them to make sense of the world, that is, ensure their success in it. And that success, whether it came from being a famous gunfighter or a money-making industrialist, was affirmed by fame. (Braudy, 1986, p. 509)

America was a new land, a new nation built on egalitarianism and opportunity rather than wealth and aristocracy. It called for new heroes, and the journalistic storytellers searched out new areas in which to locate and exploit heroic acts suitable to this unique nation. The penny press with its sensational scandal sheets was an ideal medium for creating hero/celebrities to fulfill the mythic needs of the middle and working classes crowded together in the anonymity of burgeoning industrial cities. What better place to find heroes than in those places where ordinary persons rose above ordinary circumstances and achieved heroic proportions?

The great John L. Sullivan, heavyweight boxing champion of the world, was an ideal American hero/celebrity of the late 19th century. Without formal education and without the benefit of family name and fortune he came out of the workplace to become a real-life John Bunyan and a mythic warrior conquering all opponents, overcoming the barriers to fame and fortune. His boxing prowess, his super-human strength, his voracious appetites, and most of all his rugged good looks and knowing smile made him an ideal candidate to be celebrated by the modern press. His every act, from pummeling an opponent, to felling a tree, to consuming 12 dozen oysters and 15 steaks in one sitting was dutifully and solemnly reported by the press. Photographs and sketches of him hung in every barroom, police station, firehouse, and theater. Crowds followed him, and he was welcomed in city halls and state houses.

Sullivan represented the new American hero, not one who had defended the Republic in battle or created a great invention or made great personal sacrifice, but rather one with whom the working class could identify: a rugged individual who became more celebrated than any priest, politician, or general by means of his own cunning and strength. He was everyman, at least what every factory and farm worker could aspire to if he just had the strength and the right opportunity. It was, of course, the mass media that brought this image to the public and kept it foremost in people's minds with hundreds of inches of newsprint and thousands of photographs and drawings. Sullivan recognized it was more than his victories in the ring that brought him notoriety. It was being available to the press, it was being on stage at all times, it was being able to perform the role the press had created to fill the public's demand for a working-class hero.

> American popular entertainment had transformed the show of monarchy, whose point was to watch someone who is clearly inimitable and different, into the show whose point was to watch an extension of oneself, in a performance put on for one's special benefit. . . . Thrust forward by the popular press's new resources for focus and celebration, it was a style of social behavior consonant with the aspirations of the age, and both the self-made man and his publicists were intent on transforming the internal sanctions of the old morality into external structures of behavior and self-display. (Braudy, 1986, p. 510)

There were still traditional heroes to be found in textbooks and patriotic speeches, but they were being supplemented by the new heroes whose deeds were actions (performances) of the moment rather the past. These new heroes who were created by the daily press often had performed great deeds, but their notoriety was based in large part on their ability to keep performing for a public anxious to have its own fantasies verified. Buffalo Bill Cody—the frontiersman, Indian scout, and buffalo hunter without peer—was an example of the new hero/celebrity. He gained fame when the railroads and telegraph lines moved west, accompanied by journalists eager to bring tales of the frontier to the public's doorstep each morning. These print storytellers needed a hero on whom to hang their narrative of the conquest of the Wild West, and Buffalo Bill admirably filled that need. His lean frame and steely eyes capped by flowing golden locks made him an ideal "image" for writer, photographer, and sketch artist alike. The telegraph wire made it possible to speed daily reports of his exploits to thousands of readers who could see in him the representative

American who had left behind the old oppressive ways of Europe and who was pushing forward the boundaries of freedom and opportunity.

Had Buffalo Bill died fighting off an Indian attack he might have become just another folk hero. Yet, it was his showmanship that made him into the new breed of celebrity hero. After the railroads were built and the buffalo and the Indians slaughtered, he created an enormously successful road show and rodeo that kept him in the public eye and heart for many years. On a daily basis, with the help of publicists and the press, he recreated his own image as a frontier hero. He was now performing on stage the deeds that first brought him to public attention. Throngs eagerly awaited his arrival. They rose and shouted hearty hurrahs as he rode into the ring in glittering attire, carrying high a huge American flag. They bought their tickets and cheered mightily with each reenactment of his gallant defense of the wagon train against the heathen Indians. It was no longer necessary to recall the original deed of heroism. The celebrity performed the role of hero every day, and the press celebrated the performer rather than the deed.

THE NEW MEDIA AND THE DOMINANCE OF CELEBRITY

It was the invention of the motion picture and its development as universal storyteller that ended the connection between heroic act and hero. The ability of the motion picture medium to create a realistic setting and deliver an audience to that time and place made it possible for performers to become surrogate heroes. John Barrymore and Douglas Fairbanks, Sr. did not have to actually defeat the armies at Agincourt or subdue the Barbary pirates; they could do it on the silver screen. They did not have to do anything more heroic than undergo the rigors of acting and collecting their paychecks. Yet, they became celebrated in the same sense that all heroes are; they were made notorious, and they became famous because they were so well known. They used the same means of notoriety that Alexander the Great had used—a technological medium of communication that kept their visual image and personage foremost in the public's mind. In this case it was the motion picture, photographic, and lithographic media that made them visible and noble (known). It is probably more accurate to say they were used by the media that needed known performers to sell commercial products to a heterogeneous and diverse public who lacked a common cultural heritage and who were adrift in a burgeoning, impersonal industrial society. The mass media in both form and substance gave these performers a persona and image that transcended the drudgery of the public's workaday life and held out the possibility that ordinary Americans might have the media spotlight suddenly shine on them and turn them into celebrities (Gamson, 1992).

The new motion picture camera in the hands of cinema technocrats could produce the most fantastic adventures from a Hollywood backlot. Hollywood was, and is, the supreme storyteller. Whatever people needed for inspiration or distraction—*The Birth of a Nation, Mr. Deeds Goes to Washington, Tarzan of the Apes, Singing in the Rain*—could be made in Hollywood, shipped to every town and city, and be viewed simultaneously by almost all Americans. The performance on the screen was better than reality. Thanks to the form of the cinematic medium, every scene could be reshot and reedited to create a seamless story that no witness to an actual event could ever describe. Heroism, adventure, romance, and comedy could all be achieved in an hour and a half. For viewers there were no distracting miscues, no pretending the proscenium arch did not exist, no frantic scene changes, no difficult lines of print to read, no fear of imagining the event other than as it actually was, and no need to trust it to the unsure memory of a human storyteller. The event and the hero was there on the screen where everyone could see what "actually happened" and every viewer could know that her or his view of it was as good as anyone else's.

TO BE SEEN IS TO BE FREE, TO BE HEROIC, TO BE AMERICAN

America had to organize a culture from the ground up, and in that organization the unifying and crystallizing function of faces was of prime importance. America was a vast land of diverse peoples disconnected from the European villages and cities which had circumscribed their role and identified their class. Americans rejected the concept of class, and more resolutely, images of monarchs and aristocrats were emphatically rejected. Even images of saints and saviors were set aside eventually for failing to provide appropriate celebrity for people's daily lives. Instead it was the faces of ordinary Americans who performed in extraordinary circumstances that provided the inspiration and unification appropriate for this new egalitarian culture. The power of the visible spirit in America absorbed religious sanction instead of competing with it. To be seen as an ordinary American, and at the same time, be recognized as a notorious frontiersman or industrial baron was a transcendent role appropriate to the genuine American hero. However, as the frontier receded and the romanticism of the self-made man succumbed to the crush of immigration and the numbing anonymity of the assembly line and the urban ghetto, a universal storyteller was needed who could create fantastic adventures and mythic heroes to keep alive the promise of this new land. The Hollywood motion picture industry admirably filled that function in the first half of the 20th century.

The motion picture camera and the silver screen made an ideal technological medium for sanctifying the face of the ordinary American. The camera not only produced individual photographs in a way that appeared to capture true motion, but its lens and its mobility had an affinity for the human face. The camera lens could do what the stage and the book could not. It could bring the viewer within a few inches of the performer's face, creating an intimacy and familiarity never before available to the old heroes of oral and print cultures. The close-up shot negated the stage actor's exaggerated gestures, facial expressions, and vocal intonations and sought out the smooth features, twinkling eyes, natural smile, and intimate voice of the idealized American.

Sergeant York, the hero of World War I, was more appealing in the image of Hollywood star, Gary Cooper, than in his own plain, backwoods appearance. In the camera's eye, Gary Cooper was the way the hero York should look and talk. Gary Cooper became and remained a famous celebrity. Sergeant York became a forgotten hero, never attaining the celebrity proportions of a Hollywood star. Mary Pickford needed no great talent as a stage performer or the circumstance of a heroic deed. She became notorious as "the darling of the silver screen" because her unblemished, childlike face, magnified tenfold by the close-up lens, signified everything the new American woman should be. The motion picture camera loved the ideal face—enhanced by the make-up artist—and American audiences loved the close-up iconography of the silver screen. Viewers could stare up at huge images that dominated the darkened confines of the theater and whose actions could confirm all their social fantasies, all the while verifying that the American image was truly heroic.

The arrival of the Hollywood version of the tribe's stories set off a great "talent" hunt to locate among the common folk of mid-America the potential heroes and heroines of the motion picture screen. Those who were sought were not personages of heroic size or transcendent talent, but those who had the face that could fulfill the image of the American as "Everyman" or "Miss Liberty." The technology of the camera lens made "face" the significant attribute of celebrityhood. That such famous personages as Humphrey Bogart had to stand on boxes or wear elevator shoes while performing in front of the camera mattered not as long as they had the face—the look of notoriety. In turn, all Americans, no matter how humble their origins, how lacking in physical or intellectual qualities, could aspire to notoriety and fame if only they could be discovered by Hollywood talent scouts (Gamson, 1992, pp. 4-6). The hero of the motion picture culture is not a "heavy" figure noted for great physical strength and moral courage, nor the "lighter" figure of print known for intellectual cunning and strategy (see Strate, this volume), but rather a figure of "face"—an image that unifies all Americans into the one true and noble icon that is heroic because it is American.

The advent of another technological medium of communication served to make the Hollywood celebrity/hero even closer and more representative of the ordinary American. Radio, unlike the motion picture, is of the moment, making every listener part of the place and the event as it occurs. Radio audiences do not have to assemble in the theater nor set aside a Friday or Saturday night for motion picture viewing. Radio is where the listener is, at home, in the automobile, at the ball park. It is simultaneous with the event as it occurs. It can make celebrities of any or all of the participants in the event as we listen to their voices describing the terror, the pain, and the triumph as it unfolds.

Radio, although faceless, made it possible for every American to actively participate in heroic events. It was radio that allowed, even required, a worldwide audience to participate in the agonizing suspense of Lindbergh's transatlantic flight. Radio, and its announcer's voice, was there as Lucky Lindy prepared for take off in the Spirit of St. Louis. It was these same radio voices that kept listeners glued to their wireless sets, listening for news about pilot and plane as they flew into the storm-swept skies of the North Atlantic. And, it was radio that allowed Americans, British, French, and others to join the crowds at Orly Airport and participate in Lindbergh's moment of heroism. The actual words of the Lone Eagle could be heard by millions at the very moment of his triumph. In an instant he was a world-renown celebrity. Of course, there was the deed in Lindbergh's case, and his story would have eventually been told in print and by word of mouth, but it was radio that made the audience members feel they were part of heroic performance. It is this quality of instantaneousness that radio provides that makes people feel there is very little that separates them from the hero/celebrity.

More importantly, radio technology brings the "live" voice to us at the same distance at which we converse with our family and friends. It is an intimate voice, one that we invite into our homes and our daily lives, and when those radio voices are there on a continual basis fulfilling our needs for both information and escape, we bestow celebrity status on the radio performer as well those about whom they are talking. These radio personalities (the phrase "radio personality" was coined to describe their special status) do not have to perform great deeds or even have acting talents, they only have to be there—to be heard by millions—reassuring us that they are in touch with important events and with other celebrities.

An early radio celebrity, Arthur Godfrey, a skilled pilot, achieved great notoriety not because of his aerial exploits, but because his radio voice and his talent program provided both escape entertainment and assurance for millions of Americans. His radio personality was that of a "good neighbor," bright, cheerful, nonthreatening, caring, and sincere—an ideal American at a time when people were confined more and more to the workplace and the home and spent less time with neighbors and community (Schickel, 1985; Warner & Henry, 1948). Some of these radio voices, the Jack Bennys and the Bob Hopes, had a special talent for endearing themselves to the American audience. They were the little guy, the ordinary American struggling with a vast uncaring industrial system and pompous authority. They were, at times, foolish and funny, but always self-reliant, clever, and caring for their fellow humans.

Radio succeeded in making the storyteller the celebrity. Radio, unlike the newspaper, in which journalists are separated from the public by the printed page, makes the teller of the story more important than the story itself. The legendary Edward R. Murrow of CBS Radio News interviewed the famous from around the world and was on hand at the important events of the day. Many of those he spoke with had done great things, but it was Murrow who became a famous celebrity because he seemed to have the power to be everywhere that mattered and to command the time of the great and not so great leaders of the world. Radio, like the motion picture, favored the idealized American. In this case the technology focused on the voice. It favored a general American pattern of speech and a vocal personality that idealized the new American—direct, fluent, quick-witted, humorous, at times self-deprecating, but always in command. Interestingly it was almost always a male voice. Radio's continual presence in our daily lives made those voices so well known that they took on a celebrity status and in some cases achieved heroic proportions. The voice of the storyteller had become the voice of the celebrity/hero.

It would be wrong to think each medium of mass communication produces its own set of celebrities. More accurately, all modern mass media interact and interconnect to give celebrity status such impact that no American can live in the last half of the 20th century without a knowledge of celebrities and without being influenced by their impact on American culture (Caughey, 1986). Motion picture stars became radio personalities, for example, Eddie Cantor. Radio personalities became motion picture celebrities, for example, Bob Hope and Bing Crosby. Some were renown in all the modern media, such as Will Rogers, who wrote for the daily press, appeared regularly on radio, and made countless motion pictures while continually holding the spotlight with his unusual travels.

What photography, lithography, and cinematography had begun in the 19th century, radio and television completed in the 20th century. The public no longer had to step outside to find the hero and the heroic. They did not have to await the arrival of a new heroic story at the neighborhood theater or even walk to the front door to pick up a copy of a newspaper full of celebrity gossip and publicity. The radio and then television brought the voices and images of celebrities into people's living rooms, kitchens, and bedrooms on a nonstop basis. The voices of each new celebrity, as well as of many old celebrities, became as well known as the voices of family members. Celebrity faces that filled the TV game shows, series, soap operas, and newscasts became more familiar than that of the President of the United States and certainly more celebrated than those of historical figures who had performed heroic deeds (Langer, 1981). Image and performance became everything. The acting performance on screen and on television was reinforced by the performed "real-life" appearance on radio, television, and in fan magazines. How celebrities dressed, talked, and moved became a popular ballet imitated by millions of fans in a ritualistic plebiscite, reaffirming their status as celebrity while confirming their closeness to the common person.

If the celebrity appetite of the daily newspaper was enormous, the appetite of radio and television was insatiable. With hundreds of hours of programming to be filled on a daily basis and their very existence dependent on attracting and holding large audiences, radio, and more particularly television, had to make everyday events into celebrated performances. The activities of a few Hollywood stars were not enough. Singers, dancers, writers, magicians, and even preachers and revolutionaries had to be cast as TV celebrities (Langer, 1981). Celebrity demand and media command are so ubiquitous that there is hardly room any longer for what some think of as "traditional heroes." Television with its insatiable appetite for visually appealing, attention-commanding personae has helped produce a whirlwind of celebrities.

Each medium draws on the form and structure of each other medium to insure that celebrities achieve superstar status. Although some celebrities first achieve notoriety in one medium, they work tirelessly through press agents and managers to make sure they are seen on television, appear in motion pictures, are interviewed on radio and in print, and have recordings available for purchase. Each mass medium, on the other hand, works diligently to insure it does not miss an opportunity to gather an audience by exploiting the most acclaimed celebrities. Thus there is a synergy created, primarily, of course, for the production of profit and wealth, in which celebrities become public figures simply because every medium that every American relies on for connection and comfort depends on these personae to provide the content of the media's messages to the audiences they must ensnare. Americans come to rely on these celebrities to inform them about themselves, who and what they are, what is important, and what is to be valued (Caughey, 1986). The celebrity, in that sense, fulfills the ancient role of the hero in providing a guide to civic virtue and pride.

ooooo *5*

The Wrinkle Theory: 'The Deconsecration of the Hero

Gary Gumpert
Queens College

❐ *"See the hero run, look for the flaws, watch the hero fall, look for another hero." Gumpert asks why our contemporary heroes become so quickly tarnished and why we seem to have a growing preference for desecrated heroes. He examines the public confusion over celebrity and hero and offers an explanation for the rise of the antihero. His position is that the fascination with the flawed and contaminated hero is related, in part, to the Aristotelian notion of the tragic hero and, in part, to the transformation of the tragic flaw by our contemporary media. He describes how the comic book hero has shifted from the all powerful to the vulnerable, how radio brought the hero into the living room, and how the motion picture and TV screen brought us close enough to the hero to be able to detect physical and emotional flaws. He offers his "wrinkle theory" to explain the present shift in allegiance from the protagonist to the antagonist.*

CONTEMPORARY HEROES

Hero . . . Antiq. A name given to men of superhuman strength, courage, or ability, favored by the gods; regarded later as demigods, and immortal. 2. One who does brave or noble deeds; an illustrious warrior 1586. 3. A man who exhibits extraordinary bravery, firmness, or greatness of soul, in connexion with any pursuit, work, or enterprise; a man admired and venerated for his achievements and noble qualities 1661. 4. A man who forms the subject of an epic; the chief male personage in a poem, play, or story 1697 (*Oxford Universal Dictionary*, 1955, p. 895)

Despite this antediluvian sexist explication, the definition is cited to serve as a barometer, a yardstick, to gauge and measure the vagaries of the word. The use and application of *hero* is complex and bewildering. What is a hero? Who are our heroes? This chapter contrasts our conflicting notions of the hero and shows that our relationship to the phenomenon is linked to the intrinsic properties that define the media that are used to disseminate the legends of heroes.

The heroes of the past are generally vivid two-dimensional figures whose persona and portraits appear to have been painted with broad bold strokes. They are figures whose deeds inspire, awe, and overshadow the simple ordinary human folk. Each culture has a set of heroes of the past who represent virtue and sacrifice, whose determination against a host of forces serves as symbols of courage. These are the symbols of morality transmitted from one generation to the next. They are the nondebatable images of the past that persist and guide. But the unquestionable nature of such heroes seems to have vanished in the contemporary quest for larger-than life-individuals with whom to identify. The heroes business is not what it used to be. It has descended into the nether world of the celebrity.

Russell Baker (1990) suggests that Marion Barry's achievements as a Mississippi civil rights activist and his election as Mayor of Washington, DC placed him on a potential hero path from which temptation and greed would successfully entice him.

> Heroes are pretty well all washed up in the United States these days. In place of heroes, we now have celebrities, which is to say, junk people.
>
> The celebrities' social mission is to have their frailties, peccadilloes and vices lavishly recorded by press and television to keep the uncelebrated mass titillated. Their purpose to keep us happy with our anonymity.
>
> Saving yourself from becoming a celebrity is hard once you acquire a taste for seeing your name in headlines. (p. A27)

Women, drugs, and corruption undid the good mayor. Baker suggests that Mayor Barry failed heroism because he succumbed to the less than noble enticements of celebrity status.

Writer Fred Bruning (1990) contrasted the hero worship of Nelson Mandela, as he was released from prison and returned to Soweto, with John Gotti, who returned to his admirers after being acquitted (in the 1989 trial) on charges of hiring assailants to assault and batter a fellow gangster. Bruning, like Baker, expresses a concern about the shortage of heroes.

> Americans may feel they have no choice but to entertain applications from just about anyone—killers, thugs, and hijackers included. We have the peculiar luxury of choosing our heroes badly and elevating the least worthy beyond their fondest dreams. To a prosecutor in New York, John Gotti may be "a badly articulate lowlife, a thug by even Mafia standards." To those easily dazzled, however, Gotti is irresistible—a strutting and disdainful dandy in slick suits who waves to admirers from behind the windows of a burgundy Cadillac, who sneers at the law and those who enforce it, a movieland character as apt to spend his hours in local hangouts as in the city's finest restaurants, a smoothie

who three times in four years has faced criminal charges and all three times beaten the rap, a consummate practitioner of streetsmanship who proved with his swagger and style that only suckers settle for the legal limit. (p. 13)

Then there is the tale of Toyohiro Akiyama, "A Japanese Innovation: The Space Antihero" (Sanger, 1990). For a number of years in the late 1960s and early 1970s the space program and its astronauts captured the imagination of many people. After all, to be propelled into space and weightlessness, to orbit the earth and walk on the moon, are feats of courage that require adventurers larger than life. It was the hope of the Japanese Television System that having the first television journalist to orbit the earth would boost its ratings. So, they paid the Soviet Union $12 million to have Toyohiro Akiyama accompany Soviet astronauts in space.

> Struggling through the first of his nightly live broadcasts from the heavens, Mr. Akiyama spent a lot of time describing the uglier details of space sickness. A chain smoker, he repeatedly longed for a cigarette. His brain, he complained, felt as if it was "floating around in my head." Told to pack light, he failed to bring along enough underwear . . .
> At dinnertime he mused, "I wish I had brought some natto," the smelly, fermented soybeans that even many Japanese say they cannot bring themselves to swallow . . .
> Mr. Akiyama seems like a man who wants nothing more than a chance to get back home, open a beer, and light up. He worries that his children are spending too much time in front of the television, even if it is to watch their father bounce into his astronaut colleagues. (p. 1, 5).

What do Marion Barry, John Gotti, and Toyohiro Akiyama have in common? Probably very little, except the consensus that somehow their stature and nobility does not measure up to the larger-than-life dimensions of the likes of Mahatma Gandhi, Abraham Lincoln, Jeanne D'Arc, George Washington, and Thomas à Becket.

Reporter Charles Leerhsen (1990) asked teenagers in a military academy in Indiana, in a girls' school in Dallas, in a high school in the Midwest, and on an Indian reservation to list their heroes. The number one choice by consensus of all the students was the Chicago Bulls' basketball star, Michael Jordan (p. 44) The group of eclectic achievers selected by Culver Academy students included, perhaps predictably, a military array of Ulysses S. Grant, Robert E. Lee, Alexander the Great, Chuck Yeager, Audie Murphy, and Sergeant York, in addition to the noncombative roster of Mother Teresa, Martin Luther King, Jr., Houdini, Winnie the Pooh, Lucille Ball, Margaret Thatcher, Superman, and Jane Goodall. Students at the Hockaday School for girls in North Dallas mentioned Martin Luther King, Jr., Michael Jordan, Superman, James Dean, Anne Frank, Oliver North, and Sineaed O'Conner. Pupils at a high school in the Bronx mentioned fashion model Elle MacPherson, Bart Simpson, God, Arsenio Hall, Michelangelo, Larry Bird, Mayor Dinkins, and Public

Enemy. The Indian reservation students included native American heroes such as Fools Crow and Chief Red Cloud, but Michael Jordan got the most votes. In addition, Donald Trump, Michael Milken, and Maury Povich were mentioned.

The Leerhsen survey reveals a tendency to select individuals who are often less noble and more ordinary, but with characteristics more commonly shared by most of the teenagers than the individuals who are generally associated with heroes. Leerhsen mirrors his fellow journalists' observation that the contemporary heroes chosen are a somewhat tarnished and often tawdry group.

> Thanks to TV and celebrity journalism, kids all over the country are choosing from the same menu of celebrities—and rarely with any great enthusiasm. The problem is not that fame comes, these days, to those who don't deserve it. The shortage of really inspiring heroes probably has more to do with the dearth of pure fans. So many kids today are so informed about pop culture—and about who's cheating on their mate and who's cheating on their taxes; who's been to Betty Ford and who still hasn't—that it's as if they have one foot in the audience and one behind the scenes. Such familiarity must inevitably breed at least a little contempt. (p. 47)

Even though the confusion between *hero* and *celebrity* is self-evident (they serve different functions), one is struck by an increasingly different perception of the role model as expressed by the polled teenagers from previous periods in time. The loss of the untarnished, traditional hero is the critical and mystifying issue that needs to be explored.

The position taken in this chapter is that the rise of the celebrity, the fascination with a flawed and contaminated hero, and the strange appeal of the villain as hero is related to the effect of contemporary media developments on the Aristotelian notion of those necessary characteristics that constitute the tragic hero.

THE TRAGIC HERO

The nature and status of the hero became an important dramatic theory issue in theatre several years ago as scholars debated whether contemporary playwrights could create a modern protagonist with whom the audience would identify in the heroic sense. Can today's playwright emulate the heroic tragedies of Aeschylus, Sophocles, Euripides, and Shakespeare? In the late 1940s the debate was stimulated by the production of Arthur Miller's *Death of a Salesman*. In response, Joseph Wood Krutch, the dramatic critic for the *Nation*, wrote "The Tragic Fallacy." For those who claimed that salesman Willy Loman was a contemporary tragic hero, Krutch dissented stating that there could be no common tragic hero without the requisite fall from heights of grandeur; the modern-day hero does not have the necessary eminence to accompany the great fall which evokes our pity and fear (Krutch, 1947).

The original and primary work which articulated the nature of the tragic hero was Aristotle's *Poetics* (1954) in which the hero of Greek drama is described as a great person who falls from "reputation and prosperity" through "some error in judgment," a flaw in his or her character.

> The perfect Plot, accordingly, must have a single, and not . . . a double issue; the change in the hero's fortunes must be not from misery to happiness, but on the contrary from happiness to misery; and the cause of it must lie, not in any depravity, but in some great error in his part. (p. 239)

Aristotle's protagonist is a person of such stature and nobility that his or her fall arouses in the audience the "tragic pleasure of pity and fear" (p. 240) (referring to the process of catharsis or purgation which purifies the spirit of that audience as they witness and learn from the downfall of that grand and majestic figure). For the Greek audience the tragedy mirrors reality.

The question posed by contemporary critics is whether for a 20th-century audience this extraordinary sense of a dramatic relationship can ever exist. The Greek and Elizabethan tragedies can be appreciated as works of art, but Krutch (1947) maintains that their therapeutic nature is diminished because the social and psychological structure of modern times is radically different from those early periods in history. "For while to us the triumphant voices come from far away and tell of a heroic world which no longer exists, to them they spoke of immediate realities and revealed the inner meaning of events amidst which they still lived" (p. 518).

Instead of "tragedy" the contemporary theatre achieves the "tragic"—an experience quite different from the elevation of spirit which characterized earlier dramatic experience.

> The term [tragedy] is a misnomer since it is obvious that the works in question have nothing in common with the classical examples of the genre and produce in the reader a sense of depression which is the exact opposite of that elation generated when the spirit of a Shakespeare rises joyously superior to the outward calamities which he recounts and celebrates the greatness of the human spirit whose travail he describes. (p. 518)

Krutch uses as a basis for his argument the Aristotelian view that tragedy is the "imitation of noble actions," contending that contemporary society has no real conception of a noble action. An action which is considered noble depends upon an understanding of nobility; it relies on believing oneself capable of having a grand and heroic nature.

> If the plays and the novels of today deal with little people and less mighty emotions it is not because we have become interested in commonplace souls and their unglamorous adventures, but because we have come, willy-nilly, to see the soul of man as commonplace and its emotions as mean. (p. 519)

The tragic fallacy is the assumption or illusion that an individual's soul is an integral part of the universe, that for the moment we detach ourselves from a pessimistic view of the nature of human beings in order to empathize with the dramatic hero.

Whether it is possible to have a tragic hero in a contemporary age may be somewhat of an esoteric question, but its answer provides some clues about an age in which Toyohiro Akiyama, Freddy Krueger, and Darth Veder join Abraham Lincoln, Moses, and John F. Kennedy as either role models or heroes.

THE COMIC BOOK HERO

Heroes are not the same to all people at all times in their lives. Cultural history and diversity shape the portraits of heroes. They serve different functions and needs at particular periods in time and during stages of individual growth and maturation. It seems that during childhood and adolescence especially a cadre of heroes is required, perhaps to satisfy inner frustrations, perhaps to provide secret visions and dreams in contrast to the external pressures imposed by growing up in an adult world. Therefore, the heroes of youth act as fascinating barometers of attitude. One area in which the dynamics of change can be seen is in the world of comic strips and books.

Stan Lee, one of the impresarios of the comic book, realized in the early 1970s that economics and the times required a change in the persona of the comic book hero. With this in mind he created a number of comic book heroes, all bordering on the edge of the heroic and pathetic. Marvel Comics and Stan Lee produced the Fantastic Four: "The Invisible Girl," "The Human Torch," "Mr. Fantastic," and "The Thing" (later they become "Iron Man," "Thor," "Spiderman," and "The Thing"). Lee's reasoning behind the creation of these strange characters is extremely revealing.

> Let's let them not always get along well; let's let them have arguments. Let's make them talk like real people and react like real people. Why should they all get superpowers that make them beautiful? Let's get a guy who becomes very ugly. That was the "Thing." I hate heroes anyway. Just because a guy has superpowers, why couldn't he be a nebbish, have sinus trouble and athlete's foot? (cited in Braun 1971, p. 43)

The most successful of Lee's antiheroes is Spiderman, an immediate hit. "Spidey," as he is known to his fans, is actually Peter Parker, a teenager who has the proportionate strength of a spider and yet, in Lee's words, "can still lose a fight, make dumb mistakes, have acne, have trouble with girls and have not too much money." Someone says to Spiderman, "Don't you feel like a jerk parading around in public in that get-up?" Spiderman questions himself, "Can they be right? Am I really some sort of crackpot wasting my time seeking fame and glory? Why do I do it? Why don't I give the whole thing up?" (p. 43). So,

THE WRINKLE THEORY

this strange hero has an identity crisis—one that was symptomatic of an age of anxiety—the strange 1960s.

In an earlier period the comic book hero was a character of a vastly different sort, responding to a differently woven cultural tapestry. One shift in comic strip history occurred in the 1930s when the adventure strip first appeared. Prior to that time, the comic strip primarily celebrated the comical, rather than the serious narrative of adventure. Of the 22 comic strips that originated in the 1920s, only 2 stressed the power of the main character: "Buck Rogers" and "Tarzan." In contrast, 21 strips were begun in the 1930s, and 12 of them were about powerful people including: "Joe Palooka," "Dick Tracy," "Terry and the Pirates," "Flash Gordon," "The Lone Ranger," "Alley Oop," and "Superman." One explanation of this trend was offered by Sales (1972), writing in *Psychology Today*:

> When we are afraid . . . we turn to strong leaders who can protect us. We become intolerant of outgroups and of those who differ from us. We admire power and those who wield power; we come to despise weakness and ambiguity. We are cynical about mankind, and we become superstitious. In short, when we are threatened, we become authoritarian. (p. 94)

What is particularly significant in the Marvel Comic shift is the transformation of the traditional comic book hero from the "all-powerful" to the "vulnerable somewhat-powerful" character. Suddenly, instead of superheroes who make no mistakes, superheroes emerge with flaws in their character.

In 1970, Denny O'Neil revived the adventures of two superheroes, "Green Lantern" and "Green Arrow." The revival took place at a time of social turmoil in the United States, at a time when activism, protest, and disillusionment had become commonplace.

> FOR YEARS HE HAS BEEN A PROUD MAN! HE HAS WORN THE **POWER RING** OF THE **GUARDIANS**, AND USED IT WELL, AND NEVER DOUBTED THE RIGHTEOUSNESS OF HIS CAUSE. . . . [The box of narrative accompanies the image of the muscular masked hero in green swooping over a crowed urban street full of cars and trucks.]
>
> IN THE NEXT **DOZEN SECONDS**, AN EVENT WILL OCCUR WHICH WILL SIGNAL THE END OF HIS GRANDEUR, AND THE BEGINNING OF A LONG TORMENT . . .
>
> THERE WILL BE NO HAPPY ENDING FOR THIS IS NOT A HAPPY TALE . . . NOR A SIMPLE ONE, BUT WHAT WE ARE ABOUT TO WITNESS IS, PERHAPS INEVITABLE—HIS NAME, OF COURSE, IS— **GREEN LANTERN** [in bold green large letters]—AND OFTEN HAS VOWED—**NO EVIL SHALL ESCAPE MY SIGHT!** [in large bold red letters silhouetted in yellow] . . .
>
> HE HAS BEEN FOOLING HIMSELF. (*Green Hornet/Green Lantern*, 1970, p. 1)

That is the introduction to the April 1970 issue that traces the journey of the superheroes from the all-powerful to the doubting to the superhero social activist status. It is a questioning hero who must face the realization that he has defended a middle-aged man being attacked by a mob, only to find out that he rescued a slum lord. In that issue's epilogue the Green Arrow berates his friend the Green Lantern: "YOU CALL YOURSELF A **HERO!** CHUM . . . YOU DON'T EVEN QUALIFY AS A MAN! (p. 21).

THE CELEBRATION OF THE FLAW

Apparently the time of the superhero has passed and perhaps Krutch was correct in suggesting that the distance between hero and audience has grown so far that a frame of reference, a required ingredient for the assessment of greatness, has virtually disappeared. Yet the need for heroes persists. Meyrowitz (1985) states:

> Still we hunger for heroes, and perhaps our search beneath social masks is filled with the hope of finding people whose private selves are as admirable as their public ones. But since most of the people who make enduring contributions to our culture remain under our scrutiny too long to remain pure in our eyes, we have also begun to focus on people who make one grand gesture or who complete a single courageous act that cannot be undermined by scrutiny. (p. 311)

Heroes are useful only as long as they are icons with whom an audience can identify, when one's social and psychological needs are not fulfilled elsewhere. The unemployed hero is one who does not survive scrutiny, either because his or her persona is out of date and too remote, or because familiarity has bred contempt. The audience is too close to the former superstar. Instead of the traditional noble hero, the contemporary champion, even if he or she is not one of the average folks, must now exhibit some ordinary traits.

There is yet another aspect of the deconsecration of the hero that is linked to the traditional depiction of the hero. Aristotle described the tragic hero as someone who, through "some error in judgment," a flaw in his or her character, falls from prosperity and stature to destruction and despair. The flaw, in this case, is the pivotal attribute around which the circumstances of the fall revolves. It is the flaw that connected audience and hero and that facilitated the complex emotional relationship in the "tragic pleasure of pity and fear" between audience and hero. The result of that relationship was spiritual and psychological elevation, the celebration of the moral order. The shift in the contemporary approach to the hero requires that not only must the hero share in our ordinariness, but that we discover the less-than-virtuous traits with which we can identify. In short, the flaw is the thing, the trait to be discovered and, perhaps, to be celebrated.

Yet, why should this strange disenchantment with the grand and noble

THE WRINKLE THEORY

hero emerge at this time? Certainly, time and circumstances change attitudes and perspectives, but additional factors have been instrumental in altering the psychological distance between hero and audience. Assuming that the potential of the heroic is still a part of contemporary society, the extent to which the public has access to heroes or, as Meyrowitz suggests, the degree to which heroes can survive scrutiny, becomes a central controlling factor. This chapter maintains that it is the technology and organization of the media of communication that promote scrutiny and deter, alter, and facilitate the heroic relationship.

THE MEDIUM AND THE HERO

The materials of heroes are legends: tales passed from one generation to the next, surviving the coloration of time, that are eventually gathered and chronicled by masterful tellers of tales. The medium of the traditional hero was memory. Havelock (1963) points out the form of the tale was directly connected to the nature of the medium:

> The psychology of oral memorization and oral record required the content of what is memorized to be a set of doings. This in turn presupposes actors or agents. Again, since the content to be preserved must place great emphasis on public and private law, the agents must be conspicuous and political people. Hence they become heroes. All non-human phenomena must by metaphor be translated into sets of doings, and the commonest device for achieving this is to represent them as acts and decisions of especially conspicuous agents, namely gods. (p. 171)

Just as memory is a determinant of heroic form, the very nature of the hero would be transformed over time along with the evolution and development of media technology.

Each medium is defined by the intrinsic properties, the technical and scientific components, that determine transmission and artistic potential. The sensory components of a medium establish a relationship between audience member and event, based upon the nature of that which is transmitted, the actual distance bridged, and the psychological distance that exists between them. Thus, the reader of a book can achieve a level of intimacy with writer, character, and scene because the auditory and visual components of the literary experience are created by words which are decoded from the printed page. The radio listener stimulated by the creative manipulation of sound generates an auditory and visual theatre of the mind, based upon the absence of the visual. As the comic strip relied upon a nonphotographic visual mode, it stylized the visual into either comedic or heroic genres because it could transcend the realistic. Still photography isolates and magnifies detail and stimulates the imagination by freezing details in time. In contrast, the motion picture, with both auditory and visual components, is particularly defined by both the large dark auditorium and the size of the screen upon which the images are projected. Therefore, spectacle, pageantry, and the hero are particularly connected with the cinema because of its potentially larger-than-life capability. In contrast, the relatively small television screen miniaturizes spectacle and emphasizes intimacy and detail. There is an obvious connection between the small television screen and cameras, lenses, and the editing system used to capture minute details magnified and transmitted on that screen.

In "I Am A Camera: The Mediated Self," (1986) Cathcart and I pointed out that media technology altered the interaction of individuals and groups. We argued that "not only are the media substantively altering the relationship among individuals, but that the formulation of the individual's *self image* is, in large part, media dependent" (p. 90). Similarly, the sensory components of a medium increase or decrease the psychological distance between the mediated event and the auditor of that event. Thus, the intrinsic properties of each medium determine an ideal aesthetic relationship which is imposed upon the content being transmitted. The "star" system of the motion picture can be related to the scope and proportions of the screen and the necessary cameras, film, lenses, and projector simultaneously developed. Television would, however, reduce cinemascopic legends into 17-inch neighbors. It is this transformation of magnitude that is examined in Langer's (1981) analysis of television's "personality system." "What is the significance of the fact that whereas the cinema established a 'star system,' television has not? There are stars of stage, screen *and* television, but no stars of television alone. Instead we encounter what television calls its 'personalities'" (p. 351).

If familiarity can breed contempt, intimacy may erode nobility. Ong (1977) notes that with the electronic age, "when the possibility of storing detailed verbalized knowledge becomes virtually infinite, the hero has almost vanished as a major conservator of culture" (p. 205). Yet, the details are not only cumulative. Magnified minutia are the essence of intimate media. Sociologist Richard Sennett (1974) has written that "intimacy is a field of vision and an expectation of human relations" (p. 338). It is an intimacy which is, in some part, based upon the defining ability of media technology to bridge distance, either by saturating us with cascades of data or by confusing the public and the private as the camera invades and places the subject under scrutiny, revealing the ordinariness that is shared with others. Although Langer (1981) distinguishes between "star" (rather than hero) and "personality," there is a link between the larger-than-life attributes of the "star" and the grandeur and nobility of the "hero."

> Whereas the star system operates from the realms of the spectacular, the inaccessible, the imaginary, presenting the cinematic universe as "larger than life", the personality system is cultivated almost exclusively as "part of life", whereas the star system always has the ability to place distance between itself

and its audiences through its insistence on "the exceptional", the personality system works directly to construct and foreground intimacy and immediacy; whereas contact with stars is unrelentingly sporadic and uncertain, contact with television personalities has regularity and predictability; whereas stars are always playing "parts" emphasizing their identity as "stars" as much—perhaps even more than—the characters they play, television personalities "play" themselves; whereas stars emanate as idealizations or archetypal expressions, to be contemplated, revered, desired and even blatantly imitated, stubbornly standing outside the realms of the familiar and the routinized, personalities are distinguished for their representativeness, their typicality, their "will to ordinariness" to be accepted, normalized, experiences as *familiar*. (pp. 354-355)

No medium operates in isolation. Individuals function with, react to, and think in terms of, multiple media. We telephone, listen to the radio, work with a computer, watch television, fax a letter, listen to audio discs, watch video discs, and remember when once, not so long ago, records were sold instead of cassettes and discs. The psychological influence of media is both cumulative and interconnected. The point is that one functions in one medium with an awareness of others. Each person perceives the world through a mediated sensorium—a sensory collective created by an awareness and dependency on all operative forms of communication.

Similarly, mass media content influences programming concurrently and over time. Thus, radio, television, motion pictures, and the print media of books, magazines, and newspapers are interconnected in terms of subject matter, content, and treatment. The content featured in one medium often is adapted to the technical and social needs of another.

THE TRANSMOGRIFICATION OF THE HERO

Nowhere is that interconnection of media forms more clearly demonstrated than in that former world of the hero celebrated in the late 1930s, 1940s, and early 1950s. Batman, Superman, The Lone Ranger, Tarzan, The Green Hornet, Wonderwoman, Terry and the Pirates, Dick Tracy, and Flash Gordon were some of the protagonists who captured the imagination of young children and teenagers, who believed in the adventures of their heroes as they loyally followed their exploits in comic strips, comic books, radio serials, and motion pictures (some times in animated form, other times in realistic serial form). Most of the heroes began their strange careers as comic strip or book adventurers who would simultaneously display their deeds in radio and film. By the end of 1938, six serials featuring comic book characters were on the national radio networks: Dick Tracy, Don Winslow of the Navy, Jack Armstrong, Little Orphan Annie, Terry and the Pirates, and Tom Mix (Barnouw, 1968, p. 98).

Many more joined that group before the rise of television in the late 1940s would alter the form and shape of all the other mass media and, in many cases, displace radio programming. Some of the superheroes would attempt the trauma of television (and later, for some, a return to the motion picture medium) adaptation, but few would succeed in the transition without major adaptation and alteration—genre and persona could not escape radical redefinition. It does seem strange that the panoramic setting of the West would so easily be accommodated to the television screen, but it was primarily the Western genre that migrated successfully from motion picture to television screen (Hopalong Cassidy, Gene Autry, Roy Rogers, Tex Ritter, Wild Bill Hickok, Wyatt Earp, etc.). Perhaps this was because the Western hero was more grounded in limited combat, requiring less heroic (spectacular) deeds, or because the producers understood that the artistic and economic demands of television required a different variation on the theme of heroism.

Several of the original comic book heroes were revived from wherever the remains of superheroes are placed to rest to become curious dopplegängers of their earlier selves. *Batman,* with Adam West, would become a popular television series and would later be produced as a major motion picture starring Michael Keaton. Superman (Parts I, II, III, and IV), with Christopher Reeves as superhero, became a box office hit beginning in the late 1970s. In the summer of 1990, *Dick Tracy* appeared with Madonna and Warren Beatty. Did this renaissance signal the possible return of the superhero genre to the motion picture and television screens? The answer is "no"! Whereas the success of the earlier "Batman", "Dick Tracy", and "Superman" characters was based on a naive belief that evil could be confronted and disarmed by the extraordinary, often fantastic (in the literal sense) deeds of individuals who transcended simple mortality, the college students who flocked to the all-night showings of the old reissued *Batman* film serials celebrated the joy of camp. The Adam West television series was a spoof, a satire, not necessarily intended for children, but meant for adults who revered the old ghost of a hero. Superman took form in many media—as a radio serial (successful), a motion-picture cartoon (moderately successful), a television serial (uninspired boredom), and as a major motion-picture spectacular. The motion picture was a Hollywood extravaganza in special effects, which reduced Superman to enduring the experience of such ordinary base emotions as love and passion. At the same time, the antagonists of those films achieved new heights of revelry.

THE WRINKLE THEORY

The medium did them in. The medium was not only the message, but it was the culprit, the force that inadvertently unmasked the superhero by revealing the hero's lack of perfection. Comic book superheroes were painted in grand bold strokes, articulated muscles stretched out and held in by luminous uniforms which accentuated sleekness, power, and cut down on wind resistance as they glided from deed to deed. These were the heroes who did not sweat, whose hair was never out of place, whose omnipotence reassured fragile young minds that rescue was always just around the corner, that anything could be overcome if you believed. Superheroes could not withstand the scrutiny of the all-seeing television lens which revealed not major culpability, but minor corporeal disarrangement. Superman probably could withstand the devastating revelation of his double identity, but not the wrinkles which marred his uniform and suggested that perhaps behind that frayed exterior could be found a torn and tattered soul—someone closer to us.

In an age in which even the average mortal can jog down the street in an unwrinkled spandex outfit, in which basketball star Michael Jordan can swoop, glide, and remain suspended in mid-air for what seems like minutes, with athletic skill once thought impossible, the superhero's survival was threatened by the photographic resolution of the television medium. It is the combination of photographic acuity, media's ready access (particularly newspapers, magazines, radio, and television) to event and persona through miniaturization and mobility of equipment, and the extraordinary amount of programming that is required by media organizations and devoured by the American public that dissolved the distance that protects heroes from an invasion of privacy. The aura of necessary invincibility cannot withstand constant and penetrating visibility. The role of heroes has changed. It is not catharsis that the audience seeks, but rather revelation. Most persons, even heroes, would like to protect their wrinkles from public exposure, but it is the collective medium that has created a national pastime—the revelation of the wrinkle. An audience nurtured by penetrating media comes to expect the elimination of the public face and demands insight into the private. Heroes cannot withstand such scrutiny.

One alternative is to transform the hero into a more human and believable force, to transform that symbol of the impossible into something more probable. The results are often comedic with superheroes such as Superman and Batman becoming caricatures of their former selves—to be enjoyed, but never taken seriously as they were when an audience suspended their disbelief and believed.

Another, somewhat bizarre, alternative is to shift one's dramatic allegiance from the protagonist to the antagonist (or for the protagonist to take on the features of the antagonist). This is exactly what began to happen in television and film and even in the comic book. In major motion-picture releases the almost comic/grotesque antagonists such as the Joker, Penguin, Flattop, and Lex Luthor vie for the affections of the fans and replace and dominate the nominal hero. The syndrome is evident in the James Bond films in which high-tech destruction and incarnate evil oppose the predictably debonair James Bond character. Goldfinger and Dr. No, though doomed, charm the audience. It is difficult to explain why and how an audience develops a fascination with two-dimensional representatives of evil, rather than identifying with the agents of morality and virtue. It is the flaw that grips the imagination instead of the ideal of unblemished virtue. It is the blemish and imperfection (often a combination of physical and psychological defects) exemplified in such characters as Darth Veder (*Star Wars*) that dominates the screen.

In *Superman III* the hero experiences a personality crisis induced by exposure to Kryptonite. The "man of steel" is reduced to a common beer-guzzling destructive low-life. Kael's (1983) review of that film is revealing about the state of heroes:

> So when the soul-sick superman is being prankish or surly—putting out the Olympic torch or straightening the Leaning Tower of Pisa or punching a hole in a tanker and causing an oil spill—we don't know how to react to this lecher with stubble on his chin and a soiled-looking cape. A funky, sexy sheik Superman could have audiences squealing with pleasure, and a Superman with a vendetta against the world could be awesomely neurotic, but the movie has no sooner suggested the possibilities than it drops them. (When he sits alone in a bar, boozing and exploding bottles by flicking roasted almonds at them, we get more of a sense of how dangerous—*and attractive*—Superman could be than at any other time. The *bad* superman has burning dark eyes; he looks like an Etruscan warrior. (p. 90, emphasis added)

Superman does recover and in the end virtue conquers evil, but Kael's reaction that the evil Superman is potentially more interesting and attractive than either the immaculate good Superman or the wimpy Clark Kent supports my contention that the attraction of the flaw outweighs simplistic righteousness. Whether Superman as antihero is more attractive because the role is more believable, or because we are fascinated by the darker side of human behavior, is difficult to determine, but certainly the character and appeal of the protagonist has changed.

CONCLUSION

Marvel Comic fans have grown up and perhaps also have their heroes. In "Modern Comix: Goodbye, Superheroes and innocent mirth. Hello, angst, bent humor and post-modernism," Mernit (1989) reports that about 20% of the 20 million Americans who regularly read comics are older than 25. The average comic book customer is a college-educated 20-25-year-old male, who buys six comics a week (p. 17). The interconnectedness of media and the coming of age of the superhero is succinctly articulated by Mernit:

> Modern comics have even begun to devour their own sources. Winter 1987 saw the appearance of a book-length comic novel called *The Dark Night Returns* . . . featuring none other than Batman. However, this Batman, written by Frank Miller, was utterly unlike the noble crime-fighter you may remember from childhood. He is tired, close to burn-out, and he's become the kind of violent vigilante that Charles Bronson often portrays. He not only kills his enemies, he occasionally misses and kills innocent bystanders. The book's tone is cynical and bleak with more in common with Raymond Chandler and *film*

> *noir* than with the rosy optimism of bygone superheroes. Obviously, comics can now be just as ruthless in exploiting and reworking their sources, as any other kind of post-modern art. (p. 20)

The new superhero is not someone you would care to bring home to mother. The new superhero is not someone whom you will emulate when you grow up. The superheroes of our childhood are no longer what they once were. It is not only that the superhero has changed, we all have. There is no one definitive cause that explains the fall of the superheroes and the rise of the flawed, if not corrupted and disillusioned, prototype antiheroes. However, there certainly has been an escalation of the vigilante (*Death Wish, Death Wish II, Rambo, Rambo II*), the unsavory, anti-administration police officer (*Dirty Harry, Dirty Harry II, Shaft, Shaft II*), and the postnuked, devastated Earth and alien warrior (*Road Warrior, Mad Max, Beyond Thunderdome, Terminator I, Terminator II*) genres.

It is a long way from the Aristotelian hero as a person "not preeminently virtuous and just, whose misfortune, however, is brought upon him not by vice and depravity but by some error of judgement" (Aristotle, 1954, p. 238) to the vigilante. The audience learned from the hero of old that a moral system governed the universe. The vigilante, the self-appointed representative of law and order, also teaches—and the lesson is alarmingly clear—that when authority is no longer capable of governing lawlessness and disorder, any means necessary is sanctioned for the restoration of law and order. All heroes are linked to their times.

A number of interrelated factors can be cited for this national preoccupation with the flaw and the descent of the traditional Mr. Clean superhero from the pantheon of greatness. There are a host of complex social, psychological, and economic elements that influence and alter the need for, the relationship with, and the function of heroes. The argument that media technology is somehow linked to the fall of the hero is seldom offered as another variable, but in our contemporary world, values and beliefs are filtered through a media screen, and the impact is not fully understood. Ralph Waldo Emerson once said that "every hero becomes a bore at last." In a media age, the life of a hero lasts only until all but boredom is revealed.

6

The Life and Death of Media Friends: New Genres of Intimacy and Mourning

Joshua Meyrowitz
University of New Hampshire

❐ *The author of this chapter analyzes the new sense of intimacy with strangers that has been created by those modern media that simulate the sights and sounds of real-life interactions. This sense of intimacy drives the attachment to "media friends"—those celebrities, rock stars, actors, sports figures, etc., who become part of our daily existence. Meyrowitz explains how new technologies reduce the distance between us and our media friends, blurring our response to their talents with our response to their personalities. He suggests that the "unreal" relationships with media friends are, ironically, often deeper and longer lasting than many real-life ties. He then explores these "intimate" relationships to the point of loss and shows how new forms of grief have been developed to cope with the death of media friends.*

At the time they split up, I too broke away from my family, my friends, the places I had known all my life, to attend school in California. As I drove over the hills into the Los Angeles basin, a new song by John Lennon crackled on the car radio, as if the Beatles were saying, "We're with you. You haven't left us behind." (Schaumburg, 1976, p. 3)

Because we were so used to the way he thought, the habits, the turns, the surprises of his mind, we can enter him as we remember his last moments, to let it be us in the car, pulling up to the curb, opening the door, stepping out, breathing the night. Someone said he was happy that night, and we somehow know what his happiness felt like, and we can imagine ourselves resurgent, electric with energy. (Spencer, 1981, p. 13)

Four days after . . . when I woke up to find . . . the story off the front page, that process by which the mind struggles with a fact it will not accept was still working. I scanned the front page again to see if I'd missed anything. . . . Nothing. Does this mean, I thought, that it's over? That he's not dead anymore? (Marcus, 1981, p. 27)

"John Lennon Killed by Stranger" screamed the headlines in December 1980. But for assassin Mark David Chapman, John Lennon was no stranger. Although Chapman had never come within a hundred miles of the former Beatle until that week, he knew him very well, so well that he often seemed to believe that he was John Lennon.

As a teenager, Chapman wore his hair like Lennon's, learned to play the guitar, and joined a rock group. He played and sang Lennon's songs over and over again. Chapman, like Lennon, married an older Japanese woman. At his last job, as a security guard at a Honolulu condominium, he even taped Lennon's name over his own on his identification tag. On the day he quit, he signed out as "John Lennon" in the logbook (Clarke, 1980, p. 29; Mathews, with Abramson, Morris, & Maier, 1980, p. 34).

Yet, Chapman must have been acutely aware of the gap between himself and his alter ego. The last stroke of his pen in the logbook crossed the name out. Within a few weeks, Chapman was on his way to New York to close the open psychic circle. First he played the adoring fan, asking for and receiving an autograph outside Lennon's apartment building, the Dakota. Then he returned later in the day to empty his gun into Lennon's body, thereby defining the rest of his own life in relation to the life he ended.

In a sense, John Lennon was killed by the sinister side of the same force that makes millions still mourn him and other dead media heroes: a new sense of connection to selected strangers created by those modern media that simulate the sights and sounds of real-life interactions (Horton & Wohl, 1956).

As a culture, we are still lacking in the terminology and conceptual frameworks to analyze fully these strange bonds. In this chapter, I draw on several familiar terms, including *celebrity* and *media hero*, but I focus primarily on my concept of *media friend*. Each of these terms addresses an aspect of these complex, media-fostered relationships. The term *celebrity* captures the fact that modern media enhance the possibility of someone's being widely known for being widely known. The term *media hero* embraces the sense of awe that one may feel concerning the accomplishments of a person one knows about through the media. But, to my thinking, the concept of *media friend* addresses the strangest and most significant dimension of these relationships: the sense of intimate knowledge and empathic connection. One feels a direct, one-to-one tie to a media friend that exists apart from, and almost in spite of, how widely known the person is. Further, as with real-life friends, one feels bound to the person not simply because of what they can do, but based on a more personal set of feelings about who they *are*—and how their "presence" makes one feel.

What we expect from heroes is often different from what we expect and accept from media friends. Great heroes may make boring or uncomfortable friends, and media friends may make poor heroes. Indeed, a revelation that would destroy heroic aura may only deepen the sense of intimate connection with a media friend. The natural mental space for a hero is at a distance and on some sort of pedestal. The imagined space for a media friend is at our sides—hanging out together at home, riding in the car, sharing an adventure. The multifaceted role that John Lennon and others have played in our lives has all these dimensions—celebrity, hero, and friend.

Unfortunately, Mark David Chapman is not the only unbalanced person to push the media relationship to extreme ends. There have been many other similar attempted or realized assassinations that grew out of this new form of intimacy. John Hinckley, Jr. attempted to assassinate Ronald Reagan in order to impress actress Jodie Foster. "You'll be proud of me, Jodie," he wrote to her. "Millions of Americans will love me—us" ("An innocent life," 1989, p. 64). Robert John Bardo, obsessed with *My Sister Sam* star Rebecca Schaeffer, shot and killed her in 1989. Dozens of other celebrities have been threatened, stalked, or attacked. Michael J. Fox received more than 5,000 letters and death threats from one fan who was upset about his marriage, and Olivia Newton-John has twice been followed to Australia by an Illinois mental patient ("An innocent life," 1989). David Letterman's home has been broken into several times, and his sports car has been taken for drives by a woman who calls herself "Mrs. Letterman" (Toufexis, with Lafferty, & Sachs, 1989, p. 43).

Fan reaction to the sudden death of a media friend can be equally strong. Following John Lennon's murder, a teenage girl in Florida and a 30-year-old man in Utah killed themselves. Their suicide notes spoke of depression over Lennon's death (Cocks, 1980, p. 18).

Because simulated intimacy drives the attachment, celebrities who present the sweetest personae to the public are, ironically, the ones most prone to violent threats and acts on the part of obsessed fans. These celebrities appear more approachable, more seductive. Performers who present harsher fictional or nonfictional personae may receive more hate mail, yet are less likely to be stalked and killed by those who see themselves as jilted lovers (Toufexis et al., 1989, p. 43).

One does not have to be mentally unbalanced, however, to feel a close bond with celebrities. Except for the attempts to hurt these media heroes or to demand that they return the personal attention and affection, the behavior of these "obsessed fans" is often not that different from the behavior of ordinary fans. (Indeed, the word *fan* itself is derived from the word *fanatic*.) When Chapman was a teenager, for example, he was only one among millions who felt devoted to Lennon and emulated aspects of his appearance and behavior. More than 600,000 fans a year still make pilgrimages to Graceland, Elvis Presley's home in Memphis, TN (S. Marshall, Media Coordinator, Graceland Mansion Tours, personal communication, November 20, 1991) and 4 million people visit John Kennedy's grave each year (Grunwald, 1991). Over the last century, the evolution of communication media has fostered an increasingly intense sense of intimacy with those who would otherwise be strangers.

EVOLUTION OF THE MEDIA RELATIONSHIP

Every era may have had its heroes, but a new relationship between the adored and the adoring was born with the rise of the film industry. Audiences could see the facial expressions and body movements of performers with greater clarity than from a front row seat at a live performance, and individual performers could gain a following larger than would be humanly possible through a lifetime of live appearances. Early filmmakers were taken by surprise by the strong emotional attachment that developed between performer and audience. At first, film companies, such as Biograph and Bison, did not even bother to share the names of the performers with the public. But when audience members wrote fan letters to the "Biograph girl" and their other favorites, film producers quickly realized the economic value of "stars" (Sklar, 1975, p. 40).

The nature of media relationships changed again with the addition of sound to film, which reduced some of the mystery surrounding movie stars. In some cases this demystification destroyed careers; in others it enhanced the closeness of the relationship between star and fan. In both silence and sound, however, film fostered a relatively distant closeness. Performers were seen sporadically, from afar, and much larger than life in an oversized room in the public sphere. Such settings generated awe along with a new sense of personal bond. Indeed, many early movie theaters were designed as splendid palaces for Hollywood-created royalty.

The radio era also fostered its own unique media relationships. Radio personalities were close in aural space and often entered people's homes daily, but their "presence" during these visits had no visual dimensions except in the listener's imagination. Media performers who were experienced through the radio were like friends at a pajama party who came after the lights were turned off and left before morning. There was an odd mix of intimacy and distance, of knowledge and mystery.

LIFE-LONG VICARIOUS INTIMATES

Compared to the film and radio eras, our own time is characterized by a greater intimacy, encouraged by the closeness and smallness of the speakers and TV screens in our homes and cars and by the many media through which we experience the same performers. As a result, a broader array of social performers has more fully entered our personal spaces on a more regular basis.

The more we see and hear them, the more actors, sports figures, newscasters, singers, politicians, and talk show hosts become part of our extended network of social ties (Caughey, 1986; Rosengren & Windahl, 1972; see also Drucker and Cathcart, this volume). Some of them are there to say "Good morning" to us, others to whisper "Good night." Our media friends are cheerful with us at breakfast, and they solemnly and reliably fill us in on the day's news over dinner. We can find reflective or playful media buddies to hang out with in the evening. There is always a media friend who will sing for us as we jog. The voices and faces of our media friends often provide a backdrop even to the most intimate scenes of our lives.

Through media experiences, we come to feel that we really know a John Kennedy or a John Lennon, a Magic Johnson or a Woody Allen, that we have met some of their family members and friends, that we understand something about who they are as people. There are obvious surface differences among our relationships to different types of media friends—presidents, rock stars, sports heroes, actors, and news anchors, for example—but there are also some important underlying commonalities.

We often feel that our media friends share themselves with us more easily than other people do and that we know them better than most of the people we see in our daily lives. We can watch and listen to them closely without being distracted by concerns over how we look, what we say in return, or what they think of us.

We follow celebrities through various phases of their personal lives and public activities, and their life stages often become some of the key signposts we use to mark and recall the different periods of our own lives. With the help of programs such as *Entertainment Tonight* and publications such as *People* magazine, we keep up with their romances and problems, their good years and bad years, their changing hairstyles and different phases of dress, the birth of their children and the death of their family members, their successful and unsuccessful plastic surgeries, their addictions and recoveries. With some performers, such as Cher, we are allowed to see new tatoos. With John and Yoko, we even saw them naked.

Our relationships with media personae frequently outlast our relationships with many of our neighbors, coworkers, lovers, and real-life friends. Indeed, our permanent relationships with media friends often form part of the shared experience that binds us to our temporary real-life friends. Conversely, a lack of sharing of similar media friendships can immediately terminate the negotiations for friendship with people we meet (such as when a Sinead O'Connor fan discovers that the guy sitting next to her is humming Tammy Wynette tunes; or a Barry Manilow fan dismisses the notion of becoming close to a devoted David Bowie fan).

Relationships with media friends compensate for the impermanence of many real-life relationships. Yet, they may also increase the instability of real-life ties by making it easier to end them. As difficult as it remains to leave one's home, get divorced, or travel to another part of the country or world, each of these changes is now made simpler by the fact that not all our social relationships are severed. Wherever we are, whether living alone or among others, we may continue to enjoy the company of our media friends. How can we feel completely alone when Bill Cosby, Bruce Springsteen, Elizabeth Taylor, Oprah Winfrey, George Burns, Roseanne, Michael Jordan, Paul McCartney, Joan

Rivers, Paul Simon, Cyndi Lauper, Peter Jennings, Willie Nelson, Phil Donahue, and scores of other fascinating and talented people are eager to be our companions? (Similarly, our young children always live near Mister Rogers' neighborhood and just down the block from their friends at Sesame Street.)

SELECTED PERSONALITY FACETS

Of course, we see only selected dimensions of the personalities of our media friends. Those who watched Johnny Carson's first program after the death of his son realized how much of Carson's personality and emotional life remained hidden, even after thousands of late-night chats. Similarly, David Letterman and Arsenio Hall, for all their irreverent humor, reveal very little about their personal emotional lives. As Horton and Wohl (1956) suggested in the 1950s, talk show hosts "play themselves." That is, what we see is often a genuine dimension of a media friend's personality, but it must be "played" to the extent that other dimensions of his or her personality remain purposely hidden. Indeed, the general consistency of our media friends' behaviors may be what makes them often seem to be more trustworthy and reliable than the people we interact with in everyday life. Unlike real family and friends, our media friends let us into their personal spaces (however constructed or controlled) and entertain us with high energy, without making any reciprocal demands on us. In fact, one of the factors that seems to separate "normal" fans from "crazed" ones is that the latter often react as if some personal demand on them *were* being made, only to become angry and violent when they feel themselves ignored or rejected.

In addition to selected dimensions of personality, media friends' performances often rely on other means of "staging" as well. When we watch a singing performance "taped live" in front of a studio audience, for example, we are rarely told that what we are watching may actually be the best takes from two or more sequential performances. Similarly, politicians often arrange to speak in front of largely supportive audiences so that "live and unrehearsed cheering" can contribute to an upbeat media performance. In such situations the pictured audience members are not actually those for whom the performances are designed; indeed, they function as extras in a drama constructed for a mediated audience of millions.

Media production variables are also manipulated to shape a celebrity's image. Soft filters are used to cover lines on faces (especially for female media friends) and to create a warm, glowing feel. Camera angles are used to establish the desired image (low angle for power and level camera for intimacy, for example). Visual editing, equalization filters, echo, multiple tracking, and other variables add dynamism, enhance positive features, and mute negative ones.

Increasingly sophisticated technologies have reversed the relationship between live and recorded performances. In the early days of image and sound recordings, the live performance was the standard by which the quality of the recording was measured. Now, sound and image technologies can yield recordings that are beyond anything that can be produced without them, and we often evaluate our media friends' live performances by how well they reproduce the aura of their mediated performances. With such a difficult goal to reach for, many singers now "perform live" by lip syncing to their recordings or singing along with prerecorded vocals. If the visual performance is strong enough—as in Madonna's stage shows—the fans do not seem to mind all that much.

The public's awareness that a media friend may be "performing" for them rather than simply "being" with them leads to a lively trade in offstage anecdotes. That is, stories circulate about how media friends behave in situations in which the cameras and microphones are off—or in which they think they are off. These behaviors, it is often believed, reveal or confirm the media friend's true personality. One hears about the performer with the caring public persona who is abusive toward an airplane attendant, about the "sensitive" actor who is charged with beating his wife, about the politician who condemns others for using bad language and then curses with the worst of them, and so on. There is, for example, the old story of "Uncle Don" who, after closing his children's radio program and mistakenly thinking the microphone was off, said: "I guess that will hold the little bastards" (Goffman, 1981, p. 267). Such incidents can weaken or destroy a media friendship. But there are also the frequent tales about offstage behaviors that confirm a public persona and strengthen fans' devotion.

Ironically, media performers are often so aware of the power of offstage behavior to enhance onstage personae that they may work hard at shaping their seemingly unshaped behavior. Jay Leno, for example, not only shakes hands and signs autographs almost everywhere he goes, he also chats with other drivers through his car window and even telephones some of the people who write him letters of complaint. Leno believes in LBJ's dictum that "every handshake is worth 250 votes" because, as Leno says, "each person then goes and tells someone else you're a good guy and then they go and tell more people" (Stengel, 1992, p. 58).

INCREASING EXPOSURE OF THE "BACKSTAGE"

Although it is clear that media friends selectively reveal themselves to us, it would be a mistake to miss the increase in personal revelation that has been fostered by changes in media. In the past, if national figures were seen at all, it was usually from afar, where facial expressions were invisible. In newspaper quotes or transcripts the flesh and blood person was absent. Even still photographs did not commonly replace engravings in newspapers until the threshold of the 20th century (Sandman, Rubin, & Sachsman, 1982, p. 51). At first, motion pictures were missing the key component of sound, and even early sound movies required a cooperative subject who was willing to move into the light and step up to the microphone.

Today, smaller and more sensitive cameras and microphones create less disruption of ongoing occurrences and thereby encourage greater revelation of what was once part of the "backstage" aspects of *all* social performances (Meyrowitz, 1985). Even the most formal of our media friendships have become more intimate as media have entered many social arenas from which they were once banned: presidential press conferences, Senate hearings, and courtrooms, to name a few. The pictures and sounds also have become more revealing: President Nixon shoving his press secretary, President Ford tripping over words and down stairs, President Carter collapsing while jogging, President Reagan falling asleep in an audience with the Pope, and President Bush passing out after vomiting at a Japanese state dinner.

Citizens once knew the actors in the public, political realm primarily through their words. Words can be used to talk about anything, distant or close, abstract or concrete. But the images and sounds in modern "presentational" media are always, in basic ways, about the performers themselves (Meyrowitz, 1985, pp. 93-114).

A common response to the reading of a speech in a newspaper, for example, is to ask whether the statements are logical, whether the facts mentioned are true, and whether we agree with the arguments. But a typical response to a similar speech viewed on television is to think about the personality and performance of the speaker: "Does he seem nervous?" "Is she forceful?" "Is he sincere?" Thus it somehow makes sense that polls of voters in recent presidential elections have found that people will vote for someone they disagree with on the issues, or vote against someone they agree with, based on whether they "personally like" the candidate (see, for example, Clymer, 1982). Television gives us that feeling of personal connection.

With the focus on personal style and image, rather than on words and ideas, mediated relationships cross language and cultural barriers more easily than many other types of relationships. Attachments to rock stars have fostered the sense of an international youth culture. Americans of all ages have displayed feelings of personal caring for members of the British royal family, Lech Walesa in Poland, Cory Aquino in the Philippines, Mikhail Gorbachev, Boris Yeltsin, and many others. Such mediated relationships sometimes have an impact on international diplomacy. Ronald Reagan found that he had to tone down his talk of an "Evil Empire" as the public gained a sense of Gorbachev as a "nice person." Similarly, when Americans saw thousands of Aquino supporters facing down Ferdinand Marcos's tanks, Ronald Reagan retreated from his position that Marcos's declared election victory should stand because "there was cheating on both sides." During the failed Soviet coup of 1991, George Bush reportedly found that his own negative views of Boris Yeltsin were transformed by watching television images of Yeltsin shouting defiance from atop a tank (Mathews et al., 1991, p. 42).

The sense of personal knowing of our media friends may explain why the public is now rather tolerant of ghostwriters and the explicitness with which they are relied upon. In a newspaper era an explicitly ghost-written speech would have seemed rather odd, even insulting to the public. After all, the public could only know a national figure through his or her printed words. Today, it matters more who performs the words than who writes them. It would be unacceptable for a president today to do what the shy Thomas Jefferson did with his State of the Union addresses: He crafted the words himself, but had the speeches read aloud by a clerk.

Yet, the public does not seem at all disturbed by the fact that media friends Peter Jennings, Tom Brokaw, and Dan Rather typically perform news scripts that are written by others (as did Walter Cronkite). Newspaper reporters, in contrast, are expected to write their own material, and small scandals erupt when newspaper articles are shown to contain passages written by someone other than the bylined reporter.

Even when Ronald Reagan's speechwriters had him reading a letter from a little girl within a speech that was itself ghostwritten—and thus speaking words two steps removed from his own—Reagan's performance appeared to tell the public a great deal about his personal being, beliefs, and passions. We saw tears well up in his eyes, we heard the catch in his voice; some of us sensed personal conviction, others sensed deceit. With such a rich conveyance of personal attributes, it did not seem absolutely necessary that the words had to be his alone, any more than Elvis and Madonna fans would insist that the singers perform only songs they have written completely on their own, or any more than we insist that our friends tell us only those jokes they themselves have crafted. In these real and vicarious associations we seem to crave the intimacy of interaction more than the artistry of invention.

Of course, the sense of intimate knowing can be even greater when the content of the performance is also created by our media friends. There was a special deepening of the relationship with the Beatles, for example, when they moved to recording only their own songs. Fans' devotion to singer-songwriters such as Bob Dylan and Phil Ochs in the 1960s had very little to do with their skill as musical performers. Those music critics who could not understand why these songwriters did not license their songs to technically superior singers and musicians missed the whole point.

As we come to know new media friends or deepen our relationships with old ones, we also come to know ourselves in new ways. The self, after all, is not simply something that resides *within* each of us. Although we often prefer to think of ourselves as autonomous individuals who march to our own drummers and shape our own destinies, most of the concepts we use to define ourselves are relative and social. When we think of ourselves as being short or tall, hesitant or daring, smart or dumb, kind or harsh, we must compare ourselves to others. Each of us develops a social self as we begin to see ourselves and judge our actions as they would be viewed by "significant others"

(Mead, 1934). Our sense of self is changed, then, as we gain new significant others—live or mediated—from whose vantage points we can view our own actions. When Mark Chapman experimented with drugs, for example, he knew that his parents would be horrified—but John Lennon would understand.

BLURRING OF PERSONALITY AND SKILL

We become emotionally tied to our media friends as *people*, apart from our reactions to their artistic or professional activities. Or perhaps it is more accurate to say that it often becomes difficult to separate the personal and the professional dimensions of the relationships as media friends push their art to service the media relationships themselves.

After the Beatles broke up, for example, the individual members of the group, particularly John Lennon, recorded songs that were increasingly personal in nature. One Lennon song called to his Mama "don't go" and to his Daddy "come home." Thus, his own art began to comment on the biographical details known to every dedicated fan: that after Lennon's father abandoned the family, his mother had left him to be raised by an aunt and then, just as mother and son began to become reacquainted, she was killed by a drunken driver while she waited for a bus. Other songs commented on publicized feuds with Paul McCartney and on Lennon's devotion to his wife Yoko, who was not well liked by Lennon's ex-partners or by many Beatles fans.

Fans' evaluation of the "quality" of Lennon's musical artistry, then, was difficult to separate from their sense of intimate knowledge of his life and problems. What in other contexts might be considered an unpleasant scream on a song, could be cherished as an invitation to share the emotional discoveries of the primal therapy through which a close friend was passing. Perhaps the most ironic paradox arose when Lennon's later songs tried to puncture the myths that surrounded him and the Beatles. Thus he increased his intimacy with fans by ridiculing the process through which the intimacy was established and developed. What would otherwise seem absurd comes to make some sense when one realizes that media friends tend to promote the relationship with their fans by speaking to millions of us at once as if they were speaking to each of us alone (Horton & Wohl, 1956). Lennon, then, could seem to be saying to each one of us that his relationship with all the other faceless fans was somewhat silly and overblown.

With the media's primary focus on personality, we see an increasing overlap of entertainment, sports, journalism, and government. Actors become politicians (Clint Eastwood, Sonny Bono, Ronald Reagan), and politicians become part-time actors (Jesse Jackson, Tip O'Neill, Mayor Ed Koch, and others have all played themselves on TV comedy programs). Sports figures turn to acting in advertisements, TV shows, and movies, and famous actors participate in celebrity sports competitions and in shows such as *The Circus of the Stars.* Similarly, TV journalists such as Mike Wallace, Ted Koppel, Tom Brokaw, and Peter Jennings have all appeared recently as celebrity guests on talk shows, and five newswomen appeared as themselves in the baby shower episode of the situation comedy *Murphy Brown.* The talk show circuit played an unprecedented role in the 1992 presidential election, including the launching of the "Perot for President" drive. Of course, major media stars, such as presidents and popes, can create their own "talk shows" at any time and in any place by granting exclusive interviews or creating other media events. Even fictional characters who are seen often on television may develop a personal following. During his five years on network television, for example, "Dr. Marcus Welby" received a quarter of a million letters, most requesting medical advice (Gross & Jeffries-Fox, 1978, p. 247).

Because we experience TV journalists' personal expressions and their responses to events, we now often feel as close to them as we do to the public figures they cover. After revealing the personalities and homes of many world leaders and celebrities, Barbara Walters apparently felt it only fair and sensible that she do a television program on her *own* home and personal life. Similarly, Walter Cronkite's retirement from the *CBS Evening News* and Dan Rather's troubled attempts to fill the role played by "Uncle Walter" were themselves major news stories. Ironically, Cronkite was considered "the most trusted man in America" and was viewed as a viable presidential candidate, even though no one knew—until years after his retirement from the news—what his political views were.

CALCULATED INTIMACIES

The degree to which our sense of intimacy with media friends is coincidental or calculated varies tremendously. Early filmmakers seemed genuinely surprised by the personal attachments to the "hired help." Later, however, film studios devoted much energy to courting and shaping the emotional attachments of fans. The Beatles' manager Brian Epstein probably helped make the group more acceptable by softening their rough edges before introducing them to the world, but Beatlemania ultimately relied as much on what Epstein could not control about the quartet's irreverent behavior as on the aspects he could shape to his liking.

Although the media-induced bonds with Elvis, JFK, and the Beatles were planned, there remained a sense of innocence and freshness to those relationships. They were among the first of their kind, and the nature and scope of such media friendships were unanticipated by the performers, their handlers, and the public. Subsequent relationships seem more familiar and more calculated.

Now, those media friends who trade on the mystique of their "offbeat, creative personalities" more willingly expose dimensions of their lives that could remain private, as Madonna has done in her movie *Truth or Dare* and as a very different sort of media friend, Francis Ford Coppola, has done in a recent release of a revealing "home movie," *Hearts of Darkness: A Filmmaker's Apocalypse*, about his making of *Apocalypse Now*.

Even when the media attachments are calculated, celebrities often express bewilderment over their immense popularity. Perhaps it was just part of a crafted "humble, country boy" persona (or his emulation of his own media hero, James Dean), but TV interviews with Elvis Presley following his early televised singing performances seem to reveal a genuinely confused and overwhelmed person. When asked on one mid-1956 interview show, *Hy Gardner Calling*, what had been passing through his mind lately, an exhausted Presley responded: "Well, uh, everything has happened to me so fast in the last year and a half 'til, uh, I'm all mixed up, you know, and I can't keep up with everything's that's happening." It was as if he were experiencing his bodily and spiritual essence being spread over an impossibly large area, with millions of viewers suddenly feeling that they knew him, loved him, wanted him. The previously human scale of his interactions with the world had been exploded.

As everyone has become increasingly aware of the behavioral styles that work best on television, we have seen a general shift in the sense of which people have the right personalities to fill various public roles. Stiff, wooden styles rarely make a good impression on television, regardless of the accomplishments, credentials, or other capabilities of the individual. Such considerations seem to have influenced the success and failure of a wide array of performers, including newscasters, rock stars, presidential hopefuls, and recent Supreme Court nominees. Increasingly, our culture draws on "dating criteria" more than "résumé criteria" in choosing public figures. As I have detailed elsewhere, there are even indications that the Catholic Church took a good "television personality" into account in electing Popes John Paul I and John Paul II (Meyrowitz, 1985, p. 299n).

One of the more calculated media friendships in recent memory was the one created with Christa McAuliffe, the teacher who was chosen to travel on the space shuttle, *The Challenger*. Realizing that television deals better with personalities than with the abstract idea of "space exploration," NASA decided to involve us in its next shuttle flight by focusing publicly on a single person, the first civilian, someone like you and me. Christa was chosen to be our representative, the first extraordinary ordinary person to travel into space. Surely, her game-show-like enthusiasm and her picture-perfect family played a part in her selection as an appropriate television performer and media friend. Through the media attention, NASA and the press sent her into an orbit of celebrity. The six other astronauts were kept in the background.

NASA had also no doubt hoped that the very concrete, personal dimension of Christa's flight would overshadow in the public mind the more abstract Pentagon debate over the relative usefulness of shuttle and disposable space vehicles. The television teacher in space was also to provide the Reagan administration with an *image* of leadership in support for education without any actual increase in educational funding.

Then everything went wrong. The same powerful thrust of fuel and engines that promised to bring glory to Christa McAuliffe also sealed her fate, leaving her and the rest of the crew 10 miles above ground, in an inferno, without protection or parachutes. Similarly, the media blitz that thrust McAuliffe into our lives left our emotions up in the air, raw and exposed to the elements.

What was to have been both good politics and good television became instead an exposure of the dangerous symbiosis of government and news agencies, caught in the webs of their own routines and desires. The networks, enjoying their access to dramatic images, allowed themselves to be lulled into believing that shuttle takeoffs were safe and routine. NASA, dependent on the news media for publicity, allowed itself to feel the heat from the impatient media—despite the freezing weather that they knew posed a threat to the shuttle's O-rings.

Ironically, the unnecessary accident robbed McAuliffe of the very accomplishment that would have at least partially justified all the media attention she had received. Yet, beneath the since-uncovered tangle of politics and mismanagement, our contrived media relationship with Christa McAuliffe remained emotionally powerful and real, perhaps unique in its brevity and intensity.

Media relationships have also been calculatingly fostered or suppressed for ideological reasons. The blacklist, for example, made it almost impossible for performers who held certain political beliefs to establish, maintain, or enhance media friendships with the public. Similarly, the U.S. news media have historically made a greater effort to foster a posthumous media friendship with the victims of communist and Soviet-backed terror and aggression than with the victims of terror on the part of the United States and its allies. Indeed, there was more U.S. press coverage of the murder of Polish priest Jerzy Popieluszko than the *combined* coverage of the murders of *100* religious figures in U.S.-supported countries in Latin America between 1964 and 1985, including the assassination of Archbishop Romero and four U.S. churchwomen women raped and murdered by members of the Salvadoran National Guard (Herman & Chomsky, 1988, chap. 2).

Besides great variations in the *amount* of coverage, there are also significant variations in the style of coverage. Those killed by official enemies are resurrected in photos and in accounts by family and friends, and descriptions of their murders include details of wounds, torture, and abuse—which enhance sympathy for the victim and hostility toward the murderers. But such details are generally suppressed for "our" victims (Entman, 1991; Herman & Chomsky, 1988, pp. 37-86).

A NEW GENRE OF GRIEF

It is when a media friend such as John Lennon, Elvis, or John Kennedy dies before his time that the unusual nature of the relationship is most evident. For unlike the loss of a real friend or relative, the mourning for a media friend is not eased by traditional rituals or clear ways to comfort the bereaved. Attempts to attend the actual funeral or to speak to the dead person's family are, after all, intrusions by strangers.

In order to banish the demons of grief and helplessness, thousands of people spontaneously gather in the streets or parks or hold vigils near the media friend's home or place of death. Within two hours of Lennon's 11 p.m. murder, for example, nearly a thousand people had gathered outside Lennon's apartment building (Mayer, with Agrest, & Young, 1980, p. 36).

> By morning, the gates of the Dakota looked like the wall of a Mexican church, or an instant Lourdes, covered with a collage of flowers, messages, photographs, drawings. The crowd had been brought together as if to some new Holy Place, expressing a deep primitive need to mourn. (Hamill, 1980, p. 39)

Others gathered in the Boston Common, Lee Park in Dallas, San Francisco's Marina Green, the ABC entertainment complex in Los Angeles, and similar locations around the country (Mayer et al., 1980, p. 32).

The sudden death of a media friend often leads real friends—new, old, and half forgotten—to telephone each other to mourn their shared media friend. Strangers embrace and cry. Crowds stand in silent witness or chant the dead hero's words or songs. The pain is paradoxical: It feels personal, yet it is strengthened by the extent to which it is shared with the crowd.

Just as media friendships develop over national borders more easily than real friendships, the feelings of mourning for a media friend may be surprisingly deep in distant lands. The assassination of John Kennedy spawned torchlight processions in Berlin and Berne, moments of silence in Tokyo department stores, crowds that gathered around radios and television sets in Paris, and other spontaneous rituals of mourning from Nairobi to Seoul (United Press International & *American Heritage Magazine*, 1964, pp. 48-51). Similarly, John Lennon's murder led to an outpouring of emotion around the globe. Even in Warsaw—for one day at least—newspapers gave more coverage to John Lennon's death than to the Soviet troops massing on the border ("Sharing the grief," 1981, p. 73).

Millions of scattered mourners draw on a stock of shared intimacies and "secrets" that bring similar spontaneous worries, concerns, and shattered dreams. With Lennon these included the pain that stemmed from the knowledge that he had played the key parenting role for his 5-year-old son, Sean, and would not be able to fulfill the comforting promise in his just-recorded lullaby, "Beautiful Boy" ("have no fear . . . your Daddy's here"). There was the empathy for Lennon's teenage son from his first marriage, Julian (named after John's mother, Julia), who was just getting to know his father and, now, like John, had lost the same parent twice. There was the sadness felt for John's Aunt Mimi, who had raised him from the age of 3. There was also every die-hard Beatles fan's hope—often unexpressed (John, after all, would not approve) and now meaningless—that the Beatles would somehow, sometime, someplace play together again. There were even sillier shared notions, such as that we would never get to see if John indeed would grow to look like the spirited old man pictured in artist Michael Leonard's well-known picture of the aged Beatles, an illustration for the song "When I'm Sixty-Four."

Ironically, but appropriately, the media that gave birth to the relationship also provide the most ritualized channels for mourning a media friend's death. Radio and television present specials, retrospectives, and commentaries. Following JFK's assassination, television networks suspended their regular programs and commercials for four days. After John Lennon's murder, many radio stations throughout North America and Europe played nothing but Beatle music and Lennon songs and interviews, or opened their phone lines to grief-stricken callers. Even Radio Moscow devoted 90 minutes to Lennon's music (Flippo, 1981; Mayer et al., 1980, p. 32). Other media friends guide us through our grief by hosting the media memorials. But the ultimate tribute to a widely loved media hero is the suspension of all media friend magic—a minute or more of media silence.

To be prepared for their important role in mourning the heroes they have helped to create, media professionals must always be ready to turn their growing collections of the sounds and images of a living media friend into an instant memorial. The media stalk some celebrities almost constantly, not only to capture the ongoing stream of their lives, but also to be close by when the end comes. Ever since the news media had to rely on an amateur movie to replay the assassination of John Kennedy, network news cameras have kept what is grimly called a "death watch" on the president and major presidential candidates whenever they are in public (Mankiewicz & Swerdlow, 1979, p. 108).

Unlike most of us, media friends perform even at their own memorial services. In media specials, public vigils, and private rituals the mourned media friend's "live" image and voice are played and replayed as if to revive the dead. As television cameras focused on John Kennedy's flag-draped casket in St. Matthew's Cathedral, for example, the images of the ending of a relationship with a President were contrasted with the sounds of its inauguration: "Ask not what your country can do for you; ask what you can do for your country" (Barnouw, 1990, p. 337).

The final irony is that, in many ways, the media friend never dies. For the only means through which most people came to know him or her—records, films, and audio- and videotapes—are still available. Dead media friends' images and voices continue to live all around us.

Even 10 years after his death, John Lennon was still there to perform his song "Imagine" to 1 billion people simultaneously over radio stations in 130 countries, in celebration of what would have been his 50th birthday ("Lennon broadcast," 1990). Lennon was there again on New Year's Day 1992 to mark a peace accord in El Salvador by singing "Give Peace a Chance" on the rebels' radio station (Mine, 1992). Gilda Radner and John Belushi still visit us and make us laugh on late night television. Months after his death, Michael Landon was in my living room trying to sell me a program to help my children do better in school. Marilyn Monroe and Humphrey Bogart maintain an embodied presence in our media experiences, long after their real bodies have turned to dust.

When a media friend dies, the relationship is embalmed rather than destroyed. In a sense we lose nothing that we have already had, but the sense of loss is profound nevertheless. Perhaps it is the potential and hope for increased intimacy that dies, and the never-to-be face-to-face consummation of the relationship that is most mourned.

LIVING WITH THE LOSS

The feelings of loss of a media friend and the dashed hopes for a potential deepening of the relationship are partially addressed through a variety of channels. There is a steady stream of "never before published" photos, "rare footage" of personal moments, bootlegged tapes of performances that were thought to have gone unrecorded, and reprocessed and remastered versions of old recordings. There are interviews with those who knew the media friend personally. There are impersonators who recreate the live performance style of the media friend for those who want to experience it again and for those who are saddened by having missed the real thing when the opportunities were still available. There are other media friends, new and old, who write and sing tributes to the deceased. And there is sometimes growing fame and affection for those who lived with them. Priscilla Presley's successful career, for example, seems to keep alive a part of Elvis's youth; he saw something special about her when she was only 14. Similarly, Yoko Ono's prestige and appeal grew markedly after John Lennon's death (for early examples from immediately after the killing, see Brownmiller, 1981, and "Sharing the grief," 1981, p. 75). The loss of future facets of the media friendship, then, is partially offset by adding dimensions to the past.

For those who are more patient there is the fascination with the offspring of deceased media friends and the hope that they or their children will grow up to carry on the name and style. Julian Lennon, for example, rocketed to fame with a debut album in which he sounded eerily like his father. The rare glimpses of Lisa Marie Presley's slightly crooked smile, inherited from her father, are enough to give fans some small solace. The children of John and Robert Kennedy are scrutinized for hints that they may have within them some of the greatness of their fathers. Death seems to take a holiday when Natalie

Cole is able, through the wonders of modern recording technology, to sing duets with her long-dead father, Nat King Cole.

Media friends tend to be accepted more widely after they are dead. Many political differences dissolved in front of the growing JKF legend. Elvis's death brought on an interest in his music among those too young and too old to embrace him when he was alive. After his death, John Lennon—who lived on the radical side of the pop culture spectrum—was praised by conservatives (such as William Buckley) and high culture institutions (the Tate gallery in London, for example, broke precedent and mourned him even though his work was not represented within its walls; Mayer et al., 1980, p. 36).

For long-term fans of the media friend the wider cultural embrace of their dead hero is both upsetting and pleasing. On the one hand, there is a negative feeling of the relationship being diluted and co-opted: "He was my friend, not yours, while he was alive." But on the other hand, there is the positive sense of vindication for believing in the importance of the media friend while he or she was alive: "Now the whole world understands."

Fans may also hope to gain some solace by sharing their relationship with the media friend with their own children. Yet, given the origin of the strongest emotional bonds between fan and media friend—in vicarious interactions over real time in the lives of both parties—the deep mourning for a media friend is often specific to the members of the age cohort or subculture who have spent the most time "with" the media friend. Even in the case of those figures who have transcended specific ages and subcultures—such as John Kennedy and John Lennon—the sense of loss is not easy to convey to those who were very young or not yet born when the media friend died. Unlike traditional societies with relatively unchanging cultural heritages, each generation has its own media experiences and special media friends. In this sense, media friendships not only emotionally bind strangers together, they also create new emotional rifts between generations growing up in the same household.

Nevertheless, because the actual means through which the media friendship grew—mechanically produced images and sounds—still exist, the current media environment also allows for new means of sharing these experiences across generations. Perhaps even more than in traditional societies, we are able to have our children see and hear exactly those things that we saw and heard before they were born. Our children may follow in the same footsteps of discovery, watching early performances and then later ones, or they may work backward, or take a random pattern.

Of course, the context that gave some of the original performances their cultural impact and meaning is often gone. What teenager today could understand the outrage and sensation over Elvis Presley moving his legs, for example, or the disgust and excitement generated by the short bangs on the Beatles' foreheads? Further, the titillating anticipation of a new relationship of uncertain future is missing. And the often tense negotiations over the media friend's place in the culture is largely over. But some of the magic may remain.

I have found, for example, that my young daughter is enchanted by the early Elvis's sad eyes and crooked smile, by the Beatles' irreverent humor and cheeky demeanor, by Martin Luther King's powerful oratory, and by JFK's youth and dynamism.

Fans' sense of loyalty to the memory of a media friend may make them angry over the seeming disloyalty of the media friend's spouse and real friends, who may refuse to play and replay the roles set for them in the media images from the days immediately following the media friend's death. "How could Jackie remarry?" "How could Yoko seem so happy?"

In addition to placing constraints on survivors, the sense of intimate personal knowledge of media friends also places new limits on artistic and scholarly works. Even in nonfiction and history there has always been a dramatic reconstruction of dead heroes' presentational styles. We omit some things about people and invent others. Thomas Jefferson's speech impediment or Abraham Lincoln's high, squeaky, feminine voice are rarely mentioned or portrayed, and the story about young George Washington and the cherry tree was made up. But such omissions and inventions depend on *not* having a detailed visual/aural record of people. By giving us realistic visual/aural memories, modern media have been narrowing the range of believable and acceptable dramatization. When the lives of dead media friends are portrayed, we expect the directors and actors to reproduce as closely as possible the look, sound, and feel of the media images we have already experienced and of those we discover after the media friend's death. Thus, the power of the movie *JFK* derives partially from Oliver Stone's careful recreation of the scenes so familiar from news and documentaries. It was important that Gary Busey look and sing like Buddy Holly in *The Buddy Holly Story*. Val Kilmer was praised for his capturing the appearance, stage presence, and singing style of Jim Morrison in *The Doors*. And it is difficult to imagine John Lennon being portrayed by an actor who does not generally look and sound like him.

New technologies raise the question of how much time fans will devote and how far back they will go to maintain a lifelong relationship with a dead media friend. Over the coming years the available documentary material is likely to increase. Rather than having only a limited number of still photographs or brief silent home movies of the childhoods of our media friends, we are increasingly likely to have hours of camcorder-produced videos shot by parents, neighbors, friends, and relatives. We may be able to observe our politicians, newscasters, and artistic performers when they were whiny children, fighting with their siblings, making a mess at dinner, or desperately in need of a nose wiping. All this material is likely to change our perceptions of our media friends while they are alive, as well as narrow the range of artistic license in representing their lives to us after their deaths.

Even after the death of a media friend, many fans—because of a sense of personal knowledge—would rather see a documentary drawing on the images and voice of the media friend than watch a play or movie in which an actor portrays the media friend (just as many people would find more satisfaction and comfort in looking through old photographs, films, and tapes of a dead relative than in seeing an actor portray the relative). Ironically, the images of media friends are in one sense a step closer to reality than the images of real friends or relatives: They constitute the media friend's existence in our lives. One of the reasons it is difficult not to watch the television set when dead media friends appear is that these are the actual images and sounds of our own life experiences. These recordings are more like the results of a successful seance than the recollections stimulated by a moving eulogy.

CONCLUSION: UNREAL, BUT REAL

There are, in short, many things that are odd and mechanical about attachments to media friends. At the same time, these relationships have features that are very human, very warm, and very caring.

Unlike face-to-face relationships, we have limited control over media friendships. We can rarely influence our media friends directly and personally. Further, we cannot create the friendships on our own, but only respond to some of those that are offered to us. The array of widely accessible media friendships is often limited by powerful political and economic forces. Nevertheless, there are many media friends from which to choose, and they generally enrich our lives while placing few if any demands on us.

Although some fans are driven to try to see, touch, and influence their media heroes, many other fans do not seek to experience media friends in a close face-to-face encounter. For the latter, perhaps, the spell of vicarious intimacy would be weakened or broken by a media friend's real-life blank stare or a look of annoyance or fear. It is through their media performances, after all, that most media friends create the greatest sense of comfort and intimacy with each of us.

One can think of the spread of media friendships as a sad commentary on an impersonal society or as a broadening of human caring across a wider field. Media now expand the sphere of empathy that was once restricted primarily to those who shared the same physical spaces. Even brief TV-fostered relationships—with starving Ethiopian children, with a teacher chosen to travel into space, with Chinese students protesting for democracy, or with a general conducting a television war—have potent emotional impact. It is almost as if we, as a species, are hardwired to react in a personal way to those whose faces we can see in detail. When the camera moves from long shot to close up, our emotions are engaged (Meyrowitz, 1986).

For those who hound, stalk, or kill their media friends, the relationship is an all-consuming passion. But even among the general population, the array of media friendships takes an important place among daily live interactions with family, friends, and colleagues. Real friends and associates often discuss the antics of their media friends. As uncomfortable as it can be to admit it, the death of some of our media friends may hurt us more deeply than the deaths of some of our relatives.

In the world of media friends, the sacred and profane blend—in style, location, and conversation. Talk show hosts and rock stars develop devoted followings that are the envy of religious leaders, and religious leaders increasingly take on the informal behavioral styles of other media friends. Formerly distinct settings blur; the Pope and Madonna share the same airwaves. Both ends of the sacredness spectrum collide in humor by and about media friends—"John Paul Elected Pope; George Ringo Pissed," ran one mock headline.

In the final analysis, no theoretical discussion of these unreal, but real relationships can explain them away or weaken their emotional power. We may never have seen them in the flesh, and they would not have taken note of our deaths, but when our media friends die or are killed, we feel pain. We worry about their widowed spouses and fret over their children who have lost a parent. We dwell on ways the tragedy could have been avoided. Sometimes we even feel partly responsible, as if we could have saved or warned them.

I understand the absurdity of relationships with media friends, but I have also felt all these things. When a TV or radio program airs a clip of JFK, I am riveted to the screen. The negative information I have learned about John Kennedy's backstage behavior somehow coexists with, rather than mutes, the positive feelings engendered by his media persona. As for John Lennon, I continue to find it difficult to listen to the last music album he released before his death. Although it has been more than a decade since Lennon was murdered, my emotions remain raw. Yes, I never really knew him. Yes, he was never even aware of my existence. But I still miss him.

7

The Mediated Sports Hero

Susan J. Drucker
Hofstra University

☐ *Are "sports heroes" true heroes? Drucker claims it is the mass media's celebrification of athletes and sporting events that creates the illusion of heroes emerging from sports. She examines the features of the traditional concept of hero and provides an explanation for the illusion that a sports hero is a real hero. She demonstrates the ways that stadia, photography, news, publicity, radio, and television play a part in constructing this myth and points out that it is the celebrification process at work making athletes into pseudo-heroes.*

I faced a great dilemma. I had the opportunity to take the trip of a lifetime to the Amazon, or I could spend a weekend in a small town in upstate New York where I would attend a 1-hour ceremony honoring a man I have spoken with directly for a sum total of 3-1/2 minutes in my life. I rearranged my plans and made reservations for Cooperstown. Tom Seaver, alias "the Franchise," alias "Tom Terrific," star pitcher of the New York Mets, entered into Baseball's Hall of Fame. I had planned to attend since I was 12 years old. I've watched him age, I cried with him when he was traded, I ran out in the middle of college classes to call sports phone when he was pitching; I remembered his anniversary, his birthday; I've seen his children grow; I've seen his wife not age a bit in 23 years; I've seen his 300th major league victory; shared the moment when his uniform number was retired, and even listened to Yankee broadcasts. The author ultimately attended the induction ceremony. She was not disappointed. It is a relationship of intensity, durability, one which has passed the test of time and is marked by loyalty and fidelity. This brings me to the task of attempting to unravel the nature of the relationship between the professional sports hero and the fan.

All cultures have heroes, but the hero and the heroic varies from culture to culture and from time to time. What is considered heroic is a function of cultural priorities and values and, equally significant, is related to the communication medium utilized for presenting and preserving information about heroes (Cawelti, 1985; Strate, 1985). This chapter explores the nature of "hero," the notion of "sports hero," and the way they function in society as a communication phenomenon whose scope and use has been and is being altered by the rapid advance of electronic media. Despite the cries of social commentators noting the lack of "real heroes," we continue to see endless titles relating to "Sports Legends and Heroes" and we can even purchase "hero series trading cards." It is the thesis of discussion that the nature of modern sports fosters the illusion that heroes emerge from professional sports; however, these so-called "sports heroes" are actually products of the celebrification of the pro athlete rather than the creation of a hero.

THE SPORTS PSUEDO-HERO

Why do modern-day sports seem so naturally to offer candidates for heroes, and are these athletes really heroes in the classical sense of the word? An examination of traditional features of the concept of hero provides some explanation for the illusion that real heroes emerge from professional sports. There are so many definitions of *hero* that one is tempted to simply draw on Justice Potter Stewart's observations regarding censorship and say "I know it when I see it" and conclude that it is not often seen in sports. There have been many competing definitions of *hero* including:

> A central personage taking an admirable part in any remarkable action or event; hence, a person regarded as a model. (Webster's Collegiate Dictionary)

> The hero is a mass symbol, a "vehicle for the imaginings of thousands" who is transformed by imputation and abstraction more and more into what people want of public figures. (Klapp, 1962, p. 14)

The professional athlete performs, acts, and is said to be a role model. Critics have argued that sports heroes constitute a subtle form of social control when they "become the personifications of certain kinds of values and the interpretation of performances and the conduct of spectators becomes part of a wider process whereby particular kinds of life styles, values and ideas are 'sold'" (Hargreaves, 1982, p. 128).

The appearance of heroism in professional sports may also be fostered by the publicness of the acts. If "heroism is a public drama" (Edwards, 1988, p. 48), the real hero does not merely enjoy fame as a fleeting character on the public stage, but is a figure who endures the passage of time. According to Carlyle (1908, p. 312), "A hero can be poet, prophet, king, priest or what you will, according to the kind of world he finds himself born into." Today's world is a "wide world of sports" with many of those figures ever increasingly appearing on a public stage being heralded as our modern heroes. Libraries devote shelves and shelves to volumes on the "legends" *The Great Ones, The*

Hall of Famers, Boys of Summer, and the *Summer of 49* in which some of them played. Bookstores are filled with everything from *Bo Knows Bo*, to the more cerebral works of the late A. Bartlett Giamatti—Renaissance scholar, Baseball Commissioner, sports fan. Once there were merely *The Champions, Monday Night Baseball, Saturday Night Wrestling, Sunday Golf, Sunday Afternoon Football*, and *Monday Night Football*. We now have *Sports Extra, Sports Update, Sports Central*, 24-hour sports radio, Sportschannel, and ESPN. Need a break—go to the movies to see *Field of Dreams, Bull Durham, The Natural* or *Babe Ruth*. Still not satisfied—rent a tape, settle in, and turn on *Brian's Song, North Dallas Forty, The Lou Gehrig Story*, and so on.

Achievement in modern professional sports is anything but a private act. Heroes are also creations of a common will, of combined action, of collective expression (Edwards, 1988; Fishwick, 1954; Lipsky, 1975). To Robert Penn Warren (1972), no true hero can exist in the absence of a communal soul, and Michael Lever asserts that sports is an institution that holds people together (Wenner, 1990). "We" have something in common, "we" share more than physical proximity, "we" share a sport's history, a tradition, a team, a standard of excellence, records held and broken, and our heroes. Shared sports heroes can cross economic, social, linguistic, racial, and geographic barriers. The concepts of *communal* interest and *community* itself, traditionally place-based notions, have been altered by the modern world in which the electronic media of communications permit, indeed encourage, a sense of the communal based upon interest rather than place (see Gumpert, 1987; Meyrowitz, 1985). Modern professional sports has been called an interest-based community (Gumpert, Lehman, & Drucker, 1990). All communities need heroes, communities form around heroes, and interest-based communities are no exception.

The traditional hero emerged by acting within the larger social, political, religious, and economic realm. The hero has been alternatively positioned as: saint, world redeemer, emperor (Campbell, 1968), leader, lover, politician (McGinniss, 1990), writer, mythic or literary character, and warrior. The modern sports hero restores civic pride, serves as role model, plays a role in oft-repeated sports legends, is followed by groupies, writes autobiographies, runs for public office, but most often "leads the troops into battle" as teammates take the court, ice, or field. With these notions it is a small step toward equating talented athletes with heroes.

The marriage of organized professional sports and the conception of hero is natural as the traditional requisite ingredients for hero creation appear to be present. The hero is one who makes an archetypal journey. According to Joseph Campbell (1968) the hero's story is composed of elements common across time and culture:

> The standard path of the mythological adventure of the hero is a magnification of the formula represented in the rite of passage: separation-initiation-return: which might be named the nuclear unit of the monomyth. A hero ventures

forth from the world of common day into a region of supernatural wonder: fabulous forces are there encountered and a decisive victory is won: the hero comes back from this mysterious adventure with the power to bestow boons on his fellow man. (p. 30)

The journey for the professional athlete runs from the sandlots, to the little leagues, school sports, amateur leagues, minor leagues, professional competition, and finally retirement. The "hero" acts; the athlete performs. The hero is brave even if called upon to make the "supreme sacrifice": within seconds the athlete may tear cartilage, rip a tendon, break a bone, or sustain a blow to the head resulting in a career-ending injury. When the risks of unfolding action are replaced by memories of victory, sacrifice, or survival, the athlete is venerated by nostalgia, uniform numbers are retired, Oldtimer's games are attended, restaurants are opened to house memorabilia, life stories are written, and the Hall of Fame beckons. The hero performs acts of significance: "Sports are said to reflect and reaffirm such cultural values as achievement, hard work, discipline, teamwork, loyalty, and tradition" (Trujillo, 1990). According to Wenner in *Media, Sports, and Society* (1989), spectator sports also serve a therapeutic function as they can be pleasurable, heighten attachment to place, offer "a fantasized extension of self," and "provide a sense of being part of something" (p. 224).

The illusion of heroism is clearly fostered by these delineated characteristics. Yet, on close examination of the hero-creation process, the resemblance to modern-day celebrities is startling. Twentieth-century mass media have made available in the United States an unending stream of *celebrities*, and Americans have in return responded with adulation and devotion. The evolution of a media relationship based on identification without interaction can be traced to the establishment of the Industrial Revolution in America and the rise of the mass-circulation daily newspaper. The persistent presentation of "news" about individuals enabled large numbers of people to identify with them, carefully following their dramatic triumphs, their emotional setbacks, and their personal idiosyncracies, drawing ever closer toward a new form of relationship with public characters. "News" of stars of the sports world is not relegated to the sports pages alone. When reading or hearing reports on entertainers or other well-known individuals, the sports "star" is often found dining at the next table, dancing at the same club, making a cameo appearance on television or film, or promoting the same product as the celebrity.

The varied definitions of celebrity include:

A famous or well-known person. (*Random House*)

State of being renown; State of being celebrated (i.e. to perform publicly and with appropriate rites; to proclaim or publish abroad). (*Webster's Collegiate Dictionary*)

> The state or quality of being celebrated, i.e. having been made famous. (*Funk & Wagnalls*)

> The celebrity is a person known for his/her "well-knownness." The celebrity is created and maintained by media. (Boorstin, 1961)

The celebrity's fame is molded, created, and prefabricated. The professional athlete's fame and status are created through an updated process of hero making.

THE MEDIA AND THE CELEBRIFICATION OF THE PROFESSIONAL ATHLETE

> Dreaming, we are heroes. Waking, we invent them. (Edwards, 1988, p. 48)

The process of hero construction has been a function of the communication process which has undergone radical change due to developments in communication technologies. Heroes were created through the ritual retelling of the story of their great deeds. The narrative, the story, the myth, or the epic, embodying the heroes' deeds, was, to oral cultures, the means of hero creation and perpetuation (Campbell, 1968). According to Ong (1967) there exists considerable evidence that the dominant medium of the communication of a culture affects the notion of hero:

> The figures around whom knowledge is made to cluster, those about whom stories are told or sung, must be made into conspicuous personages, foci of common attention, individuals embodying open public concerns . . . These figures, moreover, cannot be too numerous or attention will be dissipated and focus blurred. (p. 204)

Print and electronic communication technologies have provided new mechanisms for hero making which in turn have changed the end product and its functions.

The ancient hero's deeds often reflected acts of physical strength and courage on a naturally occurring stage. Contrasted with the naturally occurring challenge (offered by dragons, monsters, wars, and famines), we find sport—a rule-bound *autotelic* or self-contained activity. Were gladiators the first sports heroes? Were ancient Olympians? When the stage for the heroic deed is limited or intertwined and dependent on technology, one of the few fields remaining for testing a human against a challenge is the carefully planned, constructed, and groomed sports arena. Hero creation has been modernized; heroes changed. In an oral culture the heroic is oriented toward contests and combat. Heroes are closely associated with well-known and widely remembered events such as slaying the dragon or saving the village through moral courage and individual sacrifice. The ephemeralness of spoken discourse serves to limit the number of figures selected and sharpens the focus on those figures to be remembered. Heroes' actions in an oral culture are more readily remembered because they are portrayed as having a marked influence on the outcome of events, and they must serve as inspiration to those who feel they have little control over natural forces. It is significant to note that modern-day "hero-making" is a multimedia phenomenon.

The Stadium as Communication Medium

The sports arena, stadium, amphitheater, or complex is a public place. From Greece and Rome to the Superdome that venue serves as a place of interaction. Public places were and are a medium of communication, that is, they are essential carriers of communication (Rykwert, 1978).

The stadium is a place of communal activity; the team and players "represent" a place that provides a sense of identification for fans. Professional sports take place in spaces that yield community affiliation and contact. Modern culture is populated with citizens who live their lives behind locked doors and darkened car windows, individuals who shield themselves from contact in public with others. Yet, the very same people shout, converse, pass the hotdogs, discuss the latest managerial blunder, and sing the National Anthem in unison. In this context games are won and saved, sports stories are retold, and legends are created. This context has become increasingly mediated as the PA announcer supplements the images appearing on diamond vision that are carefully orchestrated to evoke the response desired by team management. Communication in the stadium plays a part in the creation of the sports hero. Stadia offer finite capacity with access ruled by barriers of financial means and distance, but the modern micro and mass media place no such limitations on fans as functions of the arena have been augmented, if not displaced, by all-sports talk radio, ESPN, *Sports Illustrated*, and Sports Phone.

Photography

Sports figures, great and small, find themselves in team pictures, in news photos, and in the homes of millions. Posters are marketed, photographs are autographed, pictures with fans are posed for, and trading cards are sold. Posters are sold at the stadium and in malls alongside those of the hottest rock star du jour. Teams sponsor "Photo Days," providing photo opportunities for their fans. Some encourage players to make themselves available to fans before games for this very purpose. According to Al Harazin, General Manager of the New York Mets (personal communication, May 9, 1990), "everyone wants to touch the ballplayers, and I have found out that through enough camera days and other promotional days at ball parks that if you don't have a lot of people coming through the gate you can do a lot of things."

According to Tim Nolan (personal communication, October 10, 1991), proprietor of Classic Hobby Nostalgia, a sports memorabilia shop on Long

Island, posters are the province of the kids, whereas adults specialize in collecting and coveting photographs and autographed posters. Possessing photos and posters is, according to Sontag (1977), a symbolic form of control of personal relationships with others. Having photos and posters indicates "possession" of the other person, and they are an aid in maintaining a relationship by bringing closer the person in the photo. Is it possible that the ubiquitous celebrity poster is now the counterpart of the statue of the hero in the public square? The memorial statue erected to honor and remember the hero has long been a feature of the hero-creation and preservation process. Statues, dedicated by the public, were placed in public places, including halls of fame.

Images adorn the face of trading cards. Baseball trading cards were introduced in the later part of the 19th century and became an institution with the emergence of Topps bubblegum cards in 1951. By 1984, trading cards were transformed from a childhood hobby into a multimillion dollar business (Nolan, personal communication, October 10, 1991). A 1952 Mickey Mantle baseball card can fetch as much as $50,000. There are many lines of trading cards as Topps is no longer alone in the field. Different companies offer distinctive series, each with players striking a distinct pose. Fourteen different companies produce football trading cards, the sport for which cards are least popular. Why would football cards be less popular? One suggestion has been that people relate to players when they are covered in helmets and built up in shoulder pads, therefore, the close-up photos on the cards destroy the illusion (Nolan, personal communication, October 10, 1991).

Promoters organize shows. There are monthly shows at which on the average 30-40 dealers attend, and there are larger shows drawing as many as 100-500 dealers. "In some areas one could attend a different card show each night of the week" (Nolan, personal communication, October 10, 1991), and these trading card shows provide a forum for conversation based on common interests. A child's hobby has become a big-money industry with monthly price guides, magazines, price lists, and international trade associations. An owner of a sports trading cards shop says "If I had to rely on kids I'd be out of business" (Nolan, personal communication, October 10, 1991).

Writing

Writing and print have revolutionized sports and the creation of the sports hero as well. According to Guttman, to the ancients, the game on the field was a repetitive ritual or ceremony. Sports records have existed since the ancient Greeks (Guttman, 1978) and have been a significant means for creating the sports hero. With writing came inscriptions, poems, and record keeping as a means for preserving and recreating the very transitory achievement of the sports act (Giamatti, 1989). The sports record, the "record book," in and of itself may not make what has commonly been called the sports hero. Although according to traditional notions, a hero's deeds, in the record book, might be enough to create a hero, in order to be placed on the pedestal reserved for the most revered, the modern sports figure must visit the sick hospitalized child, serve as spokesperson for a charity, and answer fan requests for photos and autographs. These activities are approved of by the front office, but are not generally required. According to Gregory Bouris (personal communication, July 16, 1990) of the New York Islanders Hockey team, the personality and attitude of a player is considered when evaluating future players. Fan relations and community relations are part of the profile of an Islander. A personality system has developed in professional sports.

Like trading cards, autograph collecting has become commercialized. The collection of celebrity autographs is not new, but the formalization of the sports star autograph show is a recent innovation. Shows are organized with sports figures of the past and present paid by the hour. Interaction with fans is limited as the more signatures that are signed, the more money that is made. Conversation with fans who seek the autograph to keep, cherish, or sell at a profit is limited by financial motive. Autographs can bring large sums. A baseball autograph of Monte Irvin is worth $75 as are Carl Hubble's and Lefty Gomez's, but Ralph Kiner's is worth only $25.

Sports heroes are also created through the omnipresent sports biography and autobiography. "Autobiographical narratives are now the method by which public figures communicate the myths which audiences identify as heroic for their particular situation. Narrative analysis of these popular forms of communication reveal these new myths as hero-making strategies" (McLennan, 1989, p. 2). Autobiographies of sports heroes collaborating "with" or "and" professional writers abound. One can read *Audibles, My Life in Football* by Joe Montana and Bob Raissman (1986); *Martina* by Navratilova with George Vecsey (1985); *Billyball* by Billy Martin with Phil Pepe; *Throwing Heat, The Autobiography of Nolan Ryan*, by Nolan Ryan and Harvey Frommer (1988); and *The Perfect Game* by Tom Seaver and Dick Schapp. One will find "along withs" such as Dick Schapp, Pete Axthelm, and Neil Amdur on such works. Add to the list the works of Yaz, Winfield, Michael Jordan, Dwight Gooden, Jose Canseco, Wade Boggs, Roger Clemens, and "before and after" stories of Pete Rose and one begins to get the sense of enormity of the professional athlete autobiography genre. Coaches, managers, and sportscasters, and celebrities (if not heroes all) can be added to the list. According to McLennan, personal narratives enable these public figures to meet the ever-increasing demands placed on them to account for their behaviors and provide their own interpretation of events. In so doing they create a public image and position themselves as heroic persona. The genre formed is one in which the individual may fashion an image beyond that of the record book or repair a damaged image by presenting himself as a hero, which is often accomplished by recounting the heroic journey or quest.

Sports pages, sports magazines, and the sportswriter all provide weekly, daily, and up-to-the-minute fuel for the celebrification process. Each move, play, decision, pout, frown, and temper tantrum is recounted, retold, analyzed, and criticized. The long-established and ever-growing genre of sports writing has contributed greatly not only to the celebrification of the professional athlete, but to the myth of the sports hero as well.

Radio, Television, Telephone

The electronic media have proved the most powerful tool in the creation of the psuedo-hero of sports. The celebrated athlete grew along with the electronic media and helped provide a seemingly endless source of content for media that consumed programming at a great rate. In 1922, even before the advent of commercial radio, WEAF broadcast in New York a University of Chicago-Princeton game, taking place in Chicago (Barnouw, 1975). In 1939, two baseball games were telecast by an experimental NBC television—a Princeton game and a Brooklyn Dodger match (Barnouw, 1975).

Although initially viewed with some skepticism by team owners who feared the loss of revenue from game attendance, the economic and marketing benefits of selling broadcast rights quickly became apparent. Total revenue from television for major league baseball, for example, rose from $15.8 million in 1960, to $40.7 million in 1970 (Horowitz, 1974), to the $1.1 billion for CBS network rights alone during the 1990-93 seasons (Jassem, 1990).

The sportscaster has become friend, critic, and a major voice through which a team presents itself. According to Al Harazin of the New York Mets (personal communication, May 9, 1990), the men in the booth are team spokesmen, ambassadors, and salesmen, as well as interpreters of events on and off the field. The sportscaster walks the line between journalism and ambassador for a sport or club. For many fans there is the daily contact with the sportscaster. They may even correspond with the announcer (McCarver, personal communication, June 8, 1990). The radio call-in format offers yet another opportunity to interact with the specialist prepared to highlight, praise, elevate, and venerate the sports professional. The familiar voice is presented as expert (i.e., either professional broadcast journalist or former participant). With some degree of credibility the sportscaster helps celebrate the athlete by calling the action, placing accomplishments in the context of the omnipresent record, and instantaneously providing the enormity of a feat in terms of endless statistics. According to sportscaster Brent Musburger, "the announcer works with the action itself, presented live on television the picture is more important than the announcer . . . the announcer is secondary to the output of the truck" (cited in Verna, 1987 p. 64). The mediation of the sport itself goes a long way in explaining why professional sports has celebrities or pseudo-heroes.

The nature of broadcasting, television in particular, also contributes to the making of the celebrity athlete. The live, the unpredictable, the dramatic "are the core of TV . . . they are the one thing TV [in particular] can do that no other medium can match" (Verna, 1987, p. 41). Television coverage personalizes and creates "stars" we know on and off the field. To sportscaster Tim McCarver (personal communication, June 8, 1990), "Television takes you into the heart and soul of the players." The audience sees each bead of perspiration, each grimace, each tension-filled expression as the camera zooms in as a basketball is shot, a baseball is hurled, a football is passed, or a tennis ball is served.

As the sound quality from the playing field has been improved, the audience can hear the crack of the bat. Managers, umpires, and players have even been miked which closes the psychological distance between fan and participant as the fan becomes even more intimate with the player. Graphics provide player identification, history, statistics, and constant reminders of "heroic deeds." The actions of the pseudo-heroes are retold via hi-tech means. Replays and stop-action shots explain why things happen and provide cause and effect (Verna, 1987).

Both mass and micro media provide means for getting to know the professional athlete. The telephone allows fans to "reach out and touch" the player when they appear on a radio or television call-in program or gives fans the privilege of paying large sums to dial a 900 number to hear a prerecorded message from the likes of Jose Canseco discussing what he ate for breakfast. The ability to directly contact the player brings the sports figure closer to the fan and promotes the relationship of celebrity/fan rather than hero/worshipper.

Athletes now have agents and are seen endorsing everything from sports equipment to jockey shorts. Can any of us forget Jim Palmer's underwear? Are we not expecting all Super Bowl victors to be going to DisneyWorld immediately after the game clock runs out? The images of Joe Montana downing a Diet Coke, Bo Jackson running downcourt in his Nikes, Hulk Hogan hawking Right Guard stick deodorant, Nolan Ryan praising Advil, Magic Johnson selling subscriptions to *Sports Illustrated*, and World Series champs adorning cereal boxes are endless. The commercialization of the sports figure further "deheroizes," as it enhances the fame and celebrity status of the athlete.

It is not merely the tremendous amount of information that modern media furnishes about professional athletes that makes them celebrities rather than heroes. The rise of personal information, the "up close and personal view" of the individual, leads to the demise of the all-powerful sports pseudo-hero.

THE NATURE OF THE SPORTS HERO/FAN RELATIONSHIP OR ARE THEY REALLY HEROES?

In a culture in which one may determine how often a hero is seen (we can always go to the videotape), may own unflattering photos, may see the sweat or hear grunting and cursing, may view the majestic swing, throw, run, dunk, pass, fumble, error, or foul instantly replayed over and over again, what is the nature of the relationship between sports figure and fan?

As Boorstin (1961) contends, heroes have been replaced by celebrities.

> Before we had celebrities we had heroes. . . . Now what these types all share, of course, are admirable qualities—qualities that somehow set them apart from the rest of us. They have done things, acted in the world, written, thought, understood, led. Celebrities, on the other hand, needn't have done—needn't do—anything special. Their function isn't to act—just to be. To a large extent, celebrity has entirely superseded heroism. . . . Celebrities are passive objects of the media—created whole out of "ordinary" newspaper print, or film, or broadcast airwaves. (Monaco, 1978, pp. 6-7)

The hero is known for deeds, the celebrity for "well-knownness" (Boorstin, 1961). The celebrity hero need only be a presence, need only be the focus of media attention, someone with whom the audience can readily identify. Because we all need something to satisfy our expectations of human greatness, we produce our celebrity heroes everyday by watching them on either the big screen or the small screen, by reading and talking about them, by buying recordings and posters, and so on. The sports figure, though performing deeds, certainly performs the function of celebrity as well. The sporting contest may foster the impression of heroic deeds, all the while presenting an ordinary person with extraordinary athletic prowess and media attention.

The "heroic" nature of sports activities is questionable when held up to traditional measures. When held under the scrutiny of the modern star system it is difficult to imagine the illusion of heroism being maintained. According to Donald Ohlmeyer, Head of Ohlmeyer Communications:

> The biggest thing that sports can do right now—the biggest thing the three networks can do to try to protect themselves . . . is to rediscover the hero. We live in an era where there are no more heroes. All of our heroes are being convicted for reckless driving or for taking cocaine, for raping girls and getting thrown in jail! That's what's wrong with sports right now. . . .The heroes are gone. (Verna, 1987, p. 66)

Pete Rose, Len Bias, Otis Nixon, Lenny Dykstra, and Mike Tyson follow in the tradition of the hard-drinking, gambling, sports figures of old. On and off the field, court, or ice, behavior is examined carefully. Unlike the hero, the fall of these sports figures does not become part of the hero-making process. It is, however, a part of the celebrification process.

The word *fan*, a term derived from *fanatic*, characterizes a relationship based on an intimate knowledge of a personality created and sustained by the mass media industry and maintained by the personality's ability to control media attention rather than to control or shape events. (The athlete is never completely in control of his or her talent, the events in the game, injuries, or outcomes.) The fan relationship with the celebrity or media personality is a symbiotic one—a relationship that appears to fulfill an important need in the public psyche.

Caughey (1986) points out that the celebrity's appeal is linked to the fan's daily social relationships. It is taken for granted in our present culture that everyone knows of great numbers of celebrities including sports figures. According to Caughey, "Pseudo mutual acquaintances of this kind often provide American strangers . . . with the basis for socializing" (p. 220). This goes well beyond linking American strangers, as Michael Jordan has in capturing the imagination of children around the world.

What we see evolving from our dependence on the new relationships forged with celebrities is a shift from the traditional notion of the hero as a transcendent character dominating events through great deeds to a more ordinary but highly talented and well-publicized person who reflects our desire to escape ordinariness and gain some recognition in an impersonal, technological world. Cathcart and Drucker have argued that the reliance on the celebrity in the establishment of self (see Cathcart & Gumpert, 1986) and the involvement with celebrities to help create a place for ourselves in a modern world in which traditional concepts of place and community have been altered by electronic media (see Drucker & Gumpert, 1991; Gumpert, 1987; Meyrowitz, 1985) would seem to argue that "solitary identification" is an important and widespread person-media personae relationship (Drucker & Cathcart, 1989).

The modern sports hero is actually a misnomer for the sports celebrity. Critics have noted true sports heroes are an endangered species, whereas sports celebrities are as common as Texas cockroaches (Trujillo, 1989). On the surface professional sports seem to offer a natural source for heroes, but on closer examination they offer celebrated sports figures shaped, fashioned, and marketed as heroic.

Section II: The Making of Modern Heros

The Making of a Journalistic Celebrity, 1963

Barbie Zelizer
Temple University

☐ *This chapter explores how the retellings and recollections of journalists concerning their coverage of the Kennedy assassination have provided a stage for the construction and perpetuation of journalistic celebrity. Media stories about the assassination reveal strategies of collective remembering and forgetting that uncover patterns in the perpetuation of the celebrity status of the journalists taking part. This examination of celebrity as a communication phenomenon addresses the ways in which notions of celebrity are interchanged with more traditional notions of journalistic authority in the workings of contemporary media. To be talked about is to be part of a story, and to be part of a story is to be at the mercy of storytellers—the media and their audience. The famous person is thus not so much a person as a story about a person. (Braudy, 1986, p. 592)*

How journalists legitimate their right to present authoritative versions of events in the real world has become a problematic aspect of contemporary journalistic performance. Events such as the debate between anchorperson Dan Rather and then-Presidential candidate George Bush or the unfolding of Watergate throw into question not only the rightful boundaries of political machinery, but also of appropriate journalistic practice. In many cases, journalists use their personal status and well-knownness to turn stories about events into stories about themselves, using their own celebrity to make themselves active players in the relay of news.

This chapter appeared in *Covering the Body: The Kennedy Assassination, the Media, and the Shaping of Collective Memory* by Barbie Zelizer, © 1992. Reprinted with the permission of the University of Chicago Press.

This is an account of how journalists have made themselves into celebrities through their recollections of one specific event—the assassination of John F. Kennedy. The Kennedy assassination occurred at a point in time when television was coming into its own as a legitimate medium for news, and journalistic professionalism encouraged experimentation with new techniques, methods, and boundaries of appropriate journalistic practice. Journalists' reconstructions of their assassination coverage therefore provided a stage not only for the construction and perpetuation of journalistic celebrity, but also a way to address larger sociocultural discourses about American journalism. Celebrity, explored here as a temporally and spatially bounded memory system that gave reporters shared perceptions and recollections in retelling the assassination story, constituted a basic cornerstone of their establishment as its authoritative spokespeople and helped journalists promote themselves along with the stories they told.

This study is based on a systematic examination of the narratives by which journalists have recollected their coverage of the assassination since Kennedy died in 1963 (Zelizer, 1992). Narratives appeared in the mass media and trade literature, including journals, newspapers, television retrospectives, documentary films, books, and professional journalism reviews. The conclusions presented suggest that journalists achieved their placement as cultural authorities in part by using the memory system of celebrity to address the story of Kennedy's death.

CELEBRITY AS A MEMORY SYSTEM

Defined as "persons well-known for their well-knownedness" (Boorstin, 1961, p. 57), *celebrity* has traditionally functioned as a set of rules for all speakers and actors that gives them idealized notions about how they are expected to be or act (Dyer, 1978). Depending in large part on the mass media, celebrity has evolved into its most contemporary form through an interlinking of different mediated texts that generate extensive public discourse about certain personalities (Dyer, 1978). Constructing and perpetuating celebrity is thus as much an institutional concern as an individual one, with institutional practices helping to generate and maintain individual cases of celebrity.

In journalistic retellings of the Kennedy assassination, celebrity both helped reporters strategically interpret the significance of their coverage of Kennedy's death and highlighted the presence of certain figures within their narratives. Even though journalists used their actions as a frame of reference for retelling assassination tales, in certain cases their status as storytellers overshadowed the tales they told. These tales emphasized the importance of the individual reporter. Journalists constructed stories of celebrity by systematically "plugging" different reporters into the assassination story. This substitutional rule offered a readymade way of making sense of the significance of covering

Kennedy's death. Celebrity offered specific cues of memory, which focused on the significance of the individual.

Tales of journalistic celebrity were formed via references to two larger discourses relevant at the time of Kennedy's death—technology and professionalism. On the one hand, they reflected the technology then newest to news work—television. The uncertainty surrounding television news generated a flurry of attention around the television journalists, whose use of the new medium thrust many into the critical public eye for the first time. As television news was legitimated, the celebrity of reporters was woven increasingly into the formats of television news presentation. Celebrity status became linked with the visual, dramatic, and personalized aspects of the medium, which generated an authority characterized by style, personality, and flair (Schudson, 1982). Features such as close-ups and televised interviews, which associated news with faces, meant that the authority with which television would eventually promote the on-site recognition of journalists figured already within assassination tales.

On the other hand, a concern for professionalism also permeated journalists' attempts to promote themselves as celebrities. The fact that celebrity reflected "shifting definitions of achievement in a social world" (Braudy, 1986, p. 10) was grounded in assassination retellings, which displayed different modes of professional journalistic practice in covering Kennedy's death. Legitimating television allowed for the rearrangement of professional roles not only in television but in other media as well. Celebrity thus became established by the new professional identities and authoritative forms of storytelling that adoption of each medium made not only possible, but—if institutional intermedia competition were to survive—necessary.

In recollecting the Kennedy assassination, journalists were thereby able to promote themselves as celebrities parallel to ongoing debates about both journalistic professionalism and the legitimation of television news. Individual reporters became the pivotal point of criss-crossing discourses about the assassination, on the one hand, and technology and professionalism, on the other. As a memory system, celebrity offered assassination retellers a way of both perpetuating their tales and gaining stature from them. Certain journalistic personalities were legitimated in association with the assassination story in ways that set them up as more general cultural authorities.

THE CONTEXT FOR JOURNALISTIC CELEBRITY

The Kennedy administration, like the assassination that brought it to an end, catered to the celebrity status of journalists. In recalling his coverage of Kennedy's reign, *Washington Post* reporter David Broder maintained that the President's live television conferences drew reporters who generally eschewed institutionalized set-ups: "Some of those (reporters) Kennedy recognized regularly became TV stars themselves, and that status—reinforced by invitations to White House parties and dinners - did nothing to hurt the administration (Broder, 1987, p. 158). Kennedy's administration was "an American court where the rich, the glamorous and the powerful congratulated each other. It was a pantheon of celebrity" (Wright, 1983, p. 34). The President created an atmosphere that made celebrity a viable context for remembering his life and death.

Journalists' retellings of the assassination followed these parameters. Certain reporters became celebrities through their postassassination reconstructions of Kennedy's reign, whereas others found that retelling the assassination was a vantage point from which to perpetuate their renown. For example, writers Theodore White and Hugh Sidey were labeled "Kennedy's elegists" (Wills, 1983, p. 94). Assassination narratives often displayed the names of individual reporters as emblems of authority for the events in Dallas.

Why were narratives of celebrity so important? For a journalistic community concerned with issues of new technology and changing boundaries of professionalism, these narratives addressed concerns about how the individual reporter could succeed. Tales of celebrity constituted a type of legitimating narrative for members of the community that displayed the appropriate boundaries of journalistic practice in addressing the assassination story. These tales had two moods—the indicative and the subjunctive (Benveniste, 1981). The indicative mood documented the "as is" of journalistic coverage of the assassination. It illustrated how individual reporters had acted in recognized ways while covering Kennedy's death. The subjunctive mood documented the assassination coverage as "it might be." It focused on higher, more refined levels of journalistic practice. Taken together, these narratives showed the journalistic community how it was possible to gain personal stature through narratives about Kennedy's death.

Four particular reporters—Tom Wicker, Dan Rather, Walter Cronkite, and Theodore White—were consistently mentioned by the journalistic community in conjunction with discourses relevant to American journalism at the time of the assassination. Although they were not the only reporters to emerge as celebrities from the story, each one's rise to fame involved issues of concern to mainstream journalism. Other reporters at the same time experienced celebrity's downside, largely because the issues about journalism they raised did not fit in with the concerns of the community. This suggests that retelling the assassination has given reporters institutionally backed ways to gain and maintain personal status. Their records of the assassination have allowed them to narratively reconstruct its events in ways that reinforce not only their own celebrity but also the institutions of mainstream American journalism.

TOM WICKER

Narratives about Tom Wicker were instrumental in showing members of the journalistic community how the print media had successfully covered the assassination. These narratives told of Wicker being on the scene continuously for the first day of events until he filed his report at day's end from an airport terminal. His actions were constructed as an ideal instance of journalistic practice that showed how the goals of speedy coverage, eyewitness reporting, and terse prose could lead to professional success. Years later, colleague Harrison Salisbury praised Wicker's on-the-scene reporting by saying that:

> The coverage had begun with classic reportage—Tom Wicker's on-the-scenes eyewitness. It could not be beat. [I told him to] ... just write every single thing you have seen and heard. Period. He did. No more magnificent piece of journalistic writing has been published in the *Times*. Through Tom's eye we lived through each minute of that fatal Friday, the terror, the pain, the horror, the mindless tragedy, elegant, blood-chilling prose. (Salisbury, 1988, p. 71)

One telling aspect of Salisbury's comments is located in his final sentence—"the horror, the mindless tragedy, elegant, blood-chilling prose." Salisbury quietly moved from telling the horror of the event to telling the elegance of the writing in which it was inscribed. In so doing he reinforced an intrinsic association between Wicker's role in reporting Kennedy's death and the events of the death themselves. Salisbury made it appear as if Wicker himself were an integral part of the assassination story, a pattern frequently repeated in tales of journalistic celebrity.

Narratives about Wicker were predicated on such an association—Wicker in Dallas was part of the Dallas story. As media critic Gay Talese later observed, Wicker's reporting that afternoon "will live longer than any novel, or play, or essay, or piece of reportage that he has ever written or will ever write" (Talese, 1986, p. 34). Wicker's actions in Dallas were repeatedly referenced in subsequent stories of his own career trajectory. Talese, for example, contended that "Wicker was a product of events, an individual whose career had been advanced by the reporting of the assassination" (p. 34). Not long afterwards Wicker was selected to succeed James Reston as the Washington bureau chief (p. 37). Nearly 30 years later, Wicker's actions in Dallas were still being used for personal credentialing, as in his 1991 discussion of Oliver Stone's movie *JFK*, which was published in the *New York Times* with the information that Wicker had "covered the assassination of John F. Kennedy for the newspaper" (Wicker, 1991, p. 1).

Tales of Wicker the celebrity thus offered a professionally correct response to unresolved concerns about what it meant to be a print-media professional in the age of television. This celebrity tale brought discourses about television journalism and journalistic professionalism together with assassination narratives in a way that underscored the viability of print journalism. It showed that it was possible to become a celebrity by having been an effective print reporter. For a community then involved in altering its own boundaries of practice around the evolving technology of television, this tale upheld the continued relevance of the print media.

DAN RATHER

Narratives about the actions of Dan Rather in Dallas similarly linked ongoing discourses about journalistic professionalism and television journalism with assassination narratives, but they did so from the perspective of the television journalist. Tales about Rather addressed concerns about the ongoing legitimation of television correspondents as bona fide reporters. Rather too was at the site when Kennedy was killed, but rather than remain on the scene, he rushed to the nearest CBS affiliate where he succeeded in providing rapid up-to-date relays of what was happening in the city. As he later recalled, "among the first lessons I learned in journalism.... No story is worth a damn unless you can get it out.... I had to hotfoot it back to the station" (Rather with Herskowitz, 1977, p. 122).

The comparison between Rather and Wicker is telling. Unlike Wicker, who anticipated the deadlines of printing by following the story to the airport, where he labored to write elegant prose in less-than-ideal conditions, Rather anticipated the demands of television technology by rushing *away* from the story and *toward* the technology of its telling. In other words, he ran to the nearest affiliate. His success in filing the story depended directly on his subordinates, who remained on the scene to provide him with information.

Tales of Rather in Dallas were frequently referenced in stories about his personal career trajectory, organizational overviews of CBS News, and more generalized discussions of the legitimacy of television journalism (Zelizer, 1989). Journalistic lore held that "he came to national prominence through his coverage of the Kennedy assassination" ("November 22, 1963: Where we were," 1988, p. 70), which earned him a White House posting, "over the heads of several more experienced Washington reporters" (Gates, 1978, p. 12). The day that Kennedy died was "in career terms, the most important day in Dan Rather's life. His swift and accurate reporting of the Kennedy assassination and its aftermath that weekend transformed him from a regional journalist into a national correspondent" (p. 293).

Institutionally grounded discourse thus confirmed Rather as a celebrity, thanks to his coverage of the assassination story. Tales about Rather were important in delineating not only what was similar between print and television journalists, but also what was different. Just as tales about Tom Wicker had shown it was possible to gain celebrity status by being part of the print media, tales of Dan Rather showed it was possible to do so as a broadcast reporter.

These tales explicitly addressed the value of television journalists, thereby responding to lingering concerns about their legitimation as bona fide reporters.

Taken together, tales about both Tom Wicker and Dan Rather foregrounded the indicative dimensions of journalistic practice. They set out the appropriate parameters of such practice by showing what journalistic professionals "do." At the same time, they upheld the two subcommunities that comprised the larger community of journalism professionals—print and broadcast. Serving as a frame of reference for the larger journalistic community, these tales suggested that it was possible to assume an authoritative presence in assassination retellings, regardless of the medium in which one was employed.

WALTER CRONKITE

Whereas tales of Wicker and Rather underscored the recognized practices of journalism, other narratives highlighted the elevated forms in which individuals worked across media. Narratives about Walter Cronkite provided just such a discussion about the elevated forms of television journalism, in that they addressed the refined levels of practice to which television news aspired.

Cronkite stayed on the air for much of the first day of events, and he was responsible for conveying to the public the news that Kennedy was dead. His emotional relay of that fact was coupled with a number of activities that underscored the anchorperson's distressed state—notably, removing his eyeglasses in a distracted fashion and forgetting to put on his suit jacket. His actions evidenced how it was possible to stretch the borders of professionalism and still be labeled professional. Cronkite cried, appeared shaken and emotionally moved, and then composed himself to carry the nation through its evolving crisis. He transcended his own personal distress to guide the public throughout the 4-day ordeal.

Cronkite's activities were important in discussions about the evolving authentication of anchorpeople as journalists. Discourse centered on both his deeds and words. One 1983 *Newsweek* article contended that: "Walter Cronkite broke into a popular CBS soap opera, 'As the World Turns,' with the first TV bulletin of the attack on JFK" ("What JFK meant to us," 1983, p. 66). The next sentence noted that Cronkite was "for 19 years anchorman of the CBS Evening News," reinforcing the link between Cronkite's role in covering the assassination story and his personal career trajectory. Another discussion of coverage of the Kennedy assassination was entitled "The Age of Cronkite" (Matusow, 1983). A print retrospective of television's 50th anniversary hailed Cronkite for having taken the American people through assassinations, conventions, and space shots:

> [his] reputation for being the TV news authority had evolved in the early 60s and was underscored by his coverage of the assassination of President John F. Kennedy on November 22, 1963. For four straight days, beginning on Friday

afternoon, Cronkite sat in the anchor chair, sometimes in his shirt sleeves and sometimes in tears, through the Monday when JFK was buried at Arlington National Cemetery. (Elm, 1989, p. 31)

Seen as producing a "new personae" for American journalists, the image of solid integrity that Cronkite projected would thereafter be emulated by journalists across the country. As Gates commented in his history of CBS News, it was "Cronkite's performance that was invariably cited" when admiration was expressed "for the restraint, the taste and the all-around professionalism of TV's coverage that weekend" (Gates, 1978, p. 6). Some "of the things he did that day would pass into folklore and become part of the legend. More than a decade later, journalism professors would still be telling their students, who were mere children at the time, how Walter Cronkite cried on air when he had to report the official announcement that President John F. Kennedy was dead" (pp. 6-7, 1). The centrality of the Cronkite tale in journalistic lore was important for members of the journalistic community concerned about the burgeoning influence of television. It showed that not only could one become a good journalist via television, but one could also use the medium to reach refined levels of journalistic practice.

Discussions of Cronkite's celebrity thus became a central dimension of many assassination tales because they were central in legitimating television anchorpersons. Tales of Cronkite the celebrity underscored not only his individual status, but also the legitimate presence of television journalists and the consoling role of anchorpersons in times of crisis. This was important for evolving discussions about the relevance of anchorpersons as a separate yet functional breed of journalists. Tales of Cronkite's celebrity upheld the subjunctive mood of practice by exemplifying "what might be" to members of the larger journalistic community.

THEODORE WHITE

In much the same way that tales of Cronkite reflected the elevated forms of broadcast journalistic practice, narratives about Theodore White signified the more refined dimensions of practice in the print media. White's performance on the assassination story was co-opted within discussions of the glory of the journalistic written word, the effectiveness of which had been brought into question following what was perceived to be the successful televised coverage of Kennedy's death.

Although White was not present during the immediate events of Kennedy's death, his summons by Jacqueline Kennedy one week later drew him into the public eye. His appearance at her Hyannis Port home a week after Kennedy's death was portrayed in fictionalized form in an ABC Circle film, *Jacqueline Bouvier Kennedy*, in which their meeting was used to signify Kennedy's death. White's narrative recounting of her experiences in Dallas, coupled with the labeling—at Jackie's behest—of the Kennedy administration as "Camelot," made White one of the more visible storytellers of the time (White, 1978). White's success with the written word rapidly gained him status as a journalistic celebrity, and his archetypal narrative structure was emulated by reporters across media. One journalist said that "he invented the form. He absorbed politics and hymned it in an act of reportage and imagination that was a variation on Walt Whitman" (Morrow, 1988, p. 24).

The focus on White's prose drew him somewhat away from periodicized journalism and toward book publishing. He remained interested in the larger, more general issues that rested behind the making of current events, and his series of books on the Presidential campaigns was considered first rate by other journalists. Nonetheless, he continued to define himself and was defined by others as a journalist. His eulogy, printed in *Time* in 1986, called him "a reporter in search of history" (Thomas, 1986, p. 62).

Within larger discussions of journalistic practice and authority, narratives about White as celebrity suggested to members of the journalistic community that it was possible to stretch the boundaries of good narrative and reportage and still be defined as a reporter. His self-defined interest in history, his search for general impulses in society, his trend-setting yet laudatory style of writing, all reconfigured the supposed limits of good print journalism. In much the same way that Cronkite epitomized the anchorperson as an effector of unity and a source of consolation, White exemplified the print reporter as a person who not only wrote well, but was concerned with issues beyond the contemporaneous event of news reporting.

This suggests that whereas tales of Wicker and Rather set out the indicative dimensions of journalistic performance, tales of both Cronkite and White as celebrities upheld its subjunctive mood. In suggesting a recasting of boundaries of professional practice, both signified to members of the journalistic community what journalistic professionals "might be."

Thus, journalistic recollections of the assassination coverage produced uniform narratives that featured reporters with tenable celebrity status. In both their indicative and subjunctive moods, such tales emphasized the importance of emulation in journalistic professionalism. By weaving the lives and careers of individual reporters into recollections of the assassination story, the resulting assassination narratives reinforced institutional agendas about then-nascent features of journalistic professionalism and television journalism, as they simultaneously highlighted the professional activities of certain reporters in covering the story.

THE DOWNSIDE OF CELEBRITY

Other reporters were not so fortunate, and they witnessed celebrity's downside as a result of their association with Kennedy's death. Certain journalists lost their jobs due to their assassination coverage. CBS's Robert Pierpoint was rumored to have lost his Washington posting to Dan Rather because Pierpoint's cumulative experience did not match Rather's skill in covering Dallas (Gates, 1978, p. 169). Tom Pettit, whose on-site, on-air coverage of Oswald's murder for NBC was hailed in 1963 by *Broadcasting* magazine as "a first in television history" ("Oswald shooting," 1963, p. 46), was rarely featured in later journalistic chronicles.

Other journalists were shunted into collective oblivion, and it was in these cases that larger institutional discourses became particularly relevant. Some reporters fell from fame because their performances did not attend to larger discourses about journalism—specifically, those favored by the mainstream journalistic community. Marginalization—for being too tabloid, too local, too left-wing—denied these reporters the kind of backdrop necessary to promote their celebrity status. Reporter Hugh Aynesworth, for example, whose assistance to more renowned reporters working on the assassination story earned him the title of its "longest running" reporter (Ephron, 1976, p. 60), was rarely discussed with the same degree of interest as those reporters with greater celebrity status. Penn Jones, who uncovered a series of mysterious deaths related to the assassination, was labeled "a sign of hope for the survival of independent journalism" (Welsh & Turner, 1969, p. 63), but cries of acclaim were confined to the nonmainstream press. Geraldo Rivera first ran a frame-by-frame analysis of Zapruder's footage of Kennedy's shooting on nationwide television, in a series he hosted in the mid-1970s, *Good Night, America*, but his tabloid-style performance kept him marginalized as compared to the mainstream reporters working the story. French journalist Jean Daniel published interviews conducted shortly before the assassination with Fidel Castro and Kennedy, which pointed to a shared belief in U.S. capitalism and Cuban communism, but mainstream media discussions of Daniel's journalistic performance invariably labeled him as being "too involved in politics" ("Reporter engage," 1963, p. 70). The actions of each journalist made them marginal to the consensus about appropriate journalistic performance, substituting notoriety for celebrity status.

The fact that certain reporters failed to achieve celebrity status, whereas others, potentially less praiseworthy, did attain such status, reveals additional patterns by which celebrity works as a memory system. It suggests that the making of journalistic celebrity depended not only on the actions of individual reporters, but also on larger institutional agendas and discourses within American journalism. Thus, the above-mentioned personalities were not perpetuated as celebrities for having covered the assassination story simply because they reported or desired it, but because they addressed relevant institutional discourses.

The lives of Wicker, Rather, Cronkite, and White were woven into assassination retellings through two arenas of institutional activity—commemoration and recycling. Both were instrumental in making each reporter into a journalistic celebrity.

COMMEMORATIVE ACTIVITY

Commemorative activity offered a routine way of remembering both the assassination and its coverage. It was particularly evident on anniversaries, when both the assassination and the memory bearers were discussed. Writer Gary Wills, for example, published his book *The Kennedy Imprisonment* (1983) on the 20th anniversary of Dallas. Anniversaries gave reporters a wide range of media formats by which to associate themselves with the story.

Through commemoration, the chronicles of journalists began to emerge as an extensive record of the assassination story. In print, journalists used recognized and routinized dates to generate commemorative issues about the assassination, special sections in journals, and commemorative volumes. Similarly, the broadcast media coordinated the production of media retrospectives around assassination anniversaries. This record increasingly incorporated journalists as its narrators, a point particularly borne out by the broadcast media: Early media retrospectives about the assassination were narrated by actors such as Cliff Robertson, Larry McCann, Hal Holbrook, or Richard Baseheart; later efforts employed the skills of Edwin Newman, Walter Cronkite, Dan Rather, Nancy Dickerson, Tom Brokaw or John Chancellor. The choice of journalists over actors for the part of narrator highlighted the emerging celebrity of journalists as assassination retellers.

Journalists' celebrity was particularly highlighted by remembering the club of reporters who had originally covered the events of Kennedy's death. This community convened in November 1988 to commemorate the events of 25 years earlier (Gamarekian, 1988, p. A24). Nearly all television and print retrospectives assigned collective status to the reporters who had worked on the story, publishing long lists of their names. One 1988 PBS documentary identified people "by their positions or affiliations in the fall of 1963" (JFK: A Time Remembered, 1988), creating an "as if" mood to the recollections they embodied. NBC's "JFK Assassination: As It Happened" ended with "a note to more than 500 people who pooled their efforts to provide continuous and extensive coverage" (JFK Assassination: As it Happened, 1988). Such commemorative activity gave journalists routinized ways to promote their association with the assassination story.

RECYCLING ACTIVITY

Recycling activity also helped journalists perpetuate their own stories, presence, authority, and ultimately celebrity in conjunction with Kennedy's assassination. The technological characteristics of each medium allowed for the furtherance of the original tales that first appeared in that medium.

In the press, original assassination tales were recycled through reprinting. Special issues of magazines, journals, newspapers, and books borrowed the words of the reporters who had originally graced their pages. The dispatches of certain reporters were circulated in in-house journals; for example, Merriman Smith's dispatch of November 23 was reproduced in the *UPI Reporter* and later reissued as part of a special book titled *Four Days* (United Press International and *American Heritage Magazine*, 1964). It was also reproduced in the trade publication *Editor and Publisher*, in which it was praised as "an historic memento, an example of narrative style at its best" ("Letter," 1963, p. 8).

Other reporters whose words were frequently reprinted were Tom Wicker and Theodore White. One of Wicker's first assassination pieces, "That Day in Dallas," was reprinted in the *New York Times's* December house organ, *Times Talk* (Wicker, 1963), and again one year later in the *Saturday Review* (Wicker, 1964a). Another piece, originally penned in 1964 for *Esquire* under the title "Kennedy Without Tears," was subsequently reprinted as a book within the year (Wicker, 1964b) and in *Esquire* 10 years later (Wicker, 1973): "Tom Wicker's brilliant (and heartbreaking) coverage of the assassination moved *Esquire* to ask him to write this essay seven months later in June 1964. Mr. Wicker went on to become chief of the Washington bureau and an associate editor of the *Times*" (Wicker, 1973, p. 196). Theodore White's famous postassassination interview with Jacqueline Kennedy was reprinted in a special commemorative volume on Kennedy, 25 years after his death (Kunhardt, 1988, pp. 295-297). Other publications also reprinted or referenced parts of the original White essay (i.e., Bluem, 1964, p. 85). In both cases, the career trajectory by which the two print reporters covered the assassination and went on to journalistic glory was facilitated by the institutions that reprinted their words. The proliferation of reprintings thus reinforced associations between the assassination story and certain reporters in a way that allowed journalists to uphold their celebrity status.

Media retrospectives accomplished for the broadcast media what reprinting did for print. They helped journalists narrate, and thus reconstruct, their original stories of coverage. The incorporation of contemporary voice-overs into original film clips underscored the journalists' celebrity status.

Dan Rather was regularly featured in broadcast media retrospectives when CBS employed him as the narrator. He narrated a three-part news series in 1983 investigating the myths and realities behind Kennedy's assassination ("The Kennedy Assassination: Myth and Reality," 1983), an eight-part news series in 1988 ("Assassination: Twenty-five Years Later," 1988), and a 2-hour documentary, "Four Days in November," which aired on the 25th anniversary of Kennedy's death ("Four Days in November," 1988). Ending his narration of the documentary, Rather concluded with

> a personal note, based on the many years CBS News and I have spent investigating, thinking about those four days. It was a day we haven't shown that also has alot of meaning for me—the fifth day. Tuesday. On Tuesday, American went back to work . . . So it is Tuesday I often think of ("Four Days in November," 1988).

That line, labeled "Rather Blather" by one observer (Grady, 1988, p. 5), nonetheless reinforced Rather's role as an authoritative interpreter of the assassination story. Connections between the assassination narrative, his interpretation of it, and his status as a journalist were thus underscored by media retrospectives. Incorporating stories of his assassination coverage in chronicles of his career showed how that authority helped enhance his status as a journalistic celebrity.

Similar aims were achieved by self-quoted discourse. Self-quoting let journalists incorporate original tales within larger contemporary recollections. They were able to look back and comment on their own words and views. Like other kinds of recycling activity, self-quoting needed media backing. Journalists appearing on talk shows and documentary specials addressed the words through which they had originally reported the assassination story. Radio reporter Ike Pappas took part in the following interchange with Geraldo Rivera about his coverage of Oswald's murder 25 years earlier:

> Pappas: My job that day was to get an interview with this guy, when nobody else was going to get an interview. . . . So I said the only thing which I could say, which was the story. Tell the story: "Oswald has been shot. A shot rang out. Oswald has been shot."
>
> Rivera: Is that the single most profound or dramatic moment of your life?
>
> Pappas: It's an extraordinary story. Probably the most extraordinary story I'll ever cover. (On Trial: Lee Harvey Oswald, 1988)

The exchange referenced Pappas's professionalism and pointed to his ensuing celebrity status. Reviews of Pappas's professional career elsewhere similarly focused on his assassination coverage ("High Profile: Ike Pappas," 1989, p. 8).

Self-quoting lent an air of simultaneous presence and distance to narrative. It positioned the reporter as an interface between the past events and their later retelling. Phrases such as "the crime of the century," "the end of innocence," or "Camelot" were paraded about—and commented on—by journalists years after their original coinage. The words of *Time* correspondent Hugh Sidey were partly quoted, partly paraphrased, 25 years after the events in Dallas by the same magazine (Sidey, 1988, p. 45). Reporter Steve Bell introduced an on-air repeat of an original film clip of himself standing in front of the Texas Schoolbook Depository 25 years earlier ("John F. Kennedy Remembered," 1988). Self-quoting not only emphasized the authority of reporters for the events of Kennedy's death, but it also connected their original words, revised with hindsight, to later discourses.

All of this institutionally backed activity helped perpetuate the image of certain journalists as celebrities. Commemoration gave news organizations convenient, recognizable, and routinized ways to highlight and perpetuate the status of certain reporters. Recycling maintained a focus on their words, while deflecting attention from those of others. Tales were generally recycled in the medium in which they appeared originally, then made the subject of extensive institutional efforts to reproduce them.

RECOLLECTING THROUGH JOURNALISTIC CELEBRITY

All of this attests to the viability of celebrity as a memory system. Positioning individual reporters as pivotal points for criss-crossing discourses about the assassination and about technology and journalistic professionalism has constituted an effective means of making journalistic celebrity. Walter Cronkite's actions became important in discussions about televised journalistic practice because they authenticated the consoling role of anchorpersons. Dan Rather's coverage reflected growing attempts to legitimate television correspondents as bona fide reporters. Theodore White's coverage highlighted the glory of the written word, which faced competition following the effective televised coverage of much of the assassination story. Tom Wicker's performance promoted the old guard of American journalism, showing that traditional objectives of speedy coverage, eyewitness reporting, and terse prose remained worthy goals. Tales of celebrity have thus attested to both the subjunctive and indicative dimensions of individual journalistic practice in retelling the assassination. Narratives of celebrity have become markers of appropriate standards of action.

Celebrity, then, has constituted an effective memory system for the journalistic community, precisely because it uses the individual reporter to focus attention on issues crucial to the community. Celebrity has given reporters idealized, but institutionally correct, notions of how to act. As a memory system, it has thereby helped to mold journalists within the context of institutionally correct agendas.

In his work on celebrity, Braudy (1986, p. 585) commented that "the urge to fame is not so much a cause as a causal nexus through which more generalized forces—political, theological, artistic, economic, sociological—flow to mediate the shape of individual lives." The establishment of journalistic celebrity through assassination tales reveals such a matrix of issues. Tales that became markers of journalists' celebrity status have clustered around professional issues central to the journalistic community.

This discussion of assassination tales, as seen through the lens of celebrity, thus shows how reporters have effectively blurred distinctions between "the event" and "the event as told" in their accounts of the real world. It shows how journalists as tellers-of-the-event have become a valued part of the telling. By embedding their own presence in the tales of Kennedy's death, journalists have created a situation that references their own stature as an integral part of it. Invoking celebrity as a memory system has therefore encouraged members of the journalistic community to remember Kennedy's death by recalling the Walter Cronkites, Dan Rathers, and Tom Wickers who gave it voice. Equally important, recalling the Cronkites, Rathers, and Wickers has become a goal in its own right.

9

Autobiography, Cultural Mythology, and the Modern Hero

David Bryan McLennan
Texas Christian University

☐ *In this chapter, the author refutes the claim made by many social critics that contemporary heroes do not exist. McLennan asserts that heroes still exist for particular audiences, but that the myths and means of hero making have changed. Autobiographical narratives are one of the more recent methods by which public figures communicate the myths that audiences then identify as heroic for that person in a particular situation. Narrative analysis of the role of self-created reconstruction of reality in the process of hero-making strategies is set forth. The case of Tom Hayden's 1988 autobiography Reunion: A Memoir is used to illustrate how the hero monomyth has evolved in contemporary times.*

America in the post-Vietnam era was in need of heroic figures. Years of political and cultural strife during the 1960s, the loss of faith in government following the military stalemate in Vietnam, and the political embarrassment of Watergate left Americans feeling alienated by the politics of the period. Subsequently, many Americans looked elsewhere for their guidance. Many turned from the activism of the 1960s to the individualism of the 1970s for measures of their identity. Labeled the "Me Decade" by Tom Wolfe, the 1970s saw Americans trying "New Age" therapies ranging from acupuncture to Zen as means of transforming their lives. Also, labeled the "Therapeutic Decade," the 1970s can be thought of as a national healing period for those affected by the national failures of the previous decade.

One group particularly affected by the aftermath of the 1960s was the youth generation. Thousands of college-aged youth, previously involved in various social movements advocating radical change, lost their identities as activists when these social movements failed. As the 1970s began, many former radicals participated in the many therapies of the decade. Former counterculturists became more mainstream as they left school, joined the job market, and established families. Others remained on the fringe joining cults or Eastern religious groups or trying psychotherapies such as EST. Some movement heroes successfully transformed their public images by using these techniques. Eldridge Cleaver, leader of the Black Panthers, found personal salvation through religious conversion, as did Chicago Seven co-conspirator Rennie Davis. Yippie leader Jerry Rubin tried dozens of therapies including TM and Rolfing before settling on capitalism and becoming a Wall Street investment counselor.

The 1970s and 1980s produced popular books written by many of the 1960s' leaders who claimed personal changes. The books offered accounts of the 1960s that implicitly asked audience members to excuse their wild, often illegal, actions as youthful indiscretions. Many, such as Jerry Rubin's (1976) *Growing Up (At Thirty-seven)*, claimed the 1960s was indeed a time for sowing wild oats and that contemporary success was due to maturing beyond that period. Others, such as Eldridge Cleaver's (1978) *Soul on Fire*, asserted that personal transformation may be attained by complete mortification through religious conversion. Others, such as Tom Hayden's autobiography *Reunion: A Memoir* (1988), take a different perspective and suggest that often these youthful indiscretions were not the individual's responsibility. In each of these instances a heroic image is posited and the resulting image among certain audiences may, at least partially, be that of the modern American hero.

The claim that modern heroes do not exist is invalid. In the early months of 1991, Americans embraced many political and military leaders as heroes including George Bush and General Norman Schwarzkopf. Despite the popularity of these figures as heroes, it may be said the modern mass media have impaired traditional notions of heroes. Many public figures striving for heroic status often have their public image damaged or tarnished by revelations made or implied in the media. Sports celebrities such as Pete Rose discover their on-the-field heroics are subsumed by off-the-field allegations of wrongdoing. Political leaders such as Gary Hart find that media coverage during presidential campaigns can ruin a political reputation. Even deceased heroes such as Martin Luther King, Jr. can have their heroic status tarnished by media allegations of misadventures such as plagiarism. As a result of the way images of public figures are transmitted, the possibility of a "universal" heroic figure may be impossible. As the previous examples illustrate, however, heroes still exist for particular audiences, and the hero myths that form the basis for these images still resonate for contemporary peoples. The primary difference is that the media of transmission for these hero myths have changed and must be investigated. I contend that contemporary autobiographies are important vehicles for transmission of these hero myths and, thus, serve as important vehicles for the creation of today's heroic figures.

Traditionally, autobiographical discourse has been understood primarily as compensatory literature or as the type of communication that provides some psychological or social functions for writers and readers. For the writer, personal narratives have performed a coping function in certain situations. Religious confessionals, testimonials, apologies, and the like are examples of autobiographical discourse used by individuals as both explanatory and cathartic. Similarly, readers find therapeutic value in reading these personal disclosures as models for living their own lives.

Especially in contemporary Western culture, autobiographies have become an appropriate and important means for individuals creating a heroic image. In recent years the autobiographical narratives told by business leaders such as Lee Iacocca, political leaders such as George Bush, and media celebrities such as Shirley MacLaine illustrate how stories of personal success may translate into heroic status among certain groups. Personal narratives enable public figures to meet the increased demands placed upon them in modern times to account for their behaviors. Individuals use these opportunities to selectively emphasize and interpret important events from their lives for the purposes of offering a plausible explanation for situations threatening their public image, creating the impression that the person's "self" has been altered, or positing a heroic persona.

One important conclusion which may be drawn from examining many autobiographies, including those listed above, is that much autobiographical discourse is archetypal in nature. In the cases of many 1960s radicals who continue as heroic figures for their particular audiences, they posited a heroic image by using variations of the heroic quest archetype.

On the surface, nothing seems more appropriate for an individual with no image or a damaged image than to present him- or herself as a hero. The hero myth has stood through time as the expression of the relationship of individuals with their communities. Heroes, however fleeting in modern times, symbolize the needs and desires of people, especially during turbulent times. The 20th century, especially the 1970s and 1980s, is no exception. Stories about heroes and their deeds continue bonding cultures together.

The importance of these hero myths as a foundation for revitalization rhetoric are many. Basically, all societies have and need cultural heroes. The selection of heroes is one way in which people of a society order their world. The hero actually embodies those qualities which people of a society revere and with which they want to be identified. In acclaiming a hero, people achieve their social order by vicariously identifying with symbolic leaders and their stories. Heroes become unifying devices to promote social cohesiveness.

A hero, both in myth and modern times, is really "a single hero" (Campbell, 1949), an archetype whose story has common elements across time and culture. All heroes have survived some form of the rites of passage—a rite of separation, initiation, and return. Autobiographies of modern cultural heroes tell their stories in such a fashion.

Throughout history, heroes have been a functional element of society, not only because of the deeds which benefit that society, but because of the way in which societies have used their heroes. In a theory of dramatism, in which life is viewed as a drama in which things happen to audiences because of parts played by actors, the function of the actor or hero is to "transport an audience vicariously out of everyday roles into a kind of reality that has laws and patterns different from the ordinary social structure" (p. 24). The hero, in this role, is a mass symbol, a "vehicle for the imaginings of thousands, who are transformed by imputation and abstraction more and more into what people want of a public figure" (p. 14). For most people, a hero has a compensatory function, "consoling people as it were for a recognized lack of what the hero represents" (p. ix). The hero either makes up for what people have not got, or becomes a symbol of "what people think they ought to be but aren't really trying to be" (p. 192).

The hero then is a vicarious vehicle for society and autobiographical narratives are vicarious means for society to find the heroes for the times. Those who successfully transform their public image through the use of personal narratives employ what Campbell describes as variations of the monomyth. Different situations demand different accountings of behavior, but the accountings must always be heroic. Analysis of autobiographical rhetoric as a modern enactment of the monomyth in a popular contemporary media form shows that this type of story can produce identification with a heroic image that acts as a unifying and redemptive force for social cohesion.

Over the past several decades the variation of the heroic story has changed, indicating a great deal about culture and the types of symbols and stories it favors. In fact, the different forms of the hero myth employed by different autobiographies illustrates important truths about the culture in which it is used, as well as about the audience which legitimates the image transformation based on the myth. Although the standard monomythic form identified by Campbell and others may be the basis for many autobiographies positing a heroic image, variations of the monomyth embody a psychosocial understanding of the historical period. Those who perceive Lee Iacocca as the hero of the late 1980s understand that overcoming obstacles imposed by institutions such as government is central to modern living, whereas those who identify with former Watergate co-conspirator Charles Colson's heroic image in *Born Again* believe in "conversion" as a way of managing failure. In these two instances, as well as others, the mythic underpinnings of their autobiographical stories vary from the standard monomythic formula.

This transformation in the heroic-quest archetype reveals several interesting conclusions. First, as a popular mythic structure, the heroic-quest archetype is at a vital crossroads of its existence. Some scholars, such as Rushing (1989, p. 21), claim that the archetypal hero myth is dead and must be replaced with a new myth for humankind. Others, more optimistic about the myth's survival, such as Nimmo and Combs (1980), argue that the modern hero offers redemption for our times. They claim that stories creating a heroic image for public figures may indeed help restore the Edenic vision of the United States which was tarnished by events such as the Vietnam War and Watergate.

However, I contend that the hero myth has evolved and still remains a vital part of our literature and rhetoric. The evolution of the hero myth and its uses may be understood as part of a larger cultural revolution.

One autobiography that illustrates the evolution of the hero myth in contemporary times and how this variation in the monomyth may create heroic figures for certain audiences is Tom Hayden's *Reunion: A Memoir* (1988). Hayden's story takes a different perspective from other autobiographies produced by former 1960s radicals and suggests that the youthful indiscretions of that period were not all the individual's responsibility. Hayden's *Reunion* explicitly employs a maturation strategy to revitalize his public image, and in a sense it legitimizes the adaptation motifs of other accountings. This variation of the monomyth may be examined for how it creates a heroic image for Hayden and legitimates his audience, who also wanted to forget the realities and failures the 1960s, remembering only the nostalgic memories of the era.

The general outline of Tom Hayden's life is familiar to many Americans. He was formerly a hero of the student movement of the 1960s, author of the Port Huron Statement, and co-conspirator in the Chicago Eight Trial. Hayden now is a four-term Assemblyperson from Santa Monica, CA. He heads a large political action group, Campaign California, and with the help of his former wife—Jane Fonda—raised millions of dollars for populist causes. Many observers, until his split with Fonda, contended that Hayden had become transformed into a mainstream politician, community leader, and family man. In short, Hayden became a heroic symbol for those who were politically active in the 1960s.

Because Hayden's past actions and writings were so well known, his reemergence into the political arena was and continues to be problematic. Even today his political campaigns are forced to deal with the perception that Hayden continues to be a radical (Lee, 1986, p. 289). As Lee (1986, p. 281) has stated, "the 44th District Assembly race was a referendum on the personal qualities and political history of the Democratic candidate." Eventually, in 1982, Hayden's transformation to mainstream politician was complete as he won the first of his four terms as a Democratic Assemblyperson from California. However, Hayden's success as a politician in the 1980s is evidence for the claim that he was able to overcome these problems and become not only a viable political force, but a hero for those forced to live with their pasts. As part of his rhetorical repertoire, *Reunion* may be seen as Hayden's best way of managing his public image.

HAYDEN'S JOURNEY TOWARD MATURATION

The journey metaphor, which derives from those rites of passage that transform the child into an adult, is particularly effective at describing the exploration, stress, and attainment of a matured identity and the way in which the individual explains him- or herself within a social and historical context. It describes both the changes that take place in the maturing individual and the place, or arrival, of that individual in the world. As a metaphor of duration, the journey suggests that change is possible until death. As such, it is useful in describing adventures that occur throughout life.

Because Tom Hayden's contemporary image centers on his return to the political mainstream, how he connects present and past is important. Within his autobiography Hayden employs this return motif explicitly to convince his readers that the ideology of the past is appropriate for the present. This aggrandizement of the past fits neatly with the rhetorical climate of the times in which theories of self-change include this return motif. In fact, in writing about the advent of the Aquarian Age, Ferguson (1980) noted:

> The emergence of the Aquarian Conspiracy in the late twentieth century is rooted in the myths and metaphors, the prophecy and poetry of the past. Throughout history there were lone individuals here and there, or small bands at the fringes of science or religion who, based on their own experiences, believed that people might someday transcend narrow "normal consciousness and reverse the brutality and alienation of the human condition." (p. 45)

In the 1970s and 1980s, many people employed theories of self-change that advocated such a return to a former and more pure time. The political climate of the times, as well, was premised on this return to the past—particularly with Ronald Reagan's conservative vision based on ideals and policies of the 1950s.

Hayden's narrative strategy is tipped off by the autobiography's title, *Reunion: A Memoir*. Typically "reunions" are events at which people with a shared past gather to reflect on the past and consider how they have grown. In addition, reunions signify emotional times during which people tearfully and/or cheerfully reminisce about how they faced certain situations and benefitted from them. Hayden's reunion is no different as he reflects on events that not only shaped his contemporary vision of the world, but also on a time during which his ideology was more mainstream. Reunion, then, becomes a rhetorical ritual of not only praising the past, but also of bringing the past into the present.

Hayden accomplishes this transformation of time by linking his youthful beliefs, attitudes, and values with those of his later life. This may be seen as Hayden's motive in the autobiography. Hayden's own words (1988) reflect how his contemporary worldview is similar to his childhood worldview:

> This life has unfolded in surprising ways. I grew up in the Midwest, gave my first speech in favor of the Peace Corps, and had my first nationally circulated article published in Mademoiselle. Ten years later I was accused of violent conspiracy against the United States government. I pondered the future of prison, exile, perhaps martyrdom. Then suddenly, my accusers—Richard Nixon, John Mitchell, et al.—were driven from office under a public cloud of scandal. It took a long time for me to accept that far from becoming a police state, the system had worked. During this long odyssey I tried to make my

world fit my idealistic American values and met discord, then rejection, from my parents as well as the state. I reacted in ways which compromised my best judgment, and I experienced what Albert Camus called "the temptation of hatred." In the end, I was fortunate to reach a point of return, of political and personal reintegration. My life, and my original values, resurfaced intact from the depths of alienation. I was damaged, but a survivor. (p. xvi)

All the elements of his maturation story are present in this passage: the journey or odyssey, use of the victimage strategy, and, most importantly, the return motif found in all maturation journeys. The return mentioned by Hayden strongly links his life with the audience's knowledge of recent history as his separation and reintegration into the political mainstream is intimately associated with the rise (victimage by) and fall (healing from) of the Watergate figures. Ultimately, Hayden's purpose is to transport readers back to a time before Watergate.

In essence, the autobiography's title, *Reunion*, symbolically represents the return motif found throughout Hayden's life story. "Return" is a common motif in mythology, as argued previously, as heroes proceed on long journeys only to return home after achieving wisdom. Hayden stands as the 1960s hero returning victoriously from the political fray.

Because the "return" motif is central to Hayden's transformation, symbols of return are important for him. Nowhere is return so powerfully depicted as in the beginning and ending of the autobiography. The first pages of Chapter 1 set the tone for this motif as Hayden equates "reunion" with "return." In this opening segment, Hayden depicts an episode in which he and his 13-year-old son watch a nostalgic film about growing up, *Stand By Me*. The film's plot centers around four young boys growing up in a small American town who bind together in a group and explore the countryside looking for the body of a young boy killed after being hit by a train. They suffer many problems during the search, including fatigue brought on by the 20-plus mile walk, fear after being fired on by a junkyard owner with a shotgun, and frustration after being harassed by a band of teenage hoodlums. Ultimately, the youths find the body, only to discover that the body (success) becomes less important than the experiences of growing up and learning about the decadence of the older generation (the act). The boys' quest resembles many heroic myths as the four characters face task after insurmountable task, ultimately succeeding in their original goals, but also losing their innocent views of the world. The film ends with the two main characters reaching an understanding that one's identity is mainly determined by the experiences one has while growing up. As the closing epilogue informs the audience, one of the boys—the intellectual—actually overcomes the problems of childhood and maturation to become a respectable adult, but his values and expectations, developed during childhood, continue.

The parallels between Hayden's life and the film exist on several levels. On one level, the film's setting—a small town in the Midwest during the 1950s—

is exactly the setting of Hayden's childhood. The film stands as a visual reminder to the audience of the idyllic life of former times. Hayden's reference to the film verbally transports readers back to that time—before Vietnam and Watergate. The perfection of those times is captured by the young Hayden's comment on the film, "Gee, what a great time to grow up, Dad. You can't grow up like that anymore" (p. 1). Not only did the film symbolize Hayden's return motif, but it also legitimated the nostalgic remembrances of the past. *Stand by Me* was one of the many nostalgic films of the mid-1980s celebrating the 1950s and 1960s.

On a second level, the film symbolizes Hayden's rhetorical strategy of adaptation and growth. As the characters face difficulties and ultimately overcome them, Hayden overcomes the problems of his youth. As the four boys face problem after problem caused by external sources, Hayden faces problems, both political and personal, brought about by an evil outside of himself. Finally, as the boys return home, their problems healed, Hayden returns to his political home, healed and more mature.

Although Hayden's autobiography begins by dislocating time back to the idyllic past, he ends his story on a similar note. Instead of returning to the 1950s and his childhood, Hayden reminisces about his political childhood in the 1960s:

> As I wandered across the Wisconsin hillside where my mother lay buried, I felt a form of personal relief. I saw the fields where I had played as a boy, the railroad tracks I walked along, the blue lakes and the tiny dams where I caught bass, the green yards where I threw the ball. It was all still there beckoning me. The harmonies of my early life, disrupted by the civil wars of the sixties, were healing and reappearing, like blades of grass after a fire, in my middle years. Perhaps there comes a time for all people when they feel the end of being young and the definite onset of those middle years. So it was for me after my parents died. I experienced the very real sense of being unfettered from the past, looking backward instead of feeling part of it. It was not that I wanted to escape from the past; far from it. I could see it, accept it, reconnect it for the first time as an older, more mature human being. (p. 485)

Hayden's reminiscing parallels the closing scene in *Stand by Me* in which the main character actually appears as the grown-up storyteller returning to the scene of his youth. Both look back on a period of time, reflecting on those times and how the experiences affected that person's character.

Hayden's closing lines give his audience a sense of what his life has meant to him, which ultimately translates into a testimonial for his transformative strategy. He states, "Times filled with tragedy are also times filled of greatness and wonder, times that really matter, and times truly worth living through. Whatever the future holds, and as satisfying as my life is today, I miss the sixties and always will" (p. 507). Hayden remembers the 1960s in the same nostalgic terms as he previously used to describe the 1950s. As a rhetorical strategy, Hayden's creation of the nostalgic mood treats his current public image in the same manner that film directors and producers treat the period. Similarly, audiences respond to Hayden's nostalgic remembrances with the same fervor that they use when buying relics of the 1960s such as tie-dyed t-shirts and peace-symbol medallions.

This return motif found throughout Hayden's autobiography is actually only part of his maturation strategy. The story of his life between his childhood of the 1950s and his adulthood in the 1980s is portrayed as a heroic quest or journey. Psychoanalysts view the heroic quest as a typical feature of adolescence, denoting a stage of development that precedes the emergence of an ego identity and the transformation into adulthood and individualization. The heroic quest stands as a rite of passage between childhood and adulthood. Hayden's use of this narrative technique further enhances his maturation strategy.

Tom Hayden's heroic quest imagery in his autobiography takes him throughout the United States and to Vietnam in search of his identity. During the dangerous adventure, Hayden performs the heroic quest by surviving attacks by the corrupt institutions of the times and returning safely to his political home. His quest resembles the basic archetypal story. Joseph Campbell (1949, p. 30) summarizes the "mythological adventure of the hero" as a "magnification of the formula represented in the rites of passage: separation-initiation-return," which he says, "might be named the nuclear unit of the monomyth."

> A hero ventures forth from the world of common day into a region of supernatural wonder: fabulous forces are there encountered and a decisive victory is won: the hero comes back from the mysterious adventure with the power to bestow boons to his fellow man.

Hayden's decisive victory is won as the wounds caused by the institutions of the 1960s are healed and his foes vanquished. Hayden bestows on his contemporaries the abilities to overcome their own radical images of the 1960s and to rejoin mainstream America. His own experiences stand as evidence for the claim that people from the 1960s can operate successfully in contemporary times.

The journey Hayden undertakes in his autobiography not only resembles the monomyth described by Campbell, but also identifies parts of his life cycle with important events in the historical context.

Section	Stages in the Life Cycle	Representative Term	Quest Stage
Growing up in the Fifties	Birth	Attachments	Beginnings
The Movement Begins	Childhood	Separation	Separation
Among the Poor	Adolescence	Adjustment	Initiation
Vietnam	Young Adulthood	Responsibility	Initiation
Chicago	Mature Adulthood	Transition	Return
Reunion	Old Age	Reminiscing	Return

The parallelism between these sections of Hayden's autobiography and stages of the life cycle are anything but coincidental. By examining how Hayden symbolically links these stages of maturation with the historical situation, an understanding of how Hayden's maturation becomes tied with society's evolution will be gained. As Hayden completes the rites of passage necessary for maturation, he returns victorious from his quest and reenters mainstream society.

Tom Hayden's description of his formative years could be taken directly from the script of *Stand By Me*. He identifies with All-American values, even down to listing his successes in Little League baseball. He describes his feelings about growing up in the 1950s in the following manner:

> The fifties were indeed the best of times for the pursuit of the American dream: After the trauma of two decades—Depression and Holocaust, two wars, the atomic bomb—came a dawn of new stability and peace, along with a rising standard of living, low inflation and unemployment rates, and an explosion of single-family housing in the newly expanding suburbs. America seemed to be making progress on the still-nagging problem of racism through Supreme Court desegregation orders . . . and Vietnam [was] an unknown word in the political vocabulary. (p. 3)

However, in sharp contrast to the idyllic 1950s, Hayden contrasts the 1960s as years in which "Richard Nixon and Spiro Agnew would appeal to our 'middle American' parents to abandon their children" (pp. 4-5). Abandonment becomes a theme working throughout the early part of Hayden's story as the beginnings of his maturation journey are foreshadowed.

As part of the abandonment theme, Hayden typically employs a victimage strategy for outlining the reasons why he was separated from mainstream America politically and socially. As part of Burke's (1970) transformative process (Guilt-Victimage-Redemption), victimage works powerfully in Hayden's story as he identifies many corrupt institutions and persons, such as Nixon, as causing not only his separation from mainstream society, but also the guilt that he feels about events threatening his image. Ultimately, Hayden symbolically redeems himself as he overcomes the people and institutions victimizing him and is healed, thus rejoining mainstream society. Because "healing" is a prominent motif of the psychosocial climate of the 1970s and 1980s, Hayden's strategy throughout the autobiography identifies him with the transforming culture.

Another important symbol foreshadowing the heroic journey is the identification Hayden makes with his ethnic heritage. Hayden was a descendent of Irish families who "journeyed through the historical mists from such barren places as county Monoghan in Old Ulster, looking for a better life during the potato famines and British persecution of the mid-nineteenth century" (p. 4). By identifying with such a strong ethnic heritage, Hayden legitimates his own journey to find a better life—a journey described throughout his autobiography. The potato famines and British persecution of the Irish journeyers may be compared to the cultural strife and political persecution during Hayden's life.

During the early part of the autobiography, Hayden foreshadows his desires for a heroic journey. He writes of his identification with "Beat" author Jack Kerouac's novel, *On the Road*, as it "was published in 1957, the year I graduated from high school. In the coming three years, I too hitchhiked to every corner of America, sleeping in fields here, doorways there, cheap hotels everywhere, embracing a spirit of the open road without knowing where I wanted to go" (p. 18). Hayden identified with Kerouac's fictional character Dean Moriority who became a powerful rebel, combining the "image of the cowboy/explorer corralled in the new suburbia that now occupies the once-vast frontier" (p. 19). The "Road" exemplifies Hayden's own description of his early life in which his search for identity took him to society's frontiers as he too rebels. The road symbolizes "departure" for Hayden—not only from his youth, but also from the institutions he finds objectionable. Ultimately, as argued previously, the road returns him to his roots. However, before Hayden may return to the nostalgia of the 1950s and 1960s, the separation rite of passage must be undertaken—as the literal hitchhiker alluded to in the Kerouac passage.

College became an important turning point in Hayden's life, as it did for so many of his generation. Hayden writes that he and his friends "kept our distance from the fraternity culture, road motorcycles, and individually hitchhiked to all corners of America during vacation breaks . . . but this part of me still exploring the emotional and intellectual wilderness" (p. 29). Hitchhiking is important for Hayden because it represents a lonely journey, part of the hero's fated quest. Fate happened to lead Hayden's hitchhiking adventure to spots such as "Berkeley and the Bay Area, already known as the mecca of student activism" (p. 33). There Hayden was able to symbolically join others separated from mainstream society and begin the initiation into his identity quest.

"Wilderness," described in his college hitchhiking experiences, defines both the unknown elements which Hayden finds on his journey and radical politics. One important event during Hayden's journey—the writing of the Port Huron Statement—typifies how the journey often took him to places considered as wilderness. The place, Port Huron, was described by Hayden as "unaffected by the changes beginning in America" and consisting of little other than "a cluster of cabins, all made of sturdy oak, with screened-in porches on all sides" (p. 84). Despite the crudeness of the surroundings, Hayden considered Port Huron to be a place in which "we came to declare a crossroads in history" (p. 82). The result, in Hayden's words, was "the most widely read pamphlet of the sixties generation" (p. 102). As a founder of the Students for a Democratic Society—a pioneer group in radical politics—Hayden's use of the wilderness imagery conjures up images of the frontier and the heroic figures conquering that frontier. As a prominent myth in the history of American political rhetoric, the frontier myth serves to identify Hayden and his followers with other great conquerors of the American frontier from Lewis and Clark to John Glenn.

Tom Hayden's trip to the frontier of American politics illustrates an important rite of passage for maturation—separation. Separation occurs at several points in everyone's life: the child being separated from the mother, the adolescent leaving home for the first time, and even the death of parents. Hayden's newfound radicalism in the early 1960s reflects this former rite. After being jailed for his work on voter registration in Albany, GA in 1961 and being violently attacked by whites, Hayden describes the result: "It was a dawn of a new realism, it was also a rip in the moral umbilical cord linking us to American society. We had not lost our vision or moral fervor, but we began to suspect that our parent society had" (p. 72). The "rip in the umbilical cord" importantly symbolizes the separation Hayden feels from the older generation and their role in the problems of society. The "dawn of new realism" symbolizes a rebirth for Hayden—a new political awareness which comes as he is initiated into his journey.

Not only does Hayden feel separated from society through the acts in Georgia, but he also feels separated from his parents. As Hayden describes leaving home after graduation for Atlanta, he symbolizes the feelings many had toward the youth generation:

> Their son who was a successful student and who they had imagined as a top reporter or editor—was instead driving off in their Corvair straight for the center of social violence in America, for the purpose of helping . . . Negroes. Though he never tried to dissuade us, my father was convinced that something was deeply wrong, and I recall my mother shaking her head and saying "I don't know what you're doing." (p. 49)

By expressing movement from the "safe" world of college into the possibly violent world of civil rights, Hayden symbolizes the feelings that many felt about middle- and upper-class white students joining the civil rights movement. As such, Hayden begins his maturation journey.

Other feelings of separation and abandonment are expressed by Hayden concerning his relationship with his parents. After moving from home after college, he describes how his parents did not understand such a decision: "Whatever demon had possessed me during my years away from home, they seemed to feel, could no longer be exorcised by them. I certainly did not know how to explain my yearnings in terms that they could understand" (p. 49). The "demon" metaphor used by Hayden is a prominent archetypal image of victimage operating in literature since the story of Adam and Eve in Genesis. Hayden identifies many people and institutions as the demons controlling his destiny. Ultimately, the "demon" plays an important role in Hayden's symbolic transformation as he exorcises or overcomes the demon's influence and becomes healed.

Another event—the assassination of President John F. Kennedy—is portrayed by Hayden as an example of how the youth were abandoned. As one of his political heroes, Kennedy symbolized the guiding light for youth and liberalism in America. His death not only signaled the beginning of large-scale protests against the U.S. government and other institutions, but also that Hayden's childhood was over. Shortly after hearing of Kennedy's death, Hayden writes that the "euphoric peak of the early sixties—the civil rights march on Washington" was ended by that tragic event which signaled that "the age of innocence was ended" (p. 103). Not only was Kennedy's assassination to blame for the social unrest that followed, but also for Hayden's personal problems, including the breakup of his marriage. Hayden recalls how Kennedy's death resulted in him abandoning his marital duties: "In my political intensity at the time, I failed to invest enough time in my marriage. . . . The breakup, when it came, therefore, was understood not so much as a personal failure, but yet another example of how society dehumanized and atomized us all" (pp. 106-108). Hayden's portrayal of being abandoned by the political partnership with John Kennedy and the personal partnership with his first wife symbolizes the importance of being perceived as a youthful victim to his overall maturation strategy. This identification ties him strongly to others in society who felt strongly attached to JFK's presidency and the political turmoil felt during the years following his death.

The first two sections of Hayden's autobiography complete the separation necessary for the maturation journey. In the third and fourth sections, initiation is portrayed—Hayden's initiation into radical politics. As Campbell (1988, pp. 123-24) argues, during the first segment of the archetype, something has been taken from the hero, and the adventure continues as the hero becomes initiated through physical or spiritual deeds. Ultimately, to evolve from immaturity to maturity involves a death and resurrection. Hayden faces these physical and spiritual deeds in places such as Vietnam and Chicago, whereas his death and resurrection occur as the 1960s student movements fail and he ends up in California.

The initiation begins in Hayden's story with his trip to Newark, NJ and his work on the Education Research and Action Project (ERAP). Facing the problems of life away from parental control and guidance is reflected in Hayden's description of his initial view of Newark:

> The sight of the neighborhood, which would be my home for the next four years, left me unbalanced. None of my reading or class work prepared me to know the ghetto, or the concrete economic realities, or know the real operation of political machines. And if I was to organize, as if I knew something that those living here didn't know. I was twenty-four years old and preparing to lead the poor in an assault on the downtown power structure. But first I had to get a street map, then an apartment, and some savvy—quick. (p. 123)

"Wilderness" reappears in Hayden's story as he faces a new situation on the frontier of 1960s radicalism. Initiated into a completely different world, Hayden's journey begins in earnest as he attempts many deeds, but receives many wounds, ultimately causing the death of his immature character and the rebirth of a new character.

A second event initiating Hayden's journey, Vietnam, prominently portrays the hero having to overcome difficulties along the journey. Hayden's Vietnam experience parallels many popular sentiments about Vietnam as a "failed mission" or "failed crusade" (Kurnow, 1983, p. 9). Hayden, too, depicts many decisions he made during this period as failures. However, despite the problems caused by Vietnam, Hayden portrays a sense that he overcame the problems, much as the United States eventually took steps to overcome the lingering problems associated with Vietnam. This is another instance in which Hayden's life is portrayed as changing with the sociopolitical climate.

This theme of slowly overcoming failure may be seen in how Hayden contrasts his feelings about his trips to North Vietnam. Within the early part of his story, Hayden describes his first visit to Hanoi as permanently affecting his life: "What began as an exercise in amateur diplomacy taught me more than I could imagine about war and revolution and inflicted unhealed scars, not to mention political baggage, that I still carry today" (p. 175). However, later Hayden reflects on the Vietnam experience after years away from the situation:

> But I was also very wrong in certain of my judgments. Time has proven me overly romantic about the Vietnamese revolution. I think Paul Berman's 1987 observation in *The New Republic* was correct in saying that my writings at the time "misinterpreted the egalitarian selflessness that arises in any popular war, and in the first moments of any revolution, as an essential quality of Vietnamese communism." The other side of that romanticism was a numbed sensitivity to any anguish or confusion I was causing to U. S. soldiers or to their families— the very people I was trying to save from death and deception. (p. 243)

This transformation of feeling about Vietnam represents redemption for Hayden and the Vietnam veterans. Hayden attempts to redeem himself and those who fought in Vietnam by bringing back a new wisdom found after completing his heroic journey.

Hayden also identifies his decision to go to North Vietnam as further separating him from his family:

> Sadly, I had no chance to debate these divergent lessons of experience with my father. Perhaps I might have convinced him that the situation was not the same as in the days when I watched the San Diego skies for Japanese attackers. Perhaps not; for marine Jack Hayden, Semper Fidelis was an important commandment. My 1964 visit to my new sister was the last for a long time. As my life became more unconventional, and my image more notorious, my father stopped answering my letters. Our relationship descended into complete breakdown. My relationship with my mother was different, but no less troubled. Her loyalty was to her son, not to the U. S. Marines or any other institution, and she found the war incomprehensible. . . . But she made it painfully clear that my behavior caused her boundless embarrassment in her midwestern small-town circles. To maintain a relationship with me, she felt she had to cut her ties to her inquisitive neighbors. (p. 179)

As one of the many trials that a hero faces, Hayden's trial in the Vietnam experience was one of isolation or rejection. His parents symbolized the feelings of many in this country that those young men who did not fight were cowards. Later, as the war became exceedingly unpopular and the draft evaders were accepted back into American society after President Carter's 1977 executive proclamation, the wounds began to heal. Hayden's healing, described later in the autobiography, comes as he figuratively and literally embraces the POWs who sacrificed their freedom for their country.

The second two sections of Hayden's story describe the trials that all mythical heroes undertake and the revelations that they gain from them. The final two sections of the autobiography exhibit Hayden's death and resurrection as a matured individual. As with most heroic journeys, the hero begins his or her return with an ending—a completion or death.

The final stage in the heroic journey—the return—begins in the fifth section of Hayden's autobiography. In this section Hayden identifies the end of his radical youth with the decline of the radical student protests begun at the Chicago riots during the 1968 Democratic National Convention. The extreme importance of 1968 not only for Hayden's transformation into an adult, but also the country's transformation away from the 1960s is reflected in Hayden's words: "I felt I was living on the knife edge of history. It did, of course, turn out to be a year of extraordinary turmoil, a climax of events that had begun five years earlier with the assassination of President Kennedy" (p. 253). Within this statement, Hayden tells of the beginning of his return.

During this part of the autobiography, Hayden ties his own separation from the student protests to the overall fragmentation and decline of the effectiveness of these protests. By doing so he begins the final process of maturation—the symbolic death before the resurrection. Hayden shows his separation from the declining protesters by describing his failed vision of youth:

> I began realizing in a rush how far many of us had strayed from the original disposition of the sixties. We had become isolated, self-enclosed in a universe of political rather than human life. In this sealed universe, social relationships were contained within organizations, language turned into jargon, disputes were elevated to doctrinal heights, paranoia replaced openness, and the struggle to change each other became a substitute for changing the world. (p. 435)

The juxtaposing images of what the movement should have been and what it was portrayed the ultimate decline of radical protests for Hayden. In a final step symbolizing the return rite of passage in his maturation journey, Hayden finally "kills off" the movement and precipitates his return to mainstream life—a return that the country experienced after the signing of the Paris Peace accords ending the U.S. involvement in Vietnam and Nixon's resignation ending Watergate.

As an important transition from radical to mature politician, Hayden symbolizes both the movement and his life in that movement as reaching an endpoint. Death becomes a prominent symbol in Hayden's description of the times. Not only was the student movement in its death throes, but death symbolized the mood of the country. The pain escalates into feelings of being mortally wounded after the assassination of Robert Kennedy, who Hayden supported in the 1968 presidential race. After Kennedy's death, Hayden describes his feelings as: "I was behaving, without quite recognizing it, as one does before one's own death" (p. 289).

For example, Hayden describes the Kent State killings as "turning Main Street Americans away from war," whereas deaths in Vietnam "were softening the hearts of many of our parents" (pp. 417-418). In a very interesting move, Hayden identifies this mood of the country with his own declining political energies. After Hubert Humphrey won the Democratic nomination for President, Hayden says about the Chicago period: "I had reached exhaustion; so had the protest. So had the hopeful movement I had hoped to build only a few years before. . . . I lay upon the grass, pondering the alternatives. Reform seemed bankrupt, revolution far away" (pp. 330-331). In addition, prior to leaving Chicago after being convicted of 11 counts of conspiracy and subsequently being granted a retrial, Hayden summarizes the period in a very important statement: "It was winter in America. The sixties were over" (p. 411). The symbolism of this statement cannot be overlooked. Winter is the season when crops do not grow, a time before all organic things grow again. In the life cycle the statement symbolizes that growth is forthcoming, much as winter signals that spring is only a few months away. For Hayden, the rebirth metaphor symbolizes his return.

As a transition to Hayden's final stage of the quest, he depicts his complete separation from the radical protest movements and his ultimate return to the mainstream. Hayden's death in the movement may be read as the winter of his life after which he is reborn into the 1970s and 1980s. In the next-to-last section of his autobiography Hayden portrays his fall from radical leadership into relative obscurity in Los Angeles. He depicts his life as completely stagnant. By labeling his life and the historical period as "dead," Hayden disconnects from his radical past and begins his return. Immediately following the Chicago conspiracy trial, Hayden portrays his feelings over moving to California:

> At twenty-eight years of age, I had not lived in a college town since Ann Arbor five years before. I had missed the flowering of alternative politics and lifestyles that had swept the youth communities of the sixties. I wanted to settle in, reinvigorate myself with different friends, an infusion of energy, a fresh base. (p. 328)

Hayden returns to his point of departure from mainstream America—college towns—just as the Berkeley radicals of the early 1970s throw him out of the group for being "counterrevolutionary," after which Hayden states: "I knew that I had to leave Berkeley's claustrophobia. I drove away in my beat-up Volkswagen convertible to Los Angeles, the notorious New Left leader and national security threat alone in a world of hurt" (p. 425). At this point Hayden's journey is described as reaching the lower depths used previously to describe the era: "Los Angeles was the end of the road for me that night in 1970, as it has been for many people escaping unsolved problems and hard times . . . the artists and bohemians remained, joined by increasing numbers of schizophrenics, burglars, and/or heroin addicts" (p. 426). The symbolism in describing Los Angeles as the end of the road is important. By including himself with society's castoffs, Hayden symbolizes his own death and promises rebirth as a matured individual in the birthplace of the Therapeutic Decade.

The last section of the autobiography fulfills the return segment of maturation journeys. As archetypal stories describe the end of these journeys, the hero is renewed or reborn with a new spirit, and this section portrays this sense with Hayden as hero. Hayden's reflections on this period point out the renewal motif indicating this stage of life:

> Perhaps there comes a time for all people when they feel the end of being young and the definite onset of those middle years. So it was for me after my parents died. . . . Wandering through that Wisconsin town, having seen my mother's family, I felt a quickening interest in revisiting certain people and places—from Chicago to Mississippi and Port Huron—that were crucial to my journey through the sixties—before it became too late. From that point on, my ability and commitment to write about my life and times were created. No longer an intellectual project, but a personal need. (p. 485)

The journey at this point not only signals a return, but also the reminiscing one does at maturity, when one can look back on people, places, and events with a different perspective.

Tom Hayden's story ultimately ends with his return to mainstream society after his maturation journey is complete. He, in fact, symbolizes this return as a healing process—a strategy that identifies Hayden with the contemporary psychosocial climate. During this era, many popular discourses of personal change promoted personal and group healing. The 1970s and 1980s were pivotal decades for Hayden's symbolic maturation. Just as the psychosocial climate contained various healing motifs, many 1960s radicals, as Tipton (1982, p. 29) argues, sought various therapeutic movements to heal the damage done by the 1960s. Hayden's story at the end of his autobiography employs the same adaptation and growth that other therapies espouse, showing how Hayden grows with the times. In a real sense, Hayden's description of his own growth during this period sounds very similar to the rhetoric of the est or religious movements. Their theme was that individuals should "take control of themselves," and Hayden portrays his life as being controlled by himself, not by others. Thus, he is reintegrated into society as he is compensated for the past.

One event for which Hayden describes himself as compensated is Vietnam. Because his experiences there damaged his public image as much as any single event during his life, the way Hayden ties his personal experiences in with the national feelings serves to show how he changes with the times. Soon after being expelled from the radical movement in Berkeley, Hayden describes several teaching positions he took at Sacred Heart College and Pitzer College in the Los Angeles area as part of his new crusade: "I would form an 'information project' on the war; my renewed faith was that if the public knew what was being done in their name, they would withdraw support" (p. 436). His teaching began at approximately the same time as "the most important event of 1971 . . . the publication of the Pentagon Papers in *The New York Times*" (p. 437). By linking his experiences in with this historic event, he attempted to portray how he was changing with the times. Hayden's description of his own transformation reflects this change:

> I had come the full circle, scarred but surviving, back to what I did best. I could lead by writing, teaching, and local organizing in the mainstream—instead of distilling myself into a hardened revolutionary. I could work on being more human myself—and try to outgrow or avoid male power rivalries. I could feel better about America—instead of resigning myself to an alienated war against the system. (p. 439)

Also important in being compensated for his actions during the Vietnam War was how Hayden portrayed his changing relationship with those involved on the other side. Hayden describes an episode in 1986 of meeting a former Vietnam POW as California Republican legislators were trying to oust him from his seat on grounds of treason. In sharp contrast to how he depicted his image after his trips to Hanoi, Hayden describes his meeting with former POW James Jackson: "Jimmy and I embraced and laughed afterward. It was twenty years since we left Cambodia. The war might not end for some, but we had at least achieved our personal peace with honor" (p. 241). The "embrace" mentioned by Hayden symbolizes more than just how he was received by those who previously despised him. Embrace also describes the new ways that the country embraced the Vietnam experience during this time. Not only did the 1980s bring about a national memorial to the Vietnam veterans that redeemed their sacrifices, but also many other therapeutic events, including the release of many films, each promising to tell the war's "true story" and many public and private programs designed to allow the survivors of the war to grow beyond those years in Southeast Asia.

Other episodes depicting these healing motifs of the 1970s and 1980s include Hayden's newfound political successes and his reacceptance by more mainstream politicians. His first foray into politics after the Chicago riots was an unsuccessful campaign for the U.S. Senate in 1976 against John Tunney. However, Hayden redefines the measurement of success as he describes his rationale for running:

> Such a race would create a visible platform for debate over post-Vietnam directions like no other; it would allow me to change my status and, by implication, that of the sixties activists, from mainstream participants in national politics; and it would provide a way to build a state-wide organization after the war. (pp. 489-469)

By defining the race in such a manner, Hayden is able to portray the moral victory gained by the loss, "because of who I was, however, the defeat was interpreted as a victory, and it felt like one. It may have been the largest vote in the nation's history for a candidate so clearly defined as a 'radical'" (p. 471). Although his political races were defined as personal referendums, Hayden describes his own return to politics as representative of his generation's return.

Further enhancing Hayden's resurrection after political death is his description of his readmittance into mainstream politics. His work for California Jerry Brown's administration is described as "a symbolic bridge for Jerry Brown to the sixties generation" (p. 472). In addition, Hayden describes his second visit to Washington, DC as "part of this novel acceptance, I visited the White House for the first time since 1962, when I sounded off to Arthur Schlesinger, and was welcomed by Jimmy Carter as a 'patriotic American'" (p. 472). Clearly these associations indicate how much Hayden sees he has grown from victim of American government to participant in the system.

Ultimately, Hayden's successful campaign for the California Legislature is described as compensating himself for the 1960s. Hayden describes how this race had "considerable risks" associated with it as his "specter" precedes him, "causing reactions from discomfort to paranoia in the political establishment" (p. 477). Despite strong opposition from Democrats and Republicans alike, his election, which "was nothing more than a referendum on Tom Hayden," was evidence that he had overcome the past. As Hayden comments to his son, "Just think—we're in there now" (p. 482). His use of "we" symbolizes Hayden's feeling that not only was he compensated for the 1960s, but his generation was as well.

As further evidence of his own successful transformation from the 1960s, Hayden offers the experiences of other radicals as following similar paths as his own. He points to the successes of Bobby Seale as a Temple University graduate student and Todd Gitlin as a University of California sociologist as examples of people who changed with the times. He even compares his own transformation to a mainstream political leader to the religious transformation of Chicago Eight co-conspirator Rennie Davis as both being "adjustments to reality," and that "the difference between my 'religious conversion' and Rennie's was that I was a 'born-again' Middle American, emotionally charged by my acceptance into the political mainstream" (p. 465). Again, Hayden is identified with the rhetorical climate as many people were adjusting to the times through various techniques, including religious conversion and additional schooling.

A final event exemplifying Hayden's healing was his celebrated marriage to actress Jane Fonda. As he describes political events of the early 1960s as destroying his first marriage, Hayden depicts the new politics of the 1980s as prompting his new marriage. Fonda's newfound involvement with political causes during the 1970s and 1980s was noted by Hayden, as well as the therapeutic effects that they had on each other: "She wondered if she could be taken seriously, genuinely, as a committed person or whether she was a shallow latecomer to a decade-long movement; I wondered if there was any way to assert a public leadership role without damaging my personal relationships. We helped each other overcome these doubts" (p. 447). Although Fonda's "Hanoi Jane" image and Hayden's radical past became fodder for the tabloids, their marriage was perceived as stabilizing the images of each, at least until 1989 when the two separated amidst rumors of Hayden returning to his first wife and Fonda having various affairs.

Hayden's political resurrection fulfills the basic requirements of the heroic journey. As a final requirement, Hayden completes the "return" rite of passage within the autobiography by returning to various places on his journey and viewing them with the new gifts bestowed by the completion of his journey. By completing the circle, Hayden completes the healing process and shows how he has adapted to the times.

The gift bestowed by his heroic journey is "ego identity" or maturation. As he describes his return to the places and people of his past, he reflects this perspective. Hayden first describes his return to Chicago, for example, for the filming of a Home Box Office (HBO) special on the Chicago Trial. There he describes his former co-defendants in such a way to remind readers of how things change with the times:

> Now we were middle-aged men, no longer the notorious targets of the Justice Department but the subjects of an HBO movie. America has a funny way of turning even its outlaws into minor celebrities, I mused, as I entered the studio.

AUTOBIOGRAPHY AND THE MODERN HERO   131

> There they were, my old co-defendants, mingled in a cafeteria with their actor counterparts, offering a striking image of then and now. There were broad smiles and hugs offered by one and all, and I knew at once that our past tensions would be suspended during this collective reminder of what we stood for and what we had endured. (p. 487)

The old adage that time heals all wounds apparently rings true in Hayden's description of this reunion. Almost as if all past sins were forgotten, Hayden notes the new lives of his former co-defendants: Bobby Seale as a graduate student, Leo Weiner as a political consultant, John Froines as a professor, and Jerry Rubin as a New York yuppie. The ghosts of radicalism have been exorcised not only from Hayden, but from the others as they have adapted to the changing times.

Hayden's return also takes him further back in the past. Taking a similar approach to his Chicago description, Hayden's return symbolizes how easy it is for people to forget the past. Mayersville, MS, site of many SNCC operations, for example, represents a renewal both physically and spiritually. The location for many activities was described by Hayden as "a fading, unpainted wooden structure overgrown by bushes on all sides. . . . It was all that remained to the freedom house of the sixties," whereas contemporary Mayersville was described in the following terms, "the former climate of terror now under a one-party state was dissipated. Political life was normalized" (p. 491). Even residents, when asked what they remembered from the civil rights movement, responded with: "Nothing." Again, the adaptation theme dominates Hayden's return.

Even Port Huron, site of the 1964 SDS convention, previously depicted as a wilderness, was described as transformed. After driving down streets lined with fast food restaurants and gas stations, Hayden writes of arriving at camps, "now designated as a state park . . . we turned off a newly constructed ramp. . . . At first I recognized nothing. There were neat cement sidewalks, brick rest rooms, and a small sandy beach overlooking the still majestic coast of Lake Huron." Also missing from the former landscape were the conference buildings where the Port Huron Statement was hotly debated. As Hayden quotes a Park Ranger, "Oh, they came down years ago. All that's left is the pipes" (p. 498).

Hayden concludes the autobiography very emotionally by telling of his 30th high school reunion. He writes about how little things had changed, including the baseball diamond which "looked unchanged from thirty years before." Even his classmates had not changed as Hayden states:

> I stared at a disorienting scene from the fifties, a pleasant banquet room filled with hundreds of people, at once intimate and foreign to me. In a few moments, however, I found a table full of my oldest friends, looking not much different than they had in 1957, carrying on as if it were lunchtime in my senior year. (p. 499)

The return is complete. It is interesting to compare Hayden's description of his 1950s schoolmates and how little they had changed with his 1960s cohorts with their new occupations and new looks. Hayden's life is depicted as coming to a complete circle.

Even Hayden's closing lines resurrect the spirit of the 1950s in the 1980s:

> This life is organic. The buildings at Port Huron had disappeared, but the yearnings of youth recorded there still remained alive, like spirits in Irish legends. I could feel them in the trees, in the paths, waiting for renewal. They were in the imaginations of my high school classmates who spoke the language of understanding, acceptance, reconciliation. The change was slow but secure, gradual but real. I felt at home again and waited expectantly for a new generation. (p. 500)

Therefore, renewal is the predominant theme for Hayden's journey—a journey in which he symbolically fulfills the rites of passage necessary for maturation. People, places, and events seem renewed.

Journeys, as do stories, end with some sort of resolution. However, as Campbell and others argue, life is a series of separations and returns. Hayden's story of maturation is no different as he promises new journeys with a new generation. As in most autobiographies, Hayden's nonclosure promises that his story will continue.

CONCLUSION

New hero myths may be found in various forms of public communication in the United States, including the narratives of film and television. However, nowhere can these new forms of the hero myth be seen more clearly than in popular autobiographies. Through autobiographical discourse, public figures can remake their public image so that they appear heroic. They invoke aspects of the new hero myths in their autobiographies and, in doing so, offer themselves as a product of that myth. Not only does autobiographical discourse containing these new hero myths function rhetorically in orienting audiences toward these newly created identities, but these stories offer new symbolic resources for their publics—a therapeutic rhetoric that permits both the autobiographer and reader to cope with the difficulties portrayed in the story.

Analysis of Hayden's *Reunion* as an image revitalization strategy also helps us understand more deeply how the rhetorical climate influences image revitalization strategies in particular and rhetoric in general. Individuals hoping to revitalize their public images and even become cultural heroes for some manage their public images within an environment made up of other mediated messages about that image and about transformation in general. Hayden's case illustrates how a climate of healing allows persons with jaded pasts to revitalize their images during the 1970s and 1980s. One might recall how the case of Louisiana legislator and ex-Ku Klux Klan member David Duke was most directly advanced as a case of image revitalization through an almost identical process. That is, there were claims that events occurring in the past were merely acts of an immature person, there were allusions to a solitary figure on a heroic quest, and strong rhetorical appeals to returning to the past. Whereas media coverage of Duke's campaign included not only showing evidence of Duke's Klan activities, but also messages by Republicans and Democrats alike reputing Duke's claim of change, Duke's claims of change through continual stories of maturation told many times in speeches and interviews have unfortunately made him a hero to many ultraconservatives throughout the country. These stories evidence the claim that variations of the monomyth such as a maturation strategy are indeed alive and well in contemporary rhetoric and literature.

This case, as well as many others, point out a number of facts about the importance of autobiographies and myths in the contemporary world: (a) audiences have an implicit knowledge of the appropriate symbols and forms for image transformation, (b) the content of the message promoting change is less important than the style and structure of the message, and (c) the psychosocial environment dictates which variation of the heroic story will function as that form which allows contemporary heroes to exist.

☐☐☐☐☐ **10**

Iacocca: Chrysler's Mass-Mediated Hero (1979-1983)

Risë Jane Samra, Ph.D.
Barry University

☐ *Lee Iacocca rose from corporate obscurity to national prominence, and to some, to a position of civic hero. His meteoric rise to celebrity, if not to herodom, could happen only with the help of the mass media and its related advertising industry. Samra provides the history of the Chrysler Corporation's economic collapse and reveals how Iacocca became the center of a campaign to restore the image of the Chrysler Corporation. She then analyzes the rhetorical strategies employed by Iacocca and his agents as reflected in the media package that established his fame.*

National business leaders, for years, have been the focus of media attention, but not always to their company's benefit. An example of inappropriate corporate behavior was that of tycoon Andrew Carnegie during the Homestead strike. When labor problems in his steel plant erupted in violence, Carnegie retired to his lodge in Scotland, 35 miles from the nearest railroad or telegraph. Carnegie wanted to be known as a "cultured philanthropist," and he let the London press know that he remained aloof from the labor struggle in order to protect his company from his own generosity. Professionally he had not amassed a $400 million fortune by worrying about the living conditions of his underpaid employees, and he was content to have his right-hand man, Henry Clay Frick, crush their strike and their union with the help of the state militia (Newsom, Scott, & Turk, 1989, p. 38).

J. D. Rockefeller, in contrast to Carnegie, wanted the public to like him. Of course, he was no pushover in the world of finance, and he did not amass his vast fortune by being a nice guy. Whether out of vanity, conscience, honest generosity, or because he was disturbed by what the journalists of the time were saying about him, Rockefeller gave away thousands of dimes to children and over half a billion dollars to charities (Newsom et al., 1989, p. 39).

As Chief Executive Officer of the Chrysler Corporation, Lee Iacocca's mission was not philanthropy. His goal was one of addressing the media by publicly admitting Chrysler's mistakes, confronting his foreign competition, and instilling the spirit of cooperation between labor and management.

In the 1980s, only a handful of national business leaders starred in their companies' advertising: Frank Borman of Eastern Airlines, Frank Sellinger of Schlitz, and Frank Perdue, the chicken king, to name a few. Besides credibility, there was good reason to feature the boss in the ad. If the ad failed, the chairperson's enormous ego could be blamed because the public routinely assumes that it was the boss's idea. When Lee Iacocca assumed the responsibility for Chrysler's quality in the company's advertising, the response was overwhelmingly positive from the mass-mediated audience, and Iacocca emerged a hero. To comprehend the cause for Iacocca's mass-mediated heroism, one must look back at the recent history of Chrysler.

HISTORY

The economic analysts on Wall Street had all but signed Chrysler's death certificate when Lee Iacocca took the reins of this floundering corporate giant in 1979. Chrysler had already lost $460 million. During a 3-year period it was destined to lose a record total of $3.5 billion, the largest in the history of American business (Kelmenson, 1984, p. 16). The Chrysler product had not responded to the important changes taking place in consumer preference. Chrysler had been fulfilling the American dream by building big luxury cars during the small car revolution in 1979. Unfortunately, Chrysler could not produce enough small cars to satisfy demand. Consequently, other small foreign imports moved to fill the vacuum.

Chrysler's errors in judgment were compounded by external circumstances. In 1979, the United States experienced the worst inflation since the Civil War. A recession followed. The price of gasoline doubled within four months. President Jimmy Carter considered gas rationing as long lines formed at the pumps. Interest rates escalated; the GNP grew only modestly; the annual new car sales dropped from 11.1 million in 1978 to 7.7 million in 1982. As in other economic recessions, consumers began to postpone major purchases such as automobiles (p. 16).

In the midst of these circumstances, in 1979, Lee Iacocca appealed for help to the House Committee on Banking, Finance and Urban Affairs. When he testified before the committee on October 18, 1979, he emphasized that federal help was absolutely necessary immediately before the end of the year. He outlined how government regulation, pollution and fuel economy standards, and the energy crunch, combined with the current economic downturn, had brought Chrysler to its current crisis. He stressed that a Chrysler bankruptcy would hurt not just workers in Detroit and Michigan, but 2 million Americans across the country:

We are a microcosm of all the things that are wrong; we're just that big. Energy's impacting us, regulations are impacting us, runaway inflation on commodities are impacting on us, imports are impacting us. We're a big city (combating) unemployment. That's impacting us. I don't know where to turn. I went all out for this committee. I've done the best I can. I'm committed to it. I'm gonna turn it around one way or another. I need your assistance now and I need a vote of confidence. What else can I tell ya? (House Committee on Banking, October 18, 1979)

Florida Representative Richard Kelly's response was not atypical of the reaction of most who opposed the bail-out. He characterized the bankruptcy of Chrysler as the inevitable consequence of a foolish policy. He also argued that a bail-out would set a precedent for large-scale government intervention on behalf of sick industries:

I think what you're [Chrysler] doing is trying to wreck this country. The only way he could possibly hope to survive is to compete and for your failure, you should get with what the free enterprise promises you. It's called, "loss." There's a profit side and loss side and you're on the loss side. And those people out there are not suddenly gonna all commit suicide or quit working because you had mismanaged the company. And if they've overcharged what the labor market can afford to pay and be competitive in the world markets . . . well, this is all just pure bunk. (House Committee on Banking, October 19, 1979)

Michigan Senator Donald Riegle (Republican turned Democrat), also a member of the House Committee on Banking, argued from circumstances in another way. Ironically, in 1971, as a young Republican Congressman he had voted against aid to Lockheed. Then, in 1977, as a Democratic Senator he became a close friend of the auto industry when he led the Senate fight to relax the Clean Air Act (Moritz & Seaman, 1981, p. 264). Contrary to Kelly's statement, Riegle made emotional appeals by explaining that a Chrysler collapse would bring on a depression in Detroit. There would be economic disaster for the nation, and it would be extremely costly for the federal government:

In order to come to grips with the Chrysler issue, we must recognize it as a problem which must be understood and dealt with on two levels: At one level it is the fact that the Chrysler bankruptcy is a massive national problem. It could put 600,000 people out of work, devastate communities, swamp hundreds of supplier organizations, and create economic shock waves that can cost the federal government some $10 million in the first year alone. And yet on another level, the Chrysler situation is symptomatic of a much bigger national problem: A growing threat to industrial America where Chrysler was the tip of a bigger and more piercing iceberg. (House Committee on Banking, October 10, 1979)

On November 1, 1979, President Jimmy Carter asked Congress to grant Chrysler $1.5 billion in federally guaranteed loans. According to C.

William Miller, the Secretary of Treasury, the federal government would guarantee repayment of money loaned to Chrysler, provided that Chrysler obtained the following commitment: The company must obtain a commitment of $2 billion in nonfederally guaranteed assistance from banks, financial institutions, other creditors, dealers, suppliers, employees, state and local governments, and from the sale of assets.

In response to Miller's statements, opponents to government action said:

- On November 1, 1979, Florida Representative Richard Kelly: "The Chrysler Charity is the most blatant con job of our time."
- On November 14, 1979, Wisconsin Senator William Proxmire: "Chrysler is asking Congress to play the role of a deaf and dumb, blind Santa Claus."
- On November 15, 1979, Lee Iacocca retorted by telling the House Committee: "Give me the money I need and I'll get the job done. I won't be back."

On December 18, 1979, President Carter told both Houses that it was imperative for the federal government to bail out Chrysler with federal loan guarantees. That day members of the Michigan caucuses buttonholed congressmen as they arrived, while union representatives including Douglas Fraser and a team of black ministers added their pleas. Everybody was doing the same thing: campaigning (Moritz & Seaman, 1981, pp. 289-290).

On December 20, 1979, representatives of the House and Senate met for the Joint Committee Meeting. This marked the final opportunity for legislators to influence the terms of what had grown from a plea for tax relief into the Chrysler Loan Guarantee Act.

On December 21, 1979, Speaker of the House Tip O'Neill made the final impassioned plea before the vote was taken in Congress. He recalled the days of the Depression in Boston when unemployed workers would stand in the morning dark and beg for work shoveling snow. Apparently, the Congressmen were duly moved. They passed the Chrysler Loan Guarantee Bill by a 2-to-1 margin (271 votes to 136) (Moritz & Seaman, 1981, p. 290). The Senate vote had been much closer, 52 to 44 (Iacocca, 1984, p. 225). On January 7, 1980, President Carter signed the Chrysler Loan Guarantee Bill into law (Chrysler Corporation, 1983, p. 1233).

The government-backed loan enabled Chrysler to survive and even to thrive, although in a substantially smaller and leaner version. It grew robust enough to exceed its repayment schedule. On August 15, 1983, at a brief ceremony at the New York Waldorf Astoria, Chrysler Chairman Lee Iacocca handed a check for $812,487,500 to Edwin Heard, vice chairman of the U.S. Trust Company, the trustee. The check included $13,487,500 in interest ("Chrysler repaid," 1983, p.

13). Incredibly, Chrysler's repayment was 7 years ahead of schedule, and the company even recorded a profit of $550 million in 1983.

During its adversity the corporation became more image conscious. Iacocca realized the need to support the sales and marketing of Chrysler products. He hired the Kenyon and Eckhardt Advertising firm of Birmingham, MI as the sole agency for Chrysler's car, truck, and corporate advertising. Taking on this assignment meant that the agency had to seek new and radical ways of advertising in order to sell cars *fast*.

The paid advertising campaign began on a note of dramatic confrontation. Having made the decision that a head-on attack was the best strategy, a crucial question was posed, "Would America be better off without Chrysler?" To answer that question, the "Confidence Ad Series" was launched. The premise of the campaign was that the basic worth and latent vitality of Chrysler made it worth saving. Iacocca became the key TV spokesperson for this cause.

During the congressional hearings Iacocca had become a nationally known figure. The Chrysler story was a regular news item, and the advertising people were eager to turn the liability into an asset.

Kenyon and Eckhardt made a strong presentation to Iacocca:

Everybody thinks Chrysler's going bankrupt. Somebody has to tell them you're not. The most believable guy to do that would be you. First, you're well known. And second, the viewers know very well that afterward you have to go back to the business of making the cars you just touted. By appearing in those ads, you're putting your money where your mouth is. (Iacocca, 1984, p. 268)

It should be noted that when the Kenyon and Eckhardt ad agency first approached Iacocca for TV ads his response was totally negative (Iacocca, p. 68). Iacocca felt that producing a commercial was most tedious and time-consuming and would be taking him away from his car business. He was convinced that a CEO who appeared in his or her company's ads was on an ego trip. He was also concerned that his appearing in television commercials would be viewed by the public as a final act of desperation that would cause the entire enterprise to backfire.

Prior to Iacocca's own advertising, the celebrity route had been taken by Chrysler, but no one was as successful as Iacocca in selling the Chrysler product. Prominent personalities who extolled the virtues of Chrysler were: actor John Houseman, former Dallas Cowboys' running back Walt Garrison (Gray, 1981, p. 2), former baseball star Joe Garagiola ("Ad for Chrysler," 1979, pp. 18-19), former astronaut Neil Armstrong (Gray, 1979, p. 83), actor Ricardo Montalban ("Ad for Cordoba," 1979, pp. 94-95), and singer Frank Sinatra, for whom the Imperial FS was named (Gray, 1981, p. 71), promoted Chrysler products in magazine, newspaper, and television advertising. Iacocca was awkward at first, but as his success grew, he became a practiced artist, smoothly performing the role of star industrialist and taking on the mantle of hero.

METHODOLOGY AND THE ROLE OF HERO

What characteristics did Iacocca project to emerge a mass-mediated hero?

First, I explored some of Carlyle's chief tenets of heroism discussed in Bentley's book, *A Century of Hero-Worship* (1957). The chief tenet of Carlyle's conception of hero is: "Great men should rule and that others should revere them" (Bentley, 1957, p. 34). He relates this chief tenet to other important tenets, which in turn, this writer contends, coincide with Iacocca's heroic display of rhetorical skills of independence, dynamics, confidence, plain talk, and the mystique of faith. Iacocca's implementation of these skills helped create the new Chrysler Corporation that led to the company's success in 1983.

Ethos/Independence. The hero (i.e., person of courage) is "sincere" and does his or her "duty," that is, he or she acts intuitively, without the interference of mechanical philosophies or restrictive codes. He or she cooperates with "the real tendency of the world" and so becomes an instrument of history and progress. Through the recognition of progress, he or she becomes free (Bentley, 1957, p. 35).

Dynamism. The core of a person's feeling (unless he or she accepts death and ceases to be) must be an affirmation of the life process. In this cruel process courage will be more valuable than love. The human ideal will not be the saint but the nobleperson (Bentley, 1957, pp. 34-35).

Confidence/Plain Speaking. The philosophy of heroism is partly pragmatic. The hero recognizes facts squarely and acts boldly. He or she therefore prefers intuition to reflection, faith to philosophy, ardor to detachment, reverence to urbanity, temerity to caution, and speed to the suspension of judgment (Bentley, 1957, p. 35).

The Mystique of Faith. Organisms fail periodically. There is catastrophe followed by a fresh start. Evolution is salutatory. Individuals and societies experience rebirth.

The hero's function is dual. First, he or she is a pattern for others to imitate, in him- or herself a justification of life. Second, he or she is creator, and through him- or her history moves forward and not backward: History is the biography of great men and women (Bentley, 1957, p. 35).

The Mass-Mediated Hero

Of course, none of these skills would have had the effect on Iacocca's audiences without the profound impact of the mass media. Media, the dimension of hyperreality—a term coined by cultural theorists Umberto and Jean Baudrillard—suggests the merger of lived experience with the representation of it, the fusion of reality with media. Through mass media the essence of Marshall McLuhan's global village permeates every phase of our society. In Sharret's article, "Good, Evil, and Movie Heroes" (1990), he discusses the "mediaficiation" of history and the transformation of the hero protagonist as representing social assumption and suggesting an attitude toward history. Thus, in order for a hero to become widely known today, he or she is subject to the media's acknowledgment and, in turn, becomes a mass-mediated hero, such as, Mother Theresa, Desmond Tuto, Nelson Mandela, and Lee Iacocca.

Specifically, 98% of all American homes today have at least one television which is turned on an average of 7-1/2 hours a day (Barker, 1993, p. 393). TV commercials take up 16 minutes of every televised hour of programming, not to mention the billions of dollars spent each year on their production. Placing Iacocca as a vehicle of Chrysler on company-paid TV commercials proved to be invaluable to his image and highly profitable for Chrysler.

Iacocca's ethos. The Kenyon and Eckhardt Advertising agency made a conscious choice in making Iacocca the personification of the Chrysler Corporation. They could do this because he had a prior reputation in the automotive industry established by his creation of the Ford Mustang. One of Chrysler's main concerns was to develop another new line to advance (or, in this case, to save) a renewed company. Had Iacocca's past success been in finance, or corporate take-overs, it would not have been feasible to project his capacity for design. Chrysler's problem had been largely in archaic design. Its salvation had to come in new design, and Iacocca was designated as its savior.

Independence: Real Americans don't take charity; they are self-reliant. Iacocca had to demonstrate that he was a reluctant recipient of Congressional aid. Even though it was absolutely necessary to receive the loan, it was mandatory that he express shame and disapproval. Americans like to think of themselves as self-reliant people; the long frontier experience gave them the myth of the lone individual, and the frontier mandate was for people who could take care of themselves in hostile circumstances. These people would not become a burden to the community. The same pattern of individualism made acceptance of community aid a badge of shame. To 'take charity' was an admission of weakness. Iacocca said: "I would sell my kids before I went back to Washington for the next $300 million" (*Fortune*, 1981, pp. 145-146).

This statement referred to the fact that Chrysler's original appeal to the federal government was for $1.2 billion. Instead, the federal government determined that Chrysler's needs were greater and thus granted Chrysler $1.5 billion. Iacocca kept his word and used only $1.2 billion.

Another reason Iacocca made this statement was built around his strong conviction that there should be a program to help big businesses in trouble, without their having to go before the bar or the press:

> Each time we've gone back, it's been three months of hell. The dealers go into a blue funk, the customers hold off buying. We probably lose 50 cents in sales for $1 in loans. I don't want to say it's impossible that we'd ever go back in a crunch, but we could probably do some of those other things instead. (Fortune, 1981, p. 146)

Dynamism. It was the prestige of success. As the company turned around Iacocca was presented as a dynamic leader who had coaxed success out of failure. Success in a mass-mediated culture is measured by high visibility. The media pay attention to successful people. Also, his peers sought his advice and showered him with praise. Emphasis was placed on the sheer force of Iacocca's personality and self-confidence rather than on structural and fiscal changes in the Chrysler Corporation.

Buoyed by the immense prestige that success brings, Iacocca seemed to become a more believable actor in commercials and press conferences:

> In Lee Iacocca we not only have the most dynamic Chairman of the Board in the country, we've got a real celebrity. He's the most sought-after business executive on the scene today. On the average he receives 70 invitations every month. He gets 600 letters a week, not only from people in the U.S., but from around the world. And the media invitations come by the dozens daily. Every Monday, it seems, Bill Monroe calls to invite Lee to *Meet the Press*. And every Monday, we decline. In the last few months, we've also had to turn down *Face the Nation, Donahue, Good Morning America, Today*, and *Nightline*. Lee is also the most admired executive in the country. Well, sort of. In a recent Gallup Poll, for *The Wall Street Journal*, most businessmen couldn't name a single executive they admired. But of those who had a favorite, Lee Iacocca was the overwhelming choice. No one else was even close. As one fellow told the pollsters, "Iacocca took a company on the brink of disaster and brought it back . . . on the strength of personality. That's very appealing to the entrepreneurial spirit." (Tolley, 1983, pp. 2-3)

This kind of testimony would tell the reader that Iacocca made his mark: He proved himself by fulfilling the goals of the ad campaign. Chrysler's Public Affairs Department was able to capitalize on Iacocca's accomplishments and used them to instill public confidence in the corporation. Because of Iacocca's strong personality, entrepreneurial spirit, and risk-taking approach to business that led to financial success, he was celebrated as a hero and became widely sought after for speaking engagements.

Confidence. Self-confidence (and the extension of confidence in the product) is demonstrated by taking risks. Capitalism is a risk-taking activity, and the deepest myth of capitalistic culture is that only the risk takers become rich and successful. The great 19th-century freebooters of capitalism were gamblers who risked everything on shrewd hunches. Like the Europeans of Machiavelli's time, modern Americans still believe that Dame Fortune must be assaulted. Iacocca was a risk taker in the great tradition because he was shown to have great confidence in his company and in his product.

A series of speeches (February 25, 1983; September 27, 1983; October 25, 1983; November 14, 1983; and February 27, 1984) presented by representatives of Chrysler's Public Affairs and Public Relations Departments, just before the loans were repaid, made it apparent that the job of reestablishing credibility in the corporation was not yet complete. They now had their hero advocating a solid and reliable product, and they had to make sure he maintained a favorable profile in the sight of the press.

Television Advertisement: Iacocca On Camera

To quote Lee Iacocca:

> If a manufacturer doesn't have enough confidence in the quality of what he makes, he doesn't ask you to buy it. And it doesn't make any difference what he makes . . . washing machines, toasters, or roller skates. Me? I'm in the car business and I've been saying for a long time that Chrysler makes cars that are as good if not better than anything coming out of America, Europe or Japan. Now to show you the kind of confidence we have in the quality of our products . . . when you buy any new Chrysler, Plymouth, or Dodge, American Built passenger car, Chrysler will protect your investment three ways. One, a 5-year or 50,000 miles protection plan on the engine and power train. Two, 5 years or 50,000 miles rust-proof protection on the outside of the car. Three, 5 years or 50,000 miles free scheduled maintenance. Now that's confidence. But let's face it. If we don't believe in our products, why should you? So if you find a better car, buy it. (Kelmenson, 1984, p. 26)

Plain Speaking. A deep strain of anti-intellectualism coupled with a preference for action over thought has always predisposed us to trust plain speakers. The dogmatism of Teddy Roosevelt, the plain talk of Truman, the straight sense of Ben Franklin and others have inspired us with certainty. Iacocca utilized action-oriented discourse in broadcast journalistic style. That is, he uttered short, declarative sentences so that when the listener heard them for the first time, there was no need for him or her to search for a deeper meaning. Perhaps it was this type of simplicity in the content of the message and its unpretentious television delivery that made Iacocca convincing to his audience.

Dressed in conservative, corporate style, Iacocca's television testimonial ad for his company and product generated the most public response. He said simply that he was in the car business and that Chrysler was as good or better than its competitors. His salient point was the generous warranty plan that one would find hard to resist. To cap it off, he said, "If you can find better protection, take it. If you find a better car, buy it" (Kelmenson, 1984, p. 26).

During this period of increased advertising, Chrysler's market share went from 8% to 9.9%. In Fall 1982, it achieved a 10% share. Chrysler's share segment went from 11 to 22% (p. 27). In a business in which a 1% share increase is the equivalent of about a billion dollars, that was an increase of great magnitude.

In an exclusive interview with *Psychology Today*, Iacocca explained the dimensions of the problem:

> I've heard people say that lower Japanese prices are great for the American consumer. Maybe that's why Fuji film is the official film of the U.S. Olympics. Maybe that's why, according to the August 4 *Washington Post*, 233 out of 493 White House staff members own cars made in Japan. That kind of thinking is nearsighted, and costly to all of us. On the average, every time someone buys a Japanese car in this country, we lost $7,500 in tax revenue at the local, state and federal level. There's no free lunch. You've got to make it up someplace. (Iacocca, 1983, p. 34)

Again, in his dogmatic way, Iacocca was saying that the "Buy American" programs were not simply a matter of self-interest, they were matters of national difference and economic survival. It was clear that he wanted Japan to cease its unfair practices or America would be forced to retaliate—not only to stop their currency and trade manipulation, but to protect the American industrial base and its way of doing business. In essence, he reminded us that we did it first and we did it best when it comes to building industrial might. We did it by investing profits where they would provide more jobs and develop better products. We did it by producing a quality product that the American worker could take pride in and on which the consumer could reply. Iacocca declared, "Now our challenge is to show that we can do it again. I believe that way of doing business is coming back" (p. 34).

The Mystique of Faith. Finally, Iacocca expressed the mystical faith that is the hallmark of leaders such as Roosevelt and Churchill. The American creed is infinite in its extent. It transcends failure, resources, and circumstances. Iacocca was telling us that in economic terms, this may be America's darkest hour. However, as slow and frustrating as our system can be, it still works and works well. Even if we became fat and lazy and allowed our quality to slip, we could improve it until it is second to none in the world. Iacocca (1983, p. 34) contended, "Anything we did, we can undo." In other words, if we created a federal debt that ruined our economy, we could reduce it and get the economy going again. If we let our country fall apart, we could pull it back together again better than before.

During Chrysler's financial crisis, Iacocca engaged in the equality of sacrifice when labor, supplies, and middle management made monetary concessions. Iacocca took a $1 a year salary from Chrysler. Of course, one may argue that he was collecting a handsome pension from his previous employer, Ford. Nonetheless, Iacocca was setting an example for his Chrysler employees.

In spite of the inequities of government, the federal government guaranteed loan gave Chrysler the opportunity once again to convey to the public that it was still a viable firm. Iacocca utilized the financial resources from the federal government and made them work profitably for the company. It is in this way that Chrysler, between the years 1979 and 1983, demonstrated a remarkable capacity for change. Iacocca's crusade, at the very least, had succeeded in something that up until this time had seemed impossible: "It had distributed large economic losses and won sacrifices from all" (Moritz & Seaman, 1981, p. 347). Iacocca convinced us that today's often distrusted alliance of business, labor, and government could, when pushed, work. Chrysler's transformation pointed to changing times, to a nation nudging its resources in a different direction, accommodating itself to a different role in the world economy and displaying willingness to learn from countries it had once tutored.

To reiterate Carlyle's (1908, pp. 34-35) tenets of heroism, one can clearly see why Iacocca fit into Carlyle's criteria:

1. Iacocca was "sincere and acted intuitively without the interference of mechanical philosophies or restrictive codes," especially when he appealed to the federal government for a massive loan. He, "became an instrument of history and progress" in the auto industry not to mention the free enterprise system.
2. Iacocca was "courageous in his endeavors"; laying his own credibility on the line to sell his cars via the media.
3. Iacocca was "pragmatic"; he recognized the cold [hard] facts and "acted boldly" to solve the problem.
4. In his quest for disputing the symbol of failure, Iacocca set "a pattern for others to imitate"; he made Chrysler a testament to change—a cause for immense optimism rather than deep despair and as a consequence, he became a celebrity.

Ironically, in a magazine article, Iacocca somewhat regretfully spoke of his celebrity status:

Some people say I've deliberately pursued celebrity, but I haven't. I did the Chrysler commercials, and I turned the company around. Then I wrote a book about myself and it got a lot of nice notoriety. I miss my privacy, but I made my bed and now I have to lie in it. Sometimes, though, this celebrity business grates on my nerves. ("Iacocca," 1991, p. 4)

CONCLUSION

The history of the Chrysler Corporation—from Walter P. Chrysler to Lee Iacocca—indeed, the history of the American automobile industry, demonstrated that, far more than institutions and strategies, it is men and their ideas who succeed or fail. In particular, Iacocca's heroic display of rhetorical skills of independence, dynamism, confidence, plain talk, and the mystique of faith, coupled with the strong positive acknowledgment of the media, helped create the new Chrysler Corporation. His sound leadership and competence led to Chrysler's financial success which provided the basis for changing the company's image. Iacocca emerged not only as a mass-mediated hero, but as one whose name became synonymous with Chrysler.

Section III:
Critical Theories:
Perspectives on the Hero/Celebrity

11

Phyllis Schlafly: Great Mother, Heroine, and Villain

Karin J. Billions
Wayne College

❐ *This chapter is a rhetorical analysis of Phyllis Schlafly's Stop ERA discourse and her current public education and child care messages. Grounded in the theories of C. G. Jung, Joseph Campbell, and Erich Neuman, it identifies how Schlafly invokes the positive and negative elementary and transformative characters of the Great Mother archetype to motivate the audience to endorse her political agendas. Billions explains how the invocation of the Great Mother makes Schlafly an effective hero for some audience members but a villain to others. Finally, it describes how Schlafly's use of the media has contributed to her hero/villain status.*

"One of the greatest things about being women is that we have the opportunity to have different careers at different times in our lives," Phyllis Schlafly said in *Good Housekeeping* (Block, 1984). The outspoken critic of the women's liberation movement and the architect of the pro-life movement is described by Block (p. 80) as the "champion of motherhood [who] has also had one of the busiest public careers of our time." Block (p. 80) noted that Schlafly's mission is to save the role of the homemaker from extinction. She also described Schlafly (p. 82) as having "the knack for making fantasies real."

Among the many things Block's article on Schlafly revealed is that for six consecutive years Schlafly appeared on *Good Housekeeping's* list of the 10 most admired women. This view of Schlafly is one that emerges repeatedly in popular media. It is one that simultaneously drove women's liberationists to distraction. The reason is that Schlafly, the proponent of the traditional homemaker, established a national following at exactly the time when the women's movement was making its strongest bid for equal rights since the days of Susan B. Anthony and Elizabeth Cady Stanton. Surprisingly, just when it looked as though Congress would pass the Equal Rights Amendment, Phyllis Schlafly organized women throughout America to work actively against the bill which many people saw as the salvation of women. How could this happen? Was Schlafly a traitor to her own kind? Was she a self-interested, middle-class wife who had everything given to her? Was she a heroine, as her supporters claimed, or a villain, as her detractors claimed? What is there about Phyllis Schlafly that simultaneously engenders such loyalty and such hatred?

Because Schlafly has taken a strong stance against gender-neutral language (1977, pp. 30-31), and because her rhetoric is laden with appeals to traditional feminine behaviors, her followers would be more likely to refer to her as a "heroine" rather than as a "hero." By contrast, feminists endorse gender-neutral language. For them, the term *villain*, rather than *villainess*, could be applied equally well to males and females. To illustrate this dichotomous world view, I have used *heroine* to refer to Schlafly as she appears to supporters and *villain* to refer to Schlafly as she appears to opponents of her views.

Preliminary research revealed that Schlafly has staunch loyal followers who idolize her, which suggests she is more than a media celebrity. Most of these followers, it appeared, were not impressionable teenagers, but rather selfless women with homes and families who worked hard to do the best for their families. Why did they select Schlafly as a heroine rather than someone from the women's movement who could direct them toward feminism and being successful in a man's world? The answer, it seems, lies in part in Schlafly's adroit use of the mass media.

Several issues of *Policy Review* include Schlafly's comments in symposium articles. She has also appeared on *Donahue* twice (in 1978 and 1982), given speeches throughout the country, and continues to have her own radio show. Schlafly has taken these opportunities to discuss everything from abortion to prayer in schools and has utilized virtually every medium to do it.

Marshall McLuhan in *Understanding Media* (1964) and the *Gutenberg Galaxy* (1968), suggested that through the electronic media contemporary society is able to return to the idyllic time of village life when communication was face to face. He claimed that electronic technology provides better communication than the written word because it is not limited to the linear kind of argument construction that writing fosters. He praised the advent of a global village. Proponents and opponents of this view continue to argue the point. Whether McLuhan was right about the influence of media on people's thought patterns, he was accurate in stating that electronic media allow modern societies to have a global village. Recent technological developments allow American messages to be beamed around the world via satellite. The proliferation of videocams allows the beating by police of a motorist in Los Angeles to be viewed on New York television stations within hours after the event. Technology also allows the almost instant creation of celebrities and heroes as the media compete with each other to get the best story and dramatize those involved.

Celebrities and heroes abound in the global village. For the ordinary person they symbolize the realization of the potential existing in humanity. Celebrities arise from publicity and from exposure to the public in a variety of media. They may or may not be deserving of their fame. Heroes, on the other hand, touch people inspirationally, mirror their values, and may motivate heroic action. They also provoke action from those whose ideas and values are strongly opposed to their own. In a society as geographically sprawling and intellectually complex as America today, it is difficult to imagine that any figure could become a national hero without the attention of the media.

In some instances, the media provide information grudgingly, which may then contribute to the hero status of the person. Felsenthal (1981) cited numerous examples of how reporters, particularly women reporters, have treated Schlafly rudely. If the hero or heroine is able to portray him- or herself as standing alone as a champion for traditional values, he or she is likely to gain a large and highly supportive audience, regardless of the editorial stance of the media. Phyllis Schlafly is such a person.

In October 1972, Phyllis Schlafly declared war on the Equal Rights Amendment (hereafter ERA) by organizing Stop ERA. At the time Schlafly was known principally as a frequent delegate to Republican national conventions and as a conservative political columnist. She had already written several books (including *A Choice not an Echo* [1964] and *Strike from Space* [1965]), borne six children, waged two campaigns for a seat in the U.S. House of Representatives (in 1952 and 1970), and run for president of the National Federation of Republican Women (in 1967). However, she came to national attention with her fight against the ERA. Whereas many Americans enthusiastically endorsed legislation to insure economic opportunity and equitable treatment for women, Schlafly opposed it, thus apparently betraying her own kind.

At first feminists and the media refused to take Schlafly seriously. This was a mistake, as she quickly rose to the status of heroine for many American women and men. Perhaps Schlafly's heroine status is best illustrated by the title of Felsenthal's biography of her, *The Sweetheart of the Silent Majority* (1981). For many men and women Schlafly became a savior fighting for a way of life. Although the ERA was soundly defeated in 1982, Schlafly continues to espouse many of the same arguments she presented against it. Her rhetoric continues to contribute to a highly satisfying mythic vision for her followers.

THE GREAT MOTHER ARCHETYPE

I argue that underlying and informing the discourse of Phyllis Schlafly is the image of the Great Mother archetype which is readily identifiable in her rhetoric. Further, I argue that this archetype significantly contributes to her heroic power to enlist followers for her political battles and to participate in her mythic vision for America. By analyzing Schlafly's rhetoric I endeavor to answer the following questions: How does the Great Mother archetype function in Schlafly's rhetoric? What is the mythic vision surrounding her rhetoric? How does Schlafly's invocation of the Great Mother archetype contribute to the success of her public moral argument? Why is Schlafly a heroine to some audiences and a villain to others?

An analysis of Schlafly's rhetoric using traditional rhetorical tools leaves much in question because Schlafly's arguments are often emotional and ill-founded, but are, nevertheless, acceptable to a large and diverse segment of the population. Furthermore, Schlafly has the distinction of enlisting followers who would defend her to the death, while at the same time enraging opponents who see her as an archvillain. This intense dichotomy suggests that Schlafly can best be studied by utilizing a methodology based on a dichotomy. By analyzing Schlafly's rhetoric within the context of cultural myth, and particularly by applying the Great Mother archetype to her discourse, one can see how Schlafly's rhetoric imbues one part of her audience with a sense of power and another part with a sense of oppression as she denigrates their efforts to win equality.

By championing traditional values, Schlafly appeals to traditional women who can follow her role model. By condemning attempts to change traditional values and by portraying her opponents as villains seeking to undermine the established order, she focuses anger, shame, and rejection on them. How this works becomes more understandable if one utilizes Joseph Campbell's theory of the functions of cultural myths and then compares those functions to Schlafly's use of rhetorical strategies in the media.

THE FUNCTION OF MYTH

Campbell (1968b, pp. 4-6), grounding his view of myth in the psychological theories of Jung, identified four recurring and universal functions of myth.

1. Myths enable the individual to understand and relate to the mysteries of the universe.
2. Myths provide the individual with an image of the universe so that she or he is able to understand contemporary conditions.
3. Myths validate and enforce the moral order so that the individual is able to function within his or her particular society, thus contributing to social cohesion.
4. Myths teach the individual how to integrate the various aspects of his or her personality, how to integrate himself or herself with the universe, and how to deal with the mystery of life.

According to Jung (DeLaszlo, 1959), the psyche incorporates a personal unconscious and a collective unconscious. The personal unconscious contains materials that at one time were conscious, but have since been forgotten. The collective unconscious contains materials that have never been conscious. An archetype is an inherited format for those materials and the most basic constituent of the collective unconscious. Jung believed that these images of instincts are present in all societies and that they are represented on an individual level by dreams and on a cultural level by myths. This chapter argues that an examination of the Great Mother archetype is most appropriate to a discussion of Schlafly's discourse. Through her use of the Great Mother imagery, Schlafly attains heroic stature, presenting herself as the champion of the American homemaker. Her heroism derives from her ability to portray the typical American woman as a superior being responsible for creating and maintaining the moral fabric of America, for civilizing American men, and for insuring the continuation of the race through her ability to give birth to and rear children.

The "hero archetype" is an inherited pattern existing in both males and females that allows heroic human qualities to take shape and contact external reality through actions. The Great Mother is also an archetype existing in both males and females that allows an inherited pattern to contact external reality through actions. By invoking the Great Mother archetype in her media messages, Schlafly creates a heroine for some audiences and, simultaneously, a feminine villain for others.

A number of scholars have utilized mythic and/or archetypal methodologies. These studies suggest that myth supports a culture's ideology (Balthrop, 1984); that it provides transcendence during crises (Burkholder, 1988; Dionisopolous, 1988; Rushing, 1985); that it mediates conflicts and reifies culture (Breen & Corcoran, 1982); and that it presents cultural oppositions such as individualism versus community (Rushing, 1983), the wilderness versus civilization (Parks, 1974), the materialistic versus the moralistic aspects of the American Dream (Fisher, 1973; Frentz & Rushing, 1978; Rushing & Frentz, 1978; Solomon, 1983a, 1983b), and patriarchy versus matriarchy (Rushing, 1989). It also defines a society (Rushing, 1986a), engenders public action (Bass & Cherwitz, 1978; Bennett & Edelman, 1985), supplies rituals and symbols which promote understanding of the culture (Bennett, 1980; Newman, 1975; Payne, 1989), aids in distorting information (Balthrop, 1984; Bennett & Edelman, 1985); and provides archetypal heroes and villains (Fisher, 1982; Gibson, 1983; Hankins, 1983; King, 1974; Makay & Gonzalez, 1987; Mechling, 1979; Riukas, 1967; Rushing, 1985, 1986b, 1989). Myth can reveal the dystopian aspects of the culture (Rushing & Frentz, 1989). The media play a mythopoetic role in creating heroes (Dionisopolous, 1988), and a movie version of an archetypal-quest story can help Americans find their cultural identities (Payne, 1989).

These studies, then, support Campbell's assertions that myths function to support the moral order and Jung's claim that archetypes exist in all cultures. It is apparent, therefore, that analyzing archetypes and myths can add depth to the study of heroes by illustrating not only why heroes act as they do, but also by explaining why audiences respond as they do. Whether a person is perceived as a hero is frequently a function of how she or he is portrayed by the media (Dionisopolous, 1988).

Particularly important to this study are the analyses of ERA rhetoric by Solomon (1978, 1979), Kruse (1983), and Foss (1979). Solomon (1978) examined the negative images of ERA supporters generated by ERA opponents. Later, Solomon (1979) studied Schlafly's *The Power of the Positive Woman* (1977) as a mythic quest and found that opponents of ERA were united around a positive theme, whereas ERA supporters had no such theme to unite them. Solomon identified the most important element of the myth as its psychological impact on women, especially its ability to provide women "with an opportunity both to share their inner confusions and doubts and to purge them effectively by scapegoating the feminists" (1979, p. 271). As Solomon explained, much of the power of Schlafly's rhetoric derives from her espousal of traditional values and roles, which Schlafly herself claims to represent and which many women would see themselves as representing. Thus, Schlafly and her supporters achieve status by accepting the traditional role of woman as wife and mother and, through these roles, as savior of society (Solomon, 1979, p. 272). Solomon suggested that the power of Schlafly's mythic rhetoric may reside in its underlying component—the archetype.

Kruse (1983) further explored Solomon's conclusions and found that ERA supporters could not invent a mythic rhetoric to combat the mythic rhetoric of their opponents. Foss (1979) utilized a fantasy theme analysis to discover the world views of ERA supporters and opponents and noted that ERA opponents saw themselves as more feminine than their counterparts and as fulfilling a sacred duty by maintaining their homes and families. Although these studies reflect the power of Schlafly's mythic vision for her followers, they do not adequately explain how Schlafly became such a heroine (or villain, depending on one's point of view). This chapter traces Schlafly's rhetoric from her Stop ERA discourse through her rhetoric on women soldiers in the Persian Gulf. The Great Mother archetype has been activated by Schlafly, making her a heroine to some audiences and a villain to others, while her use of a variety of media disperses her message to various levels of society to gain support for her mythic vision.

Schlafly's argument against ERA, which appeared in many editions of the *Phyllis Schlafly Report*, is summarized in *The Power of the Positive Woman* (1977), hereafter referred to as *The Positive Woman*. (It is important to note that the themes developed in this book are the same ones developed in contemporary rhetoric by Schlafly. This is illustrated by her comment to reporters in February 1991 [Huckshorn, 1991] that having young military mothers fighting in the Persian Gulf is scandalous.) By portraying ERA as destructive to the home and consequently threatening to women, Schlafly directed women on how to attain and utilize power, noting that her knowledge comes from living and loving life as a woman (Schlafly, 1977, p. 8). Because *The Positive Woman* emphasized the importance of the home, and specifically the role of the woman in the home, an archetypal analysis of Schlafly's discourse, based on the feminine archetype of the Great Mother, seems particularly appropriate. Underlying and informing the rhetoric of Phyllis Schlafly is a symbolic image of women; this image may be understood as the archetype of the Great Mother. The Great Mother archetype is symbolically manifested throughout Schlafly's discourse and significantly contributes to the mythic vision evoked by the rhetoric. The symbolism of the Great Mother provides the motive Schlafly needs to engage the audience in the culture myth she espouses and through which she becomes a cultural heroine.

METHODOLOGY

To study Schlafly's rhetoric, one needs a methodology appropriate to its unusual characteristics. The most unusual characteristic of Schlafly's rhetoric is that the same sentence or phrase can be wildly endorsed by one audience and wildly denounced by another. This dichotomy suggested that a methodology based on two such polar extremes could be highly explanatory. The Great Mother archetype neatly fits this requirement. Like other archetypes, it has existed in Eastern and Western societies throughout time. Because the dominant archetype invoked by Schlafly's rhetoric is the Great Mother, and because of the archetype's suitability for explaining the dichotomous effects of Schlafly's rhetoric, it alone will be investigated here. The Great Mother is examined in terms of Erich Neumann's concept. Neumann (1963, p. 4) described the Great Mother as consisting of a structure (elementary and transformative characters), sense material (perceptions), symbols, and the emotional-dynamic component (psychic energy). Although each of these components separately contributes to the Great Mother, the components are intertwined. Hence, they must be examined in relation to each other.

The structure is usually visualized as a great circle containing the elementary and transformative characters of the archetype, each of which has both a positive and a negative aspect. The circle also contains the sense material or perceptions through which the symbols reach the unconscious. These symbols then produce affects [sic] that release energy, which is in turn directed by one of the characters of the archtype's structure. It is the release of this energy that engenders the myth. Thus, a rhetor who invokes an archetype activates a myth, which then reaches out to the audience in much the same way that the archetype reached out to the rhetor's consciousness. The difference is that the archetype engenders identification with the rhetor and consequent participation in the mythic vision.

Essential to understanding the Great Mother as an archetype is its conceptualization as round. It may be visualized more graphically as a sphere containing the elementary and transformative characters operating as a kind of double helix. Containment is the primary function of the elementary character. Containment can be either positive or negative; that is, containment can (a) nourish and promote health, or (b) stifle development. Growth is the primary function of the transformative character. The transformative character is more complex and represents the Great Mother's ability to convert matter or spirit into a higher form. It too has both a positive and a negative aspect. Positively it transforms basic matter to mature matter or an undeveloped spiritual state to a highly developed one. Negatively it perverts growth by encouraging the development of the animal nature of humanity or by fostering the spiritual degeneration of the person. (This is most often seen in sexual symbolism, as, for example, Circe's activities in mythology.)

The interplay of the two characters as they respond to sense material or symbols generates the dynamic energy that gives the Great Mother her power. Thus, within the sphere of the Great Mother archetype, there is constant motion as each character seeks dominance over the person. Indications of the Great Mother in Schlafly's rhetoric appear in the form of sense material and symbols that activate psychic energy within the auditor.

Sensory perceptions allow the audience to obtain information through synthesizing images into logic (Neumann, 1963, p. 4). Neumann (p. 8) further explained that the function of the material component of the symbol is to activate consciousness so that it can comprehend sensory images. Images, then, guide the auditor or reader to the development of ideas. Similarly, analytical psychologist Edward C. Whitmont (1969, pp. 27-28) identified the image as the basis of mental functions and noted that images allow one to separate oneself from the psychic reaction to a safe distance. The Great Mother archetype, then, is invoked when one of its characters is activated by a particular image or symbol. The dynamic energy that is released enables that character to contact consciousness through the image. In other words, the archetype serves the function of synthesizing sense material through its elementary or transformative character and utilizing this energy to create an image which the unconscious can relate to appropriately. In this way, the archetype functions on a personal level and, representationally, on a cultural level, as when a powerful archetype forms the basis for a culture myth. Schlafly's discourse is dominated by images of the Great Mother, which provide the basis of a mythic vision exemplifying Campbell's functions of myth: validation of the moral order, harmony with oneself, harmony with the universe, and understanding of contemporary conditions.

SCHLAFLY AS HEROINE

Campbell (1968a) identified the hero's mission as one of separation from society, initiation through trials and temptations, and return to society with the ability to grant boons to people and thereby improve the social order. Solomon

(1979) traced Schlafly's rhetoric through the stages of just such a romantic quest and illustrated how Schlafly's advice provided guidance to women who felt at odds with the new society recommended by women's liberationists. Similarly, Rushing (1985) noted that when society is in danger of disintegrating, a transcendent myth with a cultural hero may emerge to bring wholeness to the society. Schlafly's activities against ERA may easily be seen as creating just such a transcendent myth.

Campbell (1968a, p. 388) further delineated the mission of the modern hero as that of "questing to bring to light again the lost Atlantis of the co-ordinated soul." A hero for our society, then, would offer resolution of conflict, supply an image of security, and provide the follower with the ability to function in harmony with society. This is, in fact, what Schlafly attempts to do by espousing traditional values and roles for women and men. In espousing these roles she invokes both the positive elementary and the positive transformative characters of the Great Mother archetype.

Positive Elementary Character

Neumann stated (1963, p. 5) that it is through the symbol that psychic energy is activated, causing the elementary or transformative character to direct the individual. Some common symbols Neumann lists as representative of the Great Mother elementary character include *house, bed, table, kitchen,* and *breast*. These symbols, he contended, clearly represent the containing aspect of the elementary character. References to them activate the preserving, nourishing character of the auditor. The importance of this aspect of the Great Mother to Schlafly's discourse can be illustrated with a few representative examples of this "vessel motif" from *The Positive Woman*.

Early in *The Positive Woman*, Schlafly (1977, p. 11) stated: "The Positive woman will never travel the dead-end road. It is self-evident to the Positive Woman that the female body with its baby-producing organs was not designed by a conspiracy of men but by the Divine Architect of the human race." Later she noted: "[C]aring for a baby serves the natural maternal need of a woman. Although not nearly so total as the baby's need, the woman's need is nonetheless real" (p. 17). Schlafly here related the birthing function of women to the natural order, but she also identified it as an important need women have. Her discourse often activates the positive elementary character (containing, nurturing) of the archetype in a very straightforward manner. "Another feature of the woman's natural role is the obvious fact that women can breast-feed babies and men cannot" (p. 11).

Schlafly also frequently pointed out the exclusivity of women and the value of holding onto what they have as when she stated, "Many talented women may want to have some of both careers, but home remains primary in their scale of values, while a business or professional career is secondary" (p. 44). Schlafly enhanced this idea by assigning status to the homemaker, whom she described in this way: "A housewife is a home executive: planning, organizing, leading, coordinating, and controlling" (p. 56). She further asserted: "One of the most valuable property rights that a wife has under present laws is the right to be provided with a home in accord with her husband's means" (p. 99).

Schlafly emphasized the consequences of rejecting her values in the following quotation: "The flight from the home is a flight from yourself, from responsibility, from the nature of women, in pursuit of false hopes and fading illusions" (p. 60). This can be contrasted with her picture of the joy of being a woman:

> In the business or professional world, a man or a woman may labor for years, or even decades, to acquire the satisfaction of accomplishment. A mother reaps that reward within months of her labor when she proudly shows off her healthy and happy baby. She can have the satisfaction of doing her job well—and being recognized for it. (1977, p. 57)

Although Schlafly's language appeals to her audience on this very basic, sense level, it also functions symbolically. More recently, Schlafly (1985b, p. 27) extended the scope of this nurturing aspect of the Great Mother to politics. She organized women of the Eagle Forum to send to Nicaraguan Contras kits containing toothpaste, insect repellent, and hard candy. The caring, nurturing aspect of the Great Mother is activated as women who feel they have little or no political power may experience some power by offering direct help to the victimized. They simultaneously participate in a salvation myth and become heroines themselves. Cuthbertson (1975, p. 156) argued that:

> Myth-custodians are power-holders. Myth establishes moral consensus in the community and is accompanied by social sanctions. Myth stabilizes the relationship of the individual to politics by restricting the purely organic state with the element of moral purposiveness.

The positive elementary character of the archetype, then, is activated when sense material or symbols create a need for nurturing, to which the person then responds. For Schlafly and her supporters, the nurturing is directed outward. Schlafly's invocation of the Great Mother through sense material and symbols of the transformative character is also skillful.

Positive Transformative Character

Schlafly frequently has advised her audience that the positive woman is responsible for keeping America good. She developed this idea by asserting, "The Positive Woman must be a patriot and a defender of our Judeo-Christian civilization. She, therefore, must support the legislation, the legislators, and the funding necessary to defend the values of home and country against attack by aggressors who respect neither" (1977, p. 219). Similarly, "Time and again,

God has given women the mission to save their country" (p. 220). In an address in Stow, OH, Schlafly (1990b) identified this as her mission, which she attempts to accomplish by talking to and training people. Schlafly invoked the archetype in both its characters. Just as having children and preserving home and country represent the elementary, containing character of the archetype, keeping America good represents the transformative character's ability to elevate the quality of humanity.

The transformative character, as Neumann (1963, p. 29) pointed out, is often contained within the elementary character. Thus, symbols such as *home, food,* or *kitchen* can represent both characters. Other transformative symbols Neumann (pp. 227-234) identified are *fabric, weaving, spinning,* and *cooking.* These symbols can be used to represent either physical or spiritual transformation. Schlafly frequently has alluded to the spiritual character. "It is on its women that a civilization depends—on the inspiration they provide, on the moral fabric they weave, on the parameters of behavior they tolerate, and on the new generation that they breathe life into and educate" (1977, p. 177). Similarly, "A Positive Woman cannot defeat a man in a wrestling or boxing match, but she can motivate him, inspire him, encourage him, teach him, restrain him, reward him, and have power over him that he can never achieve over her with all his muscle" (p. 17). She also stated: "The Positive Woman accepts her responsibility to spin the fabric of civilization, to mend its tears, and to reinforce its seams. No matter how wide or how narrow is the scope of her influences, this is her task" (p. 177).

The letter Schlafly and Paul Weyrich (1987, pp. 16-17) sent to members of the committee sponsoring a banquet to honor Surgeon General C. Everett Koop further illustrates how the positive transformative character can be used to serve society. Schlafly and Weyrich asked the committee to reevaluate their support of Koop because of his advocacy of condom use to prevent AIDS, his refusal to sponsor legislation against people infected with AIDS, and his desire to include information on AIDS in public school curricula. The letter stated: "Dr. Koop's proposals for stopping AIDS represent the homosexuals' views, not those of the pro-family movement" (p. 17). Schlafly and Weyrich took an action that could be interpreted as redeeming society.

These examples drawn from sense material not only illustrate the presence of the archetype, but also reveal the close relationship of this component to the Great Mother's structure. The integration of these elements, together with the integration of symbols and psychic energy, provide Schlafly with a pattern of mental activity that she can invoke through the Great Mother.

Once she has invoked the Great Mother, she provides women with what Campbell identified as an orientation to society (one of the basic components of a cultural myth stated earlier). The Great Mother functions as a legitimizer for the actions Schlafly advocates. Furthermore, Schlafly instructs women on how to use their power to preserve and transform America. In *The*

Positive Woman (1977, pp. 224-235) she advised positive women to maintain their rights to be full-time homemakers, to accept their responsibility to care for their preschool children, to take an interest in schools so that voluntary prayer can be permitted and textbooks extolling the traditional roles of men and women can be used, to discriminate against those who choose "immoral" lifestyles, and to grant the right to life of the fetus.

Further legitimization of the positive woman is offered in Schlafly's assertion (1977, p. 87) that women who follow these precepts will find a particular and secure place in society, which their husbands will be compelled to provide. That there are still women who fear the loss of traditional values was evident when an audience member in Stow, OH, revealed to Schlafly that she was teaching her children to read using a 19th-century text (Schlafly, 1990b). She asked Schlafly to recommend something more modern that would still uphold traditional values, to which Schlafly replied that anything written before 1955 would probably be good.

It is evident that Schlafly's discourse is very much concerned with maintaining the established social order and keeping women in harmony with it. Invocation of an archetype which is a part of the basic structure of that social order is an effective method of promoting social cohesion. Schlafly portrays the ideal woman as nurturing and caring for those she loves, protecting and keeping them safe, and thus insuring the continuation of the race. By doing this woman is protected. In this way the positive woman incorporates the positive aspects of both the elementary and transformative characters of the Great Mother. By maintaining this quest Schlafly becomes a cultural heroine for many traditional women and men.

Negative Elementary Character

Yet, Schlafly also activates the negative aspects of the Great Mother. A key concept here is the idea of holding onto (containing) that which one already has rather than allowing it to grow toward independence. Utilizing the Hatch amendment as a basis, the Eagle Forum, which Schlafly founded, launched an attack to preserve the traditional public education curricula. Under the headline "Please Excuse Johnny From Death Ed.," the May 1985 *Harper's* printed a letter from the Eagle Forum which parents could copy and send to their school boards. The letter itemized unacceptable subject matter for classroom discussions and textbooks. Among prohibited items were information on death, alcohol and drug abuse, human sexuality, interpersonal relationships, guided fantasy strategies, and organic evolution. The implication was that all of these items are harmful to the child's development and should be discussed only within the home, if they are discussed at all.

Later Schlafly devoted the February 1990 issue of *The Phyllis Schlafly Report* to an attack on current school curricula. Entitled "A 'New Age' for Privacy-Invading Psychiatry," the newsletter characterized New Age philosophy as a cult and advised parents to "be on guard against school courses about 'stress,' 'self-esteem,' or 'human potential.' They usually contain elements which are unconstitutional because they use religious practices or psychological/psychiatric treatment" (Schlafly, 1990a, p. 4).

Arguing against the comparable worth bill, Schlafly stated: "Statistical proof that the aim of comparable worth is to reduce the relative earning power of blue-collar men is abundantly available in the job evaluations commissioned and approved by the comparable worth advocates" (1986, p. 12).

On an intellectual level it is evident that Schlafly is making inappropriate use of statistical evidence. However, the ordinary person may well accept the "proof" and react with fear to the loss of power and value which she claims exists. Schlafly thus becomes a heroine not only for women who stay at home to care for their children, but also for the men who want them to do so. Her appeal to traditional men and women was intensified when she stated: "One of the techniques by which this [discriminating against the traditional family] is done is the devaluing of the physical and working-condition factors so important in blue-collar jobs" (p. 13).

In recent years Schlafly has utilized the same archetypal motivation when arguing against the act for better child care services. Preying on the fears women have of losing control of their own children, Schlafly (1988, p. 275) stated: "This bill is the first step of the long-range plan of the child developmentalists who want to bring all children under Government control." In arguing for a tax credit for all families with children, she characterized the child care bill as being beneficial to women who choose to work and harmful to those who wish to stay at home and care for their families. She characterized governmentally approved day care centers as "custodial warehousing" (p. 273) and the bill itself as a means of establishing "a Federal Administrator of Baby Sitting" (p. 275). She intensified the psychic energy thus evoked through activation of the negative elementary character when she stated that this bill favors working mothers and discriminates against those who stay at home, thus encouraging traditional women to hold on to what they have.

A second way to invoke the negative elementary character is through the negative orientation directed toward women's liberationists and liberals who, she implies, refuse to nurture humanity. Upon them she projects many of the evils of society. According to Schlafly, "By its very nature, therefore, the women's liberation movement precipitates a series of conflict situations—in the legislatures, in the courts, in the schools, in industry—with man targeted as the enemy" (1977, p. 10).

In this case women's liberationists are identified as eroding the social order and thereby endangering traditional women, their husbands, and their progeny. Schlafly further evoked energy, which she then channeled, by utilizing the negative transformative character. If the positive transformative character promotes spiritual and physical growth, the negative transformative character promotes spiritual and physical destruction.

Negative Transformative Character

Schlafly chiefly used the negative transformative character by references to unwarranted personal freedom and sexual license, as represented by women's liberationists. She portrayed them as modern-day Circes deserving of whatever punishment they receive:

> The women's liberationists and their dupes who try to tell each other that the sexual drive of men and women is really the same, and that it is only societal restraints that inhibit women from an equal desire, and equal enjoyment, and an equal freedom from the consequences, are doomed to frustration forever. It just isn't so, and pretending cannot make it so. The differences are not a woman's weakness but her strength. (1977, p. 15)

By contrast, positive women who do not endorse this lifestyle retain power and respect. Schlafly also described the negative results of ignoring the positive aspects of the transformative character:

> The most tragic effect of ERA would thus fall on the woman who has been a good wife and homemaker for decades, and who can now be turned out to pasture with impunity because a new, militant breed of women's liberationist has come along to alter the terms of her marriage contract. (p. 100)

Schlafly drew this conclusion for her audience:

> Thus, if ERA is ratified, the aged and faithful mother, who has made her family her lifetime career, would have no legal right to be supported in her senior years. She would have to take any menial job she could get or go on welfare if her husband and children did not voluntarily choose to support her. (p. 101)

Because the sexual liberation of modern society is often closely linked to women's liberation, and because the National Organization of Women has a contingent of lesbians, many women are suspicious of the women's liberation movement. Women also fear the loss of youth and, implicitly, sexuality. Both of these fears are negative and anxiety-producing. Thus, whereas the actual arguments Schlafly presents function on an overt level, working on a more affective, covert level are numerous invocations of the negative elementary and transformative characters of the Great Mother.

By framing her views within mythic structure Schlafly offers women an explanation of the existing order and of the forces opposing it. She orients women by utilizing elementary and transformative aspects of their Great Mother archetypes to accept or reject public issues. By so doing she pulls them into the circle of security, safety, and continuity which American society has known for 200 years.

Schlafly's discourse utilizes the Great Mother archetype to relate women to reality and to the mysteries of the universe. By identifying and espousing a traditional place for women in the universe, Schlafly promotes social cohesion, which contributes to the establishment of the cultural myth. In this instance it also makes the role of the traditional woman very attractive because it advocates activities that traditional women can engage in without a change in their lifestyles. Conventional wisdom suggests that stability is easier for most people to deal with than change; therefore, the person advocating tradition and stability becomes a kind of cultural heroine. As Schlafly also directs attention to the evils of modern society and to the need for someone to save mankind, she becomes a kind of savior to many people. Through following her example, they too can become saviors of society.

The implications of this for society may now be summarized: If women accept traditional values (as illustrated by the positive elements of the two characters of the Great Mother), society will survive. Conversely, if women reject these elements and adopt instead the values of liberals, women's liberationists, and ERA supporters (as illustrated by the negative aspects of the two characters of the Great Mother), society will degenerate. Schlafly, then, becomes a cultural heroine through her advocacy of the established order. While rearing her own family she has battled the women's liberationists, endured the hardship of separating herself from her family as she campaigned for what she believes in, and made the world safe for the American homemaker and breadwinner by contributing to the defeat of legislation she believes to be designed to change the moral order of things. More importantly, she invites her audience to also become heroes and heroines—within their families if not within the larger community.

Schlafly's symbolic images call forth both positive and negative aspects of each of the Great Mother's characters and enable her to identify with her audiences through invocation of the archetype. The symbols are important for another reason; they directly activate the emotional-dynamic, energy producing component of the archetype.

The energy generated by these symbols, when guided by the negative aspects of the Great Mother, produces self-absorption, imbalance, anxiety, and discontent—common conditions in modern society, especially as traditional male and female roles are questioned. Schlafly provides a target for this energy: Negative emotions can be focused on the destruction of women's liberation, on the defeat of the ERA and the federal child care bill, and on the local control of textbook selection. On the other hand, if a woman responds to the energy drive by procreating, remaining safe and secure at home, or by attempting to transform her mate into the best person he can become, she attains power without risking the destruction of society. Either way, Schlafly's values are endorsed.

The energy generated by positive symbols of the Great Mother, however, is directed by Schlafly not only to enable women to achieve harmony with society and the universe, but also within themselves. According to Jungian psychologist Ulanov, "To see one's problem in a larger human context frees the energy drive of the archetype to flow into new channels. Then the ego can relate to the energy in new ways" (1971, p. 31).

Schlafly activates this energy through symbolic invocations of the Great Mother, which adjure positive women to attain and retain power. Power is identified as arising (a) from their ability to birth and nurture children, and (b) from their ability to transform men spiritually. Schlafly further suggests that this transformative power can be extended to include the community, the nation, and, by implication, the universe. In Schlafly's discourse both characters of the Great Mother are invoked to generate power to be used to contain and control, and above all, to preserve traditional society. Her use of the Great Mother facilitates the accomplishment of this fourth function of a cultural myth—harmony with the universe.

Given the foregoing, it is understandable that Schlafly has become a heroine to many people. The next question to be considered is how and why Schlafly is seen as a villain by a great many people. Earlier I described how Schlafly utilizes sense material and symbols to invoke emotional-dynamic (psychic) energy which she uses to achieve rhetorical ends. I explained how the archetype works outside logic on an emotional level. It is this strong emotional and illogical appeal embedded in conventional reasoning that so incenses Schlafly's critics. Although Schlafly utilizes appeals to the value of a traditional lifestyle, her own life reflects many paradoxes.

SCHLAFLY AS VILLAIN

Despite its title, much of *The Positive Woman* is devoted to the rather negative task of pointing out what is wrong with women's liberationists and others who support the ERA and all those who deemphasize the role of motherhood. As a heroine, Schlafly exemplifies the positive transformative character in terms of her self-development—author, attorney, political activist—and in caring for those who are dependent on this character. At the same time she has identified as immoral and uncaring those who wish to pursue similar goals, thereby activating the energy of the negative elementary character in the form of the shadow. Whitmont (1969) suggested that the shadow provides us with an enemy or someone to blame: "In other words, to the extent that I have to be right and good, *he, she,* or *they* become the carriers of all the evil which I fail to acknowledge within myself" (p. 160). Schlafly stated that "If man is targeted as the enemy, and the ultimate goal of women's liberation is independence from men and the avoidance of pregnancy and its consequences, then lesbianism is logically the highest form in the ritual of women's liberation" (1977, pp. 10-11).

As one of the goals of the women's movement was nurture and development of the self, many women responded to the movement through their positive transformative Great Mother characters. Schlafly's equating this self-nurture and self-development with lesbianism produced a strong energy drive which needed direction in order to dissipate. As Kruse (1983) noted, women's movement rhetors did not provide a positive mythic orientation. Nor did they take into account how frequently and effectively Schlafly did provide one.

According to Ulanov (1971, p. 179), devoting too much time to the physical nurturing of others and neglecting to develop oneself can be harmful:

> Instead of developing a hunch or momentary "conception" into a new psychological attitude or creative contribution, a woman may project the totality of her capacity to realize conception into actual pregnancy and motherhood. She will then live out her sexual penetration, impregnation, and nurturing only on a literal plane. Then her femininity is lived outwardly, not inwardly, lived only physically, not at all psychologically.

Those women who were seeking to develop conceptions intellectually instead of physically represented a threat to Schlafly and her followers, which she dealt with by activating the negative elementary character of her followers. Schlafly affirmed: "Motherhood provides children who, in their turn, will honor you in your declining years" (1977, p. 57). This containing aspect of the Great Mother's elementary character is emphasized throughout *The Positive Woman* as Schlafly lists things women are entitled to, simply because they are women with the capacity for motherhood. Through these descriptions Schlafly offers her followers a heroic image on which they can model their lives. The image does not require change or growth of the individual, but rather endorsement of traditional values and the security of a revered place in society. Those who saw society as in dire need of a change, those who wished to grow and develop intellectually, and those who rejected child bearing as the best way of finding fulfillment became the targets of Schlafly's rhetoric.

An example from *The Positive Woman* perhaps best illustrates why many women view Schlafly as a villain. Schlafly (1977, pp. 30-31) utilized Dr. Benjamin Spock as an example of the evil results of using gender-inclusive language. According to Schlafly, changing the pronoun references in his classic work on child care from "he" to "he or she" to eliminate sexist language so liberated Dr. Spock that he left his wife of 48 years for another woman. Pointing out that the logic of this claim is questionable somehow lacks the force of the emotional reaction it engenders in many traditional women. Conversely, women who are seeking to nurture their intellectual development (the positive transformative character of the Great Mother) are insulted by such leaps in logic.

The dangers of accepting only one's physical role were noted by Schlafly when she stated that a wife can force her husband to support her by buying what she needs on credit and letting the store collect from her husband as best it can (1977, p. 96). Ethical considerations aside, many women would find this approach likely to keep the woman in a subjugated state. Again, this conflicts with the positive transformative character many women were utilizing to change their lifestyles. Furthermore, feminists found themselves under attack as not being *natural* women because of their desire to develop intellectually and to compete with men rather than just to nurture men.

A number of contradictions in Schlafly's own life provide a basis on which to perceive her as a villain. Despite her protestations of the overwhelming benefits of being a housewife, Schlafly has pursued many interests outside her home: earning a law degree, running for president of the National Federation of Republican Women, becoming a lecturer and columnist, and founding the Eagle Forum, to name a few. Many liberated women interpret these activities as illustrating exactly the kind of life that they want all women to be able to have. Consequently, they criticize Schlafly as recommending a lifestyle that she does not exemplify. Typical charges leveled against her are that she espouses a lifestyle available only to middle-class women and that she abandons less fortunate women.

In a 1983 *Newsweek* article Schlafly stated: "I'm a housewife, but not *just* a housewife" (p. 10). Implicit in this statement is the idea that there is something wrong with being "just a housewife." Later, Schlafly (1986, p. 12) began her testimony to the House subcommittee on comparable worth as follows: "My name is Phyllis Schlafly, president of Eagle Forum, a national pro-family organization. I am a lawyer, writer, and homemaker." One might have expected the founder of a pro-life movement espousing the value of homemaking to identify herself first as a homemaker and later as a professional woman. This is, after all, the woman who said she spent the first six weeks after each child was born devoting herself totally to nursing the child and nurturing herself (Block, 1984). For her, it would seem, motherhood is not always the first priority.

Schlafly's amazing energy and her ability to create and utilize positive symbols (Foss, 1979; Kruse, 1983; Solomon, 1979), combined with her absolute assurance that she is right, make her a formidable rhetorical opponent and one easy to attack. She is just as willing to create negative symbols as positive ones, but is careful to use them against those she has identified as evil or untrustworthy because of their lack of traditional values. Her willingness to recruit ordinary women to carry her message, utilizing strategies requiring traditional skills, further contributes to her heroine status for her followers and exasperates her opponents. For example, Schlafly developed a number of strategies to convince legislators to vote against the ERA, such as taking legislators home-baked bread labeled "from the breadmakers to the breadwinners" (Felsenthal, 1981, p. 260). This use of labels and slogans is, of course, much easier to understand than an argument, which frustrates Schlafly's opponents.

Perhaps more to the point, Schlafly's rhetoric openly extols womanhood and makes women feel good about themselves as they are, whereas much of the rhetoric surrounding the ERA and the women's movement criticizes women who stay at home and accept the traditional role. Her verbal messages, coupled with the covert message of the Great Mother archetype, leave those opposing Schlafly with the task of debunking a cultural heroine engaged in a mythic quest.

CONCLUSION

Schlafly is ever alert to news events that present a contemporary focus for her perennial messages, as her comments on the Persian Gulf War and on textbook revision illustrate. She has used the media by conducting her own radio show, establishing the Eagle Forum and publishing its newsletter, writing for prestigious journals such as *Policy Review* and *Congressional Digest*, testifying before congressional committees, and appearing on television. She continues to travel and give lectures, and a report in the local newspaper usually follows such a lecture. Therefore, she is able to keep herself known to the public years after the defeat of the ERA when many of its proponents are forgotten.

The Great Mother archetype permeates Phyllis Schlafly's rhetoric, thereby endowing it with motive power. By drawing forth the vast emotional-dynamic resources of the Great Mother present in all people, Schlafly invokes audience participation in her mythic vision of harmony, happiness, and fulfillment. Like the structure of the Great Mother, the mythic vision orders the participant's life by offering a contained, secure, and spiritually rewarding life. Because the appeals of the Great Mother function on an unconscious level, participants in the mythic vision are largely unaware of them and consequently vulnerable to their dynamic energy. Therefore, the mythic vision Schlafly has created through utilization of the Great Mother archetype is indeed a powerful one, virtually invincible to logical, argumentative refutation. The fact that Schlafly has utilized newspapers, magazines, books, speeches, radio, and television programs to carry her message to the public insured that she would become a celebrity. Yet, it is her use of the Great Mother archetype that has made her a heroine to some and a villain to others.

12

Rhetorical Devices for Hero Making: Charles Lindbergh and John F. Kennedy

Carol Wilkie Wallace
University of Scranton

❏ *Wallace argues that we still have heroes, but the rhetoric of hero has changed. The author juxtaposes the monomythic rites of passage narrative set forth by Joseph Campbell in* The Hero with a Thousand Faces, *with Kenneth Burke's dramatistic narrative of symbolic salvation through victimage. The author asserts that both rhetorical rituals help order society: one rhetorical ritual does this through identification with the hero who redeems us via great deeds, and the other through a hero who saves us by becoming a victim. She then describes how the mass media created a hero in Charles Lindbergh by making his transatlantic flight into the symbolic rite of passage ending in a great deed. This example is followed by an analysis of the media's role in establishing John Kennedy as a hero through victimage. She concludes that, although we still need heroes, the media have changed and society has changed so that now we are left with the hero as scapegoat.*

For many decades we have failed to acknowledge our heroes until after they are dead. Cynics may say "the only good hero is a dead hero," and indeed, we live in an age of cynicism. But more careful critics would notice that our modern heroes have all been something else—they have all been unifying symbolic leaders who strove in life to bring people together, but who accomplished this only by their deaths. Martin Luther King, Jr. toiled mightily for racial unity and achieved some measure of it when he was assassinated. The whole nation sat in universal shock and sorrow at the assassinations of John and Robert Kennedy, even though, moments before the fatal bullets struck, that same nation was divided in its support of these two men.

RHETORICAL DEVICES FOR HERO MAKING 169

This chapter contends that heroes do still walk the earth, but in a new disguise. The rhetoric for hero making, as embodied in the mass media, has changed. Whereas heroes of old (and as recently as the first decades of this century) were created through a ritual retelling of their great deeds as a survival of the ancient rites of passage, our modern media's rhetoric, instead, describes the hero's journey to greatness in terms of the age-old scapegoat ritual. Today we perceive heroes when they have been sacrificed for the greater good of society, whereas formerly we celebrated live heroes and held them up as role models during their very human life spans. I examine the rhetoric of the heroism of Charles Lindbergh and John F. Kennedy and demonstrate how Lindbergh fulfilled the monomythic hero described in the theory of Joseph Campbell, whereas Kennedy fulfilled the scapegoat hero described in the theory of Kenneth Burke.

In *The Hero With A Thousand Faces*, Joseph Campbell (1968a) reveals that a hero, both in myth and modern times, is really an archetype whose story has common elements across time and culture. All these heroes have survived some form of the rites of passage—a rite of separation, initiation, and return. This rhetoric seems to have been used in media retellings of heroic deeds right up through the Camelot comparisons of the early Kennedy era.

More modern media stories of heroes, however, seem to be concerned with Kenneth Burke's theory of identification. In Burke's theory identification is achieved "in the enactment of guilt redeemed through victimage, in social order expressed through hierarchy" (Duncan, 1969, p. 356). In other words, some symbolic leader of the social order must symbolically die in order to unite and redeem a guilt-ridden (disordered) people. In Campbell's theory the hero goes through a process of symbolic death and rebirth in order to return to earth bringing boons to mankind. In Burke's (1961) theory order is achieved either suicidally, by mortification, or homicidally, by the slaying of scapegoats more or less clearly identified with the traits of human personality (Burke, 1961). A *scapegoat* is a person who represents the social order; the people within that order seek to achieve salvation and unity by symbolically laying communal sin and guilt on the scapegoat. The scapegoat is then removed from that society, either by death or banishment; in leaving the society he or she also carries away the sins that have been laid on him or her. The scapegoat ritual unites people in a common belief that virtue will triumph over evil, that society has been purified from guilt, and that the perfect social order can be maintained.

In short, the old-style American hero created by a media retelling of his or her deed as a reenactment of the rites of passage unified Americans by showing us our better selves, embodying our values and the ideals to which we aspire. The new heroes—the Kings and Kennedys—unite us in guilt. We make of their martyrdoms a symbol of our culpability for social disorder and renew our idealism in pledges to try to right those social evils.

Both theorists provide a model for ordering society through identification. In Campbell's theory we achieve social order by identifying with a symbolic hero who will redeem our sins and social ills by great deeds. In

Burke's rhetoric we seek to achieve order through a symbolic victim who will redeem our sins (thus restoring our virtue) through victimage.

In ancient times hero and victim were often one and the same. According to Frazer in *The Golden Bough* (1913), unity and salvation were achieved by making the hero (the king, the god) the victim (scapegoat). By killing the god or king (the equivalent of today's hero), our primitive ancestors felt that they were purging themselves of their sins and restoring order to society. The king was, after all, a perfect symbol of social order, as he had authority over that order and great power in creating whatever state of order existed.

The scapegoat is an *elected* unifying device. He or she must be a chosen representative of the people. Society's redeemer, whether hero or scapegoat, must both be selected by that society and perceived as a symbol of that society. Without that recognition, neither hero nor scapegoat has any function.

The last two people generally acknowledged as great American heroes are Charles Lindbergh and John F. Kennedy (even though Kennedy's heroism has now been debunked). Lindbergh's flight, as written in the contemporary press, was a modern reenactment of the rites of passage detailed in Campbell. Kennedy's brief reign as hero was told in the rhetoric of Burke's theory of identification through victimage.

THE ACKNOWLEDGMENT OF HEROES

In order to redeem us, heroes must be recognized, indeed publicized. Unless the public is aware of a person, his or her deeds, and embodied values, the hero serves no function. If acknowledged, the hero can bring together groups of people in common agreement that this hero stands for the values that they, as a people, admire and aspire to. Once the noble deeds are accomplished, the hero moves on to a more important function: serving as a symbol of unification. In acclaiming heroes, people reaffirm the public mores of society. They are unified through vicarious identification with symbolic leaders who appear to be what they aspire to or feel.

Throughout history, heroes have been a functional element of society, not only because of their deeds which benefit that society, but because of the way in which societies have used their heroes. The function of the hero, in Klapp's words, is to "transport an audience vicariously out of everyday roles into a new kind of reality that has laws and patterns different from the ordinary social structure" (1964, p. 24). The hero, in this role, is a mass symbol, "a vehicle for the imaginings of thousands" who is transformed "by imputation and abstraction more and more into what people want of a public figure" (1962, p. 14). For most people a hero has a compensatory function, "consoling people as it were for a recognized lack of what a hero represents" (p. ix). The hero either makes up for what people haven't got or becomes a symbol of "what people think they ought to be but aren't really trying to be" (p. 139).

MASS MEDIA AS HERO MAKERS

To be acclaimed by society and to become vital unifying forces, heroes must first reach the attention of that society. In days of yore, *society* referred to a multitude of diverse and widely separated communities, each with their own customs and culture. Before the invention of the automobile, communities were widely separated from each other but close within its specific population. Heroes capable of unifying a single community could be recognized by their physical presence, and their deeds could be publicized by word of mouth. Today, however, with the Concorde making Europe a morning's journey and with instantaneous satellite transmission making the world a global village, the country is, in one sense, a single large community. This large, geographically and demographically vast collective must rely on the mass media to learn about heroes noble enough to act as symbolic leaders.

The mass media are everywhere. Thousands of magazines, newspapers, cable, and broadcast stations compete to bring us news of people and places around the world. Every day we hear about new people who have done good, if not great, deeds. Astronauts take off for the moon, young teens risk their lives to save people from burning buildings, laboratory scientists choose to forego lucrative private practices in order to find a cure for cancer. A former first lady courageously reveals her battle with drugs and alcohol, then establishes a clinic to help others benefit from her experience. Catholic priests defy Church and public opinion to counsel and console AIDS victims. All of these people embody values that we claim to cherish; all show courage and nobility. Yet, despite the vast menu of role models proffered daily by the media, heroism seems to belong to history. No individual today seems capable of symbolizing this vast collective, of standing up to the scrutiny of the media, or of standing out amid the proliferation of information which bombards us each day.

A question we might well ask is: What has changed since the days when we had real heroes and acknowledged them freely?

Certainly we have the phenomenon of the global village. Society is vast now, and it is hard to conceive of any entity, no matter how noble, capable of unifying such an amorphous mass of individuals. At the same time, society is more homogeneous than ever before; despite our differences, the national character of the media has brought the same images, ideas, and ideals to all of us, whether in New York City or in Podunk Junction, IA. America is made up of many disparate publics, each with its own definitions of such commonly revered God-words as freedom, democracy, and equality.

The world is smaller and its publics larger and more diverse than ever before. The media are greater and more powerful and prolific than ever before. This has two major effects on heroism. First, the media offer an overabundance of role models. The public hesitates, confused by so many choices, until most candidates' brief spark fizzles and finally fades. There are hundreds more waiting for their 10 minutes of fame. Second, those who do capture popular attention risk being trivialized by the same media that brought them to our attention. Should we appear to hail someone as a hero, we can also be sure that person will appear on the covers of *Time* and *People*, perhaps be featured on *Lifestyles of the Rich and Famous*, and sooner or later turn up on *The Tonight Show*. How heroic can someone seem when we know what they eat for breakfast, how popular or unpopular they were in school, and what their current love life is like? Yet the media, fueled by the public's apparently insatiable appetite for information on those we choose to honor, will persist in feeding us more tidbits, until we know not just the hero's shining qualities, but also his or her warts. Can heroes have warts and still be heroes, or does that make them too much like us? One fears, along with Daniel Boorstin, that the media will always trivialize even the most genuinely heroic of heroes into a mere celebrity (1962, p. 62).

Yet, even in the days before television, when there were fewer radio stations, fewer magazines, and no cable at all, the media gave the same intense scrutiny to its heroes, albeit in a different manner. The hero or villain of any hour in the 1920s press was likely to command not columns, but *pages* of type, and not seconds but *hours* of air time. As historian Frederick Lewis Allen describes it, "the national mind had become . . . an instrument upon which few men could play. And these men were learning . . . to play upon it in a new way—to concentrate upon *one tune at a time* (Allen, 1931, pp. 188-89).

THE LAST AMERICAN HERO—RITES OF PASSAGE

When Charles Lindbergh made his legendary solo flight to Paris, he was the tune on which, linked by a network of press associations, syndications, and radio, the national mind focused. Writer Fitzhugh Green estimated that, as a result of Lindbergh's flight, newspapers used more than 25,000 extra tons of newsprint in May and June 1927 (Mosley, 1976). For weeks his deed occupied most of the first three pages of the *New York Times*, as well as many miscellaneous items scattered throughout the inside pages (Wilkie, 1978). We learned that his mother was a biology teacher in Detroit, that the family had changed its name from Manson when they immigrated to the United States, that his nickname was Lucky Lindy, and that he took five ham sandwiches along on the flight. We learned that he arrived in Paris with no passport and luggage and that the first thing he did when arriving at the American embassy was ask for a glass of milk.

After the flight, the public was treated to stories about "What 'Dear Lindy' Found in His Mailbag" (1927) and "The Joyous Game of Sending Gifts to Lindy" (1929). By the time his engagement to Ann Morrow was announced, the press hounded Lindbergh so incessantly that he was forced into hiding, prompting the *New York World* to bewail the fact that "to the tabloids, a Grade-A celebrity is a man who has lost all ordinary human rights" (Literary Digest, 1929, p. 41).

During this torrent of triviality, the public even learned that, back in his days as a barnstorming pilot, Lindbergh played a trick on his roommate, putting kerosene in his water jug and watching him drink it in unfeigned glee (New York Times, May 20, 1927). Such a cruel joke would appear to do more than merely trivialize a would-be hero, but its impact was lost in the welter of romantic details scattered throughout the paper.

By the time Lindbergh's infant son was kidnapped, press coverage was so intense that critic Heywood Broun commented that "it took far fewer columns to tell readers that America had gone to war" ("Child murder as entertainment," 1935, p. 642).

Clearly Charles Lindbergh was subjected to media scrutiny as intense as that of the modern-day celebrity. Yet, he is often cited as the "last American hero." If so many tons of newsprint and so many hours (days, literally) of air time did not trivialize him out of existence, as they do the celebrities of today, then something else was at work in the telling of the Lindbergh saga that is not at work today. That "something else" I contend was the rhetoric employed by the press in the telling of the tale. The rhetoric necessary for hero creation is a mythic one. Both the heroes of yesteryear and those of contemporary America are eventually viewed in mythic terms, but the rhetoric employed in creating those stories, the myths that are retold, have changed. Myth is the necessary element in hero creation because myths, as Campbell has pointed out, as Jung has claimed, and as Rank, Raglan, and as many other theorists have demonstrated, are universal and archetypal—common to all mankind. From culture to culture, throughout time and space, the same myths appear and reappear. Whether we understand their meaning or not, they appear to have a universal significance which unites all humankind, despite our individual differences (Campbell, 1964; Frazer,1913; Jung, 1959, 1964; Klapp, 1956; McGee, 1975; Neumann, 1973; Rank, 1964). To be a symbolic leader, to unify the public as a representative of desirable values, the hero must be perceived as having mythic elements in his or her make-up.

Charles Lindbergh had this mythic quality, at least as his flight was presented in the 1920s' press. Journalistic style in the 1920s was much more florid than it is today. Reporters did not hesitate to wax poetic, even in a straight news story. Lindbergh was repeatedly referred to as a young Galahad or an Icarus who did not fall. Even the staid *New York Times* told Lindbergh's story as a reenactment of the ancient rites of passage described by Campbell in his book *Hero With A Thousand Faces* (Wilkie, 1978).

The rites of passage are called a *monomyth* because they are essentially one myth, told through time in endless variation. They involve three elements—separation, in which the hero "ventures forth from the world of common day into a region of supernatural wonder"; initiation, in which the hero encounters fabulous forces and wins a decisive victory; and return, in which "the hero comes back from this mysterious adventure with the power to bestow boons upon his fellow man" (Campbell, 1968a, p. 30). These rites are similar to Burke's theory of identification in that they involve a form of rebirth, in which the hero is, in the process of initiation, swallowed "into the belly of the whale," a symbolic dying of the old way of life, and emerges transformed, a hero with redemptive powers. In the process all of his or her more human traits are sloughed off, refined out of existence, until nothing but the symbolic remains. The following is the story of Lindbergh's flight as it emerged from press coverage.

CHARLES LINDBERGH: THE RITES OF PASSAGE

The ritual account of Lindbergh's flight may not be found in any single account in the press, but emerges from the coverage as a whole. F. Scott Fitzgerald described the social context into which Lindbergh emerged as hero; significantly, he describes it through the top news stories of the day.

> In the United States, prosperity was unprecedented. The revolt against Victorian puritanism was in full swing. People were releasing their inhibitions, consuming large quantities of illegal liquor in the process. The press of the nation had altered its concept of what was fit to print. Lurid and explicit stories of blood and sex became daily fare. Scandalous murder cases followed one upon the other. The Stillman case, Fatty Arbuckle, Loeb and Leopold, the Hall-Mills murder case, the Snyder-Gray case. There was old '"Daddy" Browning and his adolescent sweetheart, Peaches. On the bloody side, there were the exploits of criminals, racketeers, and gangsters, whom the Prohibition Amendment had produced and enriched. (Fitzgerald, 1956, p. 21)

Thus, Fitzgerald describes the background against which Lindbergh flew, a scene for which every adult who had either voted for Prohibition and ignored it or who followed the law but turned a blind eye to those who violated it shared some guilt. It is fitting that Fitzgerald gives us the newspapers' method of presenting social order—for it is media that form public perception of the way in which the world is ordered. And in this order, in 1927, Charles Lindbergh heard the call to adventure for a redeeming hero—the first portion of the separation rite.

Separation

> The first stage of the mythological journey—which we have designated as the call to adventure—signifies that destiny had called to the hero and transferred his spiritual center of gravity from within the pale of society to a zone unknown. The fateful region of both treasure and danger may be variously represented as a distant land, a forest, a kingdom underground, beneath the waves or above the sky but it is always a place of strangely fluid and polymorphous beings, unimaginable torments, superhuman deeds and impossible delight. (Campbell, 1968a, p. 58)

At this stage the hero must capture the attention of the population he will eventually redeem. If his deed, at this point, is made significant enough to the populace so that they can vicariously participate in the adventure and as such identify with the hero, he becomes the people's chosen symbolic leader, and thus their chosen redeemer.

Lindbergh's response to the call to adventure came when the press announced that he, a complete unknown, would compete against such acknowledged aviation greats as Clarence Chamberlin and Admiral Byrd in the race to make a nonstop New York to Paris flight. The zone in which he would fly was, to the reader on the ground, a "region above the sky." It was definitely an unknown region because the *New York Times* reported that Lindbergh proposed to fly the shortest route, the Great Circle route, so that he would not even be traveling the shipping route where ocean traffic could take note of his progress and come to his aid should disaster strike. Finally, judging from the many published predictions of disaster, the deed Lindbergh proposed was considered superhuman. Aviation experts were quoted as saying that Lindbergh could not possibly go so long without sleep, that he would be overcome with fatigue and lose control of his plane. Unlike the other competitors, he was flying solo and so would have no co-pilot to rescue him or help keep him awake. When headlines reported that Lindbergh had only 2 hours of sleep in 60 before he reached Paris, the deed seemed even more bold (New York Times, May 20, 1927). Add to this that six lives had already been lost in the race to cross the Atlantic, and the necessary tension, the color, and drama that gripped the people and comprised the call to adventure is established.

The second step in the separation portion of the rites is an encounter with supernatural aid, usually in the form of a protective figure. This figure represents a benign, protecting power of destiny. "Having responded to his own call, and continuing to respond courageously as the consequences unfold, the hero finds the forces of the unconscious at his side. Mother Nature herself supports this mighty task" (Campbell, 1968a, p. 69). Not only must the hero offer himself to the people as a redeemer, but he must be approved by the forces of nature.

Mother Nature was the most apparent figure of protection in the Lindbergh story, and the media were not reluctant to point out the almost supernatural way the elements behaved. "For even as Lindbergh prepared his plane, the fog that had choked his path to Newfoundland rolled back. Even the sun came out as he started, and it seemed that the fates which deal with brave men's lives were smiling at the youth who had defied them" ("Report conditions favor Lindbergh," 1927, p. 3).

The hero must next cross the first threshold, beyond which is "darkness, the unknown and danger" (Campbell, 1968a, p. 77). This is the point of no return. According to the *Times*, Lindbergh crossed this threshold early in his flight—at the takeoff point. The field was muddy, the engine damp and running below full power.

> The boy had to make it or die. It did not seem possible that he could get off. And then, at the last moment, the plane began to go up. Those on the field felt as if Lindbergh, with his great courage, were lifting it from the ground, making it take the air. Defeat and death stared him in the face, and he gazed at it unafraid. ("Lindbergh speeds across North Atlantic," 1927, p. 1)

The plane rose uncertainly and barely cleared several fences and obstructions in its path. "It could barely be seen to rise, and men watched with anguish in their gaze" ("Lindbergh speeds across North Atlantic," 1927, p. 1). Lindbergh made the takeoff successfully, and the first threshold had been crossed.

> The idea that the passage of the magical threshold is a transit into a sphere of rebirth is symbolized in the worldwide womb image of the belly of the whale. The hero, instead of conquering or conciliating the power of the threshold, is swallowed into the unknown and would appear to have died. (Campbell, 1968a, p. 90)

Burke points out that the ideal redeemer is the perfect victim and finds that Christ is the perfect victim (Burke, 1961, p. 217). People, however, create their own god victims, creating cleansing rites for them that make them too good for this world, and so of the very highest value. In Burke's theory, then, the vessel is made worthy in order to become the perfect victim. In the monomyth he is made worthy in order to pass from the realm of ordinary man into that of heroic redeemer. Each involves symbolic death and rebirth. Lindbergh appeared to experience this symbolic death when he was lost to sight over the ocean.

Because Lindbergh chose to fly the Great Circle route, there was a long stretch of time when he was out of sight of land or of passing ships who could report his whereabouts. The nation's people showed great anxiety during this period, besieging the *New York Times* office with phone calls demanding reassurance (New York Times May 22, 1927, p. 1). During this time Lindbergh seemed to have been swallowed up into the unknown, and many feared that he had died. Before Lindbergh's crossing, French aviators Nungesser and Coli attempted to fly from Paris to New York. They died trying. The French aviators' flight had been reported as nearing success, with erroneous reports claiming that they had been sighted over Boston. Instead, the two fliers were swallowed into the belly of the whale and did not return. When Lindbergh was in flight the public was almost afraid to believe reports that the plane had been sighted, for fear they would prove equally false.

With this temporary disappearance over the ocean, Lindbergh had completed the separation element of the rites of passage and moved into initiation. This stage involves the road of trials.

Initiation

> Once having traversed the threshold, the hero moves in a dream landscape of curiously fluid, ambiguous forms, where he must survive a succession of trials. . . . The hero is covertly aided by the amities and secret agents of the supernatural keeper he met before his entrance into the region. Or it may be that he discovers for the first time that there is a benign power everywhere supporting him in his superhuman passage. (Campbell, 1968a, p. 97)

In the road of trials the hero is voluntarily submitting himself to mortification in order to emerge purified and return to earth with redemptive powers. Although I very much doubt that Lindbergh saw redemption as the inevitable outcome of his flight, the press chose to portray it that way, just as they portrayed the flight as a road of trials with supernatural aid.

The dream landscape which Campbell mentions is symbolic of the womb from which the hero must fight his way in order to be reborn. Flight, too, is essentially motion through fluid, ambiguous cloud forms. Lindbergh described these in his firsthand newspaper account of the flight (New York Times, May 22, 1927 p. 1). In addition, he had to deal with the fluid wind, which, traveling as he was with no radio or navigational equipment (a voluntary choice), threatened to blow him off course should he nod off to sleep. The public perceived sleep to be the greatest trial Lindbergh would face, whereas newspapers warned that "even to close his eyes might have meant death" (p. 1).

Lindbergh's newspaper account of the flight tells of another, more dramatic trial. "I had sleet and snow for over one thousand miles. Sometimes it was too high to fly over and sometimes it was too low to fly under, so I just had to go through it as best I could" (p. 1).

Significantly, we have to rely on Lindbergh's account of the road of trials. The press and public knew only that he was lost in the belly of the whale at the time he was fighting his way out of a womb of ice and sleet. But, as another article in the same issue reports, the benign powers of fate came to his aid, and a miracle was performed for him. "Suddenly, the wind changed, and all cleared, and new wind that blew him to Ireland sprang up" (New York Times, May 22, 1927).

Return

Having fought his trials bravely, the hero is now symbolically aided by benign fate to a symbolic rebirth. He may now return to earth to redeem the waiting public.

> If the hero in his triumph wins the blessings of the goddess or god and is then commissioned to return to the world with some elixir for the restoration of society, the final stage of this adventure is supported by all the powers of this supernatural patron (Campbell, 1968a, p. 193).

Lindbergh won the blessing of the gods and received aid from his supernatural patron, Mother Nature. According to *The New York Times*, "The gods who rule the weather heard that Lindbergh was coming. The rains stopped and the clouds parted over Paris" (New York Times, May 22, 1927 p. 3). The hero's journey and symbolic rebirth are now complete. He has flown with destiny and emerged triumphant from the belly of the whale. However, the myth continues. The hero must face another, more enduring problem. He must now, after a satisfying vision of fulfillment, accept once again "the passage of joys and sorrows, banalities and noisy obscenities of life" (Campbell, 1968a, p. 218). This must be the ultimate, although probably unanticipated, mortification. He must return and accept this because the ultimate purpose of the ritual journey is the redemption of mankind.

Lindbergh described his reception at the Paris airfield as "the most dangerous part of the trip" (James, 1927b, p. 2). *New York Times* reporters wrote that "it seemed that the excited French men and women would overwhelm the frail figure which was being carried on the shoulders of half a dozen men. Then followed an almost cruel rush to get near the airman" (New York Times, May 22, 1927, p. 1). This rush to touch is reminiscent of the crowds who rushed to touch the hem of the garment of medieval saints or to collect relics—an attempt on the part of many to share in, to identify with, the life of the one. Lindbergh had been purified through the ideal of flight and mortification. The crowds hoped to purify themselves vicariously through touch. Such frenzy must have been a cruel shock after hours of solitary flight. Lindbergh catapulted into the joys, sorrows, and noisy obscenities of life with barely a moment for reflection, whereas people immediately began to assess the great good that they felt resulted from the impetuous flight. President Domergue of France wired that Lindbergh "brought the air union of two great lands with his deed" ("Report conditions", 1927, p. 3). U.S. Ambassador to Paris Herrick told reporters that Lindbergh was "a boon to national amity" ("Lindbergh does it," 1927, p. 1). The *New York Times* claimed that "what he had done for Franco-American relations cannot be reckoned" (p. 1). This boon, too, arose to redeem a highly polluted situation.

> Part of the explanation for Lindbergh's impact upon the public lies in the character of the times. The United States, previously a debtor nation, had emerged from the World War as creditor of the world. Gold flowed from the coffers of Europe in a steady stream to the United States treasury. While the United States prospered, Europe suffered. Large sections of the population were reduced to bare subsistence, and some, as in Russia and Germany, to starvation. Americans were hated and blamed. . . . Any mention of the war debt to the United States raised European temperatures by several degrees. By 1927, the economic conditions of Europe had somewhat improved, but hatred of Americans remained. Bad manners, condescension, misconduct—fancied or real—on the part of any American tourist was spotlighted and labeled typically American. (Morris & Smith, 1953, p. 261)

When Lindbergh landed, all this hatred was flung aside. His integrity deeply impressed the French, who hailed him as a "real American" ("Lindbergh does it," 1927). Thus, Lindbergh's symbolic death and rebirth redeemed the nation in the eyes of Europe. Other comments in the *New York Times* showed that some people felt that he had redeemed mankind. Reverend Russell Bowie's sermon was quoted. "We see manifested that indomitable heroism that . . . has made possible the progress of the human race toward mastery of the world" ("Lindbergh does it," 1927, p. 1). University of Wisconsin president Glenn Frank cabled: "You have proved that the modern world has become an intimate neighborhood, in which we no longer dare tolerate narrow nationalisms that delay the moral and intellectual reunion of mankind" (p. 1). More importantly, according to one reporter he gave the people of America a new sense of self-worth, a new ideal of purity of spirit:

> We shouted ourselves hoarse. Not because one man had flown across the Atlantic. Not even because he was an American. But because he was as clean in character as he was strong and fine in body; because he put ethics above any desire for wealth; because he was as modest as he was courageous—and because—as we know now beyond any shadow of a doubt—these are the things which we honor most in life. To have shown us this is the biggest thing Lindbergh has done. (Mullet, 1963, p. 82)

All that Lindbergh had really done was to fly the ocean in a plane to win a $25,000 prize—certainly a courageous stunt, considering the state of aviation in 1927, but not an act which would cement foreign relations, show hope for the intellectual reunion of mankind, and reveal and reinforce the best facets of American character—unless one looks to the rhetoric of the press, which gave Lindbergh to the public not as a stuntman, but as a savior whom the gods themselves had blessed.

The public reacted accordingly. The *New York Times* reported that it received 100,000 phone calls for news while Lindbergh was in flight ("10,000 telephone inquiries," 1927, p. 3). An estimated 150,000 people turned out at Le Bourget airfield when he landed, where "ranks of policemen and steel fences went down in a mad rush as irresistible as the tides of the ocean" (James, 1927a, p. 1). Theaters halted while audiences cheered. One writer described the road to Paris as "the answer to that old conundrum of what happens when an irresistible force meets an immovable body" (New York Times May 29, 1927, p. 4). In addition, Lindbergh received 3,500,000 letters, 14,000 postal parcels containing gifts, and 100,000 telegrams and cablegrams between May 21, when he landed in Paris, and June 17, when he arrived back in St. Louis.

This praise turned to deification as people rushed to get some souvenir of the new American hero. Everywhere he went, crowds rushed to touch him, to collect Lindbergh souvenirs, stripping his plane of everything that could be taken off, including cutting pieces of fabric from the wings. The week after his flight the *New York Times* reported that people actually made grabs at Lindbergh's hair in order to have some relic of their revered hero (New York Times, May 28, 1927, p. 2).

Lindbergh did not remain an untarnished hero forever. When he left America for England after the execution of Bruno Richard Hauptmann, the alleged killer of his infant son, many took this as a betrayal of his role as a great American hero. When he accepted a medal from the Nazi leader Hermann Goering, his fall from grace was complete. Yet, even today, Charles Lindbergh is revered as a hero for that one shining moment when he survived the rites of passage and emerged as a symbol of all that America wished to revere.

In the old regime, then, a hero was someone recognized for his deeds and for the noble virtues that these deeds and his character appeared to personify. Apparently, the deed does not have to accomplish much, as long as it is presented to the public as something larger than life and mythic in character. When media accounts are cast in mythic language they become archetypal, striking a responsive chord in the public. The public responds vigorously, attempting to share vicariously in the deed and to associate themselves with all of the good that the hero and his deed represent. In this way, they feel uplifted, better than they normally seem to be. This uplifting reaffirms the basic good of the social order.

JOHN F. KENNEDY: THE SCAPEGOAT HERO

There is another hero myth more prevalent today: the hero as scapegoat. The scapegoat's function is also to affirm the basic good of the social order, but rather than performing heroic deeds to redeem that order, the scapegoat achieves redemption by becoming a symbolic vessel to hold the sins of society and carry them away through symbolic or actual death. The scapegoat, too, is mythic, a ritual that has been performed since before recorded history. The second man whom this century has, at least at one time, hailed as hero, more rightfully fits the role of scapegoat.

John F. Kennedy, once the nominee for successor to Lindbergh, no longer seems to be regarded as a hero by many. When the usually prosaic modern press threw caution to the winds and wrote mythically of Kennedy, they could point to no single great deed, no rite of passage other than his heroism on PT-109 as an act which might rival Lindbergh's flight. War heroism, unfortunately, is all too commonplace.

For the brief shining moments of Kennedy's Camelot, the press made him a symbol of romance, glamour, sophistication, youth, and progress. He was young and handsome, had a beautiful family, and appeared to have a fairy tale marriage. He was rich, and the life he and Jackie led seemed glamorous and sophisticated. Lest that remove him too far from the common person, he was also a Catholic—the first and so far only Catholic to be elected president—a reminder of the old log cabin myth that assures us that we are a democracy in which every individual has the potential to reach the Oval office. All of these qualities seemed to be important in the early 1960s as we emerged from the staid and complacent Eisenhower years.

Kennedy himself furthered his mythic image with his symbol of the new frontier which would help us to pass the torch of liberty from generation to generation.

The Camelot symbolism is archetypal, as demonstrated by Rank in his *Myth of the Birth of the Hero* (cited 1964, in note 17); the new frontier as a symbol was uniquely American. The mythic Kennedys, our new Arthur and his Guinevere, seemed to be a symbol of the new, prosperous America, with its twin values of success and security.

The public was treated to the same wealth of detail about Kennedy as the press gave it when hailing Lindbergh. We learned the Kennedy family history, why Jack needed a special rocking chair in the Oval office, how Jackie was redecorating the White House, how many points JFK scored in the family touch football games, and how many people got pushed into the pool at family parties.

For many, this had the inevitable trivializing effect—the effect that had not worked with Lindbergh, but does with so many modern candidates for hero. There are several possible reasons for this. First of all, Kennedy was not elected to even his temporary position as hero because of a single deed, but because of his position, his image, and what was inevitably described in the press as his charisma. Any heroism attributed to him was constantly measured against the ups and downs of his day to day image as president.

Second, his position as a publicly recognized potential hero came through normal channels—he was elected to the presidency in the same way as acknowledged greats such as Roosevelt and Lincoln, but also as ill-remembered chief executives such as Warren G. Harding, Andrew Johnson, and Herbert Hoover. His elevation to fame was not the result of any ritual of passage and certainly no guarantee of symbolic leadership.

Third, although in fact Kennedy had survived a form of the rites of passage during his PT-109 days, an adventure avidly read by schoolboys and loyal democrats in books, and familiar to any reader of the daily press, this rite was too long ago and far away. Hindsight reminded the doubtful that even a Lindbergh could fall from grace; there was no reason to accept Kennedy as anything more than a duly elected leader until he had proven otherwise.

Following the debacle of the Bay of Pigs, and with increasing national unrest over the civil rights movement, the legend of Camelot grew somewhat tarnished. One might say with confidence that Kennedy did not unify the nation; rather his policies divided it. Only his character, the qualities for which he stood in the abstract, received anything like national admiration—and many may have failed to recognized these during Kennedy's brief reign. Then came Dallas.

Almost everyone today who was alive then can remember what they were doing when they heard the news that Kennedy had been shot. The news had a profound, unifying impact. Businesses closed, schools dismissed early, and the nation spent the next few days glued to their television sets, united in shock and disbelief.

Kennedy's death, rather than any action in his lifetime, was the act that reminded us of those values that we held most dear. The assassin's bullet reminded us of how insecure we were and how inadequate the trappings of wealth and power were in the face of enmity.

Death has a way of purifying away the trivial details that bothered us during someone's lifetime. Suddenly the pool parties and extravagances—even the Bay of Pigs—were forgotten; we remembered instead the young leader who refused to ride in a bubble-top car because he wanted to be close to his people. He had paid dearly for that democratic impulse. We remembered the young and devoted family man. We recalled with grief the bright promise of the new frontier, now shattered and bloody. We remembered, through Kennedy's death, all that we cherished in life: family, freedom, security, and relative prosperity. We remembered them and held them to us more tightly because suddenly we feared for them.

John F. Kennedy became a hero by becoming a scapegoat. In life he was unable to unite his countrymen; but in death he achieved at least a temporary unity, a temporary examination of consciences and of values. In death he seemed to carry away our transgressions to bring us together as a kinder, gentler nation. For awhile, at least, we felt cleansed and redeemed by his death.

The press, in deifying Kennedy after his assassination, shaped a new rhetoric for heroes—the scapegoat king. This is the Burkean rhetoric for hero making—one that does not require symbolic death and rebirth, but only symbolic (or actual) death.

The hero is a vicarious vehicle for maintaining social order. The scapegoat, too, is a symbolic leader. Burke's candidate for restoration of order is ideally a perfectly fitting victim who symbolizes humanity to such a degree that his sacrificial deed vicariously carries away all the guilt within the social order. The victim need not be the sort used in ancient Greece—criminals condemned to death but kept imprisoned until redemption was needed—nor need they be the idealized perfect enemy that Hitler made of the Jews. The ideal redeemer, as Burke states, was Christ, a figure ideally symbolic of purity, good, and social order (Burke, 1961, p. 219). Kennedy was both hero and victim, immortalized by an assassin's bullet. The death of the hero scapegoat unified the American people for a time and gave them a common enemy and a common sense of what one should most revere. As numerous articles and editorials pointed out, Americans were united by Kennedy's death by a common sense of guilt because we had lost sight to those ideals and turned a blind eye to the unrest in America.

HIERARCHY

Unrest, civil disobedience—all of the problems that America struggled with at the time of Kennedy's death—pose a threat to the established social order. They pollute the hierarchy. In Burke's theory of identification, the first element in the election of a scapegoat is that of disorder or pollution. The idea of order dialectically implies the negative—disorder. Following this disorder comes guilt, which Burke claims is intrinsic in the idea of order (Burke, 1961, p. 224). "Guilt intrinsic to social order is not actual, but analogous to original sin" (p. 192). In other words, all people in a society share a common guilt because of disorder, such as the common guilt shared by all through original sin. Whether actually guilty or merely consenting members of the social order, all citizens need redemption from this guilt. Burke claims that this is the atmosphere that compels emergence of a villain symbolic of that pollution.

> In order, implying the possibility of disorder, implies the possible act of disobedience, then there must be an agent so endowed, or so minded, that such an act is possible to him—and the motives for such an act must eventually somehow be referred to as the scene out of which he arose and which thus somehow contains the principles that in their way make a "bad" act possible. (p. 192)

If a polluted social context can create an agent of disorder, so it can bring an agent symbolic of desired order. This agent becomes the hero redeemer. In the case of the social order of 1963, the agent of disorder was Kennedy's assassin, Lee Harvey Oswald. Oswald's act was the catalyst for the great examination of conscience that followed. He was also a perfect symbol of social disorder. This occurred not because he in fact actually stood for all the evils rampant in society, but because so much suspicion and mystery surrounded him that people were able to believe whatever best suited them about his character. If we feared Communism, he was an agent of the Communists, but if we feared the lone stranger threatening us from a dark alley, there were plenty ready to claim that Oswald's was a warped and twisted soul that acted alone. His act, at any rate, created for us his equal and opposite number; in death he made of Kennedy a symbol of desired order—a hero redeemer.

Burke points out that the ideal redeemer is the perfect victim and finds that Christ is the perfect victim. People, however, create their own god victims, creating cleansing rites for them that make them too good for this world, and so of the very highest value.

In Burke's theory of identification social cohesion is achieved through sacrifice, which requires a victim. The victim may be a god; he must also be a goat to carry away the common guilt. In Campbell's theory cohesion is produced by the symbolic death and rebirth of a hero who redeems the people and creates unity by virtue of his deeds. Although he must undergo trials to reach his end, he is not a victim, but rather the victor.

Over the past two decades in America it seems that when any one member of society threatens to become too potent a member of the hierarchy he has been a victim, not of symbolic killing, but of an actual assassination or assassination attempt. This killing is a symptom of severe social disorder, but it does have the effect of uniting society.

This unification effect is apparent in the reaction to the death of

Kennedy. Member after member of Congress gave his eulogy; many pointed out that they had disagreed with his policies and politics, but not with the ideals for which he stood. Countless newspaper stories were read into the Congressional record, many giving evidence of the lack of unity which existed in the country—the struggles for civil rights, the war against crime in our own streets.

Guilt

Guilt is the great unifier, not because we revel in the shared dishonor, but because we instinctively work together to rid ourselves of guilt. We seek to slough it off, to find some common vessel to contain that guilt, well away from our own lives and consciousness.

Kennedy was not universally admired while president. In at least one classroom of 10-year-olds, the announcement of his death was greeted not with tears, but with applause (*Memorial Addresses*, 1964). Much of the legislation that Kennedy failed to get passed concerned civil rights and equal rights—the basic tenets of democracy. Riots and demonstrations abounded, and the nation was divided. Many normally staid citizens turned blind eyes to the abuses of law and order committed over this issue, for suddenly the placidity of everyone's lives was threatened. Faced with busing and integration, our own intolerance and hypocrisy became all too apparent. The first seeds of guilt began to sprout.

Usually we live our lives in blissful ignorance of the common guilt that we bear for polluting the social order. But when some great act occurs that causes us to focus on that disorder, we begin to examine our consciences. Or, if we are too self-centered to do that, the nation's press will be glad to do it for us.

No sooner had Kennedy been pronounced dead then the press rushed to lay the blame for his death at the feet of the American people. Not that we had pulled the trigger, but because we had allowed the social order to become so polluted that such a deed was possible. The Carson City (Nevada) *Appeal* was relatively gentle in pointing out that "as the people of the Nation pray for the soul of our beloved late President. . .they also search their own soul for an answer to the insanity and sickness that allowed such a tragedy to strike" (*Memorial Addresses*, 1964, p. 60). The Nevada State *Journal* was much more direct.

> Yes, we are morally responsible for the act of assignation, either by ignoring or condoning the turmoil within our nation today built on a foundation of violence.
>
> In the larger sense the guilt for the death of John Kennedy must rest with each of us who has permitted the spread of ignorance and fanaticism, who has joined in the flabby spirit of complacency or who has permitted the preacher of hatred to appear respectable.
>
> Yes, all who assume the self-righteous attitude that labels those who disagree with us traitors and dolts prepared the way for the vile deed that snuffed out the life of our President. (p. 61)

The Benson (North Carolina) *Review* charged that "the fact that it happened points up the venom of hatred that exists among us—class, racial, ethnic and even religious. It speaks of the sickness of our national morality" (p. 81). The *New York Times* commented that "America wept tonight, not alone for its dead young President, but for itself. The grief was general, for somehow the worst in America had prevailed over the best" (p. 220). The Paintsville (Kentucky) *Herald* suggested that "our citizens turn guiltily to look within their own hearts for the causes" (p. 274).

Perhaps John F. Kennedy was not universally mourned, but the deed that took his life left us all uneasy and unable to deny the disorder that threatened America. Charged with guilt for this disorder, we began to look for ways to redeem ourselves.

PURIFICATION AND REDEMPTION

Because Kennedy's death was the catalyst for this national call for redemption, it was fitting that he became the instrument of purification. As quick as the media was to point out the national guilt, it was equally quick to tell us that Kennedy's death should not be in vain, that it should become, for us, a redemptive act. Many pointed out that, in itself, the national examination of conscience was enough to bring some national good from Kennedy's death. Many also hoped that Kennedy's death would remind us of those high ideals to which we aspired.

The Buffalo (New York) *Courier-Express* begged, "May God grant that life will not go on as before, that each of us will be able to view the death of John Fitzgerald Kennedy as a symbol of the futility and corrosiveness of hatred" (*Memorial Addresses*, 1964, p. 821). The Manchester (Connecticut) Evening *Herald* called for the nation to "try to cleanse ourselves, not merely by condemning and punishment but by trying to make some of our own living a tribute to the memory of this clean, gallant, humor-gifted, excellence-dedicated young leader" (p. 607). Editorial after editorial called for us to learn the lesson of humanity and brotherhood from this tragedy and from the character of the martyred hero.

> From the ashes of our sorrow and anger rises a new sense of dedication. The lawlessness of the jungle will not prevail. . . . This Nation draws together in shock and adversity. The democratic ideal is as tough as it is rational. It will grow stronger until mankind learns that the world cannot live without it. (p. 507)

So, from tragedy grew a sense of at least temporary unity, of hope, and of resolution to do better. This is scapegoat redemption, and it leaves an unpleasant taste in the mouths of the redeemed. The nation unified under a Lindbergh looks only up to idealism and greatness. The nation unified under the scapegoat king feels purged, but the lingering sense of guilt, of vulnerability, the memory of personal failure, remains.

As with the monomythic hero we refine the scapegoat king's traits until he becomes a pure and perfect vessel for bearing away guilt. In tributes and editorials we choose to honor the qualities of greatness in the chosen vessel and to ignore imperfections. When our rhetoric has made the scapegoat worthy and symbolic of our best hopes, we use his or her death as a catalyst for recalling lost virtues and failed ideals.

THE SCAPEGOAT OR THE MONOMYTH?

The monomythic hero gave us something to strive for; the scapegoat hero gives us only a sense of failure. The sad way of the world is for us to fail, for there to be division and discord. As this inevitably occurs, despite our resolutions at the ritual sacrifice of the hero scapegoat, we feel, once again, a sense of guilt. There may be some purification for Americans in the ritual eulogizing of the martyred hero, but there can be no real redemption unless humankind itself changes drastically, unless societal problems find some magic and instantaneous solutions, and unless our ethic of upward mobility finds some way to function without stepping on the toes of others.

When Lindbergh fell from grace, we felt betrayed; we felt as though some vital part of the American fabric had been irreparably damaged. When the inevitable historical muckraking gave lie to the image of Kennedy the virtuous, we seemed more apt to breathe a sigh of relief. We no longer had to confront our sense of failure in trying to live up to some pure and seemingly unattainable ideal.

Perhaps it was Lindbergh's fall from grace, his seeming betrayal of the principles of democracy, that made us wary of heroes. In part, too, the ruthless scrutiny and trivializing perpetrated by the media (in response to our own endless appetite for details about those to whom we look up) has made hero worship difficult. Only in death do we forgive our moral, spiritual, and political leaders their human foibles and allow their virtues to shine forth unimpeded.

The media play a large part in this. It is true that the heroes of the early part of the century were subjected to barrages of reporters and gallons of ink, but the average reader had few media from which to choose. Confronted with hundreds of column inches in the daily paper, it was easy for people to exercise selective attention and perception and to find only those aspects of the coverage that enhanced their perception of the hero. In the case of Lindbergh there were stories that detracted from his pure, shining image, but they were buried on inside pages and seemed not to have been perceived as meaningful.

In the case of Kennedy these human foibles were seen and discussed daily, but were dismissed at his tragic death in favor of eulogistic praise and adulation. Partially we were more capable of perception because today we have more choice about the amount and type of information to which we expose ourselves. If the preponderance of coverage in our hometown press is favorable, but we somehow doubt the latest candidate for hero, we have only to check the newsstand for some other publication with views that match our own.

Journalistic style has also changed, favoring a terse factual style over the lyricism allowed in the press of the 1920s. True, we have feature stories and columns that may occasionally indulge in mythic hyperbole, but the possibility of straight news stories couched in mythic terms, as was the coverage of Lindbergh's flight, seems remote. Today's lead story may talk of heroic deeds, but in prosaic language that obscures the mythic potential of the heroic act. Mundane details will always dilute our portraits of potential heroes.

Only in eulogies are the modern media apt to resort to the rapturous rhetoric that characterized the coverage of Lindbergh's great deeds. The eulogy is an almost unfailing source of heroic rhetoric, especially when it follows the death of a person of national prominence—but only if the character of the deceased in some way exemplifies basic American ideals. Our emphasis, then, has shifted from act to actor, to character rather than great deeds. We no longer have some specific act, some symbolic story, to remind us of those values that we supposedly hold dear.

Society has changed. As a people we are better informed, but we are also victims of an information explosion. To focus our attention on a single individual long enough to recognize that person's extraordinary qualities is difficult.

People, however, have not really changed. We will always give pause when we learn of the death of a leader; we will probably always eulogize even the less worthy, but certainly lionize and elevate to at least temporarily heroic status those whose ideals we can admire. The problem is that a dead hero is just that—dead. He or she is no longer there to lead us, even symbolically. We have no day-to-day examples to inspire us to try to be our better selves.

Yet, in all of this talk of the death of heroes there is one saving grace. When we worshiped the monomythic hero, we were often content to let the hero be our symbol. We could be content ourselves with admiring an individual who seemed to have achieved what we ourselves could not. In worshiping the scapegoat we have at least learned to turn inward and to find within ourselves one great quality—that of forgiveness. For a time, at least, we can lay aside ideological differences and acknowledge the worth of the individual and the value system within which that individual operated.

13

From Celebrity Entrepreneur to Civic Hero: Donald Trump's Campaign of Self-Transformation

Brenda Cooper
Kean College of New Jersey

David Descutner
Ohio University

Sandra Alspach
Ferris State University

☐ *Is there a process by which celebrities can transform themselves into heroes? This chapter, along with others to follow, offers various answers to this question. The authors take a critical view of the case of Donald Trump, billionaire developer and media celebrity, who used an editorial to increase his fame and launch himself into political and heroic prominence. Cooper, Descutner, and Alspach detail the scenario in terms of the American tradition of the man of self-made wealth who is a civic hero. Data on Trump's image were compiled through a questionnaire administered to individuals both within and outside the New York metropolitan area. Using Bormann's fantasy theme analysis, they examine the effects of attempts at self-transformation and conclude that he is not yet perceived as having achieved hero status.*

Few crimes in recent years have generated as much media coverage or public outrage as the April 19, 1989 assault of a 28-year-old woman jogger in Central Park. The woman was raped, beaten repeatedly, and then left for dead by her teenage attackers. She suffered permanent brain damage and faced lengthy rehabilitation. Six males, ranging in age from 14 to 16 years, were indicted on charges of assault, sodomy, rape, and attempted murder (Foderaro, 1989, p. B6). One of the most publicized and controversial reactions to the rape was billionaire-developer Donald Trump's $85,000 full-page "open letter" that ran in *The New York Times, The Daily News, The New York Post,* and *New York Newsday* entitled: "Bring Back The Death Penalty! Bring Back Our Police!" (Trump, 1989a, p. A13). Trump demanded punishment for the attackers: "I want to hate these muggers and murderers. They should be forced to suffer and, when they kill, they should be executed for their crimes." Trump insisted that his motivation was to express "a deep-seated feeling that what's happening in society has to be stopped" (Foderaro, 1989, p. B6).

Although Trump's prestige and influence have fallen in recent years with the revelation that his financial empire is collapsing, his headline-producing divorce, and subsequent relationships, in 1989 he was an exceedingly famous person whose fortune and prospects seemed limitless. The Trump of 1989 serves as a vehicle for the examination of a historical moment when, with his fame at its apex, Trump the celebrity decided to speak to the people of New York City about civic issues in a most public forum.

The focus of this study is on the difference between hero and celebrity and how a celebrity may become a hero. Narrative, the medium through which we come to know celebrities and heroes (Boorstin, 1961; Braudy, 1986; Wyllie, 1954), is examined in an effort to explicate the American tradition of the self-made person of wealth who is a civic hero. Donald Trump's life and efforts at self-transformation are employed to illustrate the process. Fantasy theme analysis is then suggested as an appropriate methodology for the study of the transformation of celebrity to hero.

BOORSTIN ON HEROES AND CELEBRITIES

Boorstin (1961) contends that the preeminent role once occupied in our culture by heroes is now occupied regrettably by celebrities. Heroes are noble models of "greatness" who distinguish themselves by their "achievements." They win public admiration and reverence because they act virtuously and "because they reveal and elevate ourselves" (p. 50). Their noble and virtuous achievements make them heroic, which to Boorstin means "all heroes are self-made" (p. 48). He is especially distressed with the tendency to equate greatness with fame, against which he mounts the following objection:

> Celebrity-worship and hero-worship should not be confused. Yet we confuse them every day, and by doing so we come dangerously close to depriving ourselves of all real models. We lose sight of the men and women who do not simply seem great because they are famous but who are famous because they are great. We come closer and closer to degrading all fame into notoriety. (p. 48)

Out of this confusion we have developed a lamentable appetite for "big names" and "artificial fame" that demands a ceaseless parade of "mass-produced" and therefore ersatz heroes whose hallmark is not virtue and morality, but "human emptiness" (p. 49).

Supplanting the heroic is a "new kind of eminence" that Boorstin calls "celebrity." The celebrity is a "morally neutral" person who "is made by all of us who willingly read about him . . . and talk to our friends about him" (Boorstin, 1961, p. 58). The celebrity thus is not truly "self-made," but instead manufactured for our consumption by the strategic practices of public relations, advertising, and the mass media. Boorstin (1961) summarizes the primary differences between the hero and the celebrity accordingly: "The hero was distinguished by his achievement; the celebrity by his image or trademark. The hero created himself; the celebrity is created by the media. The hero was a big man; the celebrity is a big name" (p. 61).

What is significant is that Boorstin is not alone in his conviction that to be a hero in American culture requires being a self-made person of achievement. Wyllie (1954) concurs with Boorstin that being "self-made" is the definitive attribute of American heroes:

> The legendary hero of America is the self-made man. He has been active in every field from politics to the arts, but nowhere has he been more active, or more acclaimed, than in business. To most Americans he is the office boy who has become the head of a great concern, making millions in the process. He represents our most cherished conceptions of success, and particularly our belief that any man can achieve fortune through the practice of industry, frugality, and sobriety. (p. 6)

Wyllie claims that no public belief "enjoys such universal favor in America as that which equates success with money" (p. 4). Braudy (1986, p. 591), in his celebrated history of fame, agrees with Boorstin and Wyllie, noting that "only if businessmen are clearly self-made men . . . or if, like Howard Hughes, their wealth reaches some figure so outlandish that it can no longer be considered 'money'" will they be seen as more than mere celebrities.

Given the consensus of conclusions reached independently by Boorstin, Wyllie, and Braudy, it is hardly surprising that the story Trump (1987) tells in his first autobiography features both his supposed status as a self-made man and the many possessions he has accumulated as a result of his "outlandish" wealth. Indeed, a story of the sort Trump narrates has long struck a resonant chord in Americans, and perhaps at no time in their history were Americans more receptive to such a story of a self-made man of great wealth than in the decade of the 1980's. Money and personal wealth were publicly flaunted in ways that outstripped even the excesses of the Gilded Age of the 19th century. Phillips (1990) confirms that the "1980's were the triumph of Upper America—an ostentatious celebration of wealth, the political ascendancy of the rich and a glorification of capitalism, free markets and finance" (p. 26).

No one better than Trump symbolized this decade of "plutography,"

Wolfe's (1987, p. 57) apt term for the "graphic description of the acts of the rich" that seemed to pervade forms of popular culture. As Mills (1990) remarks: "For a figure like real estate mogul Donald Trump, it was not enough to be seen in all the right places. It was essential to brand the world one occupied: to live in Trump Tower, to sail on the Trump Princess, to fly Trump Shuttle" (p. 13).

Beyond question is that Trump is a celebrity whose wealth and flamboyant style of inscribing his name on planes and buildings fits perfectly with the plutographic ethic of the 1980s. What is open to question, and the question fundamental to the present study, is how Trump tried to move beyond being merely a celebrity to becoming a civic hero with political aspirations. What this study also seeks to determine is whether Trump's campaign of self-transformation succeeded or failed. Before these questions can be addressed, however, we first must discuss Trump's career as a public figure.

THE TRANSFORMATION OF TRUMP

Trump, before 1986, was a celebrity in the exact sense Boorstin uses the term. Trump's fame had less to do with his achievements and more to do with the image he promulgated of a self-made billionaire. Although the buildings he erected were achievements, their justification was not the heroic one of moral inspiration, but of personal profit and image embellishment. The trademarks of his image were his "avarice, venality, and thrusting ego-centrism" (Gerard, 1989, p. 93), all of which he backed up with his gaudy displays of property and possessions. Even the story he told of making a fortune on his own was more falsehood than truth, more the "typical American wealth-breeds-more-wealth story" than Trump would ever admit (p. 89).

That the accuracy of Trump's story was questionable did not seem to harm his public image, just as the proven inaccuracy of many of Ronald Reagan's statements did not hurt the President's public image. What insulated both Trump and Reagan from damaging criticism was the similar way in which both cultivated and controlled the media to insure ceaseless and uniformly favorable coverage. In Boorstin's (1961, p. 60) phrase, Trump knew how to "get into the news and stay there." One magazine writer complained that it was a rare day when at least one article about Trump did not appear in some New York newspaper, whereas another appealed to editors and writers "to give the city a few days of Trumplessness" (Hammond, 1989, p. 30).

Starting in 1986, Trump began to broaden his deal-maker image in order to pursue national recognition and perhaps political office. His book, *Trump: The Art of the Deal* (1987), became a best-seller, boosted in part by his national promotional tour. In 1988 Milton Bradley issued Trump's eponymous board game, which has sold more than a million units. He also received national coverage in 1989 for his protracted but successful campaign to purchase Eastern Airlines' shuttle service. The final testament to his national celebrity came when Ted Turner announced that he was producing a film entitled "The Donald Trump Story" (Gerard, 1989, p. 86).

Although Trump had long intimated that he aspired to political office, he might have surmised that his deal-maker image alone would not qualify him for public service. If he wanted political office, he would have to develop a complementary image of the activist citizen committed to improving the quality of life in New York City. What he needed was a symbolic opportunity to launch this image, and Central Park's unfinished Wollman ice skating rink provided that opportunity. The city had been struggling for seven years to complete the remodeling project when Trump volunteered his services in 1986.

Under his management the rink project was completed in four months, and he used this accomplishment to symbolize his commitment to the people of New York City. Furthermore, the Wollman project symbolized his own managerial talents, specifically his ability "to get things done." In Trump's (1987) own words:

> The rink came in at $750,000 under budget and opened a full month ahead of schedule in November 1986. More than a half million skaters enjoyed the rink during the first year. Before the opening the city had predicted a major operating loss. For the first full season of operation, we earned almost $500,000 in profits—all of which went to charity. (p. 237)

Trump's rink triumph demonstrated his ability to solve a public problem as well as he had always solved deal-making problems in the private sector. Speculating about Trump's motives for taking on the Wollman project, Tuccille (1987, p. 254) remarked that Trump likely was trying to build public "goodwill" because of his interest in a "race for political office later on." The Wollman rink, in Boorstin's (1961, p. 46) words, became a "monument to command the attention of a whole people."

Speaking of himself in the third person, Trump boasted of the political credibility that he gained with "voters" as a consequence of the rink success:

> They tell me the results of the polls, that Donald Trump has a great deal of credibility with the voters. The reason he has the credibility is because they think he's somebody who can get things done and he's somebody who's competent. And people like that in a city that's got a lot of problems. There are many ways of solving those problems, whether it's a skating rink that took seven years and couldn't be built and I was able to build it in four months; that's one example of what can be done. It turned out to be an incredible example, the ultimate example, because everyone was watching and saying, "no, it can't be done." (Gerard, 1989, p. 86)

This "incredible example" precipitated Trump's move to place himself in the heroic tradition of wealthy individuals engaged in civic leadership, a tradition exemplified by Carnegie, the Mellons, and the Rockefellers. These individuals all sought to improve their cities with "good works" monuments such as museums, universities, and libraries.

In keeping with his new image, Trump began to speak out on a number of important municipal issues such as government mismanagement, corruption, drugs, and crime, all of which were part of his general message that "the problems of New York City are difficult and deep" (Trump, 1989b, p. 15). Developing that message further, Trump noted that the city has had "major breakdowns in all of its services" and faces economic ruin because of unsound fiscal policies. Trump criticized then Mayor Ed Koch, a former ally, and other city officials for their failure to halt the city's decline (p. 15).

Trump's dark portrait of New York City and its officials was used to justify his call for new municipal leadership. Not coincidentally, Trump's *New York Times* editorial description of the type of person who could lead the city out of its morass corresponds precisely with the attributes he prizes in himself (Trump, 1987). According to Trump, the new municipal leader should be a "person of multifaceted talents" who is "tough on crime." That ideal leader also must have a "great and detailed understanding of business" as well as be a "man of compassion." Furthermore, that leader must have a "deep and abiding understanding of people." Above all, the next mayor must be willing to exercise "real leadership" if New York City is to "remain the greatest city in the world" (1989b, p. 15).

When Trump specifies what class of individuals is most likely to bring "proper leadership" to the city, it should not be surprising that its members all resemble Trump in being highly successful businessmen. He asserts that for members of that distinguished class, which certainly includes himself, "working for the government would be an honor" ("No band-aid," 1989b, p. 15). The Trump speaking in this editorial, and in the "open letter," adopts the voice of the hero who appears deeply committed to what Braudy (1986, p. 592) calls the "community good." He expresses that commitment by volunteering to lead his city out of the morass of governmental incompetence and social problems into a better future. Regardless of the ostensible subject of this editorial, however, Trump's actual subject is himself and his proclaimed capacity to solve any civic or commercial problem. Trump's editorial typifies his attempt to transform himself from a celebrity known only for his wealth into a contemporary version of the hero who receives praise for his achievements, values, and leadership. His transformation, then, may not be authentic, but it does represent a paradigm case of how such transformations are attempted in this age of facile heroism. It is precisely because Trump's transformation may not be authentic but is still persuasive that it merits critical inspection.

METHODOLOGY

Fantasy theme analysis of narratives was chosen as it supplies information regarding the common beliefs about Trump implicit in the personal statements solicited from individuals in response to a short questionnaire. Fantasy theme analysis assumes that sociocultural and individual narratives are the principal elements of public discourse, an assumption shared by Boorstin and the other sources that constitute our study's base, who all assert an inextricable link exists between the public's view of heroes and the stories disseminated about such persons and their heroic acts. The questionnaires were employed to explore the relationship between fantasy themes individuals hold about Trump and his own rhetorical efforts to transform himself from celebrity to civic hero.

The methodology utilized is based on the model proposed by Foss and Littlejohn (1989) in their study of the relationship between the "vision of nuclear war present in society" and the vision of nuclear war presented in the film *The Day After* (p. 312). Evidence of what is "present in society" was obtained from a survey of personal discourse written in response to a single open-ended question. In this study we solicited personal responses to two open-ended questions from individuals residing in and outside New York City's metropolitan area. The questions sought to establish how well known Trump was and whether the queried individuals thought he could solve New York City's problems. Then, in accordance with the Foss and Littlejohn approach, we identified the fantasy themes about Trump implicit in the respondents' personal discourse in order to uncover any connections between those themes and the fantasy themes we discovered in our analysis of his "open letter."

Fantasy theme analysis (Foss & Littlejohn, 1989) involves five steps, with the first requiring critics to determine if in fact a fantasy theme exists. One way to establish a fantasy theme's existence is to look for the repeated ideas or themes found in the media, organizations, social movements, or in the speeches of public figures. For example, "waging a war on drugs" has had wide circulation in the media and recent political campaigns and is one fantasy theme evident in Trump's "open letter."

A second step requires coding the themes within the artifact into one of three categories: setting, character, or action. Statements telling where the drama is taking place and/or describing the tone of the scene are categorized as setting themes. For example, analysis of the first two paragraphs in Trump's "open letter" shows that "New York City" is one site of the drama, and the "world ruled by the law of the streets" is one example of the setting's tone. Usually a discourse constructed around a fantasy theme will include both villains and heroes. Themes that dramatize the behaviors of the characters are action themes.

After the themes are categorized, they are divided into major and minor themes, the third step of the criticism. Major themes are those that appear most frequently and are used to derive the rhetorical vision. In the fourth step, a motive is suggested for the rhetorical vision based on the theme that receives the most emphasis or has the most impact on the discourse. Finally, the rhetorical visions within the personal discourse and within Trump's "open letter" were evaluated. According to Foss and Littlejohn (1989), the goal of the two-phase analysis is first to compare the public and private discourse in terms of fantasy themes, and second, to construct an overall rhetorical vision from the two discourse types.

For the first phase, personal statements were collected from undergraduate students drawn from five colleges and universities. Students were given instructions to write brief essays in response to two questions. Their statements were then coded according to the type of fantasy theme they represent. The unit of analysis was the simple statement, which Foss and Littlejohn (1989, p. 315) define as "a declarative proposition with one subject and a simple predicate" constituting a "single, undivided thought" about some aspect of either Trump or his potential as a civic leader. If more than one thought was expressed in the same sentence, they then were separated into two statements. Additionally, student statements were placed into two classifications, one dealing with Trump himself, and one that specifically mentions his suitability for political office. We now turn to the task of critical analysis.

FANTASY THEMES AND RHETORICAL VISION IN TRUMP'S OPEN LETTER

Three different settings appear in Trump's "open letter" (1989a, p. A13). The rape itself represents the foreground setting, that which occurred to provoke Trump's message in the first place. The present setting is the deplorable state of New York City where, as Trump declares, "the complete breakdown of life as we knew it" is all too evident. Trump takes a tone of moral outrage in his depiction of both the foreground setting and the present setting. His reference to "life as we knew it" suggests that the city was once a place where "respect for authority" prevailed, and he uses that reference to introduce the third setting of an idealized past.

He recounts a brief anecdote, which sounds apocryphal in its perfection, telling of an incident during his boyhood when two of "New York's finest" disposed of "bullies" who had threatened a waitress in a diner. This anecdote is strategic because it shifts the focus to Trump as a person who not only knows the solution, but has seen it work in the recent past. Trump implies that this idealized past can be recovered, and who better to lead that recovery than someone who has been a witness to that past. His tone here is wistful, encouraging readers to recall that better time before "the feeling of security" was lost. As in the editorial discussed above, Trump again is talking about himself indirectly although seeming to talk about the problem of crime.

Two character themes operating at two levels also figure prominently in Trump's "open letter." Primary villains are the accused rapists whom Trump characterizes as "roving bands of wild criminals" whose motives are their "twisted hatred" and "distorted inner needs" (p. A13). What makes them even more purely evil for Trump is their remorseless act of laughing at the victim's family. These are the "crazed misfits" whom Trump "wants to hate" and execute. Trump's tone at this point is one of utter revulsion, which he expresses through his graphic description of both the crime and the criminals.

The secondary villains are the favorite targets of conservatives everywhere. They are the defenders of civil liberties and those who seek to "understand" criminals instead of punishing them. Again invoking a golden past, Trump observes that civil liberties once were a "fine and noble pursuit," but unfortunately that pursuit is now in the hands of extremists who helped to create the "reckless and dangerously permissive atmosphere which allows criminals of every age to beat and rape a helpless woman and then laugh at her family's anguish" (p. A13). He similarly denigrates anyone wanting to "explain the 'anger in these young men,'" (p. A13), appealing to the conservative shibboleth that coddling criminals will not deter crime. The motives of secondary villains may well be honorable, but they are certainly misguided and erroneously based on a "soft" approach to crime.

Primary heroes are the police and especially the "neighborhood cop we all trusted" (p. A13). Using that "we" and "our" to forge identification with citizens, Trump recalls a better time when "cops" walked the beat, and the "chant of 'police brutality'" was never heard. The "law and order" of the past could be restored if "politicians" would both "give back our police departments' power to keep us safe" and reinstate the death penalty in New York state (p. A13). Notwithstanding problems such as police corruption, Trump leaves readers with the impression that the motives of police are always above reproach.

Secondary heroes are people such as Trump who have had enough of criminals, civil libertarians, pandering apologists, and ineffectual politicians. These heroes are the "we" and "us" noted above, the citizens living in fear of crime who with Trump "want to hate these muggers and murderers" (p. A13). Boorstin (1961) writes that heroes historically have shown a flair for the "common touch," and Trump here is supplying evidence of his "common touch." In trying to establish consubstantiality with citizens, Trump says that he hates criminals and wants to see them "forced to suffer" (Trump, 1989a, p. A13), assuming without question that citizens also share these views. What he is also doing is pandering in his own way to the base instinct of hatred. In effect, he is saying that it is good to hate criminals because Donald Trump hates them too.

Action themes follow from character themes, and they delineate the dramatic conflict between the villains and heroes in Trump's letter. Primary villains generally act to "terrorize" citizens and specifically to "rape and maim and kill" (p. A13). These reprehensible criminals, who "prey on innocent lives," are given succor by the actions of the secondary villains. While the civil liberties extremists act to protect criminals' rights at the expense of citizens' rights to be safe, the other group unwisely seeks to "psychoanalyze or understand" criminals instead of punishing them. Both groups' actions, according to Trump, amount to "pandering to the criminal population of this city" (p. A13). The actions of the two kinds of villains represent, on different levels, the civic and moral deterioration against which Trump rails in his letter.

The primary heroes act "to safeguard our homes and families" and "to help us in times of danger." The actions of the police are the focal point of Trump's diner anecdote, as they "rushed in, lifted up the thugs and threw them out the door" (p. A13). Their power to act has been circumscribed, to the detriment of citizens' security. Secondary heroes' actions also have been circumscribed but in their case because of their fear of crime. "White, Black, Hispanic, and Asian" citizens have had to curtail their normal actions of going "to the playground with their families" or "sitting on their stoops" because they are "hostages to a world ruled by the law of the streets" (p. A13). Trump in this case simultaneously encompasses the major racial groups of the city, thereby insulating himself from the charge that his letter is racist, and shows his "common touch" by invoking traditional New York neighborhood scenes of playgrounds and apartment stoops. Note the dramatic contrast Trump draws between the wholesome family actions of citizens and the repugnant, "vicious" actions of criminals. A more subtle contrast appears in Trump's criticism of "politicians" who oppose the death penalty and impede the police. The clear implication is that were Trump elected to office, he would act to support the police and reinstate the death penalty.

Taken together, these themes tell a story that tries directly to reflect the experiences of citizens and indirectly to suggest why someone similar to Trump is needed as a civic leader. Combining these themes, as Bormann (1982) recommends, yields the rhetorical vision of a city at siege with no effective leadership to save it. The remorseless criminals laying siege have been aided and abetted by politicians who shackle the police and by civil liberties apologists who are "soft" on criminals. Significantly, the politicians and apologists that Trump indicts are all institutional representatives. Unlike Trump, or so he says, they are divorced from the experience of ordinary citizens. They do not understand citizens' fears of crime and their justifiable hatred of criminals. In contrast to Mayor Koch, who "stated that hate and rancor should be removed from our hearts," Trump (1989a, p. A13) makes the citizens' impulse to hate seem altogether legitimate and moral.

In the editorial previously noted, Trump proposes indirectly that he would be a superior mayor because he has a "deep and abiding interest in people" (p. A13). The subtext of his open letter is that same oblique reference to an "interest in people," which he uses to certify that he has a unique awareness of their worries and wishes. Moreover, he suggests that he would be able to transcend the institutional constraints that constrict effective government action. He also understands citizens to believe, as he does, that accommodation and compromise will not save the city from its criminal siege. What is needed is a pragmatic, competent, and tough leader who supports the police and the death penalty. As in the editorial, the letter's underlying message is that Trump is just such a leader, although he never directly makes that claim.

It seems, then, that there are interdependent explicit and implicit motives within this rhetorical vision. Trump's explicit motive is to sound an alarm about crime and to urge support for the police and the reinstatement of the death penalty. His tone of moral outrage accompanies his condemnation of criminals and his pointed objections to officials and others who have failed in their responsibility to make the city safe. He draws his portraits of criminals and officials with vivid language strokes in order to alert citizens to the need for change. Only to the extent that he persuades citizens that change is necessary, however, does his implicit motive become relevant. That implicit motive is to present himself, without openly declaring his interest, as a civic leader capable of bringing about those changes. We now turn to the task of determining if Trump's implicit motive bears any relation to the fantasy themes about him we located in the personal discourse. We want to discover if those fantasy themes offer any clues about the relative success of Trump's attempted transformation from celebrity to civic hero.

FANTASY THEMES AND RHETORICAL VISION IN THE PERSONAL DISCOURSE

The analysis of the personal discourse seeks to identify "some basic and salient themes" about Trump that "seem prevalent in contemporary society" (Foss & Littlejohn, 1989, p. 315). Specifically, the character and action themes about Trump in the discourse of individuals from the New York City metropolitan area were compared with the character and action themes in the discourse of individuals from outside that area. Setting themes were not addressed in our question, and only rarely did they surface in the personal discourse.

Question One

Students were asked to briefly describe their thoughts on the query: "What do you think about Donald Trump, the multi-millionaire New York real estate developer?" In response to this first question, two affirmative character themes about Trump appeared with nearly the same frequency across the personal discourse of both groups. One such theme was "Trump as successful businessman"; this theme appeared in 38% of the New York group's discourse and in 34% of the other group's discourse. He was described variously as "the ultimate role model," "brilliant," "powerful," and as someone who "symbolizes what America stands for."

Another affirmative character theme recurring with nearly equal frequency across the discourse of both groups was that Trump exemplified the pragmatic values of the "work ethic." This theme appeared in 20% of the New York group's discourse and in 21% of the other group's discourse. Evident in this theme was widespread knowledge of and belief in Trump's story of making his fortune on his own through hard work. Trump was viewed as "working hard for what he has"; he was also described as a "self-made man" who "built his empire from the ground up." Interlaced through this "work ethic" theme was praise for Trump in "getting things done" and his willingness "to do anything to succeed."

One affirmative character theme found in 16% of the New York group's discourse referred to Trump's "concern for New York." The Wollman rink was mentioned in relation to this theme, as was the constructive impact of Trump's business ventures on the city's economy. Interestingly, the New York group defined Trump's "concern" partly in terms of how his business successes have led to improved economic conditions in the city. Nowhere was Trump's "concern" defined in the moral and political terms typically associated with civic leaders. Not surprisingly, this theme surfaced in only 5% of the other group's discourse.

One negative character theme appeared in 24% of the New York group's discourse and in 19% of the other group's discourse. That negative theme was "Trump as self-serving person." The attributes ascribed to Trump in expressing this theme were his "selfishness," "greed," and "arrogance." Also linked to this theme were attributions that Trump is "materialistic," "ruthless," "egotistical," and "obnoxious." The agreement across the groups on this negative theme is not unexpected, given that Trump invites these attributions with constant references to his opulent lifestyle and his "take no prisoners" attitude toward deal making. Perhaps the most telling statement related to this theme came from a person living outside New York, who disparagingly observed that Trump flaunts his wealth "to make everyone think of him as an American hero."

Question Two

The second question sought responses to the following inquiry:

> Donald Trump has repeatedly been critical of efforts to stop crime in New York City and has advocated a much harder line toward criminals, including increased use of the death penalty as a means to deter crime. Do you agree with Trump that the death penalty would deter crime? And what kind of a job do you believe Trump could do in cleaning up New York City as compared to the present administration of Mayor Koch and Governor Cuomo?

In response to the second question, the two groups continued to show marked similarities. One affirmative action theme in particular appeared in 24% of the discourse from both groups: "Trump's money equals effective reform action." The more complete statement of that theme is that Trump's money would permit him to do a better job than current officials in cleaning up the city. Both groups thus equated Trump's "financial resources" and the "power and influence" resulting therefrom with his ability to make a difference in the city. What makes this theme unusual is the individuals' assumption that Trump would use his own money in acting to improve the city. Moreover, this theme demonstrates the extent to which Trump's wealth, regardless of its relevance to the question being asked, remains the screen through which he is perceived and discussed.

One negative action theme pertaining to Trump's lack of qualifications appeared in 21% of the New York group's discourse. "Trump is not qualified to lead the city" was the form this negative theme took in both group's discourse. This reservation was expressed in statements such as "Trump's niche is business, not politics"; "he lacks the understanding of the complexity of the city's problems"; and "I find it ridiculous and offensive that a real estate developer should even think of imposing his opinions on others about subjects he is inexperienced in." Furthermore, one person from the New York group wrote that "just because someone has more money doesn't make him a good leader, it just allows him to speak a little louder and throw his weight around." One person from the other group echoed that opinion by asserting that "being a good businessman does not make all of his political and moral views ultimate."

Also in response to the second question a number of the individuals from both groups were more neutral in neither affirming or denying unequivocally that Trump could clean up the city. Their statements either said Trump may help, in which case the reason cited was his money, or that he may not help, in which case the reason they cited was his absence of qualifications. Even these more neutral individuals, then, supported their respective positions with reasons identical to the ones given above to support decidedly nonneutral positions on Trump.

The degree of agreement across the two groups suggests that a relatively uniform set of themes is prevalent about Trump as a person and as a prospective civic leader. What that agreement also suggests is evidence of a shared rhetorical vision of Trump. That vision centers on Trump's values and the issue of qualification. The "self-serving" values of greed, ambition, and ruthlessness that allowed Trump to succeed in business are the very values that most individuals think should disallow him from becoming a civic leader. Trump is admired almost exclusively for his "work ethic," business acumen, and wealth. Even those who curiously thought Trump would use his personal fortune to help the city did not embrace his values or describe him as qualified for public office. They seemed to be attracted solely by the powerful agency his money represents and by the possible good it could do if it were applied to the right ends. Trump's polls may well report that he has "credibility with the voters." With respect to his suitability for political office or civic leadership, however, evidence of such credibility in the personal discourse we collected was quite thin.

CONCLUSION

On the basis of our survey of personal discourse we conclude that Trump's attempt to transform himself from a celebrity entrepreneur to a civic hero thus far has failed. His status as a celebrity is indisputable, however, as nearly every individual surveyed was familiar with his reputation for business skill and great wealth. Perhaps Trump succeeded too well in promoting his image as the flamboyant deal maker who made his fortune on his own. That image is what most individuals summoned when asked for their view of him. Perhaps his campaign to acquire a new image was too subtle and indirect, especially when it seems the public expects him always to be blunt and outspoken in his pronouncements and intentions.

More likely, though, the explanation for his campaign's failure lies with the skeptical stance most citizens take toward celebrities with pretensions to heroic recognition. Boorstin (1961, p. 49) calls this stance a "suspicion of heroic greatness" that is characteristic of a democratic nation. Consider his account: "We have become self-conscious about our admiration for all models of human greatness. We know that somehow they were not what they seem. They simply illustrate the laws of social illusion" (p. 51).

Certain anomalous figures such as Ronald Reagan may be permitted to break those "laws of social illusion" because of their singular ability to win the country's respect and good will. Other figures such as Donald Trump do not find those same laws so easy to transgress. The authors previously speculated as to whether Trump's attempt at self-transformation might prove persuasive, even if it were not authentic. That it has not proven persuasive to date is due mainly not to a lack of effort on Trump's part, but to the suspicious attitude we hold toward celebrities with grand designs outside the arena in which they have gained fame.

A final problem in our findings warrants discussion, and that concerns surveyed individuals simultaneously admiring Trump as a self-made man and yet refusing to see him as having the stature of a civic hero. Although this finding seems to contravene the shared views of Boorstin, Wyllie, and Braudy, it indicates that being self-made is a prerequisite to, but not a guarantee of, gaining the status of a hero. Individuals perceived Trump as having unappealing qualities, most notably being self-serving, arrogant, and greedy, that mitigated the importance of his supposedly being self-made. Those unappealing qualities, as Schickel (1985) has observed, often lead the public to discount business celebrities such as Trump, particularly "when they presume to inform us on current political and social issues" (p. 259).

An anecdote reported by Meyer (1989) in his book *The Alexander Complex* supplies additional evidence of how Trump is perceived, and it supports the findings of this study. Meyer asked Steven Jobs, former head of Apple Inc., if he would agree to be interviewed for a book to which Jobs inquired about who else was to be included. Meyer mentioned a number of leading business figures, including Trump. Jobs' response was harsh and dismissive, as recounted by Meyer's description:

> "Donald Trump?" Jobs winced, shook his head, jerked his feet off the table in a paroxysm of pained incredulity. "I don't want to be in a book with Donald Trump! What's he ever done?"
>
> I replied that, among other things, Trump planned to build the tallest building on Manhattan's Upper West Side.
>
> "So what?" interrupted Jobs.
>
> So, he wants to give New York a building that would be as he puts it, a "great, true, vital symbol." A visual reminder that New York is the best, most vibrant city in the world.
>
> "Bullshit," said Jobs. "Are gambling casinos in Atlantic City heroic? Is Trump Tower on Fifth Avenue a monument to architecture? Trump's buildings are junk—garish, badly designed, big gold initials all over the place, a blight on the city. All Trump wants is money and power," Jobs declared. "He'll never do anything good." (pp. 18-19)

Given Jobs's denunciation and the mixed reviews Trump received from the individuals we surveyed, to say nothing of his recent financial problems, the possibility that he will ever wear the mantle of the hero in Americans' eyes seems more remote all the time.

ooooo *14*

Theorizing Postmodern Stars: George Michael and Madonna

Florence Rogers
San Diego State University

Michael Real
San Diego State University

❐ *MTV is postmodern television, so assert Rogers and Real. It is where we find the new celebrities—the postmodern stars such as Madonna and George Michael. It is also where we find the big advertising bucks. The authors set forth theories of film stardom, semiotics, and the postmodern that explain the symbiotic relationship between advertisers and "star" endorsers. They go on to examine how MTV with its musical/visual form has produced a new order of celebrities that appears to empower the audience, because audience members can consume both the product and the star simultaneously. They demonstrate how this occurs with a postmodern critique of MTV's Madonna and George Michael.*

MTV is where we find today's celebrity stars, and previous theories of stardom cannot accommodate them. The binary oppositions of fan and star or of star image and real person imply a sense of real life and film culture that are distinct. Yet, the styles, stars, and advertisements of MTV cannot be set against a separate everyday life and reality, nor are they real life. Its conventions construct what we think of as reality and our relations within it. The advertisements that have adopted MTV styles, namely, those featuring the stars that MTV created, destroy those distinctions. Our everyday relations become a function of identity, desire, and empowerment.

MTV has existed for a decade. It is not just music television, it is postmodern television. For better or for worse it has changed the way we think about popular music and our new celebrities—the pop stars. MTV introduced a style of video making that influenced advertising. In its underlying function MTV is nothing but advertising, but not advertising as we previously knew it. MTV is symptomatic of the postmodern condition that does away with the real and the imaginary cores of meaning and authenticity.

A theoretical background of the conventions of pop music and MTV relating to postmodernism and film theory is provided and applied to two particularly good examples of pop music star endorsers—Madonna and George Michael—to analyze how far they characterize the postmodern condition. To assess the contemporary popular music star we draw on many different areas. Employing diverse areas of theory provides a means of understanding what they mean, why they mean, and what the pervasiveness of their images indicates about relations of production and consumption.

THEORIES OF FILM STARDOM AND POPULAR MUSIC STARS

The tag *star* indicates something high up and far away, something we reach for; the very notion of a celebrity or hero being called a *star* comes from film. Film stars are literally up there on the screen and out of reach through the nature of the projected image. Star theory, then, has predominantly been about film star images in particular and audience/film relations in general. It is worth examining how much of this work can explain pop star images such as Madonna and George Michael. Richard Dyer's book *Stars* (1979) and, more recently, *Heavenly Bodies: Film Stars and Society* (1986) are both valuable texts on stars and what they mean. Dyer (1979) asks if stars are a phenomenon of production or consumption. As a phenomenon of production they represent capital: part of the bargaining power of Hollywood, an investment, and outlay, used to organize the market. This, he notes, leads to the idea of manipulation—Hollywood uses star images for its own ends (pp. 9-12).

Dyer (1986) notes Marcuse's thesis that stars are a feature of a one-dimensional society in which heroes are not those of the ideal but the ordinary. Instead of heroes being a sign of another way of life (the ideal), they are signs of the existing, average way of life. Dyer warns us not to think of the influence of stars in a relationship with some "collective unconscious" (p. 21), a term that conjures images of a quasi-spiritual communion with one another. A more appropriate way of expressing this would be as the fantasies of capitalism: the myths that everyone can succeed and enjoy boundless wealth and, therefore, happiness. These myths are strengthened every time we read of a star's divorce or heartbreak. The myth ensures that we continue to view them as individuals with human souls who are subject to the anxieties we all face. Thus, the possibility of attaining their fabulous excesses becomes all the more feasible and acceptable. They suffer as we do, but their individual charisma and talent helps them overcome, just as we could under the apparent freedoms of capital. As Dyer puts it:

> Because stars have an existence in the world independent of their screen/"fiction" appearances, it is possible to believe . . . that as people they are more real than characters in stories. This means that they serve to disguise the fact that they are just as much produced images, constructed personalities as "characters" are. (p. 22)

Dyer suggests that the star image, for all its changes, retains a coherent core. This is what we feel is "really" the star. He notes the importance of the close-up and that stars embody the dichotomies of private/public and individual/society so that although the audience realizes that stars are manufactured, there is still an irreducible core of being which confirms individuality (p. 11). This is where the fascination of the star lies: "they enact ways of making sense of the experience of being a person in a particular kind of social production . . . with its particular organization of life into public and private spheres" (p. 17).

Returning to the question of stars as production or consumption, Dyer notes Lowenthal's position that contemporary heroes come from leisure not labor (Dyer, 1986, p. 48). This complements Marcuse as previously mentioned: Stars are the ordinary made special, rather than the extraordinary as an ideal. Both these writers presuppose capitalism and mass culture as cause and effect. The contradictions that star images offer resist a reading of stars as mere reflections of dominant ideology. This is clearly the case with Madonna and George Michael and many of the other stars used in commercials. Although part of their image plays out the idea that anyone can make it to the top, many aspects are resistive and challenging to convention.

This returns us to the question of a star's contradictory and ambiguous image. Can they offer the audience empowerment through resistance of the dominant, or are they merely 'holidays' from the dominant ideology (Dyer, 1979, p. 59)? Dyer suggests that the rebel hero type that appears in film (James Dean, Marlon Brando) should be broken down into the types of resistance he is offering. First, is he an "anomic" hero, to use Marx's term, who suffers from being outside of society in general, or an "alienated" hero who is removed from the means of production and the ruling classes? Second, he asks, do these stars promote rebellion, or do they act out imaginary solutions to the feelings of anomie or alienation they have? For George Michael and Madonna a discussion of youth clarifies the issue.

In acting out the inevitable rebellion of youth, the implication is that they will grow up and out of it. But Madonna and George Michael, in their constant image changes, are forever stuck in that youthful opposition. They are not bound like Dyer's examples of Paul Newman, Marlon Brando, and Albert Finney to the narratives of their films that assuage class, generational, and political rebellion. Only James Dean is perpetually young through the fate of his short career. The star image and character image are distinct in the case of the film star, but the looser structure of video promotes a blurring of the star image into whatever the video necessitates. How often is Madonna referred to as "the Material Girl" after she acted out a pastiche of Monroe's character in *Gentlemen Prefer Blondes?* Many accounts merge her with the Monroe persona and speak of Madonna as if she were Marilyn Monroe.

The images used by music stars often locate them in a standpoint of specific resistance against convention, for example, Madonna's expressive sexuality against prevailing mores. The idea of anomie seems to override an articulated opposition to the dominant order. Dyer cites anomie as inarticulate and therefore unable to analyze its situation (Dyer, 1979, p. 61). This characterizes the pop or rock star. Rarely are they granted an opportunity to express any opinion or attitude in an articulate manner. The industry of rock provides interviews and television appearances that provide superficial data on the likes and dislikes of a star essentially with the aim of promoting an upcoming concert tour, album, or the like. The teenage fan magazines offer idealized and stylized versions of the star's life. If these stars are aware of the resistance they offer, then the lyrics of their songs would be an outlet for this. Yet, the conventions of song and video only allow for a generalized feeling of angst focused around desire, articulated in terms of heterosexual relations and the individual. It can be said that using film theory to examine rock and pop star images may be useful, but there are differences between film and other media.

Theories of The Postmodern

There is no doubt we are in the postmodern. Cultural forms and outlook for social structures in the postmodern are variously defined and evaluated by writers who broadly equate postmodernism with freedom from the high and low culture dialectic or a descent into the chaos of late capitalism. The crisis in modernism arose from the realization that a single discourse of reason and a linear search for "truth" did not exist. Unlike Modernism, postmodernism does not have a "practice." Collins (1989, p. 113) suggests it is a "context without a Zeitgeist." The postmodern embraces competing discourses.

In characterizing postmodernism one may begin with a breakdown of the high and low culture distinction in art between the avant garde and mass art. Grossberg (1988) points out that "art works or 'texts' can now either be authentic because they are outside of the commodification of art and life, or 'coopted' works which 'allow' and even celebrate their own commodification" (p. 173). The text seems to define its own consumption, and there is an assumed reflection of contemporary history in the cultural practice. Thus, textual fragmentation is exemplified by MTV in its two constituent parts—the rock videos and, more recently, the advertising that appears to be a rock video except that a product endorsement comes from outside the singer/song itself. This textual fragmentation mirrors economic fragmentation. It articulates our experience of it and is a sign of the fragmentation of our subjectivity, tainted throughout by ideology (Grossberg, 1988, p. 174). The whole premise of modernism, of cinema, and narrative was that there was some real intrinsic value to things. As Baudrillard (1983) suggests: "[T]here was already the dream of symbolic exchange, a dream of the status of the object and consumption beyond exchange and use" (p. 126). There was, it seemed, an exterior to copy. On to this our own inferiority could be projected. There was a separation of the public and the private, of the sign and signifier, the subject and the object. Baudrillard says: "What used to be lived out on earth as metaphor, as mental or metaphorical scene, is henceforth projected into reality, without any metaphor at all, into an absolute space which is also that of simulation" (p. 128). This space is "hyperreality" and it contains only simulations or "simulacra." Everything is reduced to image, a celebration of the look. Instead of living under the "sign of alienation" that at least provided a spectacle and an other to strive for via consumption, Baudrillard suggests that we are now in a perpetual present that does away with every representation and private inferiority. The primacy of the signifier, the surface, the image, renders the reality that once informed it redundant. With that "reality" fast receding, the idea of a sign that has a spectator to interpret it in terms of a reality is nonsense. The image is more real to us than the reality.

Kaplan (1987, p. 45) suggests that this timeless present is parallel to the prelinguistic imaginary state (p. 45). This ever-presentness is produced exquisitely by MTV, and it exhibits Jameson's (1983) description of how signifieds begin to look in this environment. He says:

> The experience of the present becomes powerfully, overwhelmingly vivid and "material": the world comes before the schizophrenic with heightened intensity, bearing a mysterious charge of affect . . . the signifier in isolation becomes ever more material—or, better still, literal—even more vivid in sensory ways, whether the new experience is attractive or terrifying. (p. 120)

Any prolonged viewing of MTV seems to produce this effect, with periodic "centering" by formal devices in the videos or the structure of the channel described below.

Jameson points to pastiche as a postmodern form. He distinguishes pastiche from parody as there is no knowing humor in the former. Old styles are chopped up without reference to mass and high culture divisions. The schizophrenic character of postmodernism avoids the need to acknowledge high or low culture forms and, as Kaplan (1987, p. 47) points out, speaks from no particular place or position. This lack of positioning in forms such as MTV has been argued as progressive by Fiske and Grossberg versus the idea of individuality as bourgeois myth.

MTV AND SELF-REFLEXIVITY VS. TRADITIONAL NARRATIVE

It has been widely discussed that MTV exhibits many of the above postmodern characteristics. The focus of this chapter is the advertisement that utilizes the music star within the conventions of the music video. For purposes of this discussion the music video and such ads are seen as equivalent.

Three Types of Self-reflexivity

Many music videos reject traditional narrative forms. The rejection occurs through a self-reflexivity that can take three forms. First we are often shown the video being made. Guns n' Roses, Phil Collins, U2, and Paula Abdul are a few of the artists who have used this technique. Caricatures of record company executives are included, as are technicians and hangers-on. The band/artist is presented rehearsing the song, cut together with a performance being filmed.

From this the second type of self-reflexivity deals with the whole show/rock business myth in a self-conscious manner. The band or artist's performance is intercut with the behind-the-scenes preparations and after-concert festivities such as drinking, tour buses, hotel rooms, and groupies. As much as these videos undercut traditional time and space continuities, they are mainly about promulgating the rock-and-roll lifestyle myth of hard living, hard lovin' men.

The most dramatic form of self-reflexivity is the video in which the finished video is played while the singer still performs, often on multiple screens behind the head (i.e., George Michael and Arthea Franklin's duet, "I Knew You Were Waiting"). Their faces magnified on a huge screen behind them reduces their faces to the lines on a TV set. In a variation of this, a narrative featuring the singer is watched by the singer standing outside the 'character' as in Phil Collins's "Groovy Kind of Love" in which he projects a film of himself that is excerpted from his film *Buster*.

All of this militates against traditional narrative structure. There is no narrative position from which the action unfolds. The artist tells (sings) the scenario, acts it out and watches simultaneously. Editing style mimics Hollywood genres, documentary clichés, and home video/movie effects. Both result in the flattening out of the distinction between image and reality. Within the video text it is unclear what is image and what is the internal "reality."

Videos make up the larger MTV text that is continuously broadcast without end. Baudrillard's (1983, p. 132) "state of fascination and vertigo linked to this obscene delirium" is further complicated by endorsement advertisements. The television program is available as a fictional representation in between the hard business of commercials, the "reality" in which we as consumers can participate. The advertisement featuring a music star in the style of a video further flattens the distinctions between program and commercial and between image and reality.

Hollywood Genre in Postmodern Music Videos

Kaplan notes the heavy reliance on Hollywood genres, especially the musical, horror, and western styles. Some films inspire a look or scenario: Brian de Palma's *Body Double* is echoed in Rod Stewart's "Infatuation", Ridley Scot's *Bladerunner* is evoked in Duran Duran's "Wild Boys." The same band makes use of James Bond-style exotica in their video "Rio" and comes full circle with their theme for the Bond movie *A View to a Kill*. In frequent attempts to create a feeling of absolute fan adulation in a concert scene, Leni Riefenstahl's *Triumph des Willens* is brought to mind. The anthemic music of Simple Minds and U2 lends itself to stadium-shot videos that seem to move out of a celebratory image into blind idolatry. Individual films as illustrated by Michael Jackson's "Beat It" recreate *West Side Story*, Madonna's "Material Girl" refers to Marilyn Monroe in *Gentlemen Prefer Blondes*, David Bowie's "China Girl" restaged the well-known beach scene in *From Here to Eternity*.

The use of established film conventions in rock video is complimentary to the idea of postmodernism. On one level, to recreate film styles is to acknowledge their sources, even if only at the level of affect noted by Grossberg. Although the viewer of MTV may not be aware of specific references, the feel of the film genre is communicated with shared conventions and codes of representation.

Jameson's (1983) suggestion of pastiche is significant as the appropriation of such conventions is the wholesale and random sampling of film history, cutting up former styles and putting them back together with technology that gives the impression of something new. This "neutral practice of such mimicry, without parody's ulterior motive, without satirical impulse" (p. 114), characterizes the music video. It at once breaks with Hollywood rules and replays over and over its most cliché moments.

The music video appropriates from both high and mass culture. As Jameson notes, there is a fascination with all that is trashy, glitzy, and downmarket. In Madonna's video for "Open Your Heart" she appears in a peep show. George Michael's Diet Coke ad utilizes a bull fight motif, a theme that has served in both high and mass art, a sport at once noble and barbaric.

The distortion of narrative and character in music video prevents traditional identification with the image. The subject, according to Kaplan (1987, p. 47), is denied the climax of Hollywood cinema narrative and instead is positioned constantly at the moment preceding plenitude by the sensation of ever-presentness. This, of course, ensures continued consumption.

MTV as Avant Garde

Kaplan argues that the antinarrative features described above could constitute an "avant garde aesthetic." Other writers also have suggested the possibility that MTV and the videos that constitute it are resistive and avant garde. However, there are features that root the audience back into capital and traditional forms of consumption; in relation to endorsement advertising the audience is offered a seemingly resistive experience while being positioned firmly as a consumer.

In arguing that the advertisement using the music star in the video format is a more accurate embodiment of postmodernism, it is necessary to explain how Music Television very nearly becomes a radical form.

Fiske (1986, pp. 74-75) places the music video text of MTV in relation to that of ordinary television by saying it is like comparing youth to middle age. He contrasts them thusly:

MTV	*TV*
Signifier	Signified
The Senses	Sense
Body	Mind
Pleasure	Ideology
Freedom	Control
Resistance	Conformity

He suggests that capital may have provided an anticapitalist mode. The primacy of the signifier resists the sense-making aspect of signs. The private pleasure of signifiers is outside of sense. It is not an alternative to sense (therefore, MTV can never be radical), but is non-sense. "[N]ot sense but sensation . . . it produces the presence of itself, not a representation of the absent: it is, it does but it does not mean" (Fiske, 1986, p. 77).

MTV is not a major threat to capitalist ideology. Many of its characteristics are derived directly from economic considerations: a single continuous feed for all time zones, the voracious appetite for styles and forms which demands recycling the old ones, and the impossibility of locally formatting a nationwide channel. All these economically driven characteristics are a "barrage of decontextualized information" (Tetzlaff, 1986, p. 82). Tetzlaff says that this apparently resistive form is, in fact, hegemonic. MTV, like rock and roll, acts by helping us imagine we are free to be oppositional, when, of course, it ultimately supports the system that produces it. If we view MTV as oppositional, it cannot be at the same time postmodern (Kaplan, 1987, p. 52), for the celebration of surface indicates that there is nothing behind the image.

Within this flow of non-sense there are markers to prevent us getting too carried away with the signifier as body and resistance analogy. Kaplan noted the continuing idea of the star and his or her close-up as preventing avant garde unpleasure (Kaplan, 1987, p. 48). Kaplan views the close-up as a way of bringing us back into a traditional subjectivity by establishing the viewer and star in a voyeuristic relationship. Mulvey's (1975) thesis in "Visual Pleasure and Narrative Cinema" is that the close-up of the female star mitigates against the action of the narrative and turns into spectacle. The spectator's voyeuristic relation with the image is moved to fetish as the female presents a reminder of the threat of castration. The formal properties of the close-up help this overvaluation, the magnification of the face, and the flattening of the field.

The close-up that holds up the narrative in cinema holds no currency for the music video as there is no traditional narrative flow. The close-up is certainly an important element of the video and does serve as a center for the spectator as Kaplan suggests. In the endorser advertisement the product serves the same purpose. The special image of the cola can, be it Coke or Pepsi, has the same currency as the star image, but there is no narrative flow for the close-up to interrupt.

In the postmodern form of the video in which the signifier abounds and denies history or sense, the close-up does not fulfill the traditional function of reminding us that the star is a unique private person. To Balazs (cited in Dyer, 1979, p. 17), the close-up is a "silent monologue . . . a tongue more candid and uninhibited than in any spoken soliloquy, for it speaks instinctively, subconsciously. The languages of the face cannot be suppressed or controlled."

In Hollywood cinema the illusion remains that the star has a private identity, that he or she has an ordinary life as we do. The close-up captures that identity. In music video and the advertisements that use the format, the primacy of the signified destroys this aspect. The whole premise of Madonna is that she is more about being a star than being a person. The same is true with George Michael. We do not need nor get the feeling that there is a private person behind the star image. In *Truth or Dare* Warren Beatty kids Madonna about wanting to live her whole life on camera. The image is enough, like the cola can.

The ever-present character of the postmodern form, together with the spectator being forever on the verge of plentitude, demands that these artists constantly update their images. They have no history or meaning behind the image so they must constantly re-image themselves in a simulacra of development.

The video medium has produced, like rock, male erotic stars who are detached from ideas about the male protagonist as a more perfect ego-ideal. The erotic male star of pop and rock—George Michael, Jon Bon Jovi, Michael Hutchence, Bobby Brown, and Prince, to name a few contemporary examples—is available as star and erotic image for women. Of course, the orientation of women as consumer is paramount, but they nevertheless transgress the ideas regarding Mulvey's thesis of the star image. If the subject/object relation is obscured, can the gaze still be regarded as male? Owens (1983, p. 62) suggests that postmodern forms reject Mulvey's binary oppositions of male and female, active and passive, controller of the look and object controlled. This may explain why we can view George Michael as an equally erotic object as Madonna.

POSTMODERN STARS: MADONNA AND GEORGE MICHAEL

Madonna and George Michael were chosen as examples for purposes of this discussion as they epitomize the type of celebrity stars who rely on MTV for their success. The focus of this chapter is on the advertising that utilizes the music star within the conventions of the music video.

Madonna

Successive Madonna looks have been variations on these themes. The first incarnation of the Madonna look was cemented by her role in *Desperately Seeking Susan* released in March 1985, which propelled her albums *Madonna* and *Like a Virgin* to the top of the charts in both the U.S. and U.K. At this time Madonna was wearing "thrift shop chic" (Subjic, 1989, p. 33): lace, pork pie hats, crosses, beads and ripped tights; her hair was long and heavily highlighted and her trademark eye make-up and lipstick were the first indications of the Marilyn Monroe influence that was later to surface. Fiske (1989) examines the fan's relationship with this image through letters in teenage magazines. Madonna's confidence in her own sexuality, her acknowledgment of traditionally submissive poses and looks turned against themselves is recognized by the girl fans. The Madonna "wanna-be" is clearly not a cultural dope.

Madonna's next look came with the video for "Material Girl" in which she plays out a convincing pastiche of Marilyn Monroe as Monroe sang in *Gentlemen Prefer Blondes*. Kaplan (1987, p. 20) suggests that Madonna's version of the sequence for "Diamonds are a Girl's Best Friend" foregrounds the conventions of classic cinematic gaze and look. She notes the curious discrepancy in the video and the song lyrics. The video is the opposite to the Marilyn piece: Madonna eventually chooses the poor boy, yet in the song she will refuse anyone who does not give her "proper credit." This further serves to confuse her image as simultaneously bad and good girl and highlights her knowing manipulation of that fact. Fiske (1989) notes how the lyrics of "Material Girl" place the female in charge of relationships and pleasure. This reverses the heavy male dependency in the lyrics of Monroe's "Diamonds Are A Girl's Best Friend."

Such is the mythology surrounding Madonna that the spurious information about her from gossip magazines has welded itself to her star image. Such is the currency of Monroe's image that Madonna only needs to take the distinctive eye make-up, lipstick, and platinum hair to take on board everything Marilyn Monroe signifies. How this look departs from Monroe is in the knowingness with which Madonna plays with the image. Instead of the innocence there is the gutsy postfeminist woman of the 1980s. Her aggression is doubly shocking when it utilizes the compliant Monroe look. For a time in 1989 Madonna turned the image inside out and dyed her hair brown to utterly confuse her good girl/bad girl status. Even her name creates a tension between her female confidence and what might be expected of someone who has taken on the star image of Monroe. In this case the "evil demon of images" that Baudrillard talks of "precedes the real to the extent that they invert the causal and logical order of the real and its reproduction" (Baudrillard, 1987, p. 13); postmodernism indeed.

The commercial "Make a Wish" for Pepsi-Cola can therefore use Madonna with the product of Pepsi (a similarly full/empty sign) in a way that provides space for both images. Directed by Joe Pytka the commercial was judged the best of its genre (Garfield, 1989) and premiered her single "Like a

Prayer." Madonna is seen watching a home movie of herself at a birthday party. They look at each other and travel in time. So Madonna the star does have a history, even if it is specially shot; there was once a Madonna child. Madonna dances in her high school and in the street wearing a bustier top and black pants that reveal her muscular body. Her hair is dark with a quirky blond streak that cleverly combines her good and bad images. Similarly the convent school is reminiscent of Madonna's own ambiguous use of crucifixes and the tension between repression and Madonna's boy-toy image. The gospel choir in the song appear, and when they are all dancing the effect appears genuinely uplifting. But, so it should be. Fiske (1989) suggests that the metaphor "consumerism-as-contemporary-religion" is "too glib to be helpful," yet notes that a cliché such as this is only so because of its centrality to common sense. Despite the revelation that the MTV video of *Like a Prayer* is a play and the "cast" takes a bow, the confusion between this and "Make a Wish" was too much for some, and the resulting opposition led to the withdrawal of the Pepsi spot.

George Michael

George Michael's image began with his duo Wham! which was successful both in the U.S. and U.K. The appeal was teeny bop based on winsome good looks and catchy dance songs. Wham! videos presented George Michael and Andrew Ridgeley in typical boy meets girl scenarios or rebelling against their parents. Post-Wham! Michael's image changed convincingly and smoothly from teenage heart throb to serious singer/songwriter. As his audience grew up he changed with them; his appeal was based on a more adult sexuality. Gone were the tennis shorts and heavily highlighted slightly *bouffant* hair, in came the famous stubble and ripped jeans. He wears mirrored sunglasses, a motorcycle leather jacket, and a large, silver cross earring. Likewise, the themes of his lyrics became more mature. From "Wake Me Up Before You Go-Go" he went to "Hand to Mouth" about poverty and the controversial "I Want Your Sex," which was banned in the U.K. but which celebrated monogamy.

The first element in this image that Coke found so attractive is the rock'n'roller as a youthful rebel. George Michael is still young enough to play this part convincingly (unlike older stars such as Mick Jagger or Alice Cooper). This image comes direct from the early Brando and James Dean, "the first teenager." His song lyrics speak of internal conflict, but like Dean's *Rebel Without a Cause*, his resistive stance is just that, a posture. A second element can be traced back to Elvis; Michael's aggressive stance, as in the "Faith" video in which he uses a semi-acoustic guitar (the only form of electric guitar available in the 1950s). Michael's dancing is overtly sexual, the hip thrusting with which Elvis outraged 30 years before.

The precise manner in which Michael's image is constructed is an acknowledgment of it's own artifice. The stubble says he has no desire to conform, yet we know no one's stubble really looks the way his does. His cross earring is a product of punk and a convenient gimmick for "Faith." It also shows confidence in his own sexuality to wear a female piece of jewelry so noticeably. Both are signs of nonconformity and assertion of his masculinity.

In the same artificial way Michael takes on signs of an authentic proletariat. Like Dean before him, and notably Bruce Springsteen, Michael often wears a plain white T-shirt. Part of his metamorphosis included the acquisition of a new physique. Although his muscularity is labor, rather than the thing labor produces, it is a sign both of his masculinity and that he is working at entertaining us. (Dyer, 1986, uses this phrase in relation to stardom itself.) In this way he aligns himself back to the 1950s idea of a rocker, rather than with the indulgences of the pop business during the 1960s and 1970s. His jeans and T-shirt appear the same as ones we can purchase; he appears to be one of us, his dress being a great leveler. In the spirit of Andy Warhol (1975, p. 100), we might say, "No amount of fame will get you a better pair of Levi's than I buy, nor a better white tee shirt."

Michael's Diet Coke commercial was introduced with teasers that played heavily on this iconography. The audience is given glimpses of Michael's spurred cowboy boots, his jacket, his leather and studded gloves. The theme of the commercial is the bullfight. There is an obvious link between the ritualization of the fight with the star presence. It is also a text about stylized and extreme masculinity.

The color scenes of the bullfight, with the appropriate music from the Gypsy Kings, are intercut with a dark and moody George in concert backed by his own music. The pace intensifies until Michael explodes with "Just give me a break, why don't you give me a break, now." Here we have a full face shot of Michael smiling next to the Diet Coke logo which has not appeared until that moment.

This commercial appeared before Madonna's Pepsi "Make a Wish" spot and is less successful. The matador has been equated with sex and death, themes which articulate the star phenomenon. If you are to be forever young, you must die like Dean. If you conquer the bull, you are truly a man. To some audiences, however, this metaphor may be slightly distasteful and a bad choice. As for the product, it is not quite synthesized into the piece. Michael's star image is a bit too overwhelming to allow for it. Nevertheless, this commercial exhibits all the postmodern conventions of the star image and the video format as a medium for presenting it. The pastiche of the bullfight theme, the foregrounding of self as a commodity, and the ordering of affect (the pleasure in Michael's image) surround the product. Both of these commercials are examples of an emergent postmodern form that not only draws on the conventions of MTV and the music video, but uses their empowering elements for directing the audience toward consumption. All the conditions for the postmodern form are fulfilled; it is fragmented, simultaneously full and empty. It depends for effect on a semiological history that has no reality except for its function as implied reality for the spectator. That is, it calls on the media world of brand names, stars, and images. It takes for granted a shared code of editing style, self-reflexivity, and distorted narrative. This is a form that acknowledges its own postmodernism, and these two examples are used extensively in the discussion below.

Audience/Text Relationships

The pessimistic views of postmodern forms suggest semiotic chaos. What can the audience/text relation be if there is little distinction between text and spectator leaving only a perpetual stream of fragmented signifiers? Collins (1989, p. 117) critiques both Jameson and Baudrillard when he asks, "Signs may be exhausted for Baudrillard, but are they for everyone?" The masses, he argues, are not unable to make choices or differentiate, "without differentiation there can be no desire" (p. 118). Tezlaff (1986) notes:

> The environment is one of apparent chaos. We revel in an orgy of fascination . . . Yet, society as a whole has not collapsed, only changed. Cultural chaos is accompanied by behavioral order. . . . The young search only for success within the system. (p. 83)

As both Tezlaff and Collins point out, the MTV text, the music video, and further, the endorser ad, are not entirely negotiable texts. Communication does take place in this semiotic mess. If MTV as a postmodern form has elements of the oppositional within it, the advertisement that utilizes those forms also incorporates to the fullest extent those signifying practices that pull us back from the resistive into the consumer and text relation that ensures we buy, and buy again.

The pleasure-producing aspects of the music video are used to position the spectator in relation to the product available in their own empirical reality. If this could not occur through communication, no one would attempt to produce these commercials. It is Barthes's (1973, p. 150) notion of inoculation that is more completely exemplified with MTV. With the music video the product is presented; with the advertisement that looks like music video that presentation is foregrounded. In the former, the disguise of entertainment communication is worn. With the latter there is an admission of the simulacra of entertainment.

None of this could take place without the shared conventions and signs of language—Saussure's *langue*. Even with the collapse of the signifier/signified relationship, shared images exist. The text must somehow call the spectator to it, to present itself as "the language of truth" (Collins, 1989, p. 86). Importantly, Collins takes this into the realm of the postmodern saying: "Once individuals are exposed to multiple interprellations [the fragmented postmodern (MTV) experience for example] interpellation becomes inseparable from self-legitimation" (p. 87).

Again we are caught up in a relationship in which the text directs our own subjectivity, an area in which the star image is powerfully emotive. With the endorser advertisement that private condition of identity, aspiration, and dream is firmly rooted back into commodity capitalism.

Whether or not MTV is false consciousness is almost irrelevant. On the one hand, it serves to inoculate the masses with a shot of resistance. On the other, it does not present a coherent set of facts to obscure the truth of capitalism. In those instances in which MTV presents itself as reality, the advertisement using the video format articulates that "presenting as a reality" by grounding us back into the real relations of our existence: Consumption. The music video-style advertisement is clearly a very sophisticated text that demands audience knowledge of music video conventions and of what MTV means.

What can be said about how MTV functions in the day-to-day lives of its viewers? It has been suggested that MTV can somehow reduce a person's capacity to experience "life" (Sun & Lull, 1986, p. 115). The video and musical material has been criticized as violent and sexist (Jhally, 1990). At one time MTV was attacked for its underrepresentation of black music styles. However, research suggests that the audience is selective in its use of MTV. Sun and Lull found a general liking for music and visual interpretations of the songs in the video format in their survey of teenagers. Interestingly, the respondents noted MTV as "just there." This is congruent with Baudrillard's ideas on postmodern forms. MTV cannot reduce your capacity for life because it may well be real life.

The fixed range of image choices for the audience provides a vocabulary (purchasable, of course) to enable one to feel part of a subculture or club. The latest looks, bands, exclusive video clips, and interviews with the hottest stars are the elements that can be seen as empowering in the way Grossberg (1984) described pop and rock music. This can be seen as meeting a real need. Both MTV and the products available in the commercials relieve alienation and produce pleasure. It is an imaginary solution to a real contradiction. Pleasure which only seems outside of ideology is directed back toward the products of the system. "Hegemony need not structure the semiosis, only affect" (Tetzlaff, 1986, p. 86). Tezlaff points out the enclosure of this resistance; it does not promote action. Nevertheless, the resistive element that comes out of MTV and is present in the music video-styled ad cannot be discounted, and it appears and feels real to those who watch.

CONCLUSION

There is no other form so postmodern as MTV. Even though avant garde art and cinema may play with and expose the characteristics of postmodernism, MTV is a mainstream popular form. MTV has no difficulty in synthesizing elements that art and cinema find problematic. Whereas modernism was worked through in successive artistic movements, MTV has none of the real-life baggage that accompanied that stylistic struggle. Postmodernism has as a characteristic impersonality, which does not distinguish between the real and imagined, yet is able to hail the audience effectively. Avant garde art and cinema may be able to use the imagery of popular culture, but cannot be regarded as postmodern. They continue to present "high" and "low" culture distinctions for an audience able to tell the difference.

Using film theory can only partially theorize stars such as Madonna and George Michael. It is useful as a starting point to explain audience and star relations. How pop stars like Madonna and George Michael deviate from traditional star theory, looking at a theorization of how pop music operates in the lives of its fans, becomes important in understanding why these particular star images are so persistent in MTV. Meanings around identity, difference, and sexuality are articulated through pop music and personified in pop stars such as Madonna and Michael. The MTV environment presents itself as a medium of difference, the alternative to ordinary television and its conventions. The elements that make up MTV—the antinarrative videos, the continuous stream of images with no distinction between program and commercial, and the music star images—create an inherently postmodern environment. Through MTV, pop stars are colonized and mystified by capital. To the audience they appear just as star-like as movie stars, but ideas of unique talent are grounded directly in lived capitalism. Pop star images or music are a fact of postmodern life, at home, at work, or in the car. Movie star performances exist in a more discrete environment—the cinema or on video cassette—and are tied up with character: Sylvester Stallone portrays Rocky, Harrison Ford appears as Indiana Jones. Madonna and George Michael need none of this: their image changes are different versions of the same star.

The combination of a postmodern environment and a direct relation to the lives of the audience makes these stars easy to appropriate for use in advertising. The crowded semiotic space of a music video-style advertisement still means something to an audience because the star and the product are understood conventions of MTV. In this case, a signified outside of MTV is unnecessary, and a succession of flat signifiers makes room for Coke or Pepsi. Sexuality, identity, and difference are articulated directly in terms of consumption of the product. It is an articulation that appears to be empowering to the audience because music stars retain the idea of being apart from sense and ideology.

The removal of distinctions between star image and its later mutations, between product and endorsing star, the elimination of classical narrative structures and personas, and the generalization of sexuality, these and other characteristics of MTV, pop music stars, and music video commercials mark these pervasive cultural phenomenon as inherently postmodern. The star images of George Michael and Madonna seem transparent, but contain the contradictions of both capital and postmodernism. With Coke and Pepsi as the product we have the opportunity to innocently internalize the postmodern.

In the two years since Michael's Coke and Madonna's Pepsi commercials aired much has happened to confirm the assertions of this dissuasion. Into the 1990s Madonna remains visible in all media, undoubtedly a trendsetter in fashion and video. In a traditional sense of stardom the market for lurid details of her past indicates a desire to confirm she is human, although her postmodernness ensures there is no actual revelation. Music video has continued to be the site of Madonna's image. This works as evidenced by the furor when "Justify My Love" was banned by MTV.

George Michael in comparison has not been visible. From his biography *Bare* (Michael & Parsons, 1990, pp. 143-145) it appears the George Michael that was created turned out to be a monster, a huge brittle surface manifested via MTV. For a moment Michael was on the cusp of New Man, strong and sensitive. He now talks in terms of his songwriting craft and refuses to be just an "image."

Their very postmodernness makes these stars difficult to theorize. The star images of George Michael and Madonna are perfectly colonized by capital. It is impossible to separate what is real or imagined, what is artistry or artifice. The persistence of Madonna's image in particular demonstrates how intangibles such as sexuality and identity can be successfully coopted into maintaining an ideology of consumption.

Section IV: The Celebrity-Hero Connection

☐☐☐☐ **15**

From Wild Western Prodigy to the Ageless Wonder: The Mediated Evolution of Nolan Ryan

**Nick Trujillo
Leah R. Vande Berg**
California State University, Sacramento

☐ *When Texas Ranger pitcher Nolan Ryan struck out his 5,000th hitter, posted his 300th victory, and pitched his record 7th no-hitter, he was assured a place in the Hall of Fame as one of the legends of baseball. In this chapter Trujillo and Vande Berg examine the case of Nolan Ryan as a sports hero and celebrity in American culture. They discuss the role of the sports hero in society and review the arguments made by Boorstin (1978) and others regarding the demise of the hero and the rise of the celebrity in contemporary society. They then examine how media coverage of Ryan evolved over his 27-year baseball career to help shape his identity as hero and celebrity in American culture.*

In ancient times the hero was a legendary figure who possessed attributes of great stature, such as strength, bravery, and magic, and who performed acts of great significance, such as discovering brave new worlds, parting seas, and killing fire-breathing dragons. Heroes were thought to be favored by the gods and often they were deified by members of their culture. Narratives about the hero were passed from generation to generation, and the hero, in death more than in life, became an exalted figure in the culture's history (see Campbell, 1949).

For better or (more likely) for worse, mediated heroes in contemporary times possess attributes of far less stature and perform acts of far less significance than the mythological heroes of ancient times. Today's heroes are rarely exalted or deified; rather, they are seen as being more "down to earth." Even so, the contemporary hero in American society still is understood to be, as Boorstin

(1978) described, "a human figure . . . who has shown greatness in some achievements." In other words, today's hero still "is a man or woman of great deeds" (p. 49). The true hero, thus, is not merely an entertainer or a great performer for a day, but is someone whose greatness has withstood the test of time.

Many scholars agree that heroes are individuals who symbolize mainstream ideals of a given society. As Calhoun (1987, p. 330) summarized, the "true hero is a moral hero" who reflects and affirms values considered to be positive in society. Heroes, thus, are used as models through which members understand and integrate themselves into the social structure. Klapp (1969) has argued that society's dominant groups also use such heroic models to "recruit, train, and control members of the society in accordance with these models" (p. 18).

Although heroes themselves are persons of great deeds, the process by which they are understood to be heroic is an interactive one. The process of hero construction, as Fairlie (1978) argued, is two-way: "We choose the hero. He [or she] is fit to be chosen" (pp. 36-37). Thus, even though it is natural to focus attention on the individual who is interpreted as heroic, it also is important to pay attention to the interpretive processes by which members of the culture, including members of the mass media, identify the hero and share in his or her heroism. Klapp (1962) has suggested that when a member of society aspires to the ideals represented by the hero he or she "worships," that member establishes a "yearning relationship in which a person, in a sense, gets away from himself by wishing or imagining himself to be like someone whom he admires" (p. 211). In this way, members of a culture help define the hero, and, through the mass media, they participate vicariously in the acts of heroism they worship. Sports heroes long have been used as mass-mediated models for socialization and integration. Scholars argue that sports play a potent role in reflecting and shaping the values of a given culture (see Duncan, 1983; Leonard, 1980; Novak, 1976). American sports are said to reflect and reaffirm such cultural values as achievement, hard work, discipline, teamwork, loyalty, and tradition (see Nixon, 1984; Stone, 1973; Trujillo & Ekdom, 1985). Thus, as Smith (1973) wrote, "athletic hero worship has been accepted and even encouraged because sport represents major cultural values" (p. 112).

Critics have argued that sports heroes also constrain members of society because they serve as a form of social control. Those most critically inclined have suggested that sports and sports heroes function as "opiates" which narcotize participants and spectators and which obviate concern with important social and political issues (see Hoch, 1972). Other critics have argued that sports heroes constitute a more subtle form of social control when they "become personifications of certain kinds of values and the interpretation of performances and the conduct of spectators becomes part of a wider process whereby particular kinds of life styles, values and ideas are 'sold'" (Hargreaves, 1982, p. 128).

In contemporary society the mass media serve as primary vehicles through which the cultural values of sports and sports heroes are presented to audiences. "Sports tend to be presented in the media as symbolic representations of a particular kind of social order," wrote Hargreaves (1982), "so that in effect they become modern morality plays, serving to justify and uphold dominant values and ideals" (p. 127). The mass media also have led to the proliferation of the sports celebrity.

FROM HERO TO CELEBRITY: WHERE HAVE YOU GONE, JOE DIMAGGIO? ASK MR. COFFEE

Daniel Boorstin (1978) and others have suggested that true heroes, including sports heroes, are in short supply and that they have been displaced by media celebrities who are known not for their great deeds but for their well-knownness. Boorstin argues that although the mass media give us the capability to communicate the heroic deeds of individuals to more people than ever before, they ironically make it harder for individuals to be viewed as heroes.

First, there is so much coverage of so many individuals that "the titanic figure is now only one of thousands" (p. 54). Because the media make many individuals well known, those who perform large-scale acts stand only a few column inches taller than those who act in small-scale performances. As Crepeau (1985) argues about sports heroes:

> Too many teams, too many players, too many events, and too much coverage have produced two extremes, the blandness of the mass and a preoccupation with the unusual or bizarre. It has also led to celebrity proliferation, an important commodity in American consumer culture. (p. 81)

Second, there is too much coverage of particular individuals. We read about the mundane practices of our sports figures, including how fast they drive, how much they sleep, and what cereals they eat for breakfast—in fact, they sometimes are on the cereal box itself. Despite the mass (mediated) quantities of "information" about our favorite players, however, Crepeau points out that "ironically, we probably know as little about sports heroes today as we knew about them in earlier times. The difference," he concludes, "is only in what kinds of things we know. What has revelatory journalism really revealed beyond titillation for a voyeuristic age? The myth of the flawed perhaps" (p. 78).

Third, there is much negative coverage in a society whose media managers and reporters have an insatiable appetite for sensational, conflict-oriented stories that yield higher readership and viewership ratings (see Aronoff, 1979; Simons & Califano, 1979). Thus, whereas the media of the past ignored the off-the-field neuroses of sports "heroes" such as Babe Ruth, today's media spend much time focusing on such material. "It seems that the mass media which once pandered to athletic heroes," Smith (1973, p. 69) concludes, "now is contributing to their decanonization, if not their decline."

These and other concerns about mass-mediated heroism have led some scholars to argue that the celebrity has replaced the hero in contemporary American society. "The hero," Boorstin (1978) explains, "was distinguished by his achievement; the celebrity by his image or trademark. The hero created himself; the celebrity is created by the media. The hero was a big man; the celebrity is a big name" (p. 61). Boorstin concludes that even those who perform heroic acts ultimately are transformed into celebrities:

> Inevitably, most of our few remaining heroes hold our attention by being recast in the celebrity mold. We try to become chummy, gossipy, and friendly with our heroes. . . . Instead of inventing heroic exploits for our heroes, we invent commonplaces about them . . . which make them celebrities. (pp. 74-75)

Although many writers point to the demise of the hero as one negative consequence of our mass mediated society, Crepeau (1985) has suggested that the development of American life itself has diminished the need for heroes: "No longer is it possible or necessary to have heroes who appeal to all classifications of people. . . . As there is no unified system of values, there are no universal heroes" (p. 79). The optimistic view of this, Crepeau argues, is that the demise of the universal hero reveals the maturation of American society and "could indicate greater security of identity for Americans as a people, and therefore a willingness to accept differences and reject the bygone prejudices of one-hundred-percent Americanism" (pp. 79-80). On the other hand, he also acknowledges the foreboding possibility that "it may be that rather than hero worship, this envy of celebrity is all that remains for a society that has lost its sense of shared values" (p. 81).

In summary, heroes may be in short supply because there are fewer great individuals in modern society and because our current forms of mass communication mediate so many candidates (albeit in less heroic presentations). With respect to sports, it is apparent (and too often transparent) that many athletes do not reflect the ideals of society, but rather reaffirm their own marketability as celebrities for endorsements. It seems that sports reporters and sports readers often are less interested in the performances of heroic athletes in the spirit of team play and more inquisitive about the pocketbooks of sports stars in the spirit of winning at any cost. In short, we agree with Smith (1973) that the true sports hero is "an endangered species," whereas sports celebrities are as common as Texas cockroaches.

In the remainder of this chapter we examine the case of a professional athlete who may be one of the last of our endangered sports heroes: Nolan Ryan, pitcher for the Texas Rangers baseball team. We argue that Ryan stands as a unique sports hero and celebrity in American society in that his status as hero and celebrity has been established not only because of his baseball accomplishments on the field, but because of his baseball coverage in the sports media. The evolution of the media coverage of Ryan's career is examined to evaluate how it shaped his status as an American hero and celebrity.

THE MEDIATED EVOLUTION OF NOLAN RYAN

The analysis of Ryan's media coverage can be organized in four phases that correspond to the periods of time he spent with each of the teams for whom he played during his career: the New York Mets (1966-1971), the California Angels (1972-1979), the Houston Astros (1980-1988), and the Texas Rangers (1989-1993). The unique features of media coverage in each of these "phases" is discussed to show how this coverage shaped his public identity. These phases are not mutually exclusive or exhaustive; rather, they work cumulatively to construct Ryan's ultimate identity as a sports hero and celebrity.

This analysis is based on our examination of over 500 articles in popular print media, including newspapers (e.g., *New York Times, Los Angeles Times, Dallas Morning News, Dallas Times Herald*, and others) and magazines (general ones such as *Life, Time, Newsweek, Saturday Evening Post*, and sports-oriented ones such as *Sport, Sports Illustrated*, and *The Sporting News*). The dates of these print materials span the period from 1965, the year before Ryan made his major league debut with the Mets, to 1993, the year the 46-year-old Ryan announced that the 1993 season—his record-breaking 27th in the majors—would be his last.

New York Mets (1966-1971): The Unfulfilled Promise of a (Wild) Western Prodigy

Nolan Ryan made his major league debut as a 19-year-old pitcher with the New York Mets on September 11, 1966 when he went two innings against the Atlanta Braves, giving up one run (earned) on one hit while striking out three and walking one. In his next and final appearance of 1966 on September 18, however, Ryan's performance was more erratic, and one reporter summarized the outing and foreshadowed his career as a Met: "Ryan lasted only one inning, in which he struck out the side, but he also gave up four runs on four hits, two walks and a wild pitch" (Koppett, 1966a, p. 26).

The Tall Texan with "the Fastest Fastball in Town." Early coverage of Ryan focused on the unique ability of this young rural Texan to throw the ball hard and to strike hitters out. The story of his debut against the Braves noted his minor league record of 422 strikeouts in 369 innings and provided evidence of his speed in the statement that "no one succeeded in getting around on Ryan" (Koppett, 1966b, p. 62). He was "the rookie pitcher with the cannonball serve" (Durso, 1968, p. 24), the "fabled minor-league strike-out artist" (Koppett, 1968a, p. 58), and the "New York strike-out prodigy" (Koppett, 1968b, p. 3). A *Life* magazine ("Brine for Nolan Ryan," 1968) feature revealed that Ryan has "a fast ball that has been described as faster than Bob Feller's (98.6 mph)—the fastest ever timed" (p. 78). As these articles indicate, the media shaped Ryan's on-the-field persona to the public as a power pitcher who would continue to strike batters out.

Suffering "Early Inning Blues": Adversity on and off the field. At the same time, media accounts also affirmed that Ryan had to overcome adversity before realizing his rare talent. First, sportswriters reminded readers often that Ryan could not throw the ball where he wanted to throw it. He was the "tall, slim Texan . . . who has not yet mastered control and consistency" ("These are the Mets," 1969, p. 57); more metaphorically, he was "as wild as the spinning Black Dragon ride at Astroworld" (Chass, 1970, p. 59). The press revealed Ryan's own admission of his control problems when they quoted him saying that "the wildness has been a problem right from the start, right from when I was 5 years old and couldn't throw the ball to my brother who was standing 5 yards away" (Newhan, 1972, p. 7, part III).

Second, reporters revealed that Ryan was unable to play on a full-time basis. After a rare start and complete game victory in 1970, one reporter called him "the most spectacular part-time employee in baseball" and then explained why Ryan had not pitched more often:

> When he joined [the Mets] three years ago, his rocket fastball caused blisters on his fingers. He also flies to Texas one weekend a month for Army reserve duty and recently did a two-week hitch. And his father's illness and death last month caused him to be absent again. . . . As a result of all the problems, Ryan has never pitched a full season in six years of professional baseball. (Durso, 1970, p. 26)

Ryan's wildness and his status as a "part-time" player prevented him from emerging as a regular pitcher for the Mets and from establishing a mediated identity as a key contributor to the team. During the 1969 championship season of the "Miracle Mets," Ryan conspicuously was absent from the pitching mound. He pitched only 89.0 total innings that season, the second lowest in his career (he pitched 78.0 innings in his 1966 rookie season), and in the 1969 World Series, he pitched just 2.1 innings as a reliever in Game 3 (although he was credited with the save). During this time Ryan was conspicuously absent from media coverage as well. Indeed, in one article entitled "Amazing Mets: What Makes Them Win," Ryan's name was not even mentioned. This omission is surprising because one of the reasons credited for the team's success was the "good young pitching"; however, examples the sportswriter provided included Ryan's more successful teammates "Terrific" Tom Seaver, Jerry Koosman, and Gary Gentry (Durso, 1969, p. 1).

In the End, not just a Prospect, but a Suspect. When reporters juxtaposed Ryan's raw ability to throw hard with his inability to overcome adversity, especially his wildness, they created the necessary conditions for his baseball odyssey and for his ultimate status as sports hero. If Ryan could not overcome his adversity and control his unique ability, he and his "heat" would be only a "flash in the pan," and he would fail as many fastball pitchers had failed before him. But if Ryan could overcome adversity and control his unique ability, he would fulfill baseball prophecy and, as *Life* magazine put it, he "could be the next Sandy Koufax" ("Brine," 1968, p. 78).

However, Ryan did not fulfill his potential with the Mets. His last appearance in a Met uniform came on September 28, 1971 against the Cardinals, when he started the game and failed to get an out. The newspaper reported the grim details: "Ryan walked the first four men he faced, forcing in one run, and then gave up a two-run single to Ted Simmons, the Cardinal catcher." The story noted that "yesterday's defeat was the 15th consecutive incomplete start for Ryan, who now has a 10-14 win-lost record" (Harvin, 1971, p. 23).

On December 10, 1971, Ryan was traded to the California Angels for infielder Jim Fregosi. "The New York Mets finally gave up on Nolan Ryan's wandering fastball yesterday," wrote one sports reporter (Durso, 1971, p. 37). The same article quoted Mets general manager, Bob Scheffing, who said: "I really can't say I quit on him. But we've had him three full years and although he's a hell of a prospect, he hasn't done it for us. How long can you wait?" In Los Angeles, Angels general manager Harry Dalton used synecdoche to emphasize Ryan's promise: "We've obtained the best arm in the National League and one of the best in baseball. We know Ryan has had control problems, but at 24 he may be ready to come into his own" (Newhan, 1971, p. 3, part III).

Ryan expressed his dissatisfaction with his identity as prospect in a feature article before the 1972 season. "I hate to hear people still refer to me as a prospect because after four years in the majors I should have achieved more than I have," he said, adding defensively, "I'm not a prospect but neither should I be suspect" (Newhan, 1972, p. 1, part III).

Reporters used Ryan's own words to characterize the importance of this first phase in his career, a phase which established the prophecy of his potential: "I guess the suffering now will make success that much more enjoyable—if it comes" (Newhan, 1972, p. 3, part III).

California Angels (1972-1979): A Second Chance at Stardom

Ryan's trade to the Angels was welcomed by Ryan, the Angels, and the ever-present sports media. Ryan characterized his Met years as a constant trial that had ended, and he described himself as "a Rookie making a fresh start" (Newhan, 1972a, p. 1, part III).

Angel at crossroads. "No more talk of promise," declared one reporter on the day of Ryan's American League debut. "No more comparisons with Sandy Koufax in velocity of fastball or in how Ryan, like Koufax, has had to struggle with control" (Newhan, 1972b, p. 2, part III). That same article quoted Ryan's acknowledgment of both the pressure to perform and the opportunity to have another chance. "I'm simply at the point of my career where I have to prove myself," he said, adding, "I have to get the ball over the plate or I'll find myself in the same situation I was in frequently with the Mets."

However, Ryan's second chance started with familiar press coverage. His identity as a rather outstanding promising junior power pitcher was again embellished as was his status as an incomplete prospect. After a 6-3 loss to the Oakland As early in the season, one story used power-hitter Reggie Jackson's pithy description to reiterate Ryan's pitching prowess: "He's faster than instant coffee. He's faster than a speeding bullet and more powerful than a locomotive. He throws wall-to-wall heat." The same article quoted Jackson's observation that although Ryan was still a prospect, "when he finally becomes a complete pitcher . . . there will be no way to hit him" (Newhan, 1972d, p. 1, part III).

Ryan's second chance started with familiar pitching stats as well. He won his debut with the Angels, pitching a 2-0 shutout over the Minnesota Twins, but then lost his next two starts. After he lasted just two innings in a 12-2 loss against the Orioles in late April, one reporter reviewed the Ryan/Fregosi trade and concluded that "early returns are running against [Angel GM Harry] Dalton." This reporter noted that "there are whispers that Ryan's wildness stems from his unwillingness to take instruction," and he revealed that manager Del Rice was "dejected by Friday's rout" to the point that the manager had admitted: "We'll decide within the next few days if Nolan will stay in the rotation. We can't keep him there if he's going to walk 5 or 6 every time" (Newhan, 1972c, p. 5, part III).

The Leap to Stardom. Ryan did stay in the rotation, and he did improve dramatically in his first season; in fact, he ended the year with a 19-16 record and set several Angels strikeout records. Then, in the next few years, he overcame much of his adversity and became a star for the Angels. Ryan became a star on the playing field in 1973 and 1974 when he achieved the traditional measure of pitching success by winning 20 games (21-16 and 22-16, respectively). Furthermore, in 1973, he threw two no-hitters and set a record with 383 strikeouts in one season, which broke Sandy Koufax's record of 382 strikeouts. In 1974, Ryan threw his third no-hitter, and a group of Rockwell scientists timed his pitches during a game at speeds of 100.8 and 100.9 miles per hour, the fastest pitches ever recorded. Then, in 1975, he threw his fourth no-hitter to tie Koufax's all-time record.

Through these historical and mediated performances, Ryan fulfilled earlier prophecies of greatness and earned a lasting place in baseball lore. Accordingly, reporters recast the trade of Fregosi for Ryan as "one of the most one-sided trades in baseball" ("Ryan tops Royals," 1973, p. 57) and as "a trade that will live in infamy" (Anderson, 1975, p. 39).

Ryan also became a star in the popular press as he acquired more publicity with each milestone. He was a Los Angeles Press Club winner as a headline-maker in 1974. He was paid to endorse several products, including cowboy boots in a *Playboy* magazine advertisement. In 1975, he made a cameo appearance on the soap opera *Ryan's Hope*. Thanks to his appearances on the mound and in the media, he had become, as *Newsweek's* label noted, a "superstar" (Axthelm, 1975, p. 57).

Ryan was, however, portrayed as an unusual superstar, especially for a Los Angeles celebrity. The press prominently noted that Ryan was not the stereotypic Hollywood playboy, but instead, he really was the equally stereotypic "country boy" with a rural, not urban, lifestyle. One report revealed that after he broke Koufax's season strikeout record, Ryan "sipped orange juice while champagne flowed all around him" (Distel, 1973, p. 1, part III); another revealed that "when his teammates urged him to ask for a Cadillac when the Angels offered him a new car following his fourth no-hitter, he asked for a pick-up truck instead" (Newhan, 1975, p. 1, part III). A *Newsweek* article (Axthelm, 1975) contrasted his pitching style with his lifestyle, suggesting that "his pitching style is so flashy that he is called 'The Express' but his lifestyle rolls along at the leisurely pace of his pick-up truck" (p. 56). A feature in the *Saturday Evening Post* (Jacobson, 1974) asserted that Nolan Ryan was "almost too much to believe, a cliché coming true" (p. 15). This article added that Ryan stood for "what America, in its innocence, once believed of its heroes and hardly ever found to be true" (p. 15).

Sport magazine (Anderson, 1978) inaccurately predicted that Nolan Ryan would not remain a celebrity for long: "He's not the type for the gossip columns. He's too homespun, too quiet, too private" (p. 69). On the contrary, Ryan's mainstream traditional values and his understated lifestyle continued to be used as vehicles through which the media maintained Ryan's unique identity as hero and celebrity.

Still Mortal after all these Feats. Although Ryan enjoyed unprecedented success as a superstar Angel, he also suffered more adversity as a mere mortal. He experienced major back and arm problems during the 1975 season which limited the number of innings he pitched (from a league-leading 333.0 in 1974 to 198.0) and which lessened his win-loss record (from 22-16 in 1974 to 14-12). However, whereas his injuries as a Met had been cast by the New York media as obstacles to his (and New York's) success, his injuries as an Angel—and his choice to play despite these injuries—were now cast by the media in heroic terms. "The 14 games he won in 1975 and the 4th career no-hitter he pitched may one day be looked upon as his greatest feats," wrote one reporter, because "from his 4th start of the season, his arm was all but falling off" (Rapoport, 1976, p. 1, part III).

Ryan's critics charged that he was not only mortal, but that he was mediocre, at least in the win-loss column. Despite his legendary feats as an Angel, Ryan's career record after the 1979 season was 167-159, and he had been just 138-121 as an Angel. In spite of the fact that Ryan had been hampered by injuries during the time that he had pitched his 4th no-hitter and that, as a *Sports Illustrated* (Newman, 1979) article pointed out, "his teams . . . have rarely given him adequate support" (p. 17), Ryan's critics remained.

One of Ryan's toughest critics, according to the sports media, was new Angels general manager Buzzi Bavasi. When Ryan and Bavasi failed to agree on a new contract for the 1980 season, Ryan became an unrestricted free agent, and Bavasi told reporters that he could replace Ryan "with two 8-7 pitchers," a sarcastic reference to Ryan's 16-14 record in 1979.

Although Bavasi did not make a serious attempt to resign Ryan, reporters wrote that at least 13 teams were pursuing this "star of today's re-entry draft of free agents" (Heisler, 1979a, p. 1, part III). Then-Yankee owner George Steinbrenner said that Ryan was "one of the most desirable quantities in baseball" (Keith, 1979a, p. 34), a telling comment that revealed Ryan's desirability as a star pitcher and his marketability as a superstar celebrity. Ryan exercised his free agency and signed a contract with the Houston Astros on November 19, 1979.

Houston Astros (1980-1988): Coming Home to Millions, More Milestones, and More Mediocrity

Nolan Ryan signed a free agent contract worth a record $1 million per year for three years (the Astros had an option on his contract for a fourth year for $1 million). One media report stated that the contract made Ryan the "best-paid player in the history of baseball" (Furlong, 1980, p. 66); another quibbled that it made him "the game's highest-paid free agent signee" (Heisler, 1979b, p. 1, part III), noting that the Pirate's Dave Parker also was a million-dollar-a-year player.

Ryan's contract drew mixed reviews in the media. *Sport* magazine (Furlong, 1980) described it as a "$4 million gamble" (p. 68) because of his history of injuries. Even so, the same article reminded readers that there were two powerful reasons why Ryan probably was worth the money: because of the "money-in-the-bank drama in every start" that could draw fans in anticipation of another no-hitter and because "Nolan Ryan is 'home country'" who "won't simply draw fans to the ballpark; he'll draw friends" (p. 68).

The Celebrated Homecoming. After his mass-mediated odyssey from one end of the country to the other, the "eternal country boy" returned home to Texas, close to the town of Alvin where he was raised and where he still lives (and raises cattle). "Baseball has taken Nolan Ryan to both coasts, but it has never taken him out of Alvin," *Sports Illustrated* reported. "It's what he's all about" (Fimrite, 1986, p. 84). Through the media readers also returned home vicariously with Nolan. Readers went to Nolan's childhood house on Dezso Drive, the house just past the "Smile, Jesus Loves You" sign where his mom still lived (Fimrite, 1986, p. 86). Readers traveled up Gordon Street where Nolan "used to roll 1,500 newspapers a night" to help his dad earn extra money from a paper route (Furlong, 1980, p. 68). Readers met Nolan's close friends, one of whom said that Nolan "always had it in his mind to pitch in Texas" and that "everybody in Alvin is real excited about it" (Littwin, 1980, p. 1, part III).

The mediated celebration of Ryan's triumphant return as hometown hero reaffirmed this new Astro's identity as a "regular guy," despite his astronomical salary. Nolan's barber Larry, who had cut Nolan's hair for 10 years, was the perfect character witness when he said, "Nolan is a super-fine fella" who "hasn't gotten a swelled head like some of those athletes with the big money" (Littwin, 1980, p. 1, part III). The portrait the mass media painted of Ryan was that of "a modest and clean-living young man from rural American who has pitched uncomplainingly for generally mediocre teams" (Kaplan 1983, p. 34).

More Heat and More Milestones. Into his late 30s, Ryan was still throwing his trademark fastball. "This fantastic ability to still 'bring it' after all these years," wrote one reporter in *Sports Illustrated* (Fimrite, 1986, p. 91), "absolutely baffles the baseball savants." Indeed, Ryan's ability to still 'bring it' was cast as a mystery to be solved, and sportswriters sought answers from various baseball sleuths. Ryan himself opined that it was "a matter of mechanics," but Dodger pitching coach Ron Perranowski invoked a divine explanation, saying "God gave him one hell of an arm" (Fimrite, 1986, p. 92). Yankee pitcher Tommy John professed that it was his "ratio of fast-twitch nerve fibers in that arm," while Dodger pitcher Don Sutton said simply that Ryan was "a freak" (Hoffer, 1988, pp. 292-293). One sportswriter summarized it this way: "The man has a forty-one-year-old arm that's livelier than any rookie's. No theory accounts for it, or even predicts its eventual end" (Hoffer, 1988, p. 293).

Ryan continued to set new milestones in his years with the Houston Astros, two of which were special in light of earlier prophecies. In 1981, Ryan threw his 5th no-hitter, surpassing the all-time no-hit record that he and Sandy Koufax had shared since 1974. In 1983, he recorded his 3,509th strikeout against Montreal which meant that the "Ryan Express" had surpassed "Big Train" Walter Johnson as baseball's all-time strikeout leader, breaking a record that stood for 56 years.

In 1985, Ryan recorded an unprecedented 4,000th strikeout. *Newsweek* magazine (Axthelm, 1985) described this historic achievement in this way:

> As Ryan doffed his cap on the mound in an emotional Astrodome scene, all his values seemed to come together. . . . He had painted the Picasso and defined greatness on his own terms. He was home, where he loves to be. He had blended the 100-mile-an-hour flashes of brilliance with a leathery ranch hand's longevity. In the words of yet another Southern perfectionist named William Faulkner, he had not only endured but prevailed. It was time to quiet all questions about whether Nolan Ryan was a winner. (p. 67)

Still Mediocre After All These Years. Despite the achievements, questions about Ryan's status as a winner were not quieted. Critics raised questions when he first signed with the Astros for multimillions, given his mediocre record to that point. "He's won numerous battles," wrote one reporter, "but he keeps losing the war"; the reporter also quoted Ryan's own reluctant, and somewhat defiant, admission: "Maybe I've lost too many games to be considered a great pitcher. But it's always bothered other people more than it's bothered me" (Littwin, 1980, p. 10, part III). Questions also were raised after his first season with the Astros when he posted an 11-10 record in return for his $1 million salary. After nine seasons in Houston, his career record as an Astro was just 106-94, and his entire major league career record was just 273-253. One reporter summarized Ryan's career in these bottom-line terms: "He is not a winner" (Hoffer, 1988, p. 294).

Some critics wrote that his continued, albeit somewhat controlled, wildness led to many of his defeats; one article quoted Ryan's admission that "I definitely beat myself sometimes with walks" (Kaplan, 1983, p. 36). Other critics charged that Ryan was overly aggressive, that he was "too macho on the mound" because he "wanted to challenge every hitter" and "strike him out" Axthelm, 1981, p. 82). Defenders of Ryan countered that he played for weak teams throughout his career. One article during the 1983 season calculated that Ryan had a career record of 20 games over .500 although his teams had a combined record of 14 games under .500 without him. Dodger pitcher Don Sutton was a witness for the defense when he said that Ryan has "been in the wrong place at the wrong time with the right stuff" (Hoffer, 1988, p. 294).

After nine seasons with the Houston Astros, Ryan again found himself without a team as Astro management refused to sign him at the end of the 1988 season. He became a free agent for the second time on November 1, 1988. It looked as though the hometown hero would pack up again and move back to the West coast.

Texas Rangers (1989): Vindication for The Ageless Wonder

Nolan Ryan was signed as a free agent by the Texas Rangers on December 7, 1988 at the baseball winter meetings in Atlanta, an act that was described by former Ranger manager Bobby Valentine as "the one most important transaction the Texas Rangers have ever made" (Galloway, 1988a, p. 1B). Ryan signed for a reported $1.6 million salary for the 1989 season with a signing bonus and incentives that put the contract worth close to $2 million. The Rangers also had an option for the 1990 season worth $1.4 million (in April 1990, Ryan signed a 1-year contract for the 1991 season worth an estimated $3.3 million).

When Ryan first signed with the Rangers, general manager Tom Grieve, sensitive about Ryan's status as a celebrity-drawing card, told reporters that "we are not doing this for image; we are doing this because Nolan Ryan is a pitcher who can win baseball games" (Galloway, 1988a, p. 1B). Despite Grieve's assertion, reporters claimed that Ryan "gives Rangers new credibility" (Galloway, 1988a, p. 1B), that his signing was "one incredible PR coup" (Galloway, 1988b, p. 1B), and that in obtaining Ryan, the "Rangers purchase an image" (Rogers, 1988, p. D-1). In the process of covering his career with the Rangers, reporters elevated Ryan's own image to new heights.

Staying in Texas, For Home and For Family. Sports reporters revealed that Ryan had received better financial offers from the San Francisco Giants and the California Angels. But according to reports, Ryan turned down more money because of his love of home and his love of family. "I'm a die-hard Texan and want to remain in Texas," he said in one report (Galloway, 1988a, p. 1B). Another story quoted him saying that "The overriding factor was what I felt was best for myself and my family. This was a decision not just made by me.... We will be able to maintain our home in Alvin, and our kids can keep going to the schools they are in" (Rogers, 1988, p. D-1). Once again, the media featured Ryan's traditional rural values of home and family, portraying them as more important to him than the value of money. When Ryan decided to return to the Rangers in 1990, the papers reported that the decision was based solely on the value of the family and was made after an actual Ryan family vote.

A Superstar of Epic Proportions. As a Ranger, Ryan's status as superstar was enhanced when he accomplished more milestones on the mound and received greater attendant publicity (from sportswriters and from Madison Avenue) in the media. Media coverage of his Ranger milestones, including his 5,000th strikeout, his 7th no-hitter, and his 300th victory, reached new heights. For example, as he approached and then registered his 5,000th strikeout, the media covered the event as a truly historic occasion. For non-baseball-oriented observers, the game was the epitome of Boorstin's (1978) "pseudo-event" because Ryan already led the major leagues in career strikeouts, and every additional strikeout was a new milestone. Sports reporters, however, interpreted and presented the landmark figure of 5,000 strikeouts with unprecedented fervor.

The sheer volume of media coverage of this achievement was overwhelming; it encompassed stories in major dailies around the country as well as special multipage sections of Ryan in local Texas papers replete with stories, full-page color posters, and "K" sign inserts. Also extraordinary was the nature of the coverage. Reporters placed Ryan's 5,000th strikeout on the same level as other "great records in baseball history," such as Joe DiMaggio's 56-game hitting streak, Hank Aaron's 755 career home runs, and Lou Gehrig's 2,130 consecutive games played. Reporters used testimony from well-known baseball players and coaches to corroborate the historic nature of this milestone achievement. For example, the *Fort Worth Star Telegram* (Reeves, 1989, p. 10, sec. 3) used Detroit manager Sparky Anderson's assertion that "We're looking at a record that will never be touched." Reporters used testimony from unknown fans in attendance as well; the front page of the *Dallas Times Herald*, for example, quoted 9-year-old David Wyrick of Waco, TX, who said: "I'll probably tell my grandchildren it was the most exciting thing that ever happened in my life" (Henderson, 1989, p. A-1). Pregame reports even indicated that the President of the United States would be watching the game, and later media coverage presented the full text of Bush's brief epideictic address which was played on the ballpark's Diamond Vision screen after the milestone strikeout: "Congratulations Nolan Ryan. What an amazing accomplishment. Indeed, everybody that loves baseball pays tribute to you on this very special record-breaking occasion. Well done, my friend. Well done, my noble friend" ("President's message," 1989, p. 6, sec. 3). For this historic night the mediated community spanned the country from rural Texas houses to the White House.

Ryan's identity as celebrity reached new heights with the Rangers as well when he (and the Ranger franchise) received unprecedented local publicity in a football-crazed city usually dominated by the formerly almighty Dallas Cowboys. The media heaped more national publicity on Ryan when he became the second Ranger player ever to appear on the cover of *Sports Illustrated* (May 1, 1989 and April 15, 1991). *Sports Illustrated* also printed the complete list of Ryan's 1,061 separate strikeout victims during the week of his 5,000th strikeout ("K," 1989, pp. 30-32).

Ryan's identity as a commercial spokesperson also reached new heights when he signed contracts promoting national products, including Advil, Bic Shavers, BizMart office supplies, Whataburger, and Wrangler Jeans, to name a few. In fact, Ryan's commercial endorsements became the focus of a front-page story in the *Dallas Morning News* (Baldwin, 1990, pp. 1A, 6A). Other published stories focused not on Ryan's own commercial value through endorsements, but on his estimated monetary value to the Ranger franchise, to local businesses, and to the entire city of Arlington, TX. Paralleling news stories about the commercialization of celebrity Nolan Ryan were stories about his finally becoming a Hall of Fame caliber baseball celebrity.

Vindication At Last. At the time of his 5,000th strikeout, a few critics still challenged Ryan's success as a pitcher. In the papers, Hall of Fame pitcher Bob Feller offered the most stinging critique. One report said Feller had discredited Ryan's strikeout record by asserting "strikeouts are easier to get now [because] . . . players don't care about striking out" (Ringolsby, 1989, p. 10B). Another journalist reported that Feller had said that Ryan should not be inducted into the Hall of Fame because he had not won 100 more games than he had lost. Surprisingly, one report quoted the normally low-key Ryan's sharp rejoinder to Feller's criticism: "It doesn't bother me. I know where Bob Feller is coming from. He has an ego that won't fit in a ballpark and people don't talk and write about him anymore so he has to talk about himself" (Ringolsby, 1989, p. 10B).

Then, on July 31, 1990, at age 43, Nolan Ryan won his 300th game, becoming only the 20th pitcher in the history of baseball to do so. It was another milestone, and it was one that signified success and achievement in terms of bottom-line victories. The Associated Press story on Ryan's victory over the Milwaukee Brewers began with this lead: "Nolan Ryan, a pitcher defined by great numbers, finally got the number that defines great pitchers" ("Ryan gets 300th win," 1990, p. C-1).

Reporters celebrated the event in the papers with hyperbole. One national columnist called Ryan an "icon in the heart of Texas" and wrote:

"Always at home on the ranger, Ryan was destined to make history on the mound" (Gergen, 1990, p. 47). One local reporter went even further, deifying Ryan: "God is good. But Nolan Ryan may be better" (Galloway, 1990, p. 1B).

In gaining his 300th career victory, Ryan attained vindication from long-time critics, including Bob Feller who retracted his earlier statement and said Ryan now did deserve to be in the Hall of Fame. One columnist, commenting on Ryan's critics, wrote that "No. 300 cuts their vocal cards" (Horn, 1990, p. 2H); another wrote that the 300 win mark "represents a triumphant and unarguable validation of the man and his heroic career" (Casstevens, 1990, p. 1B). In these and other published stories, Ryan's 300th victory provided vindication for the Texas Ranger pitcher as well as for the many members of the sports media who had spent so much time and so many pages covering and celebrating his career.

Farewell, Finally. On Thursday, February 11, 1993, Nolan Ryan made the announcement that some fans imagined might never happen: Ryan would retire after the 1993 season. In the days following his announcement, tributes from sportswriters filled newspapers across the country. "When Ryan is gone," wrote Randy Galloway (1993) in an article for *The Miami Herald,* "there's not another one waiting in the baseball wings. Not now, maybe not ever" (p. 11C). Gordon Edes (1993) of the Fort Lauderdale *Sun-Sentinel* offered a similar tribute, writing that "when it comes to larger-than-life characters, those in the [Michael] Jordanesque category, baseball's list begins and ends with Ryan" (p. 6C).

Other sportswriters eulogized Ryan in the past tense. "What he gave the Rangers," wrote Ringolsby (1993) in the *Rocky Mountain News,* "was an official state hero . . . which puts him in a class with such historical dignitaries as Davey Crockett and Sam Houston" (p. 68). Writing for *The Sporting News,* Kindred (1993) waxed poetic about Ryan:

"Yaz is gone Rose is gone
Aaron McCovey Banks Bench Schmidt
the Beatles Elvis hot pants mood rings pet rocks
7 presidents 5 commissioners XXVII Super Bowls
Kareem Magic Bird Payton come and gone
while you, Nolan, brought the heat." (p. 7)

CONCLUDING OBSERVATIONS ON THE MEDIATION OF AN AMERICAN HERO AND CELEBRITY

Ryan clearly has been an unusual athlete with rare abilities who has attained unique accomplishments in the history of professional baseball. As described in this chapter, media coverage of Nolan Ryan also has been unusual and has established Ryan as a contemporary hero and celebrity. In fact, this analysis suggests that his mediated identity as hero and celebrity have worked in unison, rather than in opposition, to establish Nolan Ryan as a truly unique figure in American sports culture.

Mediating Ryan as Hero

The media established Ryan's identity as hero in several ways. First, the media demonstrated that Ryan has passed the traditional tests of the hero; namely, that he has performed great deeds, that he has passed the test of time, and that he has embodied the mainstream cultural values of American society (see Boorstin, 1978; Campbell, 1948; Klapp, 1962).

Ryan's various accomplishments were defined by the media as great deeds. In sports, the quantification of all players and performances throughout history allows reporters (and fans) to document the historic nature of particular players and performances. By the end of the 1992 season, Ryan had set or tied 52 major league records including most no-hitters (7), most one-hitters (12), most strikeouts (5,668), and lowest average hits per nine innings for a career (6.54). As sportswriters revealed these and other records for fans who understand the game "by the numbers," they established the fact that Nolan Ryan has been a man of great baseball deeds.

The media also presented Ryan as someone who had passed the test of time. Reports in 1992 indicated that at age 45 Ryan was the oldest pitcher in baseball. In 1989, stories revealed that he became the oldest pitcher to win an All-Star game; that year he also became the oldest pitcher (age 42) to get 300 strikeouts, beating Mickey Lolich's previous record at age 31 in 1971. In 1991, reports revealed that Ryan became the oldest pitcher (age 44) to throw a no-hitter, beating Cy Young's previous record at age 41 in 1908. During his later years with the Astros and Rangers, the media praised Ryan's remarkable and mysterious ability to continue to throw hard at his advanced age.

The media also established Ryan as a hero in stories about his commitment to mainstream cultural values. "Heroes," Klapp (1962, pp. 27-28) argues, "state major themes of an ethos, the kinds of things people approve." Throughout Ryan's career, reporters focused on his hard-work ethic—in stories about his "legendary" workouts and about his ability to play while in great pain, including reports that he threw his 6th no-hitter (in 1990) with a stress fracture in his back. Reporters displayed Ryan's commitment to home and family in stories about his return home to Texas as an Astro and about his decision to play for the Texas Rangers, even though he received better offers from other teams located further away from his family's home. Reporters also featured Ryan's wholesomeness (when he drank orange juice, not champagne, after he broke Koufax's strikeout record), his honesty and fairness (when he refused to renegotiate for more money with the Rangers after a successful 1989 season), and his humble lifestyle and respect for tradition, explicit in his maintaining his rural roots.

Second, the media revealed that Ryan had passed the test of the media, perhaps a more rigorous standard for contemporary heroism than was the test of time for yesterday's heroes. Given the media's penchant for publishing sensational, conflict-oriented "scoops" (the incentive being increased audience size and concomitant revenue increases) and the sports media's emphasis on the off-the-field excesses and abuses of professional athletes, another testament to Nolan Ryan's heroism is his emergence from over 20 years of media scrutiny virtually unscathed. Although Ryan's critics challenged his focus on strikeouts and his mediocre win-loss record, virtually no media accounts have questioned his commitment to the mainstream values noted above. Nor has any mediated report revealed any skeletons in Ryan's closet, even though such a revelation would be one of the biggest scoops in sports-writing history.

No less than *Dallas Morning News* columnist Skip Bayless (1989), who has a well-earned reputation for shredding the most revered local sportsfigures, including the legendary Tom Landry, wrote a column exalting Ryan as a genuine "hero" (p. D-1). The columnist told readers that he had checked with anonymous sportswriters about Ryan's background, assuming that "no wealthy baseball star can be as humble and clean-living as Ryan's supposed to be, and beat writers usually know every speck of dirt". The only indiscretion he discovered was that Ryan once "was accused of scuffing the ball on his change-up in the National League". In the same column in which Bayless critiqued the "baseless cockiness" of former Ranger manager Bobby Valentine, he concluded: "Nolan is Nolan—just an ol' cowpoke. And I don't mean that negatively. He's so respected in our industry because of the way he carries himself. He's as far from a prima donna as you can get".

Third, the media used Ryan's Texas roots and rural lifestyle as a motif to present him as a cowboy hero and a western warrior. Reporters demonstrated that Ryan was not merely a gunslinging "baseball cowboy" who threw heat to challenge enemy batters; he was a "real cowboy" who embodied frontier values on and off the mound, a cowboy rancher who actually raised cattle in the off-season.

Many scholars have argued that the cowboy and the western myth are central symbols of our history and image as a nation (see Carpenter, 1977; Cawelti, 1976; Rushing, 1983). In his 19th-century "Frontier Thesis," for example, Turner argued that "our national customs and character, indeed, our sources of success as a people, were largely a product of our frontier experiences" (cited in Carpenter, 1977, p. 117). The cowboy, as the central figure of the frontier thesis, stands at the heart of American culture. "Daring, noble, ethical, romantic," Maynard (1974) wrote about the cowboy, "he permeates our popular media to this day. He personifies our national self-image" (p. vi). By presenting Ryan as a cowboy who represented these and other western values, the media cast him as a uniquely American hero.

Finally, the media established Ryan as a hero by presenting the story of his career as a narrative of the quest (Frye, 1957; Stelzner, 1971). The medi traced Ryan's ongoing pitching journey from pastoral little league ba rural Texas to Major League Baseball in New York City and Los Angeles in search of the American Dream of success. During his long odyssey, the media recorded Ryan's struggle to overcome obstacles and adversity, including his pitching wildness, his injuries, and the mediocrity of the teams for whom he played. Along the way, the media recorded his performance of various feats, including his strikeout records, his no-hitters, and finally, his 300th victory which led sportswriting guardians to exalt him as a true hero and to bestow upon him the honor of being worthy of the most precious object—a place in the Hall of Fame.

In the end, Ryan achieved material success while maintaining his moral values; he become the million-dollar cowpoke (see Frentz & Rushing, 1978). Perhaps most importantly, he returned (and stayed) home to prove ultimately that if one works hard and lives clean, one can go home again as a hero. As Giamatti (1989) wrote:

> If baseball is Narrative, it is like others—a work of imagination whose deeper structures and patterns of repetition force a tale, oft-told, to fresh and hitherto-unforseen meaning. . . . It is the story . . . of going home after having left home, the story of how difficult it is to find the origins one so deeply needs to find. It is the literary mode called Romance." (p. 90)

In presenting Ryan as a uniquely American hero, the media performed a bardic function. As Fiske and Hartley (1978) note, this bardic function of the mass media is a form of ritual condensation, a way of giving abstract ideals permanence by locating them in some manifest form such as in the narratives of the heroic quests of sports figures. In addition, the media coverage of Ryan performed a compensatory function by portraying him as a hero who represented the values of America's past. Mediated heroes, as Rader (1983) has observed, have "assisted the public in compensating for the passing of the traditional dream of success, the erosion of Victorian values and the feelings of individual powerlessness" (p. 11). In fact, according to Rader, as a society becomes more complex and bureaucratic, its members may have an even greater need for such heroes.

Mediating Ryan as Celebrity

As Boorstin would have predicted, the heroic Ryan was presented by the media as a celebrity as well. Ryan received much publicity throughout his career; he won awards as a news headliner, and he made many commercial endorsements. Even though he was being exalted as the "ageless hero" in his later years, he also was called the "newest star of the Baby Boomer set" (Greene, 1990, p. 50).

Two features of the mediated development of Ryan's celebrity status are worth noting. First, in their presentation of every detail of Ryan's life throughout his career, reporters helped audiences who would never know Ryan personally to develop "para-social relationships" with him (see Cathcart & Gumpert, 1983; Horton & Wohl, 1956; Wenner, 1985). Stories repeatedly disclosed Ryan's Texas roots and provided such intimate tidbits as his favorite music ("country"), his personal transportation ("a pickup"), his hero ("John Wayne"), and the worst job he ever had ("unloading boxcars in a lumber yard during the summers when [he] was in high school") (Jennings, 1989, pp. 1E-3E). As Anderson and Stone (1981) argue with respect to sports figures, "all this detailed information enables the devotee to identify more closely with the team and to develop imaginary-intimate relationships with the players" (p. 168). Although media members may not intend for audiences to use this information to develop parasocial relationships, the choice to report this information makes such relations all the more likely.

In the case of Nolan Ryan, the information about his understated rural values made identification with him as a "regular guy" all the more likely. And, as Boorstin (1978) suggested:

> Our most admired national heroes—Franklin, Washington, and Lincoln—are generally supposed to possess the "common touch." We revere them, not because they possess charisma, divine favor, a grace or talent granted them by God, but because they embody popular virtues. We admire them, not because they reveal God, but because they reveal and elevate ourselves. (p. 50)

Thus, when country music blared from the Arlington Stadium speakers between innings during one of Ryan's 1989 starts, one fan told his ballpark neighbor, "That's Nolie's favorite type of music."

Second, the same Western myth that was used as a motif to cast Ryan as a unique American hero also has been used as a tool to commodify Ryan as a unique American celebrity. For example, in several of his commercials Ryan was not dressed in baseball attire, but in western attire. His full-page newspaper ads for Wrangler Jeans constitute perhaps the most obvious example. In these ads Ryan was pictured standing on the pitcher's mound at Arlington Stadium, wearing a baseball glove and holding a baseball; he also was wearing a cowboy hat (though surprisingly a black one), a western-style shirt, and Wrangler Jeans. One ad caption read, "A western original wears a western original"; another read, "He's won 300 games and still hasn't lost the crease in his jeans."

Thus, the same set of Western images have been used by reporters to establish Ryan's identity as hero (in order to embellish news stories and sell newspapers) and by advertisers to cash in on Ryan's identity as celebrity (in order to sell products and services). Furthermore, Ryan himself has used this identity to enhance his own marketability in order to increase his wealth through endorsements. However, unlike Boorstin, we do not believe that Ryan's celebrity status has discredited his heroic status; rather, we believe they have worked together to establish Ryan's unique mediated identity as hero and celebrity. Over time, his material value as a celebrity commodity may diminish, but his social value as a celebrity hero only will be enhanced.

In the final analysis, this case study of Nolan Ryan suggests that true

American heroes still can be found in contemporary society. However, the heroes of today can never be like the heroes of yesterday. Today's heroes must, by definition, also be celebrities. When today's heroes perform great deeds and pass the test of time, they ultimately, and inevitably, receive too much press coverage and do too many commercials. However, in becoming celebrities, public figures who perform great deeds over time do not necessarily diminish their status as heroes. In order to maintain their identities as heroes, however, public figures must pass the test of the media and rise above their temporary status as celebrity.

We believe that a cartoon from an issue of the *New Yorker* magazine (1990) summarizes this final point quite elegantly. The cartoon shows a teacher facing her class of young boys and girls. As she looks at one of these students, she praises his answer: "Very good, Gary: 'A hero is a celebrity who did something real.'"

Nolan Ryan is a hero; he *is* a celebrity who did something real.

16

Jimmy Swaggart as Hero: People of a Narrative Tradition

Kathaleen Reid
Lee College

☐ *This chapter reveals one of the significant changes in the role of the hero in today's heterogenous society. Reid shows that real heroes still exist, but they exist for circumscribed communities rather than for society at large. Reid provides a look inside the Pentecostal community revealing its particular world view, value system, and self-imposed isolation. She then furnishes a detailed analysis of the ministry of Jimmy Swaggart, clearly locating him within this community and establishing how he functions as a true hero, despite the attitude of the general public. Her study demonstrates how mass media can be used by a televangelist to create and maintain a narrative myth that gives him hero status within a relatively isolated community.*

Currently, a debate rages as to the authenticity and power of the religious personalities in the broadcast industry. No critical consensus exists as to how destructive or constructive this programming may be. Yet, while the controversies rage, televangelists continue to ply their trade.

One such figure is Jimmy Swaggart, who has appeared on over 300 television stations in over 190 markets (Gerbner et al., 1984; Horsefield, 1984; Ostling, 1986). Based on 1987 Arbitron ratings, Pullum (1988) found that Swaggart ranked number one in audience size among televangelists (p. 112). Remarkably, Swaggart's subsequent confession of promiscuity involving prostitutes did little to dampen his popular appeal. The question becomes, then, how has Swaggart maintained such mass appeal, despite behavior that is so dramatically at odds with the beliefs of his audience? Neither blind loyalty nor guileless gullibility accounts satisfactorily for this phenomenon. First, I argue that Swaggart's pentecostal audience follows a narrative myth that allows Swaggart to function as a contemporary hero for the old-line pentecostal community, and further that the mass media, particularly television, encourage and enhance Swaggart's perceived heroic character. Television makes it possible for Swaggart's original Southern followers (those existing prior to his broadcast ministry) to identify with a hero around whom their story can be told and to broadcast their story to an international community.

Second, I demonstrate how a narrative approach reflects a media phenomenon from an internal perspective, that is, from the perspective of the audience and its intrinsic characteristics that relate to the media. Critics, Pullum (1990) in particular, have offered explanations of Swaggart's mass appeal by looking only at Swaggart's rhetoric in his televised sermons. I go further by examining the phenomenon as a reflection of individuals within a vital community, and I suggest that the phenomenon can be understood only in this social context. This internal approach, according to Niebuhr (1989) in his discussion of how the study of narrative helps us to understand subcultures, allows for the perception of the tertiary qualities or values of a given subculture so that the role and function of a social phenomenon can be described more clearly (p. 32). As Niebuhr (1989) reminds us, "One must look with them and not at them to verify their visions" (p. 36).

I emphasize that I wish neither to substantiate nor to refute the claims of televangelist Jimmy Swaggart or his followers. I do wish, however, to examine the pentecostal narrative and Swaggart's role in it because he and his followers create a phenomenon of contemporary mass media.

One might ask in relation to this analysis, why Swaggart and not other televangelists? Swaggart's heritage is that of old-time Southern pentecostalism, and pentecostals of the old school find in Swaggart a voice that rings with a message reminiscent of their past. Theirs is a world marked by material deprivation and a lack of social standing, and they are not easily seduced by the self-help schemes offered by many evangelists in the name of Christianity. Stoics at heart, these pentecostals accept material life with resignation. Their hope comes not through political and economic change, but through spiritual transcendence.

Jim Bakker's Christian holiday park remains a chimera for these simple people who have little time to play. The new "gospel of getting on," of easy prosperity and health, espoused by such accommodating evangelists as Kenneth Copeland and Robert Schuller, springs from a world alien to a people who have shunned the pleasures of the world. As Bruce (1990) points out in *Pray TV: Televangelism in America*, contemporary religious programming is filled with avenues for self-fulfillment, self-satisfaction, and self-esteem, all of which easily could appear as too "self-serving" for the old-line pentecostal.

Televangelists, such as Roberts, Bakker, and Robertson, often do not emphasize a distinctive theology, so they may have the broadest possible appeal (Bruce, 1990, p. 237). Swaggart's programming, on the other hand, is more narrow, with little deviation from the traditional beliefs of the pentecostal community (Harvey, 1987, p. 94). As a long-time televangelist, Swaggart's style remains highly pentecostal in its assertiveness, boldness, and emotion.

THE PENTECOSTALS AND THEIR NARRATIVE MYTH

Pentecostalism developed at the turn of the century out of the religious fervor of 19th-century Christian revivalism. I hold that in the late 20th century, traditional followers of pentecostalism find themselves in a position of isolation on three fronts: from the broader Western society, from the overall Christian community, and from within the pentecostal and charismatic community itself. The reasons for this include their lower economic and social class and a self-imposed separation based on their theological world view. Their economic and social position has little chance of changing, according to Dabbs (1972) in his historical assessment of the religious movement. He suggests they "have no horizon" and "the rich world flows by in the shining cars, the neon signs, and on the TV screen, and the most they can do is to watch with glazed eyes" (p. 194).

Old-line pentecostals are separated from the broader community by their ideology, as well as by economic realities. Although functioning within the milieu of contemporary society, pentecostals continue to hold values of an earlier age of simpler, agrarian societal forms, structures, and ideas. Deeply embedded in this is the fierce independence of the individual which produces freedom for them, respect for the freedom of others, and leads to the conceptualization of freedom as being isolation from those who differ (Byrd, 1991). As social critics, the pentecostals believe the world is "sick and dying" and they share Joseph Campbell's (1949) pessimism that "every last vestige of the ancient human heritage of ritual, morality, and art is in full decay" (p. 388). The pentecostal reaction of isolation from the broader society may be viewed as a direct response to the changes and fragmentation within society during the last 150 years as well as a theological position.

Until recently, most pentecostals have been isolated from the traditional Christian community. They frequently and mistakenly have been viewed as simply another group of fundamentalists; however, they are more parallel to Eastern orthodoxy with its deep-rooted mysticism than Western Christianity (Land, 1989, p. 493). In the early days of their community, the pentecostals also distinguished themselves from other Christian denominations in their inclusiveness. Women and members of all races were permitted to hold significant positions in their churches. Allowing involvement of all people was, in the eyes of many mainline Christian denominations, an embarrassment and a disgrace, as well as an "incorrect" interpretation of scriptures. Perhaps the most noticeable difference between pentecostal and mainstream American protestantism is the pentecostal style of worship. They "laughed in the spirit," "spoke in other tongues," and were "slain in the spirit"—behaviors which were once part of, but by the late 19th century totally rejected by, many traditional churches. Although these behaviors can be found today in the charismatic movements of many mainline churches, the old-line pentecostal identifies more clearly with the age in which these methods of worship were totally rejected by both the broader Christian church and the secular community.

Currently, isolation comes from within their own ranks as middle-class values infiltrate their own denominations, which originated among the poorest of the poor in American society. Often from their pulpits each Sunday, today's pentecostals hear their traditional forms of worship combined with contemporary clarion calls of wealth and success, both viewed suspiciously by the old-line pentecostals. Although they continue to support and participate fully in their religious social structures, they are isolated within their own community, and the pentecostal denominations are becoming more fragmented (Poloma, 1989).

The Narrative Myth

The pentecostal narrative accounts for much of the isolation described earlier. The narrative is mythical in that these stories are transcendent and are believed by the pentecostals to be true. According to rhetorical critic Robert C. Rowland (1990), myth must be "taken very seriously by the people who tell it"; the story "need not be factual," but "there should be evidence that those who tell it believe the story to be more than mere entertainment; that it is in some sense true" (p. 105). For the purposes of this analysis, myth is defined as an anonymously developed story explaining why the world exists and why humans relate to one another as they do. It is a teaching device that lends guidance as it tells of the nature and destiny of humans (Wellek & Warren, 1956, p. 119). As such, myth provides a sense of importance that allows for individual identity and grants the hearer a place within a community (Lewis, 1987).

The pentecostal myth includes the orthodox Christian description of the origin of human life and human destiny, but is distinguished by the emphasis placed on the imminent presence of God directly intervening in the lives of community members. The pentecostal stories describe miraculous encounters, both physical and spiritual. Because of the belief in supernatural intervention, the pentecostal myth represents life as a great divine drama with all human beings participating in "God's history." In the myth, each human being is a significant actor, and each human act is endowed with meaning because it is a part of the teleological "process of suffering, healing, hope, and victory" (Land, 1990, pp. 339-343). Life is described as a journey filled with "trials and tribulations." The pentecostal journey includes an appropriation of the Hebrew journey; a "moving from Egypt through the desert across the Jordan into Canaan" is combined with the pentecostals' personal "journeys" through contemporary life. The journey takes the pentecostals into battles between good and evil, enacted in the spiritual, not physical realm. "Earthly," physical battles are anathema to the pentecostals, so much so that in the early years of the movement most pentecostals were pacifists.

The pentecostal myth tells of supernatural battles and supports their belief that change comes by spiritual transcendence, not by politics, manipulation, or coercion. All pentecostals are "soldiers" in the "Lord's Army" fighting with "spiritual weapons": prayer, both individual and corporate; fasting; and the reading of Scriptures. The enemy is "Satan" and they band together to pray for any nonbeliever who may be a "pawn of evil." Their journey is taken within the context of their community, which in their story is the strategy for transforming the world and them with it. In the myth, it is a haven for outcasts, the poor, the sick, and the suffering "servant of God." The community is a shadowed reflection of "heaven on earth" where all individuals within the community are granted dignity and value in the grand drama of the universe.

The pentecostals understand that the cosmic struggle described in their myth is offensive to many, and, consequently, they anticipate their isolation from others. They have no expectations that those outside their community will celebrate their myth. Their main difficulty is the threat of isolation within their own community. In the midst of this tension, the traditional pentecostal clings to the old myth and searches for an apocalyptic voice that "makes a space for the cry of the disposed, the languishing mass who feel . . . victimized by cultural and ecclesiastical forces which tend to shut down their historic process" (Land, 1990, p. 94).

THE HERO

Televangelist Jimmy Swaggart, in line with the myth previously indicated, is such an apocalyptic voice. He offers hope and order as he reiterates the pentecostal narrative and guides the community in the midst of social change. Swaggart's story, which replicates the genre of the hero in Western culture, is composed of the characters traditionally associated with this form. Swaggart's cast of characters includes a hero—himself, several antagonists—supernatural enemies and institutions, and the common folk—his constituency. The consistent hallmarks of a hero include his journey, humility, the self-sufficient use of weapons, and bringing culture to a community.

The solitary journey is the hero's quest to preserve the good (Parks, 1982, p. 32). This places the hero in a state of transition as he moves into the unknown, thus transforming his own life as well as the lives of others (Williams, 1961, p. 405). This common pattern of charting the unknown is represented in Jimmy Swaggart's television programs. This is a 20th-century man moving with his audience into the 21st century with its unknowns; in the process, Swaggart is changed as he prepares to move from the mortal to the immortal in his spiritual journey. He takes oral narrative forms of traditional agrarian cultures and transposes them into the 21st century via a sophisticated contemporary medium.

This journey of the hero is always a solitary one, the hero is always a loner, "poised between savagery and civilization, the desert and the Garden," belonging to neither world (Parks, 1982, pp. 57-58). Swaggart remains poised between the savage world that he constantly describes in his sermons and the institutions, such as the Assemblies of God denomination, which offer a civilizing influence as they organize their constituency. As indicated by his withdrawal from the Assemblies of God after they restricted him in 1988 because of his voyeuristic involvement with New Orleans prostitutes, Swaggart never fully participates in any institution or organization not of his own making. He is too autonomous to follow the mandates of the denomination with which he began his ministry, yet he is not so independent of this tradition that he can renounce all desire to be involved in the pentecostal community. He remains in his personal pentecostal ministry, even as his temptation to enter the "savage" world continues. Thus, he becomes an independent agent, and, in his story, he struggles between the spiritual and physical worlds, seeming to belong in neither. This struggle fits the Pentecostal myth as it suggests that Swaggart is caught in a battle between his own ideal, "spiritual self" and his "mortal flesh," as most clearly revealed with the confession of his voyeurism in 1988. Swaggart's confession became a way of overcoming evil in a great duel—his "sin" a battle with his "foe" in whom he recognizes his own fatal flaw. The confession becomes part of the myth.

The second primary trait of the conventional hero is humility. He is "an able man [who] must not glory in his cleverness," who recognizes "[v]anity or personal arrogance in any form [as] . . . taboo" (Wecter, 1941, p. 483). This trait is one that Swaggart clearly has understood. The very act of confessing his wrong-doing and his statements following the accompanying publicity were described in *Newsweek* (Hackett, 1988) as meek, modest, and self-responsible. Swaggart did not arrogantly brush aside accusations when he told his audience of 7,500, "I do not plan to whitewash my sin. . . . I have no one but myself to blame. I take the fall" (p. 30). Before the Assemblies of God board, "[H]e showed nothing but openness and honesty. . . . He showed a very humble attitude. He was repentant" (p. 31). While with the board, he reportedly said, "Here I am. I'm sorry . . . I'm at your mercy. I love you all" (p. 31).

Swaggart indicates his humility in his sermons, often referring to his lack of "cleverness" and "sophistication." Although his actions may be arrogant (i.e., refusing to obey the Assemblies of God's direct orders to step down from his ministry and to seek counseling), his rhetoric has been consistently one of humbleness. For example, Swaggart's strategic use of rhetoric turned his act of pulling away from the Assemblies into an ennobling one that was done for the sake of a higher mission—that Swaggart Ministries might continue to function and fulfill their obligations to employees and to evangelize the world. The "God-given" mission was to override any "human-made" organization. Such seeming humility and noble action are understood by Swaggart's constituency because his sin, confession, and subsequent behavior are all rhetorically presented in a myth with which the audience can identify. Using the propagandistic device of "plain folk," a very simple rhetoric and argument, is effective with this hero's followers.

A third trait of the hero is self-sufficiency and use of weapons. The solitary hero of Western society is known for being self-sufficient, for fighting alone against the enemy; any assistance from the common people is usually minor. Swaggart's independence was emphasized when he chose to lose his denominational affiliation, and his self-reliance was evidenced in his refusal to seek psychological treatment after the church organization advised him to do so. Swaggart fights for his ministry and his followers, subscribing to this code of self-reliance using an arsenal of a Bible that is reputed to be "sharper than any two-edged sword," a hymnal, fire-and-brimstone sermons, and his charisma.

According to Parks (1982, p. 57), the hero is highly skilled and "handles tools well, whether equipment or weapons" and is at home with his desolate battlefield or terrain of desert and mountains. Swaggart, too, is at home with his terrain whether it be the television cameras, spotlights, an open set, or the spiritual battlefield which he describes so vividly for his audience. He handles the verbal and nonverbal requirements of the Old Time Gospel style well and has easily adapted them for TV presentation. His highly dramatic and emotional use of words, his confessions at the appropriate times, and his actions have become weapons that he handles adroitly in the duel between good and evil.

Each hero has his antagonists. For Swaggart, the list of enemies is quite diverse: science, Satan, much of contemporary culture, political figures and issues, and even the Roman Catholic Church (Harvey, 1987, p. 88). Enemies are all clearly pointed out over and over again in his sermons. Satan is often personified and at other times takes the form of a "monster" or a "beast" (Swaggart, 1977). Listeners are encouraged to recognize the Evil One's varying forms and to be on guard against him. Institutions also can be evil enemies of faith, so Swaggart condemns Roman Catholicism (because it is a "false cult") and the U.S. Supreme Court and Congress ("institutions damned by God") (Harvey, 1987).

The last set of characters in the myth of the hero is the common folk represented by Swaggart's audience. International broadcasting makes Swaggart's mass audience heterogeneous, crossing boundaries of age, class, gender, and language. According to Abelman (1988) in his study of religious television, mass audiences viewing televangelists are varied, but for the most part they are demographically downscale, older, poorer, and less educated. No matter what the actual composition, Swaggart places the audience in two basic categories: those who believe and those who do not. The believers consist of the many regular viewers who accept the Old Time Gospel message as the one that is right and true and who agree with the need to be spiritually "born again" and to be "filled with the Spirit" to aid in their struggle against evil. They share Swaggart's interpretation of the spiritual drama, and it is to this group that he appeals for financial assistance. The other viewers are "nonbelievers," those who are not "born again," and who do not accept his interpretation of spiritual life as truth.

Interpretation of the Hero

Stories indicating that hero worship is a deeply ingrained emotion that cannot be eradicated from human nature thrive in most cultures throughout recorded history (Fraser, 1980, p. 19). Often called "gods," the heroes were superior men, directly related to the social and religious structures of their society (Rovin, 1985). They were perceived as a "gift from heaven" and "a force sent by destiny." Westerners of classic times called their heroes god-men; the medieval culture, God's men; the Renaissance, universal men; the 18th century, gentlemen; the 19th century, self-made men (Fishwick, 1983). The pentecostals are closest to the medieval culture, as they view a hero as God's person and heroic figures as chosen men and women serving divine purposes. Such figures are evidence of the persistence of the hero, suggesting that the pentecostal narrative is not just a story, but a cultural myth that speaks to people and fulfills their need for a stabilizing force and central figures who embody their values.

Embedded within the pentecostal view of heroic figures are important general traits of Western cultural heroes along with traits more specific to American heroes. Underlying both of these influences is the pentecostal 20th-century interpretation of divine heroes. The result is an eclectic or hybrid hero.

Western Culture Hero. The pentecostal myth and Swaggart's story within it contain primary elements of the Western Culture Hero paradigm as described by Campbell (1949) and Blacker (1984). They note the path a culture will follow is cut by the hero on his journey into a supernatural region in which he encounters powerful forces. The hero overcomes these forces and then returns to bestow wisdom or liberation to his followers, a function that Swaggart takes very seriously. In short, the hero's pattern is "a separation from the world, a penetration to some source of power, and a life-enhancing return" (Campbell, 1949, p. 35). Campbell (1949) suggests that all groups are looking for a hero who precedes them so that they "have only to follow the thread of the hero's path" (p. 25).

The Western Culture Hero represents us to ourselves, brings us our culture, and rescues us. The rescuer myth is the biography of an exceptional being. In this type of myth, a hero must be perceived by his followers to be an exceptional being who often is granted by the gods exceptional virtues denied average mortals. Swaggart's gifts of rhetoric and musical talent and his battles with supernatural forces are perceived as far superior to those of his audience. Along with these virtues, a hero, such as Swaggart, carries the burden of his mission and travels on his great journey, acquiring skills and knowledge that will help his followers.

American Hero. The American heroic traits found in Swaggart's story are those of the Wild West that evoke images of the isolated Lone Ranger facing the odds alone and overcoming them. The American hero is typified by the one-dimensional television image, and Swaggart's programming boldly embodies this style.

When heroes appear in the American mass media, the scene often depicted is of a solitary figure on horseback against the backdrop of a vast, empty desert. The hero's figure in stark relief is dramatic, capturing the audience's attention. Similarly, Swaggart with Bible in hand holds center stage with no other objects around him. Under stark lights, he is a dramatic figure against an unlit backdrop. He stands in bold relief, nothing distracting the viewer from his image—a major parallel between the traditional Wild West heroes and Swaggart. The convention of the lone figure in the open space is understood by Swaggart's audience, and it brings with it the expectation of the strong, solitary leader who will rescue the people from disaster. In exchange, they will provide him with the laurels and adoration befitting their hero. As he rescues the people, Swaggart fulfills his audience's expectations that a hero should lend guidance to his followers. Swaggart's image as the lone figure in the spotlight visually reinforces his verbal message during broadcasts, as he holds forth that "the man on horseback" still discerns good from evil. Much of Swaggart's emotional appeal rests on the visual recreation of the solitary man, the hero who clearly defines the enemy and leads the common people in purging their community of evil.

This suggests that the visual setting is essential in "influencing the form of the work and the audience's response to it" (Parks, 1982, p. 28) and in creating a symbiotic relationship of hope and trust between Swaggart and the audience. It helps tell the story and communicate the mood and even the plot to the viewers. In Swaggart's setting the physical light and dark reinforces to the viewers the universal drama that is occurring, the battle between good and evil. In the process they are given hope visually as they see their hero accented by the light. He appears strong, animated, filled with energy, and ready to do spiritual battle on their behalf.

The American Hero often comes from poor, humble, or obscure origins (Robertson, 1980, p. 209) and becomes a leader, an indispensable ingredient for heroic figures in our society (Hook, 1943). Swaggart's rise from poor, humble, Southern origins to become the leader of an organization that encompasses a global community reflects the common American theme of the journey from obscurity to fame.

Divine Hero. A divine hero is one whose purpose is given by a god or gods and manifested in a specific event or revelation. A message for his followers will be given to the hero, and his path will include testing in order to purify him (Butler, 1979, pp. 80-90). The divine hero—the saint, teacher, or dragon slayer wrestling with supernatural forces—fights a cosmic battle and has a divine revelation that is perceived as truth by his followers. Often, the scene of the battle is nonmaterial. The basic elements of divine heroism—the supernatural journey, divine purpose or mission, struggles with good and evil to purify the individual, and guidance for his followers—are reflected in Swaggart's story. At the same time that Swaggart is providing his audience with stories of his personal journey in which he is the heroic figure, he is acting out an important part, that of a hero within its religious tradition. Embedded within the pentecostal narrative theology is a great love of the heroic figures of the Old and New Testaments. In his narratives Swaggart becomes a modern-day version of a man wrestling with tremendous forces of good and evil, like those individuals of the past, who can best parallel the traditional Biblical figures and can become the most significant to these religious people.

Thus far, Swaggart's story is one his constituency can understand, his struggles are those with which they can identify, and his mandates are those with which they can agree. This audience does not confuse Swaggart as a divine hero with primary universal heroes, such as Jesus or Gantam Buddha, both of whom bring messages for the entire world or the means to regenerate society (Campbell, 1949, p. 38), but rather he is a tribal or local divine hero who commits himself to a single group of people as he overcomes his personal oppressors and conquers his enemy. This concept of tribe is redefined by the broadcasting media, creating an international "tribe." Whereas the oral tradition of tribes is continued via television, this mediated community differs significantly from the traditional tribe based on geographic proximity.

Swaggart continues the tradition of divine heroes by incorporating stories of cosmic struggles and battles between good and evil. In Swaggart's narratives these scenarios illustrate how evil controls all areas of society—politics, the entertainment industry, education, and other businesses. This illustration provides justification for the pentecostals' isolation from secular society. Swaggart's strictures as to which groups to follow or shun provide guidance through cultural changes. Clear simplistic lines of demarcation tied to the prevailing myth reassure and guide Swaggart's audience.

Examination of the elements of Swaggart as hero implies that a contemporary religious figure is a hero only to the extent that he characterizes the heroic traits found in his constituency's myth. For his constituency Swaggart validates the traditional story of Christianity, of sin and forgiveness. He remains a hero only as long as he continues to seek "the good" as defined by this community. Once he consistently chooses what his followers are opposed to, Swaggart can no longer be a hero to this community. Choosing "evil" shifts his role from hero to "sinner"; yet, even then, Swaggart still validates their story of how easily human beings fall victim to corruption, losing their heroic status.

Bruce (1990) supports the idea that Swaggart's story is part of the pentecostal narrative by noting the audience's response to the scandal and resulting public humiliation. He states that Swaggart followed the expectation of the pentecostal audience when he assumed full responsibility for his behavior and presented his narrative as an example that "shows that we are all in sin since the Fall, that the flesh is weak, and that we need more gospel preaching to keep us on the straight and narrow" (p. 209). In this type of narrative, Swaggart shows that "[h]is own transgressions qualify him to preach to all of us because that 'all of us' now includes him" (Bruce, 1990, p. 209). This inclusiveness reflects the pentecostals' stories involving scenes and actions of failure, sin, and forgiveness. One of Swaggart's viewers said, "Brother Swaggart is an imperfect human being but the Bible says those who love the Lord and seek the truth shall have their sins forgiven if they repent" (Ostling, 1988, p. 30). In fact, this element of sensational behavior and forgiveness that transforms the individual can be far more dramatic and imperative to the audience because the sinner who repents is a far better exemplar of the community myth than the blameless, ordinary person (Bruce, 1990).

Even in his failure, Swaggart's primary function for the old-line pentecostals is that of rescuer of their rapidly disappearing myth, and as Hook (1943) notes in his examination of historically important figures in Western culture, those who save their followers are heroes (p. 12). These individuals are saviors, prophets, or men on horseback, and their function is the key to their existence (Parks, 1982, p. 58). Swaggart often describes himself as a lone figure who clearly sees the path and seeks to save his followers and preserve their values, serving as an important social force for his time and his constituency.

THE PENTECOSTAL CONTEXT, THE HERO, AND THE MEDIUM

Contemporary heroes, including religious ones, must contend with the electronic media and its attendant celebrities who are often viewed as opposed to or as counterparts of the traditional hero (Boorstin, 1977). Electronic media with new patterns, new space, and new techniques create previously untried arenas for heroes, who now must bear the weight of the dynamic characteristics of the media—the instantaneous, the fleeting, the temporary. Fishwick (1972) notes that few individuals can withstand these forces; other critics go so far as to suggest that only fictitious heroes can tolerate the weight of the electronic media (Frye, 1957; Rollin, 1983).

In contradiction to the critics, the hero who weaves the constituency's narrative myth through the media and manipulates the media well is enhanced and empowered. For instance, Hackett (1988) states that for Swaggart the move to television proved to be a "marriage made in heaven" (p. 31). The medium of television enables Swaggart's program to perpetuate the pentecostal myth, and it reflects key characteristics of the pentecostal phenomenon. These characteristics, which are shared by television and pentecostals, include the concepts of orality, community, and fusion. Television, enhanced by orality, empowers the pentecostals through speech; television allows a global community to "embrace" one another, an essential element of the pentecostals' emphasis on relationships; and television, which fuses time and space—an important aspect of the pentecostals' theology—permits the pentecostals to be transported into the presence of their hero.

These three elements have been woven intricately within the pentecostal movement, prior to and following the introduction of television. As a result television is a natural medium for these people in contrast to the mainline churches which relied more on written, static media, such as printed materials. These elements make the pentecostals far more susceptible to the strengths and weaknesses of the medium of television. Because of this close affinity between the medium and the intrinsic characteristics of this group of people, a hero such as Swaggart can arise with ease and be embraced more quickly and maintained more easily within the people's narrative. Television enhances this role by providing the arena of the social movement and the electronic means of carrying its voice. It broadens the movement by moving it from a local community into an international one, an act which rescues the pentecostals from their isolation within local communities and gives them the opportunity to speak to a broader audience.

The foundation of pentecostal theology is an informal oral-narrative liturgy (Land, 1989). This includes various oral forms, such as concert prayer, testimonials, speaking in tongues, prophecies, and descriptions of visions and dreams. The oral narratives tell of the pentecostals' personal experiences and joys brought about by their religion (Hollenweger, 1972, p. 55). They fully expect the oral presentation of stories to be a vital part of their worship services, and in keeping with this, Swaggart fills his programs with extraordinary stories and testimonials of the divine leading in battles with evil monsters. He uses colorful details of his encounters with the supernatural as the data necessary to prove his heroic status to his audience. His stories are enhanced by the dynamic qualities of television, a medium often referred to as a myth-making or storytelling machine. Swaggart's stories come alive as he uses verbal and nonverbal skills to dramatize events. Dramatization is the natural characteristic of this medium, thus, increasing Swaggart's credibility and expertise as a storyteller and solidifying his role as hero.

In addition to the narratives, Swaggart's style of delivery, including animated facial expressions, pointing, pounding, and varied vocalics, brings about active audience participation, including oral amens and praises, the nodding of heads, and clapping. Swaggart's comfortable format of gospel rhythm and blues is one in which his constituency can participate by singing along and verbally interjecting responses to the speaker (Hoover, 1988). This format is charged with high emotional appeal in contrast to the formal, more cognitive one that attends written prayers and liturgy. Swaggart's informal, televised format indicates that he is a hero who is among them, not separated from them. He permits a limited dialogue between himself and the audience, increasing their feelings of identity with their hero. This environment encourages viewers to believe that their oral responses are being replicated by like-minded audience members with whom they share similar social and economic disadvantages, but from whom they may be separated geographically.

In the process the pentecostals intuit that their stories are lent credibility through the medium itself because television often is recognized as a highly credible source. Simultaneously, the act of seeing and hearing their oral forms broadcast to numerous countries validates the pentecostals' significance in the broader society. The result is a legitimization process with the potential for widening the influence, acceptance, and credibility of the pentecostal myth.

In his analyses of oral traditions Ong (1982) recognizes the power of speech by theorizing that the "word" is a sound event that loses its power when locked in silent space through print. The pentecostals understand this in terms of spiritual power being released, not through theological, written argument, but through the oral message. To them the resulting spiritual transformation is the important attribute brought through this power of the spoken word.

In the narrative tradition the spoken word reveals truth, and according to pentecostals, individuals are transformed by this truth into righteousness and love as they are brought into communion with God. Such ideas are based on the premise that truth is revelational, not just propositional. The spoken word in narrative form introduces truth through metaphors and experiences, not through the careful reasoning and propositions established in the traditional Western logic in much of American society. This revelational approach to truth is highly dependent on intuitive and emotional responses, methods that are used adroitly by Swaggart. His narratives show truth as revealed versus truth from reason, and his excellent use of this form reinforces his role as revealed hero.

Narrative form, not rational argument, is the primary means of communication on television. These forms are revelational in that segments become symbols of much more, and the viewer of the symbol must experience closing the gap, that is, determining the symbol's meaning. Attendant with this narrative form is the use of images and oral messages to evoke emotional responses. If television is the medium of emotion and image, then audience members' experience is more significant than their reasoning, as demonstrated by Swaggart, who projects his heroism through visual image and emotion not through reason. This places television in the same experiential, revelational category as the pentecostals. In this light, television is understood not as a transmitter of information, but as a ritual. A ritual view indicates that communication is the "sacred ceremony that draws persons together" and is the means "whereby reality is created, shared, modified, and preserved" (Carey, 1989, pp. 18, 33). Reality is transformed based on the language and symbolic forms that are used. Television, as a myth-making machine, does not just serve as a carrier of the myth, but becomes a part of the transformation process when adopted by the pentecostals. This helps explain how a figure such as Swaggart can be transformed from ordinary mortal into hero.

Another significant aspect of orality is that empowerment occurs when the authority base shifts from those with status, education, money, and judicial power to the individuals with the spoken word (Hollenweger, 1986). Any member of the pentecostal community—whether simply a local church member or a heroic figure such as Swaggart—is empowered to speak the words that he or she deems important to another person or to the entire group. With this empowerment the old-line pentecostals give *all* community members a significant voice, thereby granting them dignity. They simultaneously choose their own heroes, such as Swaggart, who speak for them. In so doing they redefine authority, which results in the old-line pentecostals not "playing by the rules" of their oppressors, but creating their own world view of society and their role within it. In this new world view the pentecostals are understood, not as the deprived, but as those with important wisdom to contribute to society.

By the use of television the pentecostals can disseminate more easily and rapidly their messages of wisdom to a greater portion of the society. At the same time these words which constitute the oral narratives of their television programs create a sense of control over this medium that, in their perception, can be more often the purveyor of evil than of good. Such control magnifies their sense of empowerment. Control is further intensified when their hero Swaggart proves to be such an excellent manipulator of this medium. Capabilities brought about through the spoken word—to have authority based within, not outside, their own community; to contribute wisdom to society; and to legitimate this authority through the pentecostals' appearance on and through their control of television, the primary medium of the 20th century—liberate the pentecostals from dehumanizing cultural, economic, and social forces.

Deprivation of the poor, although often defined in economic terms, is not the only deprivation. For the pentecostals it is the loss of speech that is most devastating. For with the loss of speech is the loss of self-worth and dignity, the loss of identity (Hollenweger, 1972, pp. 459, 462). Rhetorical forms such as those used by Swaggart give the people a voice as they allow their hero to speak for them. Television offers a place for their voices to be represented to the broader society. The empowerment and resulting sense of identity that comes through the spoken word releases the pentecostals from isolation and causes pentecostalism to be recognized by some critics as "the most vibrant . . . model of Christianity today" (Dowd, 1985, p. E3).

Community. As a guiding figure for this segment of the pentecostal community, Swaggart uses television to provide a forum so that he functions as a force and a rallying point around which his global village can find courage, faith, and communal identity. Serving as the central force embeds his role of hero within the central core of the community, a characteristic essential for heroes (Browne & Fishwick, 1983; Butler, 1979). His program draws together a disparate group of individuals into a collective unit composed of like-minded people, who share common beliefs, and via television, common experience. This provides isolated individuals with a sense of place and belonging. In so doing Swaggart grants the old-line pentecostals a significance that empowers them as they gain an arena in which their presence is valued. In return they bring Swaggart their allegiance and loyalty, and he ascends to the position of hero.

This reciprocal relationship reflects the "living theology" of the pentecostal community. A sense of community is essential to the pentecostal tradition, and Swaggart's global community is highly important to the pentecostal whose theology is described often as a "living" one because it stresses the development of relationships. The traditional pentecostals always have been noted for their warmth, vitality, and closeness. In any pentecostal community there will be lots of hugging of necks, patting of backs, and shaking of hands. As the central mediated figure Swaggart is the pivot around which a global community can "embrace" one another. In this sense Swaggart as the centralizing agent functions today as a larger-than-life hero of his global electronic village, just as the minister was the primary person in a small town in days past.

Although some televangelists have become preoccupied with political concerns, Swaggart has continued to emphasize community and everyone's part in it through videos and monetary contributions. Each Sunday he shows videotapes of people from around the world who are involved in Swaggart Ministries. The pictures show children in need, the elderly being helped, and various international locations of the ministry. Swaggart's appeal for money is based on the call for members of the community to aid these fellow members of the Swaggart community. Although the ethics regarding Swaggart's request for funding and how that funding is distributed can be debated, the key concern here is how Swaggart creates a cohesive following. One way is by inviting audience members to contribute, even if it is only small amounts. In so doing, Swaggart is giving the people a chance to participate in the lives of others in this mediated community, and he is seen as the hero who fends for the poor. This appears to reenact the poor caring for the poor, as in the pentecostals' early days. Such participation in the lives of others provides a sense of identity among Swaggart's followers and gives them a greater sense of their possible influence and power as a distinct segment of society.

One aspect of Swaggart's community is a feeling among audience members that they have indeed helped suffering brothers and sisters around the world. Other factors, often unrecognized, can work as a detriment to the audience as community. Television only provides parasocial relationships, not interpersonal ones found in a geographic community (Horton & Wohl, 1986). In such parasocial relationships found in the pentecostals' association with their hero, the struggles, responsibilities, and rewards of interpersonal relationships are not found. In the case of Swaggart's audience, the result is a paracommunity, a community that has the appearance of a true community, but in reality does not contain the essential elements that compose one. For instance, no accountability exists between Swaggart and his viewers. As a result, behaviors such as Swaggart's voyeurism go unchecked for extended periods of time, and his status as hero remains unchallenged.

Even though on one level these parasocial relationships create feelings of increased identity and decreased isolation, in reality, the individual sits alone. Instead of a personal relationship, Swaggart is not a person, but an exalted hero who appears each week as an electronic icon, simply a devotional image that is a symbol of the pentecostal story. This increases privatized worship and higher levels of individual autonomy, while it decreases the old-line pentecostal theology that emphasized relationships and community. Paradoxically, the broadcast, which decreases the pentecostals' feelings of isolation, is, on another level, encouraging higher levels of autonomy with attendant increases in isolation from local communities. Although pentecostals still may be involved in these local communities, they may be turning to a new medium to meet their needs rather than demanding change within the local community.

This suggests that appearances, in this case, are deceptive. Overall, this televised religious program with its parasocial relationships and privatized worship changes the structure of the "living theology" of pentecostals and allows their hero to be shrouded in ambiguity outside of true interpersonal relationships. The apparent international worship service is, in reality, privatized worship, and the global community is, in reality, more deeply entrenched isolation. Indeed, the experience of worship has been altered by the medium employed.

Fusion. Swaggart's role of hero is enhanced through the new "cathedral" of the electronic church. This new form allows the time and distance between the viewer and their hero to be collapsed as he appears each week via television in their living rooms. This is the concept of fusion, a basic element within the pentecostal tradition which marries well with Swaggart's electronic ministry. Fusion refers to the important coming together of key terms in the pentecostal theology (Land, 1989, pp. 489-491). Opposite, but equal terms are fused phenomenologically so that pentecostals do not have a linear, highly categorized theology. The most significant of these joined terms is the "already-not yet" eschatological fusion, which explains the relationship of space and time. This fusion recognizes a telescoping of here and there, now and then. Conceptually, fusion of space and time allows the pentecostal to participate in an "all at once" sense of being. For example, their belief in the past event of the death of Christ and the future event of His return are fused with the present event of spiritual empowerment for pentecostals. In this view spiritual and material worlds co-exist as extensions of one another.

These concepts are most clearly demonstrated in the pentecostals' narrative form. Narratives transcend temporality with the traditional beginnings of "Once upon a time . . ." and fuse personal and historical time into the timeless, cosmic, absolutes of revelational truth (Niebuhr, 1989). Instead of the old orator of the past, today television takes up this function of the narrative and allows the viewer to transcend the physical moment in a given chair in a given room in this fusion process.

The fusion of time and space and its resulting transcendence makes the pentecostals vulnerable to the confusion of "reality" as portrayed within broadcast media. Television's collapsing of time and space parallels these concepts: To see Swaggart is to be there with him. This experience of the moment will not be hindered by the question of whether it is live or a videotape created today or last year. In fact, a portion of Swaggart's heroism is based on his ability to control this medium by collapsing space and time so efficiently. This collapsing enhances the experiential nature of the medium for the viewer. Through the instantaneous, dynamic, and multisensory characteristics of television as demonstrated in Swaggart's electronic church, the viewer transcends a given time and location and can be brought into the presence of his or her hero. The "architectural" elements of this televised worship will be in direct opposition to the unchanging, static elements of traditional cathedrals and churches. The walls of the electronic church are the airwaves that surround the viewer, extending their eyes and ears and fusing time and space. Using the distinctions of Ricoeur (1971), the images of the traditional religious architecture are "fixed" (analogous to the written word), whereas those of the electronic church are "fleeting" (analogous to the spoken word). The key characteristics of this new "cathedral" are dynamic, continuous, and simultaneous, not "fixed" or static. This becomes "architecture" that is amorphous and easily adapted by a hero and his followers as it collapses the time and distance between them.

The resulting experiential nature of Swaggart's electronic church allows the pentecostals to "congregate" around their hero as space is fused through their involvement in this new form. Involvement occurs through extensions of the viewer's senses. Spotlights and cameras become the viewers' eyes and sound systems their ears. Shiny marble and metal surfaces allow viewers to "feel" with their eyes, extending their sense of touch (Reid, 1989).

Watching Swaggart's movements and mobile facial expressions requires constant involvement from the viewers. Expansive gestures, rapid pacing, and facial expressions involve the audience in the intensity of the moment and invite Swaggart's followers to participate. The mosaic of Swaggart's electronic church is an instantaneous collage of movement and light. The pentecostal audience as viewers must put together its mediated impressions. The television's abstract images require interpretation by the viewers using all their senses to participate in the transference of meaning. In so doing the viewers become "part of the system," as they become the screen on which images are projected. In the process Swaggart's followers have collapsed the distance and time between him and themselves. For them, Swaggart becomes a vibrant, living icon through whom they can fuse their here-and-now with Swaggart's there-and-then; in so doing, they become a part of the entourage of their hero.

Such analysis suggests that the pentecostals' concept of eschatological fusion fits well with the multisensory elements of Swaggart's television ministry. Actually, Swaggart developed his ministry by offering a haven for traditional pentecostal values in the midst of the cultural confusion of the 1960s, a time when "[t]he key word was . . . not oral or verbal but multi-sensory; not improvised or planned but electronic" (Fishwick, 1972, p. 2). Paradoxically, although representing the old traditional agrarian values of the pentecostals, Swaggart's televangelistic form was part of the contemporary age—the multisensory and electronic. As a result, the "Old Time Religion" preached by Swaggart functioned in a multisensory fashion, extending the senses of the individual and creating an existential bond between Swaggart and the viewer. In the process television intensified Swaggart's role as hero, not just as the heroic lone figure on center stage, but also as the one who moved the people from the known to the unknown. He used the new form of television to portray the old one of revival meetings, and, in the process, wedded new characteristics of the electronic medium to those of an established form of Christianity. This melding of characteristics has within it the power to rescue the traditional pentecostals from their isolation and move them into the electronic age. Swaggart, as rescuer of the people and manipulator of this new medium, embeds his heroism both within the content of television and within the dynamic nature of the medium itself.

CONCLUSION: WHY THERE CAN BE A HERO

As Bellah suggests (1968) in his discussion of America and religion, when institutional patterns of religion do not meet the needs of the people, a new form or variant grows, as new blossoms sprout on the trees. One form of blossoming is electronic religion with its televangelists who offer order and hope to many religious groups. This analysis indicates that televangelist Jimmy Swaggart offers hope to the pentecostals to the extent that he functions as a hero who represents their own narrative and rescues them from isolation through a medium that is compatible with their intrinsic characteristics.

Furthermore, this analysis suggests that six elements are essential for the creation of a hero. First, the audience needs a deeply entrenched grounding, a clear narrative that is consistent and stable. It must be broad enough and deep enough to accommodate many life events, scenarios, and ideas so that new stories may be added within its framework. This requires a true myth. It cannot be merely a collection of disparate stories. Second, the hero must use the forms of discourse that are most significant and identical to his constituency, such as Swaggart's use of the pentecostals' oral tradition. Third, a medium that accommodates mythmaking must be available, and, again, the medium must be one that reflects the intrinsic characteristics of the hero's population. Fourth, heroism is a question of identity in that followers must see familiar character traits that mark an individual as a potential hero within their particular community. Fifth, the audience and the hero must share the same time. When the people are ready, the hero will appear, just as Swaggart appeared to lead the pentecostals from the agrarian age into the electronic. Lastly, the hero must capture the audience's imagination. He must be larger than life for his constituency, and he must appear to be the epitome of their primary attributes.

Whether or not Swaggart can continue as a hero to the pentecostals remains to be seen. As Fishwick (1983) suggests, the highly publicized heroes of contemporary society can no longer hide their shortcomings and failures, so that their followers must accept them "warts and all" (p. 7). The pentecostals' narrative will help them accommodate the lack of perfection in a hero. For example, Swaggart's continued affiliation with prostitutes can be interpreted within their narratives, and through these, they can define his position within their society. Accordingly, if Swaggart falls from hero status, he will be remembered like a famed heroic general, such as an Old Testament King Saul who goes down in defeat during battle. The pentecostals would remember the greater, glorious days of battle and forgive the final defeat as they allow their general to rest in peace. These people with sadness, but balanced equilibrium, would understand Swaggart as a man who fought a difficult battle but could not overcome the enemy in the end. This indicates that whether or not he is ultimately victorious, Swaggart still plays a significant heroic role in the community and their narrative. In his representation of human victory and all too often, human failure, he becomes a morality play to remind the viewers of the dangers and pitfalls of life.

Swaggart's narrative mythology serves as a rich instance of a synergistic relationship between himself and his audience, resulting in a paracontractual agreement that gives Swaggart the mandate to rescue these people while, almost paradoxically, licensing him to manipulate them. This process is a dynamic one that simply does not lend itself to any single extant methodology. Rather, to access the dynamic of Swaggart's mythology, critics must appreciate the ambiguity, which illustrates how Swaggart's ministry is one of the more controversial and notorious in contemporary mass media.

Narrative explains how values, concepts of time and space, intrinsic characteristics of a subculture, and human associations aid in understanding a media phenomenon. Examination of a group's narrative indicates how members perceive their own worth and their own values as demonstrated by the characters within their stories. Furthermore, the narrative, as internal history, shows how the old-line pentecostals exist part and parcel with a hero such as Swaggart. He and his followers are not in isolation, to be studied simply as separate psychological and biological entities, but are bound through their shared narrative and medium as thoroughly as Siamese twins. Even if the pentecostals eventually reject Swaggart as a prominent hero, this man and this community are woven inextricably so that the rise and even the fall of a hero can be defined. These points of either celebration of the hero or of his excommunication can be defined when the people's narrative is as intact as that of the pentecostals. Thus, whether a fallen man or a celebrated hero, Swaggart remains a part of the pentecostals' history, and, in turn, a part of their narrative. He becomes a communal event that is described, defined, and remembered by a community.

17

The Celebrity and the Fan: A Media Relationship

Susan J. Drucker
Hofstra University

Robert S. Cathcart
Queens College

☐ *"What social and psychological needs of audience members are gratified through the consumption of messages about heroes and celebrities?" Drawing on the "uses and gratifications" research of Karl Rosengren and Sven Windahl the authors explore the typology of mediated interpersonal relationships and suggest the relationship between the celebrity and the fan is one of "solitary identification." To test this thesis the authors constructed two survey instruments designed to establish the parameters of the celebrity-fan relationship. The survey was administered to over 300 participants, and the results are presented here for the first time. The authors conclude that there is a unique celebrity-fan relationship, distinct from the relationship with traditional heroes, which better serves the needs of individuals in modern times.*

Twentieth-century mass media have made available in the United States an unending stream of celebrities. Americans have, in return, responded with adulation and devotion. Social commentators, film and TV critics, and media scholars, although agreeing that "celebrity" is a function of the rise of mass culture, mostly decry its superficiality, its commerciality, and its exploitation of the mass audience (McGinniss, 1990; Monaco, 1978). There are those who see the rise of celebrity as an inevitable result of egalitarianism and the desire to replace elitism with individual recognition (Braudy, 1986)—a conflict between the democratic and aristocratic in fame discourse (Gamson, 1992). Still others see the celebrity phenomenon as a substitute for hero worship (Boorstin, 1961) and blame the mass media for blurring the distinctions between hero and celebrity.

What is there about mass media and mass culture that produces celebrities? Of what use is this celebration to individual members of the culture? What social and psychological needs of audience members may be gratified through the consumption of messages about heroes/celebrities? Many of these questions remain unanswered, necessitating an examination of the celebrity/hero phenomenon with regard to the needs and gratifications of the fans.

Our electronic, media-dominated culture has led to an alteration in the relationship between private and public persons. The electronic/film media in particular have created an environment in which people relate to media personae in ways more similar to face-to-face interpersonal relationships than to private-citizen/public-figure relationships (Cathcart & Gumpert, 1983; Horton & Wohl, 1957). To determine the nature of the mediated interpersonal relationship between celebrities and fans we conducted a study of people's "media relationships" (see Rosengren & Windahl, 1972) with celebrities and established a framework for exploration of this form of media effect.

MEDIA RELATIONSHIPS AND CELEBRITIES

The celebrity-fan relationship is clearly a preeminent one in our contemporary society, but its function is not readily recognized. Lamentations are frequently heard citing the worship of celebrities as evidence of a society characterized by alienation and ennui, one in which heroes no longer reflect traditional values (Goldsen, 1978; Mankiewicz & Swerdlow, 1979). Media researchers of the "critical school" see celebrity as just another tool of the dominant power structure for placating the public. Yet, other explanations including the one found in media uses and gratification research (Wenner & Palmgreen, 1985) can offer valuable insights which could account for the rise of celebrity and explain its function.

Media consumption, according to uses and gratification theory, is seen as behavior that meets, or fails to meet, needs generated through the interaction of the individual's psychological dispositions and experience in her or his social situation (McQuail, 1972). Pioneering studies by Merton (1949) and Wright (1959), and the later studies by Rosengren and Windahl (1972) and Rubin (1983), into uses of mass media as functional alternatives for gratification of social and psychological needs provide a basis for understanding the new celebrity-fan relationship as a functional alternative to traditional relationships with public personae (heroes). Rosengren and Windahl (1972), examining the uses and gratifications of media, produced a typology of relations between audience and actors of mass media (pp. 180-190). In this typology, all relationships with media personalities are complemental, supplemental, or substitutional to an individual's existing interpersonal relationships. These mediated relationships vary depending on a person's social skills and the existing social environment.

The person with effective social skills who exists in a satisfactory social environment uses media personae (e.g., a soap opera character or a talk show host) to complement interpersonal interactions by using these characters and their behaviors as content for discussions with friends. They, however, remain "detached" from these media personae in terms of their interpersonal relationships. People who work at jobs that isolate them or who live in impersonal and hostile environments may use television and radio personalities as supplemental "friends" who speak directly to them (through the camera lens or the air waves) and who give them a feeling of intimacy with the character, albeit a simulated form of intimacy (Horton & Wohl, 1956). Some social isolates may even use their involvement with media characters as a substitute for actual face-to-face interpersonal relationships. Not altogether uncommon are persons who become so involved in soap opera or adventure series that they talk and act as if they were part of the fictional setting, substituting it for their own environment.

The need for social interaction can lead to four types of media relationships with media personae: detached, parasocial, solitary identification, and capture. Some viewer/listeners always maintain a detached relationship with all media characters, but many others become involved in what has been labeled a "parasocial" relationship (Horton & Wohl, 1956). The existence of parasocial interaction with media personae has been well established and supported by a considerable body of literature (Cathcart & Gumpert, 1983; Horton & Wohl, 1956; Levy, 1979; Rubin, Perse & Powell, 1985). The media relationship of capture has been the subject of studies of psychotic/neurotic maladjustment in which individuals lose touch with reality and live in a media fantasy world.

A form of complemental media relationship is solitary identification. Rosengren and Windahl (1972) explain:

> It is rather difficult to identify with somebody of the mass media . . . without at the same time interacting with the rest of the cast. But especially in the case of a one-man show, or when one person or role is very dominating, identification without interaction may, of course, occur. We have named this type of relationship *solitary identification*. (p. 171)

This media form has received little scholarly attention which may be due, in part, to the fact that Rosengren and Windahl assumed it was relatively rare. It is the central contention of this chapter, however, that solitary identification with a media celebrity is a widespread phenomenon and is exemplified in what we designate as the celebrity-fan relationship.

THE ROLE OF CELEBRITY

The evolution of a media relationship based on "identification without interaction" can be traced to industrialization and the rise of the mass-circulation daily newspaper (Gamson, 1992). Although it is often thought that Hollywood, through its "star" system, is the prime contributor to the phenomenon of celebrity, long before the movies, actors and stage performers such as Sarah Bernhardt, John Gilbert, and Lillian Russell took on the aura of celebrity. The growth of large cities and the creation of railroads enabled performers to be seen by relatively large audiences. This kind of exposure, along with the rise of the mass circulation newspaper of the late 18th century, bestowed real celebrity status on these performers. "In the middle of the nineteenth century, a series of dramatic changes in the media of publicity and communication established celebrity as a 'mass' phenomenon" (Gamson, 1992, p. 3). Media developments including the telegraph and photography fostered the emerging celebrification industry. The persistent presentation of "news" about entertainers enabled large numbers of people to identify with them and seriously follow their dramatic triumphs, their emotional setbacks, and their personal idiosyncracies as they were drawn ever closer in a new form of relationship with public characters.

Public involvement was not entirely spontaneous, but resulted from the calculated dissemination of highly personal information (later institutionalized as "Hollywood gossip" columns in daily newspapers) by the newly established publicity industry (Gamson, 1992, pp. 4-12). Lowenthal (1961) traced the expansion of biographical stories in popular magazines of the time and noted a significant shift from the "idols of production," who primarily served as "educational models," and whose success could be imitated, toward the "idols of consumption," who provided a "readily grasped empire" merely confirming "identification with normalcy." He noted that filling the pages of the magazines with publicity made it no longer contemptible to focus on the private affairs and habits, rather than the public deeds, of popular figures (p. 113).

At the beginning of the 20th century this new publicity industry linked with the new movie industry, creating ever more celebrities or "stars" with whom the common person, who attended movies rather than dramatic productions, could identify. Accompanying the industrialization and urbanization of America, the rapid and widespread development of the Hollywood star system provided a social context in which more traditional "hero worship" of the public figure began to be supplanted by "fan worship" of the celebrity.

The word *fan*, a term derived from *fanatic*, characterizes a relationship based on an intimate knowledge of a personality created and sustained by the mass media industry and maintained by the personality's ability to control media attention rather than to control or shape events (Boorstin, 1961). The fan relationship with the new film/electronic hero (i.e., the celebrity or media personality) is a symbiotic one, a relationship that appears to fulfill an important need in the public psyche.

Caughey (1986) suggests that the celebrity's appeal is linked to the fan's daily social relationships. It is taken for granted in our present culture that everyone knows of great numbers of celebrities, reflecting the individual's desire to escape ordinariness and gain some recognition in an impersonal, technological world (see Braudy, 1986; Monaco, 1978). The celebrity is relied on in the establishment of self (see Cathcart & Gumpert, 1986). Celebrities may be used to maintain a sense of belonging in a chaotic modern world in which concepts of place and community are no longer clear cut and concepts of connectedness and belonging are altered by the use of electronic media (Gumpert, 1987). Media technology have emancipated social interaction from place and redistributed it through space (Drucker & Gumpert, 1991) as the electronics of telegraphy, telephony, radio, television, facsimile, computers, and satellites transcend the walls of home and workplace. The dominance of mediated communication produces an aspatial communication orientation so that interaction occurs in those places that are perceived to be safe, controllable, and private (Drucker & Gumpert, 1991). "Solitary identification" becomes a more widespread and significant person-media personae relationship.

THE CELEBRITY-FAN RELATIONSHIP

How is solitary identification with media personae established, maintained, and utilized? What are its parameters, and how does it affect interpersonal communication and public discourse? Research based on Rosengren and Windahl's typology of mediated functional alternatives to interpersonal involvements has clearly established the media parasocial relationship (Levy, 1979; Rubin et al., 1985). In an effort to follow this line of investigation into solitary identification and the celebrity-fan relationship two survey instruments were developed to corroborate our conceptualization and help establish the areas of investigation necessary to validate solitary identification as the key to the celebrity-fan relationship. One survey questionnaire, using a cognitive approach, asked people about their behavioral involvement with media celebrities. A second questionnaire, a Likert-type attitude scale, was derived from the Parasocial Interaction Scales developed by Levy (1979) and Rubin et al. (1985). Questions in both surveys were formulated to ascertain information that would help establish the parameters of the celebrity-fan relationship. This study was a probe to learn the most useful behaviors and attitudes to measure if such a relationship was to be established.

Questions were designed to check the psychological distance that subjects perceived between themselves and their favorite media celebrity. Although the psychological relationship of viewers to mediated messages has to date received limited scholarly attention, the viewer's perspective with regard to media presentation would appear significant in understanding the nature of relationships created with and through the media. The authors assume that solitary identification with a media celebrity requires a different psychological distance than would face-to-face relationships and private citizen-public figure relationships.

Four categories of *distance* indicate different degrees of personal involvement with media celebrities: interpersonal, heroic, fantasy, and social. Questions were designed to detect the presence of these psychological distances with regard to relationships to celebrities. In seeking *Interpersonal distance* the issue was whether the subjects' involvement with a celebrity related to distance similar to that experienced in face-to-face relationships? *Heroic distance* was addressed by questions dealing with social admiration for accomplishments, whereas inquiry into *Fantasy distance* involved the issue of whether the celebrity was an object of secret desire or fantasy escape. *Social distance* was explored by investigating whether the involvement with the celebrity was similar to that with a role model in other social relationships. Additionally, some questions probed, both directly and indirectly, the uses receivers made of the media presentation of celebrities.

The survey was conducted initially in 1988 and again in 1992 to verify the findings. Two versions of the survey were administered. The first questionnaire was administered to 145 persons of diverse ages living in a large Eastern metropolis, whereas the verification survey conducted in the same metropolitan area surveyed 122 persons and focused on the 18-35-year-old age category. The second survey was administered to 53 college students.

DISCUSSION

Initial survey data substantiate a new mediated relationship based on solitary identification. Survey results support the conclusion that the celebrity-fan relationship operates on a more personal one-to-one level than does the private citizen-public figure relationship, which traditionally involved a large group of people relating to one extraordinary person. Although celebrity adulation results from millions of fans devoting themselves to each of their celebrities, the survey did not reveal a coalescing of large groups of fans around a few central celebrities, but rather a tendency for fans to identify with celebrities on an individual basis.

Celebrity-fan relationships tended to follow age and sex lines rather than grouping around particular celebrities. Older subjects named celebrities who had been popular for a long period of time, but the length of time of celebrityhood and fame did not influence middle and low age groups. A traditional public hero would be known by all age groups because older generations would spread the hero's fame to succeeding generations. These findings corroborate prior work indicating that celebrities are extremely contemporary. Older persons reported long-standing celebrity relationships, having begun when the fan was much younger, and so they continued to think of their celebrity as a contemporary.

The great number of celebrities named and their uniformity as entertainers indicate that subjects are using their relationship with celebrities to meet personal needs rather than societal needs. It would seem that it is the fan's relationship to *media* and how media are used to meet personal needs that determine the onset of admiration rather than societal recognition of the celebrity. For example, young females tended to name young male celebrities as their favorites because they were sexually attractive. Young males named young female celebrities for the same reasons, and males named male athlete celebrities whom they wished to emulate.

Subjects often listed more than one attractive attribute of a celebrity, for example, talent and looks, personality and ability, talent and style. This suggests that the way the media "packages" a personality establishes a "trademark" that makes the celebrity more widely known and more admired. The celebrity appeal and answering role of the fan appears to stem, in part, from media packaging. This result can be attributed to the so-called performance-persona principle developed by popular aestheticians. This principle recognizes that what has come to be termed *hype* is an important part of the artistic or creative work as a whole. Cawelti (1985) notes that individual works become part of complex, artistic constructions which include showmanship, promotion, and media coverage. Beyond this he claims that the influence on a particular performance of previous acts by the same persons are the phenomena of stardom and celebrity. This would indicate that when the performances or acts of the celebrity are processed by their admirers, they are processed in the context of prior performances as well as in the context of an entire constructed media package. The person becomes an admired figure for the package that is presented rather than for unusual talent or ability.

Responses concerning the psychological distance dimensions of the celebrity-fan relationship also support the position that the need for and use of the famous is changing. In the interpersonal distance area all questions about seeing, talking to, and contacting celebrities received a majority of *negative* responses. This may be due to the inaccessibility of most celebrities, but it could also be accounted for by television's ability to create "intimacy at a distance" as described by Horton and Wohl (1956) in their article on parasocial interaction. The direct address form of television and the accompanying hype asks the viewers to respond as though they are intimates of the personality. Studies of parasocial interaction reveal that viewers relate to the TV personalities as friends (Levy, 1979; Rubin et al., 1985).

Keeping up on the events in the celebrities real life was reported to be important. It was clear that getting personally involved in actual relationships with other admirers of the celebrity, such as belonging to a fan club, produced a uniform negative response. Although some young people agreed that it was important to have a face-to-face relationship with a celebrity, the actuality is that any interpersonal relationship that exists is one based on the ability of media to produce a pseudo- or parasocial relationship that makes this seem possible.

In the heroic distance category there was agreement that the celebrity be looked up to and admired by others, in the future as well as at the present. This would indicate that when fans express attitudes toward celebrities' accomplishments, they want celebrities to fill a role similar to that of admired public figures. It is unclear whether this is because fans think the celebrity's accomplishments embody the important values of the society, or whether they simply feel their involvement with the celebrity needs to be legitimized.

The fantasy distance relationship produced two clear responses. An overall majority wanted the celebrity as a "close friend" and were "not jealous of the celebrity's involvements with other persons." Fantasy distance, like interpersonal distance, may be related to the media's ability to create pseudo-intimacy (Horton & Wohl, 1956). It is rather well established that the television form brings the performer "closer" to the viewer and creates an immediate "reality" that makes viewers feel they know television personalities better than they do their friends and neighbors (see Meyrowitz, 1985).

On the social distance dimension an overwhelming majority indicated they talked about the celebrity with their friends, and a large majority of those under age 35 thought their friends identified them with the celebrity. Although any famous person, traditional hero or otherwise, might be talked about with friends, that there is a high level of personal identification involved indicates that the subject's "uses" of celebrities might be more closely related to the desire to imitate a celebrity rather than have a public figure to admire.

Survey results support Rosengren and Windahl's (1972) typology of media relationships that function as complemental, supplemental, and substitutional alternatives to personal socialization needs. They also uphold the position that the solitary identification relationship is the key to understanding the function of and importance of the celebrity-fan phenomenon. This probe into the possible dimensions of a media relationship based on solitary identification reveals that when persons become fans of media celebrities, they do so because they identify with the celebrity, and in turn the celebrity is identified with them. They think of the celebrity as their "friend"; a friend who is talented, attractive, and to whom attention is paid. They keep pictures and posters of their celebrity "friend," they continually learn more about the personal life of the celebrity, and they discuss the celebrity at length with their "real-world" friends. They want the celebrity to be admired just as they would want to be admired should the media make them well known.

There is much more to be done to establish the dimensions of solitary identification as a media effect. The discussion of this pilot study is meant to encourage future research that must be conducted to determine which forms and contents of media produce this relationship, what the characteristics and conditions of the persons most likely to respond to such media messages are, and what the best means of measuring such responses are. This will then enable us to better understand how celebrity functions in our culture and how it meets the needs of fans.

CONCLUSION

With the rise of film media, movie actors such as Mary Pickford and Douglas Fairbanks became stars in our social firmament and developed followings that lasted throughout their careers and beyond. With the rise of radio and television media, baseball players such as Babe Ruth and musicians such as Elvis Presley came to occupy celebrity status and went on to become enshrined as popular heroes. Today the range of media celebrities spans Dan Rather to Madonna, Michael Jackson to Michael Jordan, each with fan clubs and loyal groups of followers eager to know of their every appearance and every intimacy. The sources of celebrity are as varied as the population which accepts, adores, criticizes, and consumes them. It would appear that the electronic media celebrity has become the functional alternative to the action and intellectual hero of the past. Monaco (1978) concluded:

> Before we had celebrities we had heroes. . . . Now what these types all share, of course, are admirable qualities—qualities that somehow set them apart from the rest of us. They have done things, acted in the world, written, thought, understood, led. Celebrities, on the other hand, needn't have done—needn't do—anything special. Their function isn't to act—just to be. To a large extent, celebrity has entirely superseded heroism. . . . Celebrities are passive objects of the media—created whole out of "ordinary" newspaper print, or film, or broadcast airwaves. (pp. 6-7)

The celebrity does not have to be great or even heroic by deed or thought. The celebrity need only be a presence, need only be the focus of media attention, someone the audience can readily identify with. Because we all need something to satisfy our expectations of human greatness, we produce our celebrity heroes everyday by watching them on either the big screen or the small screen, by reading and talking about them, or by buying recordings and posters.

The responses obtained in this investigation indicate that personal characteristics of celebrities rather than public deeds are related to their elevated status. Identification with the looks and personal characteristics that media publicity celebrates removes the celebrity from the hallowed pedestal of the hero. "The hero may well be he or she whom every American should wish to be, but the celebrity is he or she whom every American can be" (Wecter, 1941).

Richard Schickel (1985) contends that a media celebrity community exists, and fans consider themselves part of that community. This new media community offers attributes now missing in society: a small-town life, aspects of the extended family, and so on. Although there are changes in membership and in an individual's status (brought on by increased publicity), the media community continues, and we can always participate in that media community no matter where we are. The need for this surrogate community may be necessitated by the alienating effects of the industrialized and electronic age in which obligations to others are altered by the new media communities. Living in a world in which surmounting limitations of time and space is quick, easy, and safe, media connection has been emphasized at the expense of more traditional face-to-face interactions. The result has been to shift social relationships to media communities such as those offered by the celebrity-fan relationship.

If those individuals who are most famous and most admired can be said to be codifications of a culture's values (Strate, 1985), then we have witnessed a shift from the valuing of heroic action and thought to the veneration of image "well-knownness." With oral heroes the attribute admired was action—great human deeds. The dominant medium (orality) served to determine those attributes to be admired within the constraints of that medium. With print heroes the characteristics lauded were human intellect coupled with accomplishments. The dominant medium (print) served to define the abstractions that were to serve as praiseworthy and aspirational goals. With the celebrity, values are not only formed and maintained in relation to the dominant media, as was the case with orality and print, but the present situation indicates that we value the media itself. The object of adulation, in a sense, is not the human manifestation but the power of the medium.

Ultimately, if societal selection of heroes is indicative of the values and needs of that society, then the change from traditional hero to media celebrity may well be indicative of the power the dominant media of communication has over societal needs and values.

18

Who Are the Puerto Rican Heroes?: A Cross-Cultural Study

Joseph M. Ferri
Joan M. Fayer
Alma Simounet-Geigel
University of Puerto Rico

❒ *This is a study of what happens to the notions of hero when two cultures become intertwined. The authors have long been involved in Puerto Rican studies, viewing Puerto Rico with its mix of Hispanic and Anglo cultures as an ideal matrix for cross cultural communication research. In the study recounted in this chapter the authors surveyed a sample of Puerto Ricans, determining their media usage and their choices of heroes. Results reveal a tendency in Puerto Rico to give hero status to island celebrities most closely associated with traditional Puerto Rican culture. There were also a number of "international" figures from religious, political, and entertainment worlds who were recognized for their heroic characteristics. The chapter explores whether the mass media may be creating a system for the elevation of international heroes over local heroes and what effect this may have on Puerto Rican self-identification.*

> Poets use metaphors to expand the meaning of words. Heroes are the metaphors that expand our understanding of ourselves. ("Heroes for hard times," 1988, p. 25).

This study explores the metaphors—heroes—which give definition to self. It seeks to find out how Puerto Ricans reflect themselves in the persons they name as their personal heroes and celebrities.

DEFINING THE SELF

The definition of self is a process of identity formation through direct sensory perception (comparison of self with parents and peers and with norms, averages, and members of reference groups) and through social interaction. Among the characteristics that give definition to self are physical condition and appearance, feelings, and roles (Watzlawick, Beavin, & Jackson, 1967). Everyone is actively involved in the process of definition of self. Every individual is involved in communication with self and with others on both individual and collective levels. The individual searches for his- or herself by integrating individual and group perceptions, as well as the symbols grounded in the environs of individual and group associations.

To communicate effectively the individual has to perceive the self as an integral part of a group. *Group*, as defined by Singer (1987, p. 53), is "a symbiotic relationship which exists between a group as a whole and the individuals who comprise the group." The individual has "group related perceptions stored in the memory of each individual's data storage bank" (p. 86). This study purports that it is a group memory that defines cultures and/or co-cultures, for through the use of a relatively unique symbol system the individual may be defined as Puerto Rican, North American, Chicano, Irish, or as a member of other cultures or ethnic groups.

Identity, the image the person sees when he or she looks at self, is individual and collective. One sees the "I" (subject) and the "me" (object) in addition to the "us." The "us" concept and its relationship and significance to self, as well as its significance to hero and culture, are relevant. The hero can be a role model for the process of socialization and culturalization and can serve as a reference the group may attempt to model or to imitate for a sense of identity. The hero is part of the significant others who influence humans about who they are and about what the world around them is like.

HEROES AND CELEBRITIES

It is difficult to ascertain the origin of the hero. This phenomenon may be as old as the history of human life. Heroes encompass all aspects of human life including religion, mythology, the military, literature, and so on. Traditional heroes were "extraordinary individuals with rare personal qualities who performed admirable deeds" (Browne, 1987, p. 127); they were people with real accomplishments and whose deeds had a significant impact on history. This is not true of the celebrity, for according to Schickel (1985, p. 23) "there was no such thing as celebrity prior to the beginning of the twentieth century." In contemporary society the traditional hero has been replaced by the media-created hero or celebrity. Schickel, agreeing with Strate (Chapter 2, this volume), adds that the "history of celebrity and the history of communication technology over the last century are very closely linked" (p. 28). Although today's celebrities may be known for their "admirable deeds," their fame may last only as long as their exposure in the media.

Because the mass media reflect the status quo and move with the currents of social change, the hero concept is not only a metaphor for self, it is a metaphor in the process of change. In the past in Puerto Rico, the male hero was Lincoln, Lindbergh, Franklin Roosevelt, Bolivar, or Juarez; the female hero conjured images of Dolly Madison, Amelia Earhart, Helen Keller, or Isabel of Spain. One *U.S. News and World Report* survey (McBee, 1985) identified Clint Eastwood, Eddie Murphy, Ronald Reagan, Jane Fonda, Sally Field, and Steven Spielberg as the heroes of young adults, ages 18-24, in the United States. The heroes of different age groups serve to symbolize generational differences. In addition to generational differences, there are also gender and cultural differences.

A later study of Hispanic heroes revealed that top choices were Ronald Reagan, Cesar Chavez, Lee Iacocca, and Julio Iglesias (Perez, 1986). Although heroes and celebrities of Hispanic Americans in the United States have been studied, there has been limited investigation of that phenomenon outside the continental United States.

CULTURE CONTACT

Heroes are culturally defined, and when two cultures come into contact, as they do in Puerto Rico, a traditional hero identification system undergoes change. Puerto Rico, a predominantly Spanish-speaking country in the Caribbean situated between Latin America and North America, makes possible an analysis of the media-created heroes or celebrities of both Latin and Anglo cultures. In addition to location there are other factors that make Puerto Rico an interesting country for the study of the effects of culture contact on hero formulation and self-identification.

In 1898, the island, which had been a possession of Spain was ceded to the United States as a result of the Spanish American War. In 1917, American citizenship was granted to Puerto Ricans. It is now a commonwealth associated with the United States with its own elected governor. Both Spanish and English were designated official languages, but 1991 legislation, repealed in 1993, made Spanish the only official language. The results of the last available census indicate that approximately 40% of the population is bilingual. For Puerto Ricans who have had college educations, the percentage is much higher.

As American citizens, Puerto Ricans can travel to the United States without passports which means that visiting between the island and the mainland is frequent. In addition, many Puerto Ricans have moved to the United States permanently, while others have gone for short periods of time. In a recent study it was found that 89% of Puerto Ricans had relatives in the United States. These factors make Puerto Rico an island in which there is daily contact between Hispanic and North American culture.

The study of components of culture in a contact situation, however, is not the only reason to study heroes in Puerto Rico. Hispanics are members of the fastest growing ethnic group in the United States. Fishman (1985, pp. 112,

140) states that in 1979 there were almost 8 million people who declared Spanish as their mother tongue. There was an increase of 447% from 1940 to 1970 of those who were native speakers of Spanish. The rising numbers of Hispanics could very well have an important impact on the concept of hero in the United States.

MEDIA AVAILABILITY

In Puerto Rico, as in other cultures, the media play an important role in the creation of hero/celebrity. "Electronic media are exerting an ever-increasing influence upon American culture. During the last thirty years, the electronic media have gradually become the focal point of the average American's time, energy, and attention" (Chesebro, 1984, p. 111). The following data, based on the most recent surveys compiled by Asesores, Inc. Marketing Research and Consulting (1991), reveal that daily newspaper readership reaches 82.2% of the population between 12 and 64 years old. Approximately 1,860,000 people read a newspaper at least once a week. Circulation figures for daily newspapers are: *El Vocero* at 252,700, *El Nuevo Dia* at 210,054, and *The San Juan Star* at 47,500. Of the reading population, older and more affluent groups prefer newspapers. The proportion of readers by sex is similar to that of the total population; 51.9% of these are women and 48.1% are men. Another study in *The San Juan Star* (1989) titled "What newspaper readers like to read" finds that 77.2% of all readers prefer local news and 52% prefer international news.

Surveys of media preferences reveal radio is chosen second to television (96.5%) and is preferred mostly by younger age groups and those at lower socioeconomic levels. Both male and female listeners reported a high preference for music shows, talk programs, and news shows. There is no significant difference for radio preference in rural and urban areas. Based on surveys from 1986 to 1991, radio listening has increased from 6.4% to 11.2%, and the most popular station for all age groups is one which plays rock and salsa music.

North American programming is brought to the attention of Puerto Ricans via cable television, a service first offered in 1970 in the area of the capital city, and now almost islandwide with 238,357 subscribers (Asesores, 1991, p. 5). Most of the channels on cable television are in the English language (including CNN and C-Span and the major U.S. networks) making the island part of the international television community.

CULTURE AND CHANGE

Puerto Rico is a country undergoing rapid change. Prior studies of nonverbal communication (Ferri & Hernández, 1988), food (Fayer, Simounet-Geigel, Peters, & Ferri, 1983), naming practices (Fayer, 1988) music (Chesebro &

Ferri, 1985), and clothing (Simounet-Geigel & Ferri, 1982) in Puerto Rico with different generations noted changes in progress. It can be assumed that in this changing cultural climate there would be changes in the ways in which Puerto Ricans respond to heroes and celebrities. To determine how present-day Puerto Ricans respond to the hero/celebrity phenomenon, in 1991 we interviewed a random group of 268 islanders ranging in ages from 17 to 60 and had them complete a brief questionnaire.

We wanted to learn directly from the people themselves: Who are the heroes in contemporary Puerto Rico? Has the traditional hero been replaced by the media created celebrity? Does the selection of heroes/celebrities reflect a combination of Latin American and North American cultures? Are there gender differences in the selection of heroes/celebrities? Are there generational differences in the selection of heroes/celebrities? The questionnaire consisted of questions about: (a) contemporary male and female heroes; (b) historical male and female heroes; (c) qualities for which heroes are admired; (d) national and international heroes in politics, history, religion, sports, fine arts, and entertainment; and (e) heroes in Puerto Rican folklore.

WHO ARE THE PUERTO RICAN HEROES?

Responses to the open-ended question regarding contemporary male heroes revealed the most frequently cited for almost all age groups were Mikhail Gorbachev, Pope John Paul II, George Bush, Luis Ferre (Puerto Rican statehood advocate and former governor), Nelson Mandela, and Ruben Berríos (Puerto Rican independence leader). The most cited contemporary female heroes were Mother Teresa and Victoria "Melo" Muñoz (senator and daughter of the first elected Puerto Rican governor). They were followed by the former British prime minister, Margaret Thatcher, Felisa Rincón (former mayor of San Juan and better known as Doña Fela), Sister Isolina Ferré (a nun who works with the underprivileged in Puerto Rico and sister of Luis Ferré), Corazón Aquino, and "mothers."

For most of the contemporary male heroes and for some of the contemporary female heroes the media have played a vital role in the enhancement of their public image. With the exception of Ferré and Berríos for the males and Victoria Muñoz, Doña Fela and Sister Isolina for the females, the contemporary heroes are international figures.

In the category of historical male figures, the top choices were Luis Muñoz Marín, Pedro Albizu Campos (Puerto Rican Nationalist leader), Gandhi, Christ, Martin Luther King, Jr., and Eugenio de Hostos (Puerto Rican poet, philosopher, and educator). For the historical females most admired, the first choice Julia de Burgos (Puerto Rican poet) had a far greater percentage than that of the next choice, Joan of Arc. They are followed by Doña Fela and Lola

Rodríguez de Tió (Puerto Rican patriot). As for historical figures the highest ranking male and female heroes are Puerto Rican. The top three qualities most admired in both contemporary and historical heroes are intelligence, dedication, and leadership followed by honesty and idealism. The least admired qualities are physical appearance and dedication to family.

When asked who were their "political" heroes the ranking in order of preference was Melo Muñoz, Gorbachev, Berríos, Reagan, Bush, and Rafael Hernández Colón (past governor of Puerto Rico). When asked about heroic figures in political history there was a tie for first choice—Muñoz Marín and Martin Luther King, Jr., who were chosen by every respondent. They were closely followed by Albizu Campos then John F. Kennedy, Doña Fela, Juan A. Corretjer (Puerto Rican socialist), and Eleanor Roosevelt.

For "religious" heroes Mother Teresa and Gandhi were unanimous selections, closely followed by John Paul II. For sports figures respondents placed Angelita Lind (Puerto Rican track star) first, then Michael Jordan, Mike Tyson, Fernando Valenzuela, and Hector "Macho" Camacho. There was a three-way tie in the category of fine arts: De Burgos, René Márqués (Puerto Rican playwright), and Francisco Oller (Puerto Rican painter).

Respondents were asked to name their most admired figures in the entertainments—music, television, and film. In the music category Ruben Blades, a Hispanic singer and actor, received the highest percentage of votes, followed by Danny Rivera, a Puerto Rican singer and political activist. The two male singers are followed by Ednita Nazario, Miami Sound Machine, Madonna, and Lunna. Others, too numerous to mention, were named in this category. In the television field Puerto Rican TV talk show host Luis Francisco Ojeda had almost unanimous preference. Ojeda was followed by Sunshine (Puerto Rican satirist), Gladys Rodríguez (actor in theater and TV), Michael J. Fox, Tom Selleck, and in sixth place Carmen Jovet (TV talk show host). In the film section Raul Juliá was named first by an overwhelming number of respondents, followed by Arnold Schwarzenegger and Eddie Murphy. They are followed by Charlie Chaplin, Greta Garbo, and Whoopi Goldberg as well as others.

A list of local folk heroes included the names of those who had been prominent in the media for deeds or misdeeds. Four of the six in this category were assured legendary status because of untimely deaths or martyrdom. The top three choices were Roberto Clemente (deceased baseball star and philanthropist), Sylvia Rexach (Puerto Rican composer), and Luis Vigoreaux (Puerto Rican TV celebrity murdered by his wife).

MEDIA INFLUENCE

As indicated earlier, the availability of electronic media in Puerto Rico has increased in the last decades. Puerto Rico, classified as a high-context culture with an oral tradition, has through the years sustained numerous print outlets.

To this profusion of print media have been added the electronic media. Because of its unique geographic location, its political, economic, and social associations with the United States and its technological advances, Puerto Rico receives constant media bombardment from various sources. The island is now part of the global village with immediate access to world events and personalities.

This access has resulted not only in immediacy, but also in modification of the cultural system and of the individual's definition of self within the system. A culture may be examined as a relatively unique symbol system; the individual, in terms of self, may be examined as to her or his direct sensory perception and social interaction. The individual has extensive access through the media; through the electronic media he or she can see and hear Gorbachev, Bush, Mother Teresa, Thatcher, and, in the case of John Paul II, participate in the celebration of the Mass at Plaza Las Americas during his visit to Puerto Rico. Technological advances bring the hero model closer physically and psychologically and may even allow for group social interaction. The role model then becomes not only a person in the media, but also a person one may actually see, hear, and touch without media. Of the local contemporary heroes—Ferré, Berríos, Muñoz, Doña Fela, Sister Isolina—three are actively involved in politics, particularly concerning Puerto Rican political status. Sister Isolina is active in community social work; Doña Fela in her 90s still presides over social and political activities. Therefore, their "well-knownness" on the island and by some in the United States is sustained by the media and the possibility of face-to-face personal interaction within the island community.

Responses to the questionnaire reveal that male international figures play an important heroic role in today's Puerto Rico. In contrast, most contemporary female heroes are Puerto Rican, with an interesting tie for first place between Mother Teresa, an international religious figure, and Melo Muñoz, a local Puerto Rican senator who was a 1992 nominee for governor of the island. In addition, the female vote for contemporary female hero has a higher percentage than for contemporary male hero, which could be interpreted as a more solid preference indication. Although the female subjects submitted approximately the same number of names for both, the male subjects submitted more male figures than female figures. This may be an indication of male chauvinism on the island, though similar results occur with male subjects in the United States and elsewhere.

There is an interesting competition among figures from the male local or Hispanic arena. For example, Hernández Colón and Luis Ferré receive almost the same number of votes as the TV personalities Ojeda and Chayanne (Puerto Rican singer). Gabriel García Márquez, Colombian writer and Nobel Prize recipient, appears in this grouping also. His Latin American ethnicity together with his place in world literature assure his selection by the Puerto Rican subjects. Even though Puerto Ricans have extensive exposure to British, American, and Spanish writers, they selected this particular Latin American literary figure.

Interestingly, the figure, "Mothers," received a significant vote by female subjects and a zero vote by male subjects, reflecting Puerto Rican cultural values. In contrast, there was no "Fathers" counterpart with either males or females. Puerto Rico is a predominantly Catholic country in which the veneration of the Virgin Mary is prevalent. In fact, mothers are usually seen through a similar perception of goodness, nurturing, and courage. Often this phenomenon is referred to as "marianismo." A physical manifestation of this would be the extensive wearing of medals with the image of Mary. Yet, although Puerto Rican men wear religious medals, they seldom utilize the image of Mary and prefer the cross or the image of male saints. Moreover, Puerto Rico, basically a patriarchal society inculcated with Spanish and Catholic tradition, has slowly been modifying its societal structure because of the increase in the rates of divorce, in one-parent households (namely female), and in a more liberal attitude toward sexual behavior. Therefore, the role of women has been gradually transformed from that of the docile, good, nurturing female to one which may combine the previous feminine qualities with more masculine qualities such as assertiveness, courage, and leadership. Some of this is reflected in the naming of contemporary female heroes.

Gender, however, remains an important factor in people's preferences. There are, for example, zero male respondents for Hernández Colón, García Márquez, Chayanne, and Ojeda; there are zero female respondents for Fidel Castro, Michael Jordan, and Ronald Reagan. There are zero male respondents for "Mothers," Isabel Allende (Latin American writer), and local female entertainers. There seems to be no pattern in the nonselection for male respondents; however, for female respondents one might assume females would not select a sports figure nor an elderly statesman nor a Communist leader at a period of unpopularity with totalitarian Communist regimes.

Responses reveal a tendency to nominate heroes covered extensively in the media, such as Antonia Coello Novello (U.S. Surgeon General and the first female and Hispanic in this position), Jacobo Morales (Puerto Rican screenwriter and a 1989 Academy Award nominee for Best Foreign Film), Sandra Zaiter (Puerto Rican TV personality and handicapped person), Luis Rafael Sánchez (Puerto Rican author and resident writer at New York University), and others.

We also noted a generational bias. Ferré, an elderly statesman, received nominations only from the over-30 female and male respondents. In contrast, over-30 females did not select either Berríos or Mandela, both political activists. These results affirm the tendency for the over-30 respondents to not identify with or admire nontraditional heroes.

Questions about historical male and female heroes reveal that the choices for male heroes are primarily political figures. However, the choices for female heroes list both political and tragic figures. De Burgos, who was found dead in a gutter in New York City, and Joan of Arc, who was burned at the stake, exemplify courage, leadership, and dedication to a cause. Both strove for independence from a colonizing power. There seems to be a parallelism between the tragic nature of these two women with the top male choices in this category—John F. Kennedy, Gandhi, Christ, Martin Luther King, Jr., and Albizu Campos.

There is also a parallel construct for the remaining male and female choices. Muñoz Marín and Doña Fela were influential in Puerto Rican society and politics because of their appeal to the masses, which crossed socioeconomic and political boundaries. Rodríguez de Tió and de Hostos were 19th-century Puerto Rican patriots and intellectuals who through their work strove for the independence of Puerto Rico. Over half of these choices are Puerto Rican, not international figures.

In the female historical hero category Julia de Burgos was cited by more than twice as many females than males. Perhaps the male respondent is unable to identify with the tragic nature of her life and cannot reconcile his perception of a hero as a leader with the absence of leadership quality in de Burgos.

When asked about the qualities most admired in heroes there was no significant difference in female and male responses. However, it must be pointed out that intelligence, not traditionally admired in women, is selected by both male and female respondents, as is leadership. Surprisingly, dedication to family, an alleged cornerstone of Puerto Rican culture, received one of the lowest scores. Physical appearance, an extremely important value on the island, is also deemed unimportant in this particular decision.

Looking at "political" heroes, mostly Puerto Ricans were selected with Melo Muñoz receiving an overwhelming number of votes. There is a significant gender difference for male and female student respondents to the Muñoz nomination. More young females identify with this female role model. Young males and females identify more strongly with radical political heroes. Of the "historical" heroes named, four of six top choices are Puerto Rican, indicating identification with local figures for the historical model. We note that more female than male respondents selected Doña Fela.

In the religious category not a single Puerto Rican religious leader received mention. The highest scores were given to international religious figures whose images have been enhanced by the media. In Puerto Rico and other contemporary societies the traditional religious leader is male, yet Mother Teresa is the first choice among Puerto Ricans. The Pope received higher scores from the over-30 male and female respondents; Mother Teresa received double the number of votes from the over-30 males than from young males. Jesus Christ was selected by only a very small number of young females. These low scores suggest the inappropriateness of the inclusion of Jesus in the hero category; otherwise, what explanation can be given for the selection of Mother Teresa whose life is an emulation of Christ's own life and teachings?

In sports, the only female athlete to appear on the list is Angelita Lind—first choice in this category. This is attributed to the limited participation of Puerto Rican women in sports. At present, the public school system provides a very limited physical education program. Lind received double the number of votes from young female respondents, whereas Michael Jordan obtained double the votes from young males. The fact that Valenzuela received the highest scores from both the males and females over 30 reveals the long standing popularity of baseball for this generation.

In the fine arts category, all choices were Puerto Rican. De Burgos, not voted a hero by males in the historical category, was selected for the "belles lettres" category. Her lack of leadership does not influence nomination in this category. In music, five of the six nominees are Hispanic, and one is an international figure. More females than males identify with music heroes; there is only one significant figure for male respondents—Ruben Blades. The only difference between Blades and other singers is his song lyrics, which take the form of social protest rather than romance. The over-30 females show preference for the traditional ballad singers; they strongly reject Madonna. Males over-30 select male singers more significantly than female singers.

In television, Ojeda, the Puerto Rican talk show host who covers controversial topics, received the highest score, particularly with all females. The top three choices are Puerto Rican. More females than males prefer Ojeda, Rodríguez, Fox, and Jovet. Rodríguez is more popular with the over-30 group; Fox is not significantly popular with the latter. However, he is very popular with female students who also prefer Jovet. Despite the availability of cable television on the island, the selection of Puerto Rican TV actors over English language actors seems to be influenced by the viewers' preference for Spanish-language programming.

In film, Juliá is overwhelmingly selected by all respondents, a fact which demonstrates once more the identification of Puerto Ricans with a successful, talented, Puerto Rican actor at both national and international levels. The other top nominees are Hollywood products who are identified with comedy and the "macho" image. These two figures—Schwarzenegger and Murphy—are more popular with young respondents than with the over-30 subjects. Eddie Murphy in particular is more popular among male respondents; females over-30 reject him completely. It should be noted that the classic stars Garbo and Chaplin received significant scores.

CONCLUSION

The characteristics that give definition to self are physical condition and appearance, feelings, and roles. The choices in this study affirm this; the selection of Schwarzenegger, Fox, Murphy, Selleck, Rodríguez, Jovet, Nazario, and Lunna reflect the importance of the first trait in Puerto Rican culture. De Burgos and "Mothers" clearly exemplify the trait of feelings. The roles of the selected heroes emphasize intelligence, leadership, dedication, and courage.

To communicate effectively the individual must perceive of the self as an integral part of the group. Moreover, a group memory defines a culture or a co-culture. Thus, in Puerto Rican culture, females identify with females, males with males, and both females and males identify with other Puerto Ricans. This group identity allows the individual to have access to role models within his or her physical or psychological proximity.

The hero is also a model for culture, and the selection of Puerto Rican heroes in those areas closely associated with their culture such as fine arts, music, history, and language-related media verifies this. The emergence of new heroes in this survey reinforces the belief that the hero concept is not only a metaphor for self but also a metaphor in the process of change. For example, the choices in many categories listed rising celebrities such as the U.S. Surgeon General and Puerto Rican screenwriters as well as literary figures. In fact, on March 25, 1991, the Puerto Rico Senate gave the local singer Chayanne an award for "the glory and prestige he had brought to the island and for his symbolizing the hope of Puerto Rican youth" ("Chayanne," 1991). Especially gratifying to the local population was Chayanne's statement that stardom and celebrity and Florida residency had not taken away his "Puerto Ricanness" or what he referred to as "la mancha del platáno" (the stain caused by the plantain which is very difficult to remove).

Categories that once defined *hero* such as religion, mythology, literature, and the military are no longer prevalent. Traditional heroes were extraordinary individuals of rare personal qualities and admirable deeds. Contemporary Puerto Rican society combines some of the herolike qualities (Mother Teresa, Gandhi) with media-created celebrity status (Bush, Gorbachev, John Paul II). The latter confirms Boorstin's (1961) belief that a celebrity is a person who is known for his or her "well-knownness."

This study of Puerto Rican heroes and celebrities reveals the impact of the media for contemporary figures. In some categories, however, those no longer in the news continue to remain popular. It is also evident that Puerto Rico is an example of cultures in contact, for international men and women are chosen in the categories of religion, politics, and film, and local figures are selected in fine arts and music. Television, however, combines local with international individuals. In some categories such as sports there is a combination of indigenous and nonindigenous names. It would be interesting to see if this is also true of other cultures in contact situations. Are the media creating a system for the selection of international heroes/celebrities? Would a comparison of the results of this study to one of Puerto Ricans and other Hispanic groups in the United States reveal trends in acculturation? Answers to these questions would provide valuable information for students of history, culture, language, communication, and the media, as well as those interested in the cultural significance of the hero/celebrity.

☐☐☐☐☐ *19*

"Trying to Learn How to Walk Like the Heroes": Bruce Springsteen, Popular Music, and the Hero/Celebrity*

Thomas Gencarelli
Montclair State College

☐ *In response to Boorstin's (1980) claim that the heroes of our modern mass-mediated culture are often no more than, or are mistakenly equated with, celebrities, Gencarelli argues that the popular music artist Bruce Springsteen is both a celebrity and a hero. Using Campbell's (1968) concept of the monomythic journey of the hero—separation, initiation, and return—the author shows how Springsteen's career can be divided into three discrete stages, each of which constitutes a monomythic journey in itself, whereas the three stages taken together also constitute the monomyth in their entirety. The analysis is carried out by means of a theoretical framework, suggesting that popular music as a form of communication must be examined along with content and context.*

On June 12, 1982, I was working as a volunteer at the Nuclear Disarmament Rally in Central Park in New York. This gathering, along with the "No Nukes" rally at Battery City Park some three years earlier, was one of the events that helped set the tone for a resurgence of political activism in the 1980s—an activism expressed largely in terms of such events. At the park that day was an audience of an estimated 400,000 people, a number of political action and special interest groups, and a huge stage set up for celebrity speakers and musical guest performers. At a little past noon under the late spring sun, one of

---

The Bruce Springsteen study was initiated by Tracy Schario, Ohio University, one of the original participants in the 1989 Speech Communication Association Seminar on Heroes and Celebrities. Her seminar paper is titled, "Bruce Springsteen: The Working Class Hero."

these musical guests stepped out unannounced and began to sing to the vast sea of faces, accompanied by only his acoustic guitar and harmonica. That guest was Bruce Springsteen.

I remember completely forgetting my duties and wandering off to listen during his brief, four-song set. I stood there awed, at first, by the fact that here was a guy who had captured the attention of 400,000 people—*by himself*—to the point that the park's Great Lawn was virtually silent. It was also a special occasion to hear Bruce perform solo because his live shows have always been 3-hour full-tilt rock-and-roll marathons, with the full complement of his E Street band. And yet, there was something else that caught me on that day and made me listen—something that I could not quite put my finger on at the time.

It was not just that I was listening to a star like Springsteen doing a special and intimate version of his songs (if you can call a solo performance in front of 400,000 people "intimate"). Had it been another star of the same magnitude up there—Madonna or Michael Jackson—I am not sure they could have pulled it off, or at least pulled it off to the same effect. It was not a measure of Springsteen's virtuosity as a singer or a player. Indeed, many popular artists are, technically speaking, more gifted. It was not the political message in his songs or the appropriateness of that message to the day. A number of artists are more overtly and directly political. Jackson Browne, who was also there that day (and who sang harmony on Springsteen's "The Promised Land"), is one who comes to mind, as do Sting and Peter Gabriel.

This last point, however, is not to say that Springsteen's music is not political. But there is a difference to Springsteen's politic. First, his politic is implicit in his work rather than explicit. As popular music critic Dave Marsh (1981) points out in his Springsteen biography, *Born to Run*, Springsteen has "always shied away from any specific political statements (even though there were strong political threads in his work from the beginning)" (p. 239). These "threads" that Marsh alludes to arise from the fact that, as a lyricist, Springsteen is a storyteller: one who writes about people, their lives, and how they see and experience their place in the world. As a result, according to McGuire (1984), Springsteen's politic is *descriptive* rather than *proscriptive*; his approach "is to show the audience possibilities, not to tell his hearers what to think or do" (p. 246). Second, as Marsh's quote also suggests, Springsteen's politic has always been integral to his music. Jackson Browne, Sting, and Peter Gabriel all started out doing something else with their music before they began to express concern with the political climate of the times—before they took advantage of their position in the forum of global pop music to become rock's new political statesmen. Bob Dylan's contributions in his later career have always been measured against the power and poignancy of his earlier political songs, the pedestal that he was put on as a result of these songs, and the expectation that this is how his art should always serve us. Springsteen's music, however—although it has clearly undergone changes (see Sellnow & Sellnow, 1990)—has been political since its very beginnings. It is posited in this chapter that the maintenance and evolution of this politic is inseparable from the man himself and from the way he sees and experiences *his* place in the world.

It is also argued that there is another way in which Springsteen's music is inseparable from the man. It was stated previously that Springsteen is not a virtuoso as a singer or musician. Yet, this does not mean that he is not musically gifted. First, his ability as an author and composer must be considered as part of the musical equation. From the early, elaborate constructions of "Rosalita (Come Out Tonight)" (1973b) and the operatic "Jungleland" (1975), to the plaintive strains of "Meeting Across the River" (1975) and "Racing in the Streets" (1978), to the barrelhouse rock and roll of "Cadillac Ranch" (1980), to the haunted, acoustic "Nebraska" (1982), to the blistering, immediate pop of "Born in the U.S.A." (1984), he remains a consummate craftsman. Second, this ability as a songwriter is also directly tied to the fact that he writes for his own performance. And although he is not masterful, in the traditional sense as a musician, he *is* a folk artist and a rock and roller who—to use Hebdige's (1979) succinct and appropriate term—has *style*.

Although Hebdige intends this term to refer to *personal* style (image, attitude, dress, and the accouterments with which one adorns and surrounds one's self), it can also be argued that a popular music artist's *sound* has a definite style (Gencarelli, 1990). This style is an inextricable characteristic of popular music. Because performance is the primary way in which a popular music work is experienced, if someone else performs a particular work, it becomes, quite literally, a different work. Moreover, in the case of a recognizably successful artist it can be said that this style of sound is interwoven with his or her personal style, in a semiotically coherent way. Both of these, in turn, are intertwined with his or her politic (in the widest sense of the term). The point here, however, is that Springsteen's music is more a matter of his unique, indelible style than it is about technical ability. And his success as an artist is due as much to this style as it is to his political stance.

SPRINGSTEEN AS HERO

It is with these two points in mind that the thesis of this chapter can now be presented: Springsteen is a rock-and-roll hero, but he is also a true modern hero, in the fullest sense of the term. To support this thesis, however, it is first necessary to define this fullest sense of what is meant by *hero*.

Once again, two points need to be made. First, in a modern massmediated world, all of our heroes are exploited by our media of mass communication, if they are not, in fact, created by them. Because of this, as historian Boorstin asserts in his book, *The Image* (1980), we have come to confuse celebrity worship and hero worship. Boorstin defines the traditional hero as a person "who has shown greatness in some achievement . . . a man or woman of great deeds" (p. 49). He goes on to suggest, however, that "the machinery of information has brought into being a new substitute for the hero, who is the celebrity, and whose main characteristic is his well-knownness" (pp. 59-60). Strate (1985) echoes this point in tracing the changing concept of the hero across the three epochs in the history of human communication: orality, literacy, and the electronic. He adds that: "Where we once measured a hero by his actions, and then by his ideas, we now evaluate him on the basis of his image" (p. 52). Thus, in the view of both Boorstin and Strate, the character and value of the contemporary hero has been debased by our mass media, especially our electronic media. The hero no longer lives the "individual adventure," as Campbell calls it (Maher & Briggs, 1988, p. 59), unless by this adventure we mean only becoming famous and concomitantly wealthy. Indeed, Boorstin, Strate, and Campbell might argue that it is this very achievement that our culture most esteems today. Yet, it is on this very point that the nature of today's hero becomes problematic.

To use the pop music artist as an exemplar of this problem, the rock-and-roll hero has always connoted the youth who rose up from obscurity on the sheer strength of his belief in the music, who paid his dues, and who "made it." But once you have made it, the adventure is over. What do you do for your next trick? As Strate (1985, p. 51) acknowledges: "In electronic culture, we have more heroes then ever before, but they are given the role for a much shorter period of time." The reasons for this development are as follows. First, due to the omnipresent plastering of the celebrity/hero's image and exploits across the broadsides of air, wire, and the printed page, we quickly tire of hearing about and seeing them. Or, in the case of the pure celebrity, whose image outweighs his or her exploits, we perhaps tire because he or she was not really worth our attention in the first place. Our media also need to fill their space and time with new "product" to keep attracting and holding our attention. Finally, in the age of art as commerce, the commodification of the celebrity/hero in the media arts—through what Joni Mitchell once referred to as the "star-making machinery"—cuts into the staying power of all but the most gifted, prolific, and driven of artists.

But this is just an explanation of what has become of the hero in our modern mass media world. Clearly, a more complete definition of the traditional, true hero is also necessary—the second point in outlining the full sense of what a hero is. This is important as a foundation and as a comparison for what has been said so far and because it is the intent of this chapter to argue that Springsteen is such a hero. Thus, to return to this idea, Campbell, in writing about mythic heroes in his book, *The Hero With a Thousand Faces*, notes the following:

> Such a one's visions, ideas, and inspirations come pristine from the primary springs of human life and thought. Hence they are eloquent, not of the present, disintegrating society and psyche, but of the unquenched source through which society is reborn. The hero has died as a modern man; but as eternal man—perfected, unspecified, universal man—he has been reborn. His second solemn task and deed therefore (as Toynbee declares and as all the mythologies of

mankind indicate) is to return then to us, transfigured, and teach the lesson he has learned of life renewed. (1968a, pp. 19-20)

It is in following this model that the nonmythological hero of our real world also lives his or her great adventure. That is, the standard path of any true hero must trace this same rite of passage, which Campbell (borrowing from Joyce) refers to as the nuclear unit of the "monomyth": *separation—initiation—return* (p. 30). The first step—separation—is the "call to adventure" (p. 36), wherein the hero becomes aware of his or her vocation, and moves, or is led, in its direction. The second step is the "trials and victories of initiation" (p. 36), wherein the hero battles and reaches beyond the means and limitations of common mortal existence and attains the pinnacle of his or her calling. Finally, the third step is his or her "return and reintegration with society" (p. 36), which, Campbell states, "is indispensable to the continuous circulation of spiritual energy into the world, and which, from the standpoint of the community, is the justification for the long retreat" (p. 36).

It is argued in this chapter that Springsteen is an artist who has followed this tripartite path and whose staying power and popularity throughout his 20-year career must be attributed to this lived heroism. Furthermore, this argument is made on two related levels. First, Springsteen's career can be broken down into three discrete stages, each of which can be seen as a complete monomythic journey in and of itself, and wherein he brings his experience of his place in the world to his art and returns a message with deep resonance for his audience. These stages are titled here according to the names of his songs: "Growin' Up" (comprising the albums, *Greetings from Asbury Park* [1973a], *The Wild, the Innocent & the E Street Shuffle* [1973b], and *Born to Run* [1975]); "The Promised Land" (comprising the albums, *Darkness on the Edge of Town* [1978], *The River* [1980], *Nebraska* [1982], and *Born in the U.S.A.* [1984]); and "One Step Up" (comprising the album, *Tunnel of Love* [1987]).

The first stage is signified by Springsteen's coming of age near the New Jersey shore and in New York City and is filled with stories about street life, wild youth, and about living on the verge of working class adulthood, but dreaming of a way out to something greater. The words are rife with image after poetic image, and the music is rollicking and ambitious; they seem determined to prove something—to establish the artist's greatness right away, as he crams everything he can into the grooves of the record while he has his big chance.

The second stage comes after *Born to Run* establishes Springsteen as a major talent—it became one of the most critically acclaimed records of the 1970s—and after his legal troubles with his former management kept him from releasing any new music for over three years. This stage is marked by Springsteen's having found a way out himself, but having grown up along the way by facing some of life's harder lessons. It finds him struggling with the fact that the greater something is still elusive, and still writing about the people of his roots, who grew up with him. And yet, through it all, he still finds it in himself to celebrate the joy of rock and roll. The music is also more assured—both realizing and accepting of its power and eloquence.

The third stage, which has only recently begun, finds Springsteen a full-fledged celebrity and multimillionaire after *Born in the U.S.A.* sold some 21 million copies worldwide (Holden, 1992, p. H27)—ultimately fulfilling the promise that is the reason John Hammond at Columbia Records signed him in the first place. Here is a mature artist dealing with what the dreams of life become and what the course of life leads to, when it hits us that the greater something may always be elusive, regardless of what we achieve or attain. This comes across on the one album in this stage in which Springsteen tries to comes to terms with settling down, with this knowledge, into a love relationship that may not be our saving grace either, but to which we inevitably turn for solace from our struggles. The music here is restrained and simple and at times even seems to take a back seat to the lyrics.

It is also argued, however, that these three periods in Springsteen's career *together* constitute the steps of a monomythic journey. Thus, in attempting to communicate how he sees and experiences his place in the world, within each stage in his personal growth and career, Springsteen has followed the path of the hero—and, from the same perspective, his entire career stands as a hero's journey, from which he now returns, both a hero and a celebrity.[1]

To analyze each of these stages and Springsteen's entire career and to support this claim, however, it is necessary to introduce one additional, methodological point. That is, to understand popular music as a form of communication it must be looked at on four distinct levels. First, the words to songs obviously hold meaning for us. Language is our common denominator and the most direct, immediate component of any popular musical message. Second, music itself further communicates to us through its unique brand of symbols. However, although the framework provided by Irvine and Kirkpatrick (1972), and adopted by others (Gonzalez & Makay, 1983), tries to break down the elements of music in an attempt to explain it as a rhetorical form, there are two problems with their results: (a) music winds up being secondary to the lyrics—as little more than something that supports or embellishes the message in the lyrics; and (b) most popular music listeners do not dissect music in this way. Thus, a more appropriate way of talking about music itself would simply be to address its style, as discussed above—on its own terms, without trying to fit it into any modes of discourse analysis, and as any critic or fan would. Third, in our modern mass mediated culture, personal style also communicates a great deal. It might be said, harking back to Boorstin's words, that the image of our popular artists and groups (including the aural image that is the style of their sound) is what we buy into more than anything else their art has to say to us. Finally, the context in

---

[1]This is not to argue that Bruce's artistic integrity is so pure and/or unaffected that he has not played a role in marketing himself, by manufacturing his persona to some degree. In an age of art as commerce, one simply cannot separate the two.

which we discover and/or attend to an artist's or group's music, which adds further definition to it, is a fourth source of meaning in popular music.

Therefore, to examine Springsteen's career, and extract from it evidence of his heroism in accordance with what has been said so far, it is the purpose of the remainder of this chapter to explore how the artist and his body of work communicate this heroism in the messages he brings back about his and *our* place in the world. This includes an analysis of how his politic has maintained yet evolved in his lyrics; an analysis of how his musical style has evolved in and of itself; an analysis of how his personal style has evolved to reflect or project the changes in the first two; and an analysis of the context that makes up each stage of his career.

GROWIN' UP

The first stage of Springsteen's career traces the path of the monomyth as follows. Separation can be said to be through all of his life, building up to his first record contract. Through this period, he gives up everything in quest of his singular goal: making it in music. Marsh's (1981) biography chronicles these early years, prior to Springsteen's signing with Columbia, including the bands on the Jersey shore circuit, the trips to California, the songs that led to his signing, and so on. Initiation comes with the signing of the Columbia contract and the birth of a career, all of which hinges on his ability to make commercially viable music and to make it on a regular basis. Springsteen faces up to the task and creates three albums that bring kudos from the critics and help him to build a steady following—up through the multimillion selling landmark album, *Born to Run*. Return, of course, is what he communicates, by way of his music and his burgeoning stardom, which makes his art valuable to us (and which makes us buy the records).

Lyrically, Springsteen talks about himself and the people in his immediate world during this stage. In fact, he appears in many of the songs himself, whether he is the central character telling his own story or part of a cast of characters in some larger story. This is also true whether he refers to himself in the first person or makes an oblique or third-person reference to himself (e.g., the boy prophet in "The E Street Shuffle"; Scooter in "Tenth Avenue Freeze-Out"). It does not begin to change until *Born to Run*.

The stories here are populated by colorful characters, with names like Crazy Janey and Wild Billy, Spanish Johnny and Puerto Rican Jane, Madame Marie (the fortune teller from the Asbury Park boardwalk), Little Angel, and Magic Rat. They eventually shift from Jersey shore and New York City street scenes to a less place-specific Americana of youth, motorcycles, and cars. This change coincides with Springsteen's increasing popularity and incessant touring, and, thus, with the expanding of his horizons beyond his more parochial beginnings.

Examples of Springsteen writing about himself can be found in two wholly autobiographical songs from the first album: "Growin' Up" and "It's Hard to Be a Saint in the City." "Growin' Up" is his paean to youthful rebellion and the bravado of one who believes in himself and his vision, regardless of, and even thumbing his nose at, the crowd from which as a result he separates himself. He is determined to rise above, or feels that he has already done so, by virtue of simply having the desire and taking the steps:

> The flag of piracy flew from my mast my sails were set wing to wing
> I had a jukebox graduate for a first mate she couldn't sail but she sure could sing
> I pushed B-52 and bombed 'em with the blues with my gear set stubborn on standing
> I broke all the rules strafed my old high school never once gave thought to landing
> I hid in the clouded warmth of the crowd but when they said "Come down" I threw up
> Ooh-ooh growin' up.

In "It's Hard to Be a Saint in the City," this same confidence and swagger come across still more powerfully:

> I had skin like leather and the diamond hard look of a cobra
> I was born blue and weathered but I burst just like a supernova
> I could walk like Brando right into the sun
> Then dance just like a Casanova
> With my blackjack and jacket and hair slicked sweet
> Silver star studs on my duds like a Harley in heat
> When I strut down the street I could feel its heartbeat
> The sisters fell back and said "Don't that man look pretty"
> The cripple on the corner cried out "Nickels for your pity"
> Them gasoline boys downtown sure talk gritty
> It's so hard to be a saint in the city.

Stories in which Springsteen is the main character include "Fourth of July, Asbury Park (Sandy)" and "Rosalita (Come Out Tonight)" from the second album. In both of these songs, Springsteen casts himself as a lover, trying to make the girl see his vision so that she will come over to his side and perhaps come along for his ride. In the open-ended final two lines to the first chorus from "Sandy," however, he seems to be reaching only to capture the wonder and beauty of the moment—perhaps knowing that he will be moving on; perhaps wanting to take the girl with him, but not knowing if he can, or if she will come; perhaps recognizing and surrendering to the fleeting nature of all such moments, as well as to the moment of their youth passing:

> Sandy the fireworks are hailin' over little Eden tonight
> Forcin' a light into all those stony faces left stranded on this Fourth of July
> Down in town the circuits full with switchblade lovers so fast so shiny so sharp
> As the wizards play down on Pinball Way on the boardwalk way past dark
> And the boys from the casino dance with their shirts half open like Latin lovers along the shore
> Chasin' all those silly New York virgins by the score
> Sandy the aurora is risin' behind us
> The pier lights our carnival life forever
> Love me tonight for I may never see you again.

In "Rosalita," however, he emphatically and without question invites the girl along for the ride:

> Now I know your mama she don't like me 'cause I play in a rock and roll band
> And I know your daddy he don't dig me but he never did understand
> Your papa lowered the boom he locked you in your room
> I'm comin' to lend a hand
> I'm comin' to liberate you confiscate you I want to be your man
> Someday we'll look back on this and it will all seem funny
> But now you're sad your mama's mad
> And your papa says he knows that I don't have any money
> Oh tell him this is his last chance to get his daughter in a fine romance
> Because the record company Rosie just gave me a big advance.

The songs in which Springsteen is just one among many characters in a story are relatively few, but include "Spirit in the Night" on the first album. Included in this song is Springsteen's landscape of desperate youthful abandon, of working-class kids searching for something greater in the only corner of their lives in which they can find happiness—in their freedom and escape:

> Crazy Janey and her mission man were back in the alley tradin' hands
> 'Long came Wild Billy with his friend G-man all duded up for Saturday night
> Well Billy slammed on his coaster brakes and said anybody wanna go on up to Greasy Lake
> It's about a mile down on the dark side of Route 88
> I got a bottle of rose so let's try it
> We'll pick up Hazy Davy and Killer Joe and I'll take you all out to where the gypsy angels go
> They're built like light
> And they dance like spirits in the night.

By the end of the song, however, Springsteen lets on that he knows that this is not the place or the way to search for what he is looking for, as he closes with the following: "Janey said it was time to go/So we closed our eyes and said goodbye to gypsy angel row . . ."

Finally, in terms of lyrics, there are a number of songs in which Springsteen is just an observer or narrator, painting a poet's picture of characters, their environs, their yearnings, and the events and fates in which they are caught up. These songs begin with "Lost in the Flood" from the first album and reach their climax with the closing song from *Born to Run*, "Jungleland": the story of Magic Rat, street gangs, motorcycle toughs, and rock-and-roll dreamers, living in a world that bridges Springsteen's New Jersey towns and New York City streets. Yet, one song turns up on *Born to Run* that takes a turn away from all of these other songs. In "Night," Springsteen paints a picture of a person of whose world he is obviously no longer a part:

> You get up every morning at the sound of the bell
> You get to work late and the boss man's giving you hell
> Till you're out on a midnight run
> Losing your heart to a beautiful one
> And it feels right . . .
> And the world is busting at its seams
> And you're just a prisoner of your dreams
> Holding on for your life
> Cause you work all day
> To blow 'em away in the night.

By this time Springsteen has established himself and his career. *Born to Run* was the make-or-break album in his contract, but he was on the verge of stardom, his talents were blossoming, and he worked doggedly in the studio perfecting this record. Moreover, he was earning a living from music at this point and had never worked at a straight day job in his life. Thus, "Night" stands as a transitional work. Up until this lyric, all of Springsteen's words are about the world of his youth. Whether he is writing about himself with the cocksure attitude of one who has discovered his mission in life and is working as hard as he can toward it, or about the sometimes tragic lives and longings of those around him, he takes what he knows and what he lives from day to day and puts this to music. With the release of *Born to Run*, however, Springsteen was on the cover of *Time* and *Newsweek*, and was being courted like the celebrity he was becoming. After this, he could no longer write about himself and his world and expect it to resonate for us.

However, before moving on to examine the stage in his career that follows this transitional point, the remainder of how Springsteen communicates his heroism must be included in this analysis. That is, his music, his style, and a final statement about the context that is this first stage remain to be addressed. Musically, as was noted above, the first three albums are undeniably ambitious in scope, covering a number of styles and including complex and lengthy arrangements. (It is noted that the lyrics are similarly expansive.) There is also a great deal of density, and one might say even overplaying, on many of the songs (listen, for instance, to the coda on "The E Street Shuffle"). In addition, the quality of the performances and the recording on the first two albums are somewhat ragged—all of this showing the inexperience of a young but determined group of musicians, getting by more on heart and soul than anything else. Insofar as Springsteen's style is concerned, the albums in this stage find him a combination street poet and motorcycle greaser—with his tousled hair and scraggly beard, black leather jacket, jeans, ripped T-shirts, sneakers or boots, and beat-up old Fender Telecaster guitar. Semiotically speaking, the pieces all fit.

Contextually, Springsteen's early live shows celebrate the wild abandon of the rock-and-roll dream, in 2 1/2- to 3-hour sets at small venues such as New York's The Bottom Line and Los Angeles' The Roxy; concerts as vast and ambitious as anything on his records. However, it can also be said, in terms of the context into which everything about this stage falls, that Springsteen's heroism at this point is reflected in the fact that he has taken his experience, and the experience of a typically American youth audience like him, and made art from it. As a result, he returns a message found not only in his music, but in his musical career. This message speaks of the joy of youth and of striving to achieve one's dream; it is about youth rising above in the search for something greater. In turn, Springsteen is accorded heroic status; he is idolized for achieving his dream—as one who has risen from out of our ranks and who has done so by providing us with a rich, deep picture of ourselves.

THE PROMISED LAND

The second stage in Springsteen's career traces the path of the monomyth as follows. Separation comes with the success of *Born to Run* and Springsteen achieving rock stardom. He leaves the world of his youth in two respects: he has risen above it, and he is older and more mature. This leaves him in a tenuous position, however: How can he continue to build on the persona he has established in his work and career up to this point?

Initiation is comprised of the factors that influence the evolution of Springsteen's music moving into this period. It is his attempt to live up to the mantle of his heroism. He must prove himself worthy of his status (on the same terms that he achieved it), maintain it, and strive to take it still further. The way that he does so is by maintaining the integrity of his identity. He must accept that he has moved on, that his concerns are now more adult and that he is no longer the street kid he once was. Yet, he also fights against the insularity of his success. He cannot or will not shake his identification with the typical, American working-class person and presents himself as such a person, despite the trappings of his success. Moreover, success leaves him still unfulfilled and unsettled—a factor that Marsh alludes to a number of times (see 1981, p. 182, for example). He is still searching for something that even realizing his rock-and-roll dream has not brought him.

In addition, two other factors can be said to play a part in his initiation at this stage. First, Springsteen is by no means a wealthy man at this point. Marsh (1981) points out that his total income, paid to him by his former management for the 4-year period ending in March 1976 (six months after the release of *Born to Run*), amounted to only $100,000, or approximately $25,000 per year (p. 194). Second, his troubles with his former management resulted in a protracted legal battle, which left his career on hold until the release of *Darkness on the Edge of Town* in 1978. This bitter experience was the final catalyst in Springsteen's maturation from man-child to man. He learned, firsthand, what it meant and felt like to not be in control of his own life and destiny. This served to strengthen his identification with a world and its people that he had never really left, but had just grown up alongside.

Return, of course, is once again the message that Springsteen communicates about himself and us through his music and his persona. It can also be noted, that if the first stage in his career—striving to attain this status of the second stage—is the separation step in his heroic path, then this second stage is clearly initiation. Springsteen has arrived; he must now live up to his promise.

The songs in this stage are still sometimes about the artist himself, but are mostly about the people with whom he identifies and for whom he now speaks. A primary characteristic of Springsteen's storytelling at this point, however, is how he writes himself in as the character; the songs are almost exclusively in the first person, whether they are about Springsteen or not. In addition, most of the songs are about the strife and struggle of daily living— about circumstances that people want or need to break out of, or at least dream of rising above. This, it can be said, comes in part from Springsteen's own continued restlessness and struggle. As a result, the songs he writes about himself ring true for everyman, whereas the reverse is also true, to an extent. The only exception to all of this is a series of 3- to 4-minute back-to-basics rock-and-roll songs from the first two sides of the double-record compilation, *The River* ("Sherry Darling," "Two Hearts," "Crush on You," "You Can Look [But You Better Not Touch]," and "I Wanna Marry You"). As suggested earlier, these songs are just celebrations of rock and roll, coming at a point when Springsteen is confident enough to express himself in such a simple, traditional form.

The song that announces Springsteen's arrival into this stage in his career is indeed "The Promised Land," from *Darkness on the Edge of Town*. In the penultimate line of the chorus, he sings: "Mister, I ain't a boy, no, I'm a man." Yet, the remainder of the song is wholly about someone who Springsteen is not, and presages the orientation and concerns of his work throughout this period:

> I've done my best to live the right way
> I get up every morning and go to work each day
> But your eyes go blind and your blood runs cold
> Sometimes I feel so weak I just want to explode
> Explode and tear this town apart
> Take a knife and cut this pain from my heart
> Find somebody itching for something to start.

"Independence Day," from *The River*, on the other hand, is clearly autobiographical, at the same time that it is a story of sons and fathers everywhere and of every time:

> Well Papa go to bed now it's getting late
> Nothing we can say is gonna change anything now
> I'll be leaving in the morning from St. Mary's Gate
> We wouldn't change this thing even if we could somehow
> Cause the darkness of this house has got the best of us
> There's a darkness in this town that's got us too
> But they can't touch me now
> And you can't touch me now
> They ain't gonna do to me
> What I watched them do to you . . .
> So say goodbye it's Independence Day
> Papa now I know the things you wanted that you could not say
> But won't you say goodbye it's Independence Day
> I swear I never meant to take those things away.

With the exception of the rock-and-roll love songs from *The River*, however, the rest of the songs in this stage are primarily about people striving to transcend their life's world. They are about trying to grab hold of the reins of whatever it is in life that is beyond our control and which controls us—while reaching with the same hands for that elusive, greater something that will bring us peace of mind and spirit. For instance, the title track from *Darkness on the Edge of Town* introduces us to a man who has not found what he is searching for in his material wealth or who perhaps realizes this only now that he has lost what he had. But still he searches:

> Some folks are born into a good life
> Other folks get it anyway, anyhow
> I lost my money and I lost my wife
> Them things don't seem to matter much to me now
> Tonight I'll be on that hill 'cause I can't stop
> I'll be on that hill with everything I got
> Lives on the line where dreams are found and lost
> I'll be there on time and I'll pay the cost
> For wanting things that can only be found
> In the darkness on the edge of town.

The title track from *The River* expresses the wistful longings of a young man trapped by his fate, who has only his memories left to carry him and thoughts of missed possibilities to haunt him:

> I come from down in the valley
> Where mister when you're young
> They bring you up to do like you're daddy done
> Me and Mary we met in high school
> When she was just seventeen
> We'd ride out of that valley down to where the fields were green

> We'd go down to the river
> And into the river we'd dive
> Oh down to the river we'd ride
> Then I got Mary pregnant
> And man that was all she wrote
> And for my nineteenth birthday I got a union card and a wedding coat
> We went down to the courthouse
> And the judge put it all to rest
> No wedding day smiles no walk down the aisle
> No flowers no wedding dress
> That night we went down to the river
> And into the river we'd dive
> Oh down to the river we did ride.

The title track from *Nebraska*, finally, addresses the darker, more extreme side of people who have given up, and what they can be driven to, when Springsteen tells the story of mass murderer Charles Starkweather's 1958 midwestern killing spree:

> I saw her standin' on her front lawn just twirlin' her baton
> Me and her went for a ride sir and ten innocent people died
> From the town of Lincoln, Nebraska with a sawed-off .410 on my lap
> Through to the badlands of Wyoming I killed everything in my path
> I can't say I'm sorry for the things that we done
> At least for a little while sir me and her had some fun...
> They declared me unfit to live said into that great void my soul'd be hurled
> They wanted to know why I did what I did
> Well sir I guess there's just a meanness in this world.

The most interesting and, in many ways, most significant message from this stage, however, is the title track to *Born in the U.S.A.* Here, Springsteen gives his voice to a character who is a blue-collared Vietnam veteran and tells a story that, by now, has resonance for most of us on one level or another:

> Got in a little hometown jam
> So they put a rifle in my hands
> Sent me off to a foreign land to go and kill the yellowman
> Born in the U.S.A.
> Come back home to the refinery
> Hiring man said "Son if it was up to me"
> Went to see the V.A. man
> He said "Son don't you understand."

This song is important in three ways. First, it is the public response to this song, and the accompanying album, that finally puts Springsteen over the top—bringing him superstar status and the diverse audience that such mass appeal implies. Second, however, this diverse audience reads the song and, in turn, Springsteen himself, in diverse ways. For example, McDermott and Mackey-

Kallis (1991) point out that Ronald Reagan tried to use Springsteen's music and image during his 1984 Presidential campaign to impress American voters with the values of moral strength and faith in the American Dream that his heroism represents. However, invoking Springsteen in this way completely ignores the fact that the patriotism inherent in "Born in the U.S.A." is a double-edged sword. The lyric to the song is a cry from a people who feel let down and put down by the country in which they live. Yet, to make a third point about the import of this song, such an oversight is the result of the mixed message that a surface reading of the song and the album communicates on the other three levels of popular music's communication.

To briefly address the music of this stage, it has already been noted that the songs have been stripped down to their essentials: the basic elements of the abbreviated form that is a pop-rock song. Although there are still 7-minute-plus songs on *The River*, there are no more intricate, rambling arrangements. There is no need; Springsteen has mastered the form. And yet, it must be pointed out that "Born in the U.S.A." is an anthemic piece of music. Even more important than this, however, is the evolution of Springsteen's style as this stage reaches its acme with *Born in the U.S.A.* The album covers of *Darkness on the Edge of Town* and *The River* depict the artist in stark, simple photographs. His image is toned-down, even somewhat everyday. The cover of *Nebraska* is desolate: a picture of a grey midwestern prairie. But with *Born in the U.S.A.*, Springsteen makes a stylistic shift. The cover of this album shows Springsteen's jeans-clad buttocks in front of the American flag. At this same time, he has also begun building his body—a development that can be interpreted in a number of ways. It can be argued, for one, that Springsteen simply jumped on the bandwagon of the 1980s fitness craze. It can also be argued that, at the age of 35, the toll of so many 3-hour-plus shows, coupled with a desire to stave off feeling too old to rock and roll, led him to try to get in shape and keep on rocking. Whatever the case, his style at this point comes to reflect the archetypal all-American male.

The context in which Springsteen's music is heard in this stage also influences his message. He begins by playing hockey arenas, like The Spectrum in Philadelphia, but by the time of the *Born in the U.S.A.* tour, he has graduated to playing outdoor stadiums, in front of 80,000 people. His records also sell millions of copies. The fact that he now reaches this many people can be accounted for by summing up the context that is this stage in his career. That is, this part of Springsteen's career is completely given over to speaking for us. His lyrics are direct and are aimed at universal hopes and fears and dreams. His music is also direct—and even macho—becoming powerful and elemental at the same time (as well as more polished) and reaching almost epic proportions, sonically speaking. Moreover, his image is more like that of an average working male than a rock-and-roll star. As a result, he attracts a broader base. And this base holds Springsteen up as a hero in that, as he rises toward the crest of celebrity that *Born in the U.S.A.* brings, he does so representing us and by holding on to what put him there in every way that he can.

ONE STEP UP

The third stage of Springsteen's career traces the path of the monomyth as follows. Separation comes about as Springsteen attains a stratospheric level of celebrity from which he can go no higher and as he matures toward middle age. He is far removed from the well-springs of the art of both of his earlier stages. There is no more youthful challenge, and the early songs such as "Growin' Up" begin to fade back into his history. (This may explain, in part, why the transition into this final stage is marked by the release of a boxed-set live album [1986], which stands as a retrospective of his career up to this point.) Furthermore, he cannot avoid or deny the influence of his fame and fortune or expect to still be perceived as that person who seems to be just like us, but for his special gift. And yet, he still has the drive to create his art. Initiation is once again about Springsteen attempting to come to terms with this change in his life and ascertain how he can continue making valuable, viable art out of his experience and his place in the world. Finally, return is, as always, what he and his music communicate that strikes a chord within us and is contiguous with what has always been heroic about the artist and his art.

It is also clear that, if the first stage in Springsteen's career is separation, in his mission to make music that is meaningful to people and live out the rock-and-roll dream, and the second stage is initiation, whereby he must try to make good on the promise of his early career and not be corrupted by celebrity or be diverted or burn out, then this final stage is return. Springsteen has survived the trials of celebrity relatively unscathed by remaining true to himself and his art. In doing so he has fashioned a public career of undeniable continuity and coherence. Thus, it is the legacy of this career—in which he can achieve nothing greater—from which he now returns, with the achievement that is his last album (up to this point, anyway) and the one remaining statement in his artistic evolution: *Tunnel of Love*.

The songs on *Tunnel of Love* are about an adult world and an idea or part of life that is inconsolable with youth and rock and roll: settling down. They are also about the steps beyond the solitary effort to find meaning, purpose, and contentment in one's life, and about the attempt—perhaps just as elusive—to find these things by sharing one's life with someone else. In this sense the songs can be said to be a reaction to the fact that, although Springsteen himself has found meaning and purpose, he is eternally questioning and reaching for more. It is also clear that the songs are at least in part based on his short-lived but highly publicized marriage to, and subsequent divorce from, actress/model Julianne Phillips. Thus, they are simultaneously autobiographical and universal.

The title track from *Tunnel of Love* addresses this subject in the direct terms that Springsteen's lyrics have continuously moved toward s the days of "Madman drummers, bummers and indians in the summer." The words suggest that Springsteen is still involved in the same battle as always, but that the arena has changed to love and love alone:

> It ought to be easy ought to be simple enough
> Man meets a woman and they fall in love
> But the house is haunted and the ride gets rough
> And you've got to live with what you can't rise above if you want to ride on down in through this tunnel of love.

Beyond this, the bridge from "Brilliant Disguise" contains the first and only moment in Springsteen's oeuvre in which he admits to his place in life as a celebrity (albeit, it must be noted that he does not fully enunciate the word "wealth"):

> Now look at me baby
> Struggling to do everything right
> And then it all falls apart when out go the lights
> I'm just a lonely pilgrim
> I walk this world in wealth
> I wanna know if it's you I don't trust
> Cause I damn sure don't trust myself.

To examine the rest of what this stage in Springsteen's career communicates, it is also suggested that his music has crested somewhat: the entire album would certainly fit the play list of any adult contemporary radio station. This says the following: (a) perhaps Springsteen is too old to rock and roll or, at least, the rock-and-roll form is no longer congruent with what his personal style and the context of this stage can be; and (b) his music has evolved on a continuum, from a point at which his music and words were equal in their complexity, and both in the foreground for the listener, to a point at which the lyrical message has shifted to the forefront, whereas the music simply creates a bed that provides what Langer (1959) calls a "form of feeling," to embellish and support the message of the words, and to give us the aural hook which makes the song memorable.

Stylistically, Springsteen appears as very much the adult on the cover of *Tunnel of Love*, in a dark suit and starched white shirt and with signs of a receding hairline. It is with this that the semiotic coherence of this stage becomes complete. However, to fully define the context that is this stage, the lyric to the lovely and elegant "One Step Up" has been saved to this point in the analysis:

> It's the same thing night on night
> Who's wrong baby who's right
> Another fight and I slam the door on
> Another battle in our dirty little war
> When I look at myself I don't see
> The man I wanted to be
> Somewhere along the line I slipped off track
> I'm caught movin' one step up and two steps back.

It is not the tale of hard love or the struggle to make it—like everything else in Springsteen's songs—transcendent that is important here. Rather, it is the sentiment and the notion contained in the final line. That is, after all that Springsteen's music has meant to us in what he has said and how he has said it, and after all his career has meant as he lived out the rock-and-roll fantasy and achieved greatness in all the ways we measure it, he comes back with an album that makes an eloquent statement, but on a theme that is the basis for most of the popular music known. What might be said, then, is that Springsteen cannot be expected to reach any higher. His music has always been about reaching, and his career was built by reaching. Yet, perhaps this is what his message stands as, at this stage and in the end: That for all of the struggle of human beings to live the heroic and mythic life, all we have that amounts to anything is our struggle and what it is worth. At the end of the monomythic journey, whenever it comes, we take that last step of return and find ourselves two steps back: still no more than just human beings, still shy of attaining that greater something, and with only what we have already done and given as the measure of our lives.

EPILOGUE

At the time of this writing, Springsteen has released two new albums *Lucky Town* and *Human Touch* simultaneously (perhaps taking a cue from Guns n' Roses). Thus, the closure that this analysis suggests is by no means a complete statement about his career. One can only wonder, however, how he can sustain the power that this analysis argues.

Certainly, two albums of good, strong songs would confirm his reputation once again and keep his place among the pantheon of rock gods. However, songs do not the hero make. If selling millions of albums on the basis of attractive, well-crafted, or catchy songs was a gauge of heroism, one could easily argue that Elton John or Billy Joel is a hero. Similarly, selling millions of albums is not in itself a function of heroism, but is often merely the product of a music-making and merchandising machine.

It is stated, in conclusion, that heroism in popular music can only be judged on the merit of a balanced look at the career and work of an artist or group, on all of the levels of popular music as communication suggested here. If what is communicated to us in this career and work can be argued to have a coherence that equates with artistic integrity—if the endeavor to make music amounts to more than something that clicks for us on some level, but that communicates something of import on every level—this is what separates the celebrities from the celebrity/heroes. Springsteen has clearly tried to do more with his musical career than just entertain us or make himself famous and wealthy. Rather, he has tried to make a musical statement about how people see and experience their place in the world and how they struggle for something beyond this world. Somehow, we might expect that he will continue to do so.

We shall see and hear.

References

A difference of opinion. (1981, March 23). *Fortune*, 145-146.
Abelman, R. (1988). The allure for viewers. *Critical Studies in Mass Communication, 5*, 259-265.
Allen, F.L. (1931). *Only yesterday: An informal history of the nineteen-Twenties.* New York: Blue Ribbon Books.
An innocent life, a heartbreaking death. (1989, July 31). *People Weekly*, pp. 60-62, 64.
Anderson, D. (1975, June 3). For a change, another Ryan no-hitter. *The New York Times*, p. 39.
Anderson, D. (1978, August). The Ryan Express races for the records. *Sport*, pp. 67-71.
Anderson, D., & Stone, G.P. (1981). Sport: A search for community. In S.L.Greendorfer & A. Yiannakis (Eds.), *Sociology of sport: Diverse perspectives.* West Point, NY: Leisure Press.
Arendt, H. (1958). *The human condition.* Chicago: University of Chicago Press.
Aristotle. (1954). *The Poetics.* (I. Bywater,Trans.) In Aristotle's rhetoric and Poetics. New York: The Modern Library.
Aronoff, C.E. (Ed.). (1979). *Business and the media.* Santa Monica, CA: Goodyear.
Ashen F., & Ashen, F. (1983). *Language and the sexes.* Albany: State University of New York Press.
Assassination: Twenty-five years later. (1988, November 14-23). *"CBS Evening News,"* CBS News.
Axthelm, P. (1975, June 16). Fastest arm in the West. *Newsweek*, pp. 56-60.
Axthelm, P. (1975, July 22). Ryan's fast-ball express. *Newsweek*, p. 67.
Axthelm, P. (1981, October 12). A winner in a lost season. *Newsweek*, p. 82.
Baker, R. (1990, August 15)., The loss of a hero. *The New York Times*, p. A27.
Baldwin, P. (1990, July 10). Pitchman: Rangers pitcher Ryan expected to be drafted by more advertisers. *The Dallas Morning News*, pp. 1A, 6A.
Balswick, J. & Ingoldsby, B. (1982). Heroes and heroines among adolescents. *Sex Roles 8*(3), 243-249.
Balthrop, V.W. (1984). Culture, myth, and ideology as public argument. An

interpretation of the ascent and demise of Southern culture. *Communication Monographs, 51*, 339-352.

Barker, L. (1990). *Communication*. Englewood Cliffs, NJ: Prentice Hall.

Barnouw, E. (1990). *Tube of plenty: The evolution of American television* (2nd rev. ed.). New York: Oxford University Press.

Barnouw, E. (1975). *Tube of plenty: The evolution of American television*. New York: Oxford University Press.

Barnouw, E. (1968). *The golden web: A history of broadcasting in the United States*. New York: Oxford University Press.

Baron, D. (1986). *Grammar and gender*. New Haven, CT: Yale University Press.

Barthes, R. (1973). *Mythologies*. London: Paladin.

Bass, J.D., & Cherwitz, R. (1978). Imperial mission and manifest destiny: A case study of political myth in rhetorical discourse.*Southern Speech Communication Journal, 43*, 213-232.

Bate, B. (1988). *Communication and the sexes*. New York: Harper & Row.

Baudrillard, J. (1987). *The evil demon of images* (Maria Kuttna Memorial Lecture on Film, July 25, 1984). Power Institute of Fine Arts: University of Sydney.

Baudrillard, J. (1983). The ecstacy of communication. In H.Foster (Ed.), *The anti-aesthetic*. Washington, DC: Bay Press.

Bayless, S. (1989, July 10). Need a hero? Just send for 'Old Gun Ryan.' *Dallas Times Herald*, p. D-1.

Bellah, R.N. (1968). Civil religion in American. In W.G. McLoughlin & R.N. Bellah (Eds.), *Religion in America* (pp. 3-23). Boston, MA: Beacon.

Bennett, W.L. (1980). Myth, ritual, and political control. *Journal of Communication, 30*, 166-179.

Bennett, W.L., & Edelman, M. (1985). Toward a new political narrative. *Journal of Communication, 35*, 156-171.

Bentley, E.R. (1957). *A century of hero-worship*. Boston: Beacon Press.

Benveniste, E. (1981). *Problems in general linguistics*. Coral Gables, FL: University of Miami Press.

Birnback, L. (1984, September 27). Future bureaucrats of America, leadership, and heroes. *Rolling Stone*, p. 46.

Blacker, C. (1984). Introduction. In H.R.E. Davidson (Ed.), *The hero in tradition and folklore* (pp. vii-x). The Folklore Society, Mistletoe Series, 19.

Block, J.L. (1984, April). The Phyllis Schlafly only her family knows. *Good Housekeeping*, pp. 80, 82, 84, 86, 88.

Bluem, A.W. (1964). Looking ahead: The black horse (editorial). *Television Quarterly, 3*(1), 84-87.

Boorstin, D.J. (1961). *The image: A guide to pseudo-events in America*. New York: Atheneum.

Boorstin, D.J. (1962). *The image, or whatever happened to the American dream*. New York: Atheneum.

Boorstin, D.J. (1978). *The image: A guide to pseudo-events in America*. New York: Atheneum.

Boorstin, D.J. (1980). *The image: A guide to pseudo-events in America.* New York: Atheneum.
Bormann, E.G. (1972). Fantasy and rhetorical vision: The rhetorical criticism of social reality. *Quarterly Journal of Speech, 58,* 396-407.
Bormann, E.G. (1982). Fantasy and rhetorical vision: Ten years later. *Quarterly Journal of Speech, 68,* 288-305.
Braudy, L. (1986). *The frenzy of renown: Fame and its history.* New York: Oxford University Press.
Braun, S. (1971, May 2). Shazam! Here comes captain relevant. *The New York Times,* pp. 32-33, 36, 38, 41, 43-46, 48, 50, 55.
Brecht, B. (1938/1961). Galileo. In E. Bentley (Ed.), *Seven plays by Bertolt Brecht* (C. Laughton, trans.). New York: Grove Press.
Breen, M., & Corcoran, F. (1982). Myth in the television discourse. *Communication Monographs, 49,* 127-136.
Brine for Nolan Ryan. (1968, May 31). *Life,* p. 78.
Broder, D. (1987). *Behind the front page.* New York: Touchstone Books.
Brombert, V. (1969). *The hero in literature.* Greenwich, CT: Fawcett Publications.
Browne, P. (Ed). (1987). *Heroines of popular culture.* Bowling Green, OH: Bowling Green State University Popular Press.
Browne, R.B., & Fishwick, M.W. (1983). *The hero in transition.* Bowling Green, OH: Bowling Green University Popular Press.
Brownmiller, S. (1981, January 22). Yoko and John. *Rolling Stone,* p. 25.
Bruce, S. (1990). *Pray TV: Televangelism in America.* New York: Routledge.
Bruning, F. (1990, March 5). Contrasts in hero worship. *MacLean's,* p. 13.
Bulfinch, T. (1979). *Bulfinch's mythology.* New York: Avenel Books.
Burke, K.B. (1961). *The rhetoric of religion: Studies in logology.* Berkeley: University of California Press.
Burke, K.B. (1970). *The rhetoric of religion.* Berkeley: University of California Press.
Burkholder, T.R. (1988, November). *The limits of transcendence: Kansas populism, woman suffrage, and the agrarian myth.* Paper presented at the Speech Communication Association Convention, New Orleans.
Burns, J.M. (1978). *Leadership.* New York: Harper & Row.
Butler, B. (1979). *The myth of the hero.* London: Rider and Company.
Byrd, J. (1991). Church of God beginnings: Tennessee mountain culture. *Reflections, 1*(3), 3.
Calhoun, D.W. (1987). *Sport, culture, and personality* (2nd ed.). Champaign, IL: Human Kinetics.
Campbell, J. (1948). *The hero with a thousand faces.* Princeton: Princeton University Press.
Campbell, J. (1968a). *The hero with a thousand faces.* (2nd ed.). New York: Princeton University Press.
Campbell, J. (1968b). *The masks of God: Creative mythology.* New York: Penguin.

Campbell, J. (1973). *The hero with a thousand faces.* Princeton: Princeton University Press.
Campbell, J. (1988). *The power of myth.* New York: Doubleday.
Carey, J.W. (1989). *Communication as culture: Essays on media and society.* Boston, MA: Unwin Hyman.
Carlyle, T. (1840/1940). *Sartor resartus: On heroes, hero-worshipping and the heroic in history.* London: J.M. Dent & Sons.
Carlyle, T. (1908). *Sartor resartus: On heros and hero-Worship.* New York: E.P. Dutton.
Carlyle, T. (1956). *On heroes and hero-worship.* London: J.M. Dent & Sons.
Carpenter, R. (1977). Frederick Jackson Turner and the rhetorical impact of the frontier thesis. *Quarterly Journal of Speech, 63,* 17-129.
Carroll, J.B. (Ed.). (1956). *Language, thought and reality: Selected writings of Benjamin Lee Whorf.* Cambridge: The Massachusetts Institute of Technology.
Casstevens, D. (1990, July 25). 300th will be Ryan's reply to his critics. *The Dallas Morning News,* p. 1B.
Cathcart, R., & Gumpert, G. (1983). Mediated interpersonal communication: Toward a new typology. *Quarterly Journal of Speech, 69,* 267-277.
Cathcart, R., & Gumpert, G. (1986). I am a camera: The mediated self. *Communication Quarterly, 34,* 89-101.
Caughey, J.L. (1986). Social relations with media figures. In G. Gumpert & R. Cathcart (Eds.), *Inter/media: Interpersonal communication in a media world* (3rd ed., pp. 219-252). New York: Oxford University Press.
Cawelti, J.G. (1985). With the benefit of hindsight: Popular culture criticism. *Critical Studies in Mass Communication, 2,* 363-379.
Cawelti, J. (1976). The western: A look at the evolution of a formula. In J. Cawelti (Ed.), *Adventure, mystery, and romance* (pp. 192-259). Chicago: University of Chicago Press.
Chass, M. (1970, June 11). Pepitone clouts four-run homer. *The New York Times,* p. 59.
"Chayanne." (1991). *The San Juan Star,* p. 17.
Chesebro, J. (1984). The media reality: Epistemological functions of media in culture systems. *Critical Studies in Mass Communication, 1,* 111-130.
Chesebro, J., & Ferri, J. (1985, November 24). Media event: Is there a Menudo? *The San Juan Star, Sunday Magazine,* pp. 2-3.
Child Murder as Entertainment. (1935, March). *The Catholic World, 140,* p. 642.
Chrysler Corporation. (1983). *Moody's Industrial Manual, 1,* 1233.
Chrysler Repaid Its Remaining $800 Million. (1983, August 15). *The Wall Street Journal,* p. 13.
Clarke, G. (1980, December 22). A lethal delusion. *Time,* p. 29.
Clymer, A. (1982, January 31). Poll finds Reagan popularity rating misleads. *The New York Times,* p. 22.
Cleaver, E. (1978). *Soul on fire.* Waco, TX: Word Books.

Cocks, J. (1980, December 22). The last day in the life. *Time*, pp. 18-24.

Collins, J. (1989). *Uncommon cultures: Popular culture and post-modernism.* New York: Routledge.

Crepeau, R.C. (1985). Where have you gone Frank Merriwell? The decline of the American sports hero. In W.L. Umphlett (Ed.), *American sport culture: The humanistic dimensions.* London: Associated University Presses.

Curtius, E.R. (1963). *European literature and the latin middle Ages.* New York: Harper & Row.

Cuthbertson, G.M. (1975). *Political myth and epic.* East Lansing: Michigan State University Press.

Czarnowski, T.V. (1978). The street as a communications artifact. In S. Anderson (Ed.), *On streets* (pp. 207-212). Cambridge, MA: MIT Press.

Dabbs, J.M. (1972). *Haunted by God.* Richmond, VA: John Knox Press.

DeLaszlo, V.S. (Ed.). (1959). *The basic writings of C.G. Jung.* New York: Modern Library.

Dionisopolous, G.N. (1988). A case study in print media and heroic myth: Lee Iacocca 1978-1985. *The Southern Speech Communication Journal, 53*, 227-2243.

Distel, D. (1973, September 28). 383 strikeouts! Ryan breaks Koufax record. *Los Angeles Times*, p. 1, 6, part III.

Dowd, M.B. (1985, November). *Contours of a narrative pentecostal theology and practice.* Paper presented at the Society for Pentecostal Studies.

Drucker, S., & Cathcart, R. (1989, November). *The celebrity and the fan: An exploration of a media relationship.* Paper presented at the Speech Communication Association Convention, San Francisco, CA.

Drucker, S., & Gumpert, G. (1991). Public space and communication: The zoning of interaction. *Communication Theory, 1*(4), 294-310.

Duncan, H.D. (1969). A sociological model of social interaction as determined by communication. In W. Rueckert (Ed.), *Critical responses to Kenneth Burke, 1924-1966* (pp. 355-). Minneapolis: University of Minnesota Press.

Duncan, M.C. (1983). The symbolic dimensions of spectator sport. *Quest, 35* 29-36.

Durso, J. (1968, July 4). Pirates shell Ryan and rout Mets, 8-1. *The New York Times*, p. 24.

Durso, J. (1969, July 14). Amazing Mets: What makes them win. *The New York Times*, p. 1.

Durso, J. (1970, August 5). Mets down Cubs, 4-0, as Ryan hurls 3 hitter and fans 13. *The New York Times*, p. 26.

Durso, J. (1971, December 11). Mets give up Ryan for Fregosi. *The New York Times*, p. 37.

Dyer, R. (1979). *Stars*. London: BFI.

Dyer, R. (1986). *Heavenly bodies: Stars and society.* London: BFI.

Edes, G. (1993, February 14). Ryan will leave Texas-sized void. *Fort*

Lauderdale Sun-Sentinel, p. 60.
Edwards, L. (1988). The labors of psyche. *Aperture*, Spring, pp. 48-55.
Edwards, L.R. (1984). *Psyche as hero*. Middletown, CT: Wesleyan University Press.
Eisenstein, E.L. (1980). *The printing press as an agent of change*. New York: Cambridge University Press.
Eliade, M. (1975). *Myth and reality* (W. Trask, trans.). New York: Harper Colophon Books.
Ellis, B.E. (1985, September 26). Down and out at Bennigton College. *Rolling Stone*, pp. 77-78, 80, 82, 114.
Elm, J. (1989, May 6). From 'good evening, everybody, coast to coast' to 'courage,' *TV Guide*, pp. 30-31.
Emerson, R.W. (1883). *Representative men: Seven lectures*. Boston & New York: Houghton, Mifflin and Company.
Entman, R. (1991). Framing U.S. coverage of international news: Contrasts in narratives of the KAL and Iran Air incidents. *Journal of Communication*, *41*(4), 6-27.
Ephron, N. (1976, February). Twelve years on the assassination beat. *Esquire*, pp. 58-62.
Fairlie, H. (1978, November). Too rich for heroes. *Harpers*, pp. 36-37.
Fayer, J. (1988). First names in Puerto Rico: Change in progress. *Name*, *36*(1), 21-27.
Fayer, J. (1988). *Bilingualism in Puerto Rico: Data from U.S. census reports*. TESOL of Puerto Rico Annual Conference. San Juan, PR.
Fayer, J., Simounet-Giegel, Peters, A., & Ferri, J. (1983). "Puerto Rico: Food as a communication system." *Estudios Latinoamericanos*, p. 16.
Felsenthal, C. (1981). *The sweetheart of the silent majority*. Garden City: Doubleday.
Ferguson, M. (1980) *The antiquarian conspiracy: Personal and social transformation in the 1980s*. Los Angeles: J.P. Tarcher.
Ferri, J. & Hernández, E. (1988). *Puerto Rican gestures: Generational differences*. Paper presented at the Eastern Communication Association Convention, Baltimore, MD.
Fimrite, R. (1986, September 29). A great hand with the old cowhide. *Sports Illustrated*, pp. 84-88, 90-94, 96.
Fisher, W.R. (1973). Reaffirmation and subversion of the American dream. *Quarterly Journal of Speech*, *59*, 160-167.
Fisher, W.R. (1982). Romantic democracy, Ronald Reagan, and presidential heroes. *Western Journal of Speech Communication*, *46*, 642-646.
Fishman, J. (1985). *The Rise and fall of the ethnic revival*. New York: Mouton Press.
Fishwick, M. (1972). Prologue. In R.B. Browne, M. Fishwick, & M.T. Marsden (Eds.), *Heroes of popular culture* (pp. 1-8). Bowling Green, OH: Bowling

Green University Popular Press.
Fishwick, M. (1983). Introduction. In R.B. Browne & M.W. Fishwick (Eds.), *The hero in transition* (pp. 5-13). Bowling Green, OH: Bowling Green University Popular Press.
Fishwick, M.W. (1985). *Seven pillars of popular culture*. Westport CT: Greenwood Press.
Fiske, J. (1986). MTV: Post-structural post-modern. *Journal of Communication Inquiry 10*(1), 4-9.
Fiske, J. (1987). *Television culture*. London: Routledge.
Fiske, J. (1989). *Reading the popular*. Winchester, MA: Unwin Hyman.
Fiske, J., & Hartley, J. (1978). *Reading television*. New York: Methuen.
Fitzgerald, F.S. (1956). *The crack-up* (E. Wilson, ed.). New York: Scribners. (Original work publisihed 1931).
Flippo, C. (1981, January 22). Radio: Tribal drum. *Rolling Stone*, p. 19.
Foderaro, L.W. (1989, May 1). Angered by attack, Trump urges return of the death penalty. *The New York Times*, p. B6.
Foley, L. (1990). *Saint of the day*. Cincinnati OH: St. Anthony Messenger Press.
Foss, K.A., & Littlejohn, S.W. (1989). The day after: Rhetorical vision in an ironic frame. In S.K. Foss (Ed.), *Rhetical criticism: Exploration and practice* (pp. 312-332). Prospect Heights, IL: Waveland Press.
Foss, S.K. (1979). Equal rights amendment controversy: Two worlds in conflict. *Quarterly Journal of Speech, 65*, 275-288.
Four days in November: The assassination of President Kennedy. (1988, November 17). *CBS News*.
Fraser, A. (1980). *Heroes and heroines*. London: Weidenfeld and Nicolson.
Fraser, A. (1988). *The warrior queens*. New York: Alfred A. Knopf.
Frazer, J.G. (1913). *The golden bough: A study of magic and religion* (Vol. 6: The Scapegoat). New York: St. Martin's Press.
Frentz, T.S., & Rushing, J.H. (1978). The rhetoric of"Rocky": Part two. *Western Journal of Speech Communication, 62*, 231-240.
Frye, N. (1957). *The anatomy of criticism: Four essays*. Princeton: Princeton University Press.
Furlong, W.B. (1980, April). Baseball's best paid pitcher comes home. *Sport*, pp. 66-70.
Gaither, R. (1991, January 14). *New York Magazine*, pp. 20-35.
Galloway, R. (1988a, December 8). Ryan gives Rangers new credibility. *The Dallas Morning News*, p. 1B.
Galloway, R. (1988b, December 15). Ryan's smile gives Rangers cheerful look. *The Dallas Morning News*, P. 1B.
Galloway, R. (1990, August 1). Ryan's greatness affirmed. *The Dallas Morning News*, 1B.
Galloway, R. (1993, February 14). Ryan in '93: Last chance to see the legend play. *The Miami Herald*, p. 11C.

Gamarekian, B. (1988, November 22). Hundreds are in capital for 25th remembrance. *New York Times*, p. A24.

Gamson, J. (1992). The assembly line of greatness: Celebrity in twentieth-century America. *Critical Studies in Mass Communication, 9*, 1-24.

Garfield, B. (1989, March 9). Pepsi should offer a prayer to Madonna. Advertising Age. [Review].

Gates, G.P. (1978). *Air time*. New York: Harper & Row.

Gencarelli, T. (1990, March). *"Notes from the underground": The 'death' metal audience as interpretive community*. Paper presented at the 20th meeting of the Popular Culture Association, Toronto.

Gerard, J. (1989, June/July). Trumped up. *Fame*, pp. 85-93.

Gerbner, G., Gross, L., Hoover, S., Morgan, M., Signorelli, N., Cotugno, H.E., & Wuthnow, R. (1984). *Religion and television. A research report by the Annenberg School of Communications*. Philadelphia: University of Pennsylvania.

Gergen, J. (1990, August 6). Ryanger's star an icon in the heart of Texas. *The Sporting News*, p. 47.

Giamatti, A.B. (1989). *Take time for paradise: Americans and their games*. New York: Summit Books.

Gibson, D.C. (1983). *Neither god nor devil: A rhetorical perspective on the political myths of J. Edgar Hoover*. (Doctoral dissertation, Indiana University, 1983). Dissertation Abstracts International, 44, 3539A.

Goffman, E. (1981). Radio talk: A study of the ways of our errors. In E. Goffman (Ed.), *Form of talk* (pp. 197-327). Philadelphia: University of Pennsylvania Press.

Goldsen, R.K. (1978). *The show and tell machine*. New York: Delta.

Gonzalez, A., & Makay, J.J. (1983). Rhetorical ascription and the gospel according to Dylan. *Quarterly Journal of Speech, 69*, 1-14.

Grady, S. (1988, November 22). JFK: A look back. *Philadelphia Daily News*, p. 5.

Gray, R. (1979, March 26). No backseat role for K & E: Laux. *Advertising Age*, p. 83.

Gray, R. (1981, September 7). Star power for Chrysler. *Advertising Age*, p. 2.

Green lantern/green arrow. (1970, April). No. 76. Sparta, IL: National Periodical Publications.

Greene, B. (1990, June 24). Nolan Ryan is newest star of th baby boom set. *The Dallas Morning News*, p. 50.

Gross, L., & Jeffries-Fox, S. (1978). What do you want to be when you grow up, little girl? In G. Tuchman, A.K. Daniels, & J. Benét (Eds.), *Hearth and home: Images of women in the mass media* (pp. 240-265). New York: Oxford University Press.

Grossberg, L. (1984). Another boring day in paradise: Rock and roll and the empowerment of everyday life. *Popular Music, 4*, 225-258.

Grossberg, L. (1988). Putting pop back, into postmodernism. In A. Ross (Ed.), *Universal abandon: The politics of postmodernism*. Edinburgh: University of Edinburgh Press.

Grunwald, L. (1991, December). Why we still care. *Life*, pp. 34-36, 38, 40, 42-44, 46.

Gumpert, G. (1987). *Talking tombstones and other tales of the media age.* New York: Oxford University Press.

Gumpert, G., Lehman, G., & Drucker, S. (1990). *Sports and the media community.* Paper presented at the Speech Communication Association Convention, Chicago.

Guttman, A. (1978). *From ritual to record.* New York: Columbia University Press.

Hackett, G. (1988, February 29). A sex scandal breaks over Jimmy Swaggart. *Newsweek*, pp. 30-31.

Hamill, P. (1980, December 22). The death and life of John Lennon. *New York*, pp. 38-50.

Hamilton, E. (1953). *Mythology.* Boston: Little Brown & Co.

Hammond, M. (1989, February). The Trumps: America's most glamorous two-career couple. *McCalls*, pp. 22-24, 30.

Hankins, S.R. (1983). Archetypal alloy: Ronald Reagan's rhetorical image. *Central States Speech Journal, 34,* 3-43.

Harazin, A. (1990, May 9). Senior Vice President N.Y. Mets

Hargreaves, J. (1982). Sport and hegemony: Some theoretical problems. In H. Cantelon & R. Gruneau (Eds.), *Sport, culture, and the modern state* (pp. 103-140). Toronto: University of Toronto Press.

Harvey, D.A. (1987). TV Preacher Jimmy Swaggart: Why does he say those awful things about Catholics? In M. Fishwick & R.B. Browne (Eds.), *The God pumpers: Religion in the electronic age* (pp. 87-100). Bowling Green, OH: Bowling Green State University Press.

Harvin, A. (1971, September 29). Carlton notches no. 20 as Cards beat Mets, 5-2. *The New York Times*, p. 23.

Havelock, E. (1963). *Preface to Plato.* Cambridge, MA: Belknap Press of Harvard University Press.

Hayden, T. (1988). *Reunion: A memoir.* New York: Random House.

Hebdige, D. (1979). *Subculture: The meaning of style.* New York: Methuen.

Heisler, M. (1979a, November 2). If Angels want Nolan Ryan now, they'll have to take a number. *Los Angeles Times*, pp. 1, 14, part III.

Heisler, M. (1979a, November 20). Ryan becomes Texas millionaire. *The Los Angeles Times*, pp. 1, 7, part III.

Henderson, J. (1989, August 22). 5-oh!-oh!-oh! Heroic Ryan finishes quest for historic K. *Dallas Times Herald*, pp. A-1, A-15.

Herman, E.S., & Chomsky, N. (1988). *Manufacturing consent: The political economy of the mass media.* New York: Pantheon Books.

Heroes. (1980, January 10). *Scholastic action*, p. 13.

Heroes are back. (1985, April 22). *U.S. News & World Report*, pp. 44-48.

Heroes for hard times. (1988). *Mother Jones*, pp. 25-33.

High Profile: Ike Pappas. (1989, September 10). *Philadelphia Inquirer Magazine*, p. 8.

Hoch, P. (1972). *Rip off the big game.* Garden City, NY: Doubleday.

Hoffer, R. (1988, May). Armed and still dangerous. *Gentleman's Quarterly*, pp. 292-294.

Holden, S. (1992, August). When the boss fell to earth, he hit paradise. *The New York Times*, pp. H1, H27.

Hollenweger, W.J. (1986). Pentecostals and the charismatic movement. In C. Jones, G. Wainright, & E. Yarnold (Eds.), *The study of spirituality* (pp. 549-53). New York: Oxford University Press.

Hollenweger, W.J. (1972). *The pentecostals: The charismatic movement in the churches.* Minneapolis, MN: Augsburg.

Hollenweger, W.J. (1988). *The pentecostals* (R.A. Wilson, Trans.). Peabody, MA: Hendrickson Publishers. (Original work published 1969)

Hook, S. (1943). *The hero in history: A study in limitation and possibility.* New York: John Day.

Hoover, S.M. (1988). *Mass media religion: The social sources of the electronic church.* Newbury Park, CA: Sage.

Horn, B. (1990, August 2). Expressly Ryan: In honor of 300. *The Dallas Morning News*, pp. 1H-2H.

Horowitz, I. (1974). Sports broadcasting. In R. Noll (Ed.), *Government and the sports business* (pp. 275-323). Washington, DC: Brookings Institution.

Horsefield, P. (1984). *Religious television: The American experience.* New York: Longman.

Horton, D., & Wohl, R.R. (1956). Mass communication and para-social interaction: Observations on intimacy at a distance. *Psychiatry, 19*, 215-229.

Horton, D., & Wohl, R.R. (1982). Mass communication and para-social interaction: Observations on intimacy at a distance. In G. Gumpert & R. Cathcart (Eds.), *Inter/media* (2nd ed., pp.188-211). New York: Oxford University Press.

House Committee on Banking. "Senator Proxmire and Representative Kelly at the Loan Guarantee Hearings for Chrysler (October - December, 1979), "excerpts from videotapes of ABC, CBS, and NBC News. Procured throught he Chrysler Public Relations Department, Detroit, Michigan.

High Profile: Ike Pappas. (1989, September 10). *Philadelphia Inquirer Magazine*, p. 8.

Huckshorn, K. (1991, February 24). A furor brews over military moms. *Akron Beacon Journal*, p. 16.

Iacocca, L. (1983, February). "Revitalizing America: A Proposal." *Psychology Today*, 34.

Iacocca, L. (1984). *Iacocca, an Autobiography.* New York: Bantam Books.

Innis, H.A. (1977). *The bias of communication.* Toronto: University of Toronto Press.

Irvine, J.R., & Kirkpatrick, W. (1972). The musical form in rhetorical

exchange: Theoretical considerations. *Quarterly Journal of Speech, 58*, 272-284.
Jacobson, S. (1974, June/July). Nolan Ryan: Whoosh! *The Saturday Evening Post*, pp. 14-16, 124.
James, E. (1927, May 23). Lindbergh is hero of hour in Paris. *The New York Times*, sec. 1, p. 2.
James, E. (1927, May 22). Crowd roars thunderous welcome. *The New York Times*, sec. 1, p. 1.
Jameson, F. (1983). Postmodernism and consumer society. In H. Foster (Ed.), *The anti-aesthetic*. Washington, DC: Bay Press.
Jassem, H.C. (1990, November). *American sports and the media dollar*. Paper presented at the Speech Communication Association Convention, Chicago, IL.
Jennings, D. (1989, March 26). Nolan Ryan. *The Dallas Morning News*, pp. 1E-3E.
JFK: A Time Remembered. (1988, November 21). Susskind Company, in association with Obenhaus Films, Inc. Shown on PBS.
JFK Assassination: As It Happened. (1988, November 22). NBC News. Shown on Arts and Entertainment Network.
John F. Kennedy Remembered. (1988, November 22). "KYW Eyewitness News," Channel Three Eyewitness News Nightcast, Philadelphia.
Jhally, S. (1990). *Dreamworlds: Desire/sex/power in rock video* [45 minute video]. Amherst, MA.
Jung, C.G. (1959). *Psyche and symbol: A selection from the writings of C.G. Jung* (ed. Violet S. deLaszlo). Garden City, NY: Anchor-Doubleday.
Jung, C.G. (Ed.). (1964). Approaching the unconscious. In *Man and his symbols*. Garden City, NY: Doubleday-Windfall.
K. (1989, August 28). *Sports Illustrated*, pp. 30-32.
Kael, P. (1983, July 11). The current cinema: Time-warp movies. *The New Yorker*, pp. 90, 93, 95.
Kaplan, E.A. (1987). *Rocking around the clock*. New York: Metcuen.
Kaplan, J. (1983, May 9). For Ryan, it was a very special K. *Sports Illustrated*, pp. 34-41.
Keith, L. (1979, November 19). It's fishing season for Nolan Ryan. *Sports Illustrated*, pp. 34-35.
Kelmenson, L.A. (1984). The marketing miracle of Chrysler: How a new 'partnership' philosophy helped resurrect a dying giant. *The Journal of Consumer Marketing, 1*(2), 14-27.
Kerényi, C. (1960). *The Gods of the Greeks* (N. Cameron, Trans.). New York: Grove Press.
Key, M.R. (1975). *Male/female language*. Metuchen, NJ.: The Scarecrow Press.
King, A.A. (1974). Booker T. Washington and the myth of heroic materialism. *Quarterly Journal of Speech, 60*, 323-327.
Kindred, D. (1993, February 22). Faster than the eye can see. *The Sporting News*, p. 7.

Klapp, O.E. (1956). *Ritual and cult: A sociological interpretation*. Washington, DC: Public Affairs.

Klapp, O.E. (1962). *Heroes, villains, and fools*. Englewood Cliffs, NJ: Prentice-Hall.

Klapp, O. (1964). *Symbolic leaders: Public dramas and public men*. Chicago: Aldine Publishing.

Klapp, O.E. (1969). *Collective search for identity*. New York: Holt, Rinehart & Winston.

Koppett, L. (1966a, September 12). Atlanta routs Ribant in taking third straight, 8-3. *The New York Times*, p. 62.

Koppett, L. (1966b, September 19). Ryan, McGraw are losers in 9-2 and 6-5 decisions. *The New York Times*, p. 26.

Koppett, L. (1968a, April 15). Mets sink Astros, 4-0, as Ryan and Frisella combine to pitch 5-hitter. *The New York Times*, p. 58.

Koppett, L. (1968b, April 28). Reds triumph, 5-3, on 4 Met miscues. *The New York Times*, p. 3

Kruse, N.W. (1983). The myth of the demonic in anti-ERA rhetoric. *Women's Studies in Communication, 6*, 85-95.

Krutch, J. (1947). The tragic fallacy. In B.H. Barrett (Ed.), *European theories of the drama* (pp. 517-526). New York: Crown Publishers. (Original work published 1929)

Kunhardt, P.B., Jr. (Ed.). (1988). *Life in Camelot: The Kennedy years*. New York: Time-Life Books.

Kurnow, S. (1983). *Vietnam: A history*. New York: Viking Press.

Lahr, J. (1984). *Automatic vauderville*. New York: Alfred A. Knopf.

Land, S.J. (1989). Pentecostal spirituality: Living in the spirit. In L. Dupre & D. Saliers (Eds.), *Christian spirituality: Post reformation and modern*. New York: Crossroad Publishing.

Land, S.J. (1990). *A passion for the kingdom: An analysis and revision of pentecostal spirituality* (Doctoral dissertation, Emory University). Dissertation Abstracts International, 52-04A, 1392, 00437.

Langer, J. (1981). Television's personality system. *Media, Culture and Society, 4*, 351-365.

Langer, S.K. (1959). *Philosophy in a new key* (3rd ed.). Cambridge, MA: Harvard University Press.

Lee, R. (1986). The new populist campaign for economic democracy: A rhetorical explanation. *Quarterly Journal of Speech, 72*, 280-294.

Leerhsen, C. (1990, Summer/Fall). This year's role model. *Newsweek*, pp. 44-47.

Lennon broadcast is beyond imagination. (1990, October 5). *Portsmouth Herald (AP)*, p. D8.

Letter. (1963, November 30). *Editor and Publisher*, p. 8.

Lewis, W.F. (1987). Telling America's story: Narrative form and the Reagan Presidency. *Quarterly Journal of Speech, 73*, 280-302.

Leonard, W.M., II. (1980). *A sociological perspective of sport*. Minneapolis:

Burgess.

Levy, M.R. (1979). Watching TV news as para-social interaction. *Journal of Broadcasting, 23*, 177-187.

Lindbergh speeds across North Atlantic keeping to schedule 100 miles per hour, sighted passing St. John's N.F., at 7:15 p.m. (1927, May 21). *New York Times*, p.1

Lindbergh does it! To Paris in 33 1/2 hours. Flies 1,000 miles through snow & sleet; Cheering French carry him off field. (1927, May 22). *New York Times*, p.1.

Lipsky, R. (1975). *Sports world.* New York: Quadrangle.

Literary Digest. October 1, 1927, p. 36 and May 18, 1929, p. 49.

Literary Digest. (1929, June 13). p. 41.

Littwin, M. (1980, April 17). Nolan Ryan: Fastest (and richest?) gun in Alvin. *The Los Angeles Times*, pp. 1, 10, part III.

Lowenthal, L. (1961). *Literature, popular culture and society.* Palo Alto: Pacific Books.

Maher, J.M., & Briggs, D. (Eds.). (1988). *An open life: Joseph Campbell in conversation with Michael Toms.* Burdett, NY: Larson Publications.

Makay, J.J., & Gonzalez, A. (1987). Dylan's biographical rhetoric and the myth of the outlaw-hero. *Southern Speech Communication Journal, 52*, 165-180.

Mankiewicz, F., & Swerdlow, J. (1979). *Remote control: Television and the manipulation of American life.* New York: Ballantine Books.

Marcus, G. (1981, January 22). Life and life only. *Rolling Stone*, pp. 26-27.

Marsh, D. (1981). *Born to run: The Bruce Springsteen story.* New York: Dell.

Martin, B., & Pepe, P. (1987). *BillyBall.* New York: Doubleday.

Mathews, T., with Abramson, P., Morris, H., & Maier, F. (1980, December 22). Lennon's alter ego. *Newsweek*, pp. 34-35.

Mathews, T., with Bogert, C., Coleman, F., Breslau, K., DeFrank, T.M., Waller, D., Barry, J., & Warner, M.G. (1991, September 2). The people vs. the plotters. *Newsweek*, pp. 34-37, 39-40, 41-44.

Matusow, B. (1983). *The evening stars.* Boston: Houghton Mifflin.

Mayer, A.J., with Agrest, S., & Young, J. (1980, December 22). Death of a Beatle. *Newsweek*, pp. 31-36.

Maynard, R.M. (1974). *The American west on film: Myth and reality.* Rochelle Park, NJ: Hayden Book.

McBee, S. (1985, April 22). Heroes are back: Young Americans tell why. *U.S. News & World Report*, pp. 44-48.

McCarver, T. (1990, June 8). Interview.

McDermott, I., & Mackey-Kallis, S. (1991, October). *Bruce Springsteen, Ronald Reagan, and the American dream.* Paper presented at the New York State Speech Communication Association Convention, Albany, NY.

McGee, M.C. (1975). In search of 'the people': A rhetorical alternative. *Quarterly Journal of Speech, 61*, 235-249.

McGinniss, J. (1990). *Heroes.* New York: Simon & Schuster.

McGuire, M. (1984). 'Darkness on the Edge of Town': Bruce Springsteen's rhetoric of optimism and despair. In M.J. Medhurst & T.W. Benson (Eds.), *Rhetorical dimensions in media: A critical casebook* (pp. 233-250). Dubuque, IA: Kendall/Hunt.

McLennan, D.B. (1990, November). *The autobiography, cultural mythology, and the modern hero*. Paper presented at the Speech Communication Association, Seminar on Heroes, San Francisco, CA.

McLuhan, M. (1964). *Understanding media: The extensions of man*. New York: McGraw-Hill.

McQuail, D. (1972). *Sociology of mass communication: Selected readings*. Harmondsworth, England: Penguin.

Mead, G.H. (1934). *Mind, self, and society: From the standpoint of a social behaviorist* (ed. Charles W. Morris). Chicago: University of Chicago Press.

Mechling, E.W. (1979). Patricia Hearst: Myth America 1974, 1975, 1976. *Western Journal of Speech Communication, 43*, 168-179.

Memorial Addresses in the Congress of the United States and Tributes in Eulogy of John Fitzgerald Kennedy, Late a President of the United States. (1964). Complied under the direction of the Joint Committee on Printing. Washington, DC: U.S. Government Printing Office.

Mernit, S. (1989, June/July). Comix. *Express*, pp. 16-20.

Merton, R.K. (1949). *Social theory and social structure*. Glencoe, IL: Free Press.

Meyer, M. (1989). *The Alexander complex*. New York: Times Books.

Meyrowitz, J. (1986). Television and interpersonal behavior: Codes of perception and response. In G. Gumpert & R. Cathcart (Eds.), *Inter/media: interpersonal behavior in a media world* (3rd ed., pp. 253-272). New York: Oxford University Press.

Meyrowitz, J. (1985). *No sense of place: The impact of electronic media on social behavior*. New York: Oxford.

Michael, G., & Parsons, T. (1990). *Bare*. London: Penguin.

Miller, C., & Swift, K. (1980). *The handbook of nonsexist writing*. New York: Lippincott & Crowell.

Miller, M.S. (1978, July). The Journal's teen survey. *Ladies Home Journal*.

Mills, N. (Ed.). (1990). The culture of triumph and the spirit of the times. In *Culture in an age of money*. Chicago: Ivan R. Dee.

Mine, D.G. (1992, January 2). Salvadoran guns to fall silent. *Foster's Daily Democrat (AP)*, p. 7.

Monaco, J. (1978). *Celebrity: The media as image makers*. New York: Dell.

Montana, J., & Raissman, B. (1986). *Audibles: My life in football*. New York: Wm. Morrow & Co.

Moore, C. (1989, November). *Obscure heroes*. Paper presented at the annual convention of the Speech Communication Association, San Francisco, CA.

Morgan, R. (1989). *The demon lover: On the sexuality of politics*. New York: W.W. Norton & Company.

Moritz, M., & Seaman, B. (1981). *Going for broke*. Garden City, NY:

Doubleday.
Morris, L., & Smith, K. (1953). *Ceilings unlimited: The story of aviation from Kitty Hawk to supersonics.* New York: MacMillan.
Morrow, L. (1988, October 24). Of myth and memory. *Time*, p. 22.
Mosley, L. (1976). *Lindbergh.* New York: Doubleday.
Mullett, M.B. (1963). The biggest thing that Lindbergh has done. In G. Mowry (Ed.), *The twenties: Fords, flappers and fanatics* (p. 82). Englewood Cliffs, NJ: Prentice-Hall.
Mulvey, L. (1975). Visual pleasure and narrative cinema. *Screen, 16*(3), 6-18.
Navratilova, M., & Vecsey, G. (1985). *Martina.* New York: Alfred A. Knopf.
Neumann, E. (1963). *The great mother: An analysis of the archetype.* (R. Manheim, Trans., 2nd ed.). Princeton, NJ: Princeton University.
Neumann, E. (1973). *Depth psychology and a new ethic* (trans. E. Rolf). New York: Harper Torchbooks.
Newhan, R. (1971, December 11). Fregosi "thrilled" by trade to Mets. *The Los Angeles Times*, pp. 1, 3, part III.
Newhan, R. (1972a, February 28). Ryan: Four years is too long to be a 'prospect.' *The Los Angeles Times*, pp. 1, 7, part III.
Newhan, R. (1972b, April 18). Angel at the crossroads: Ryan must prove he can control fastball. *The Los Angeles Times*, p. 2, part III.
Newhan, R. (1972c, April 29). Weaver's 'early birds' feast on Angel's Ryan, Queen 12-2. *The Los Angeles Times*, pp. 1, 5, part III.
Newhan, R. (1972d, May 23). Homer lucky blow, says Jackson, as A's top Angels, 6-3. *The Los Angeles Times*, pp. 1, 6, part III.
Newman, B. (1979, July 23). Hats off to you, Nolan Ryan. *Sports Illustrated*, pp. 12-17.
Newman, R.P. (1975). Lethal rhetoric: The selling of the China myths. *Quarterly Journal of Speech, 61*, 113-128.
Newsom, D., Scott, A., & Turk, J.V. (1989). *This is PR: Realities of public relations* (4th ed.). Belmont, CA: Wadsworth Publishing Company.
Niebuhr, H.R. (1989). The story of life. In S. Hauerwas & L.G. Jones (Eds.), *Why narrative? Reading in narrative theology* (pp. 21-44). Grand Rapids, MI: William B. Eerdmans Publishing.
Nimmo, D., & Combs, J. (1980). *Subliminal politics: Myths and mythmakers in America.* Englewood Cliffs, NJ: Prentice-Hall.
Nixon, H.L., II. (1984). *Sort and the American dream.* New York: Leisure.
Nolan, T. (1991, October 10). *Proprietor of classic hobby nostalgia.* Interview.
Norman, D. (1990). *The hero: Myth/image/symbol.* New York: Anchor Books.
Novak, M. (1976). *The joy of sports: End zones, bases, baskets, balls, and the consecration of the American spirit.* New York: Basic Books.
November 22, 1963: Where we were. (1988, November 28). *People* [special section], pp. 54-70.
On Trial: Lee Harvey Oswald. (1988, November 22-23). London Weekend Television with Tribune Entertainment Company. Shown on Fox Network.

Ong, W.J. (1967). *The presence of the word.* Minneapolis: University of Minnesota Press.
Ong, W.J. (1977). *Interfaces of the word: Studies in the evolution of consciousness and culture.* Ithaca: Cornell University Press.
Ong, W.J. (1981). *The presence of the word.* Minneapolis: University of Minnesota Press.
Ong, W.J. (1982). *Orality and literacy: The technologizing of the word.* New York: Methuen.
Ostling, R. (1988, March 7). Now it's Jimmy's turn. *Time,* pp. 28-30.
Ostling, R.N. (1986, February 17). Power, glory and politics. *Time,* pp. 62-69.
Oswald shooting a first in television history. (1963, December 2). *Broadcasting,* p. 46.
Oxford English Dictionary. (1989). Oxford: Claredon Press.
Oxford Universal Dictionary. (1955). Oxford: At The Clarendon Press.
Pagels, E. (1976). What became of God, the Mother: Conflicting images of God in early Christianity. Signs, 2, 293-303.
Parks, R.J. (1974). *Mass media mythology: The western hero in film and television.* (Doctoral dissertation, Northwestern University, 1974). Dissertation Abstracts International, 47, 701A.
Parks, R.J. (1982). *The Western hero in film and television: Mass media mythology.* Ann Arbor, MI: UMI Research Press.
Payne, D. (1989). The Wizard of Oz: Therapeutic rhetoric in a contemporary media ritual. *Quarterly Journal of Speech, 75,* 25-39.
Pearson, C.S. (1989). *The hero within.* New York: Harper & Row.
Pearson, C.S. (1991). *Awakening the heroes within.* San Francisco: Harper & Row.
Perez, P.R. (1986, March 2). Who are the Hispanic heroes? *Vista,* pp. 12-14.
Phelan, J.M. (1977). *Mediaworld.* New York: Seabury Press.
Phillips, K. (1990, June 17). Reagan's America: A Capital Offense. Pearson, C.S. (1991). *Awakening the heroes within.* San Francisco: Harper.
Poloma, M. (1989). *The assemblies of God at the crossroads: Charisma and institutional dilemmas.* Knoxville: University of Tennessee Press.
Postman, N. (1979). *Teaching as a conserving activity.* New York: Delacorte.
Postman, N. (1982). *The disappearance of childhood.* New York: Delacorte.
Postman, N. (1985). *Amusing ourselves to death.* New York: Viking.
Potok, C. (1973). Heroes for an ordinary world. In *Great ideas today* (pp. 71-76). Chicago: Encyclopedia Britannica.
Poyton, C. (1989). *Language and gender: Making the difference.* Oxford: Oxford University Press.
President's message. (1989, August 23). *Fort Worth Star Telegram,* p. 6, Sec. 3.
Pullum, S.J. (1988). *A rhetorical profile of pentecostal televangelists: Accounting for the mass appeal of Oral Roberts, Jimmy Swaggart, Kenneth Copeland, and Ernest Angley* (Doctoral dissertation, Indiana University). Dissertation Abstracts International, 49-010A, 2863, 00310.
Pullman, S.J. (1990). The mass appeal of Jimmy Swaggart: Pentecostal meida

star. *The Journal of Communication and Religion, 13*, 39-54.

Rader, B.G. (1983). Compensatory sports heroes: Ruth, Grange, and Dempsey. *Journal of Popular Culture, 16*, 11-22.

Raglan, F. (1975). *The hero: A study in tradition, myth and drama.* Westport, CT: Greenwood Press Publishers.

Rank, O. (1964). *The myth of the birth of the hero and other writings* (ed. P. Freund). New York: Vintage.

Rapoport, R. (1976, March 22). Nolan Ryan's coverup: 1975 was living hell. *The Los Angeles Times*, pp. 1, 10, part III.

Rather, D., with Herskowitz, M. (1977). *The camera never blinks.* New York: Ballantine.

Reid, K. (1989, November). *The setting and the message.* Paper presented to Speech Communication Association, San Francisco, CA.

Report conditions favor Lindbergh. (1927, May 21). *The New York Times*, p.3.

Reporter engage. (1963, December 23). *Newsweek*, p. 70.

Report from Asesores de Puerto Rico. (1991). San Juan, PR: Author.

Reeves, J. (1989, August 28). Ryan is brightest of stars. *Fort Worth Star Telegram*, pp. 1, 10, sec. 3.

Rickey, C. (1991, March 24). Too male & too pale. *The Philadelphia Inquirer Magazine*, pp. 14-16, 32-35.

Ricoeur, P. (1971). The model of the text: Meaningful action considered as a text. *Social Research, 38*, 528.

Ringolsby, T. (1989, August 23). Nolan Ryan on. *The Dallas Morning News*, p. 10B.

Ringolsby, T. (1993, February 14). Rangers happy Ryan wears their cap as he makes his way to Cooperstown. *Rocky Mountain News*, p. 68.

Riukas, S. (1967). *God: Myth, symbol, and reality: A study of Jung's psychology.* Dissertation Abstracts International, 28, 4925A. (University microforms No. 68-06166).

Robertson, J.O. (1980). *American myth, American reality.* New York: Hill & Wang.

Rogers, P. (1988, December 11). Rangers purchase an image: Ryan gives Texas a touch of class. *The Dallas Times Herald*, p. D-1.

Rollin, R.R. (1983). The Lone Ranger and Lenny Skutnik: The hero as popular culture. In R.B. Browne & M.W. Fishwick (Eds.), *The hero in transition* (pp. 14-45). Bowling Green, OH: Bowling Green University Popular Press.

Rosengren, K.E., & Windahl, S. (1972). Mass media consumption as a functional alternative. In D. McQuail (Ed.), *Sociology of mass communications* (pp. 166-194). London: Penguin Education.

Rovin, J. (1985). *The encyclopedia of superheroes.* New York: Facts on File.

Rowland, R.C. (1990). On mythic criticism. *Communication Studies, 41*(2), 101-116.

Rubin, A.M. (1983). Television uses and gratifications: Interactions of viewing patterns and motivations. *Journal of Broadcasting, 27*, 37-51.

Rubin, A.M., Perse, E.M., & Powell, R.A. (1985). Loneliness, parasocial interaction, and local television new viewing. *Human Communication Research, 12,* 155-180.

Rubin, J. (1976). *Growing up at thirty-seven.* New York: M. Evans.

Rudofsky, B. (1969). *Streets for people: A primer for Americans.* Garden City, NY: Doubleday.

Rushing, J.H. (1983). The rhetoric of the American western myth. *Communication Monographs, 50,* 14-32.

Rushing, J.H. (1989). Evolution of "the new frontier" in alien and aliens: Patriarchal co-optation of the feminine archetype. *Quarterly Journal of Speech, 75,* 1-22.

Rushing, J.H. (1985). E.T. as rhetorical transcendence. *Quarterly Journal of Speech, 71,* 188-203.

Rushing, J.H. (1986a). Mythic evolution of "the new frontier" in mass mediated rhetoric. *Critical Studies in Mass Communication, 3*(3), 265-296.

Rushing, J.H. (1986b). Ronald Reagan's "Star Wars" address: Mythic containment of technical reasoning. *Quarterly Journal of Speech, 72,* 415-433.

Rushing J.H. (1989). Evolution of "the new frontier" in alien and aliens: Patriarchal co-optation of the feminine archetype. *Quarterly Journal of Speech, 75,* 1-24.

Rushing, J.H., & Frentz, T.S. (1978). The rhetoric of "Rocky": A social values model of criticism. *Western Journal of Speech, 62,* 63-72.

Rushing, J.H., & Frentz, T.S. (1989). The Frankenstein myth in contemporary cinema. *Critical Studies in Mass Communication, 6*(1), 61-80.

Ryan gets 300th with strong backing. (1990, August 1). *The (Bakersfield) Sun,* p. C-1.

Ryan tops Royals on no-hitter, 3-0. (1973, May 16). *The New York Times,* p. 57.

Ryan, N., & Frommer, H. (1988). *Throwing heat: The autobiography of Nolan Ryan.* New York: Doubleday.

Rykwert, J. (1978). The street: The use of its history. In S. Anderson (Ed.), *On streets* (pp.15-28). Cambridge, MA: MIT Press.

Sabatini, R. (1934). *Heroic lives.* Boston: Houghton Mifflin.

Sales, S. (1972, November). Authoritarianism. But as for me, give me liberty, or give me, maybe, a great, big, strong,powerful leader I can honor, admire, respect and obey. *Psychology Today,* 94-98, 104-143.

Salisbury, H. (1988). *A time of change: A reporter's tale of our time.* New York: Harper & Row.

Sandman, P.M., Rubin, D.M., & Sachsman, D.B. (1982). *Media: An introductory analysis of American mass communication* (3rd ed.). Englewood Cliffs, NJ: Prentice-Hall.

Sanger, D. (1990, December 7). A japanese innovation: The space antihero. *The New York Times,* pp. 1, 5.

Schaumburg, R. (1976) *Growing up with the Beatles.* New York: Pyramid.

Schlafly, P. (1977). *The power of the positive woman.* New York: Jove Publications.

Schlafly, P. (1983, February 28). Schlafly soldiers on against the Feminists. *Newsweek, 101*, 10.

Schlafly, P. (1985a). Please excuse Johnny from death ed. *Harper's, 270*, 24.

Schlafly, P. (1985b). A little help from friends. *Newsweek, 106*, 27.

Schlafly, P. (1986). Comparable worth: Unfair to men and women. *The Humanist, 46*, 12-13.

Schlafly, P. (1988). Should the Congress adopt the proposed act for better child care services of 1988? *Congressional Digest, 67*, 271-275.

Schlafly, P. (1990a, March). A "New Age" for privacy-invading psychiatry. *The Phyllis Schlafly Report, 23*(7).

Schlafly, P. (1990b). *Address presented at the evening worship service of Calvary Chapel of Praise*. Stow, OH.

Schlafly, P., & Weyrich, P. (1987, August). Disowning the Surgeon General. *Harper's, 275*, 16-17.

Schickel, R. (1985). *Intimate strangers: The culture of celebrity*. New York: Doubleday.

Schudson, M. (1982). The politics of narrative form: The emergence of news conventions in print and television. *Daedalus 3*(4), 97-112.

Seaver, T., & Schaap, D. (1970). *The perfect game: Tom Seaver and the Mets*. New York: Dutton.

Sellnow, D.D., & Sellnow, T.L. (1990). The human relationship from idealism to realism: An analysis of the music of Bruce Springsteen. *Popular Music and Society, 14*(3), 71-88.

Search for Hispanic heroes: Informs, surprises, confirms. *Vista* (1986, June 8). pp. 18, 20.

Sennett, R. (1974). *The fall of public man*. New York: Alfred A. Knopf.

Sharing the grief. (1981, January 22). *Rolling Stone*, pp. 20, 73-75.

Sharrett, C. (1990, July). Good, evil, and movie heroes. *USA Today*, p. 61.

Sidey, H. (1988, November 28). A shattering afternoon in Dallas. *Time*, p. 45.

Simons, H., & Califano, J.A., Jr. (Eds.). (1979). *The media and business*. New York: Vintage Books.

Simounet-Geigel, A., & Ferri, J. (1982). Communication with clothing in the Puerto Rican Context. *Puerto Rican Communication Studies*.

Singer, M. (1987). *Intercultural communication: A perceptual approach*. Englewood Cliffs, NJ: Prentice-Hall.

Sklar, R. (1975). *Movie-made America: A cultural history of American movies*. New York: Random House.

Smith, G. (1973). The sports hero: An endangered species. *Quest, 19*, 59-70.

Solomon, M. (1978). The rhetoric of STOP ERA: Fatalistic Reaffirmation. *Southern Speech Communication Journal, 64*, 42-59.

Solomon, M. (1979). The "Positive Woman's" Journey: A mythic analysis of the rhetoric of Stop ERA. *Quarterly Journal of Speech, 65*, 269-274.

Solomon, M. (1983a). Robert Schuller: The American dream in a crystal cathedral. *Central States Speech Journal, 34*, 172-186.

Solomon, M. (1983b). Villainless quest: Myth, metaphor, and dream in "Chariots of Fire." *Communication Quarterly, 31*, 274-281.
Sontag, S. (1977). *On photography.* New York: Dell.
Spencer, S. (1981, January 22). John Lennon. *Rolling Stone*, p. 13.
Springsteen, B. (1973a). *Greetings from Asbury Park.* Columbia, 31903.
Springsteen, B. (1973b). *The wild, the innocent and the E-Street shuffle.* Columbia, 32432.
Springsteen, B. (1975). *Born to run.* Columbia, 33795.
Springsteen, B. (1978). *Darkness on the edge of town.* Columbia, 35318.
Springsteen, B. (1980). *The river.* Columbia, 36854.
Springsteen, B. (1982). *Nebraska.* Columbia, 38358.
Springsteen, B. (1984). *Born in the U.S.A.* Columbia, 38653.
Springsteen, B. (1986). *Bruce Springsteen & the E-Street Band live/1975-85.* Columbia, 40558.
Springsteen, B. (1988). *Tunnel of love.* Columbia, 40999.
Stasio, M. (1990, October 13). What's happening to heroes is a crime. *The New York Times Book Review*, pp. 1, 57-58.
Stengel, R. (1992, March 16). Midnight's mayor. *Time*, pp. 58-61.
Stelzner, H. (1971). The quest story and Nixon's November 3, 1969 address. *Quarterly Journal of Speech, 57*, 163-172.
Stone, G.P. (1973). American sports: Play and display. In J.T. Talamini & C.H. Page (Eds.), *Sport and society: An anthology* (pp. 65-84). Boston: Little, Brown & Co.
Strate, L. (1985, Spring). Heroes, fame and the media. *Et cetera, 42*(1), 47-53.
Subjic, D. (1989). *Cult heros: How to be famous for more than 15 minutes.* London: Andre Deutch.
Sun, S.W., & Lull, J. (1986, Winter). The adolescent audience for music videos and why they watch. *Journal of Communication*, 115-125.
Sunshine, the Magazine of South Florida. (1991, December 15). p. 4
Swaggart, J. (1977). *To cross a river.* Plainfield, NJ: Logos International.
Talese, G. (1986). *The kingdom and the power.* New York: Laurle Books/Dell.
10,000 telephone inquiries on Lindbergh answered by Times in eleven hours. (1927, May 22). *The New York Times*, p.3.
Ten years later: Where were you? (1973, November). *Esquire*, pp. 136-137.
Tetzlaff, D. (1986). MTV and the politics of postmodern pop. *The Journal of Communication Inquiry, 1*, 80-91.
The Kennedy assassination: Myth and reality.(1983, November 7-9). CBS Evening News, CBS News.
The New York Times, May 20, 1927, sec. 1, p.1 &4.
The New York Times, 22 May 1927, sec. 1, p. 3.
The New York Times, 28, May 1927, sec. 1, p. 2.
The New York Times, 29 May 1927, sec. 1, p. 4.
The San Juan Star (1989). Attitudes, values and habits of Puerto Rican youth. September 12, 21-23.

These are the Mets, champions all. (1969, October 17). *The New York Times*, p. 57.
Thomas, E. (1986, May 26). A reporter in search of history, *Time*, p.62.
Time. (1979, April 23). Chrysler Ad, 18-19.
Time. (1979, November 19). pp. 94-95.
Tipton, S. (1982). *Getting saved from the sixties.* Berkeley: University of California Press.
Tolley, J.L. (1983, February 25). *Chrysler: back from the brink.* Texas Public Relations Association, Dallas.
Toufexis, A., with Lafferty, E., & Sachs, A. (1989, July 31). A fatal obsession with the stars. *Time*, pp. 43-44.
Trujillo, N. (1989, November). *The meaning of Nolan Ryan: A case study of a sports hero.* Paper presented at the Speech Communication Association Convention, San Francisco, CA.
Trujillo, N., & Ekdom, L.R. (1985). Sportswriting and American cultural values: The 1984 Chicago Cubs. *Critical Studies in Mass Communication*, 2, 262-281.
Trump, D.J. (1987). *Trump: The art of the deal.* New York: Warner Books.
Trump, D. (1989, May 1). Bring back the death penalty! Bring back our police. *The New York Times*, p. A13.
Trump, D.J. (1989, July 29). No band-aid for our city. *The New York Times*, p. 15.
Trump, D.J., with Leerhsen, C. (1990). *Trump: Surviving at the top.* New York: Random House.
Tuccille, J. (1987). *Trump.* New York: Donald I. Fine.
Turpin, J. (1990). *Women in church history.* Cincinnati OH: St. Anthony Messenger Press.
25th anniversary of JFK's assassination. (1988, November 22). "Nightline," ABC News.
25 years later. (1988, October 24). *U.S. News and World Report* [special section], pp. 30-40.
Ulanov, A.B. (1971). *The feminine in Jungian psychology and in Christian Theology.* Evanston, IL: Northwestern University Press.
United Press International and American Heritage Magazine. (1964). *Four days: The historical record of President Kennedy's death.* New York: UPI and American Heritage Publishing.
Verna, T. (1987). *Live TV: An inside look at directing and producing.* Boston: Focal Press.
Wallace, R. (1989, November). *Vanishing heroes: Out of sight, out of mind.* Paper presented at the annual convention of the Speech Communication Association, San Francisco, CA.
Warhol, A. (1975). *The philosophy of Andy Warhol.* New York: Harcourt Brace Jovanovich.
Warner, W.L., & Henry, W. (1948). Radio daytime serial: A symbolic analysis. *Genetic Psychology Monographs, 37*, 3-71.

Warren, R.P. (1972). *Dearth of heroes*. American Heritage.
Watzlawick, P., Beavin, J., & Jackson, D. (1967). *Pragmatics of human communication: A study of interaction, patterns, pathologies and paradoxes*. New York: Norton Press.
Webster's Third New International Dictionary. (1964). Springfield MA: G.& C. Merriam Co.
Wecter, D. (1941). *The hero in America*. New York: Charles Scribner's Sons.
Wellek, R., & Warren, A. (1956). *Theory of literature*. New York: Harcourt, Brace, & World.
Welsh, D., & Turner, W. (1969, January 25). In the shadow of Dallas. *Ramparts*, pp. 61-71.
Wenner, L.A. (1985). Media, sports, and society: The research agenda. In L. Wenner (Ed.), *Media, sports & society* (pp. 13-48). Newbury Park, CA: Sage.
Wenner, L.A. (Ed.).(1989). *Media, sports, and society*. Newbury Park, CA: Sage.
Wenner, L.A. (1990). Therapeutic engagement in mediated sports. In G. Gumpert & S.F. Fish (Eds.), *Talking to strangers: Mediated therapeutic communication* (pp. 223-244). Norwood, NJ: Ablex.
Wenner, L.A., & Palmgreen, P. (Eds.) (1985). *Media gratification research: Current perspectives*. Newbury Park, CA: Sage.
What 'Dear Lindy' found in his mailbag. (1927, October 1). *Literary Digest, 95*, 36.
What JFK meant to us. (1983, November 28). *Newsweek*, pp. 3-91.
What newspaper readers like to read. (1989). *The San Juan Star*, p. 21.
White, T.M. (1978, July 3). Camelot, sad Camelot. *Time*, pp. 46-48. Also in *In search of history: A personal adventure*. New York: Warner, 1978.
Whitmont, E.C. (1969). *The symbolic quest: Basic concepts of analytical psychology*. Princeton, NJ: Princeton University Press.
Wicker, T. (1963, December). That day in Dallas. *Times Talk* [New York Times internal publication].
Wicker, T. (1964a, January 11). A reporter must trust his instinct. *Saturday Review*, pp. 81-86.
Wicker, T. (1964b). *Kennedy without tears*. New York: William Morrow.
Wicker, T. (1973, October). Kennedy without tears (report from June 1964). *Esquire*, pp. 196-200.
Wicker, T. (1991, December 15). Does 'J.F.K.' conspire against reason? *New York Times*, sec.2, pp. 1, 18.
Wilkie, C. (1978). *The Lindbergh-Hauptmann encounter as modern myth and ritual through media*. Masters thesis, Wayne State University.
Williams, J. (1961, November 18). The Western: Definition of a myth. *The Nation*, pp. 402-406.
Wills, G. (1983). *The Kennedy imprisonment*. New York: Pocket Books.
Wolfe, T. (1987). Tom Wolfe's walk on the wild side. *U.S. News and World Report, 103*(21), 57.

Wright, C.R. (1959). *Mass communication: A sociological perspective.* New York: Random House.
Wright, L. (1983). *In the new world: Growing up with America from the sixties to the eighties.* New York: Vintage Books.
Wyllie, I.G. (1954). *The self-made man in America.* New Brunswick, NJ: Rutgers University Press.
Zelizer, B. (1992). *Covering the body: The Kennedy assassination, the media, and the shaping of collective memory.* Chicago: University of Chicago Press.
Zelizer, B. (1989, Summer). What's rather public about Dan Rather: TV journalism and the emergence of celebrity. *Journal of Popular Film and Television,,* 74-80.

Author Index

A

Abelman, R., 247, *299*
Abramson, P.,63, *311*
Agrest, S., 75-76, 78, *311*
Allen, F.J., 172, *299*
American Heritage Magazine, 75, 108, *319*
Anderson, D., 228-229, 239, *299*
Arendt, H., 3, *299*
Aristotle, 51, 61, *299*
Aronoff, C.E., 223, *299*
Ashen, F., 25, *299*
Ashen, F., 25, *299*
Axthelm. P., 228-229, 231-232, *299*

B

Baker, R., 48, *299*
Baldwin, P., 234, *299*
Balswick, J., 34, *299*
Balthrop, V.W., 153, *299-300*
Barker, L., 143, *300*
Barnouw, E., 57, 76, 90, *300*
Baron, D., 27, *300*
Barry, J., 69, *311*
Barthes, R., 215, *300*
Bass, J.D., 153, *300*
Bate, B., 25, *300*
Baudrillard, J.,207-208, 212, *300*
Bayless, S., 237, *300*
Beavin, J., 271, *320*
Bellah, R.N., 258, *300*

Bennett, W.L., 153, *300*
Bentley, E.R., 140, *300*
Benveniste, E., 100, *300*
Birnback, L., 21, *300*
Blacker, C., 248, *300*
Block, J.L., 149, 166, *300*
Bluem, A.W., 108, *300*
Bogert, C., 69, *311*
Boorstin, D.J., 3-4, 7, 19, 23, 86, 92, 98, 172, 189-192, 196, 201, 221, 223-224, 233, 236, 239, 251, 261, 263, 280-281, 283, *300-301*
Bormann, E.G., 197, *301*
Braudy, L., 7, 37-40, 97, 99, 110, 189-190, 193, 260, 264, *301*
Braun, S., 52, *301*
Brecht, B., 1, *301*
Breen, M., 153, *301*
Breslau, D., 69, *311*
Briggs, D., 284, *311*
Broder, D., 100, *301*
Brombert, V., 1-2, *301*
Browne, P., 33, 271, *301*
Browne, R.B., 254, *301*
Brownmiller, S., 77, *301*
Bruce, S., 242, 250-251, *301*
Bruning, F., 48, *301*
Bulfinch, T., 28, *301*
Burke, K.B., 121, 169, 176, 182-183, *301*
Burkholder, T.R., 153, *301*

Burns, J.M., 3, 5, *301*
Butler, B., 249, 254, *301*
Byrd, J., 243, *301*

C

Calhoun, D.W., 222, *301*
Califano, J.A., Jr., 223, *317*
Campbell, J., 2-3, 5, 18, 30 ,32, 84, 86, 113, 119, 123, 152, 156-157, 169, 173-178, 221, 236, 243, 248, 250, 281, 284-285, *301-302*
Carey, J.W., 253, *302*
Carlyle, T., 2, 19, 83, 145, *302*
Carpenter, R., 237, *302*
Carroll, J.B., 24, *302*
Casstevens, D., 235, *302*
Cathcart, R., 56, 93, 238, 261-262, 264, *302-303*
Caughey, J.L., 45-46, 65, 93, 264, *302*
Cawelti, J.G., 2, 82, 237, 266, *302*
Chass, M., 226, *302*
Cherwitz, R., 153, *300*
Chesebro, J., 273-274, *302*
Chomsky, N., 74, *307*
Chrysler Corporation, 138, *302*
Clarke, G., 63, *302*
Clymer, A., 69, *302*
Cleaver, E., 112, *302*
Cocks, J., 64, *303*
Collins, J., 206, 215, *303*
Coleman, F., 69, *311*
Combs, J., 114, *313*
Corcoran, F., 153, *301*
Cotugno, H.E., 241, *306*
Crepeau, R.C., 223-224, *303*
Curtius, E.R., 2-3, *303*
Cuthbertson, G.M., 158, *303*
Czarnowski, T.V., 6, *303*

D

Dabbs, J.M., 243, *303*
DeFrank, T.M., 69, *311*
DeLaszlo, V.S., 152, *303*
Dionisopolous, G.N., 153-154, *303*

Distel, D., 229, *303*
Dowd, M.B., 254, *303*
Drucker, S., 84, 93, 264, *303, 307*
Duncan, H.D., 169, *303*
Duncan, M.C., 222, *303*
Durso, J., 225-227, *303*
Dyer, R., 98, 204-206, 211, 214, *303*

E

Edelman, M., 153, *300*
Edes, G., 235, *303-304*
Edwards, L.R., 5, 26-27, 29, 33, 83-84, 86, *304*
Eisenstein, E.L., 18, *304*
Ekdom, L.R., 222, *319*
Eliade, M., 16, 18, *304*
Elm, J., 104, *302*
Ellis, B.E., 21, *302*
Entman, R., 74, *304*
Ephron, N., 106, *304*

F

Fairlie, H., 222, *304*
Fayer, J., 273, *304*
Felsenthal, C., 151, 166, *304*
Ferguson, M., 116, *304*
Ferri, J., 273-274, *302, 304, 317*
Fimrite, R., 230-231, *304*
Fisher, W.R., 153, *304*
Fishman, J., 272, *304*
Fishwick, M.W., 2, 27, 32, 35, 84, 248, 251, 254, 258-259, *301, 304-305*
Fiske, J., 210, 212-213, 238, *305*
Fitzgerald, F.S., 174, *305*
Flippo, C., 76, *305*
Foderaro, L.W., 189, *305*
Foley, L., 28, *305*
Foss, K.A., 194-195, 198, *305*
Foss, S.K., 154, 166, *305*
Fraser, A., 29, 248, *305*
Frazer, J.G., 170, 173, *305*
Frentz, T.S., 153, 238, *305, 316*
Frommer, H., 89, *316*

AUTHOR INDEX

Frye, N., 237, 251, *305*
Furlong, W.B., 230, *305*

G

Gaither, R., 8, *305*
Galloway, R., 232-233, 235, *305*
Gamarekian, B., 107, *306*
Gamson, J., 8, 41, 43, 260, 263, *306*
Garfield, B., 212, *306*
Gates, G.P., 102, 104, 106, *306*
Gencarelli, T., 283, *306*
Gerard, J., 191-192, *306*
Gerbner, G., 241, *306*
Gergen, J., 235, *306*
Giamatti, A.B., 88, 238, *306*
Gibson, D.C., 153, *306*
Goffman, E., 68, *306*
Goldsen, R.K., 261, *306*
Gonzalez, A., 153, 286, *306, 311*
Grady, S., 109, *306*
Gray, R., 139, *306*
Greene, B., 238, *306*
Gross, L., 72, 243, *308*
Grossberg, L., 206-207, 216, *306-307*
Grunwald, L., 64, *307*
Gumpert, G., 16, 56, 84, 93, 238, 261-262, 264, *302-303, 307*
Guttman, A., 88, *307*

H

Hackett, G., 246, 251, *307*
Hamill, P., 75, *307*
Hamilton, E., 28, *307*
Hammond, M., 191, *307*
Hankins, S.R., 153, *307*
Harazin, A., 87, 90, *307*
Hargreaves, J., 83, 222-223, *307*
Hartley, J., 238, *305*
Harvey, D.A., 243, 247, *307*
Harvin, A., 225, *307*
Havelock, E., 55, *307*
Hayden, T., 112, 115-116, *307*
Hebdige, D., 283, *307*
Heisler, M., 230, *307*

Henderson, J., 233, *307*
Henry, W., 44, *319*
Herman, E.S., 74, *307*
Hernández, E., 273, *304*
Herskowitz, M., 102, *315*
Hoch, P., 222, *308*
Hoffer, R., 231-232, *308*
Holden, S., 286, *308*
Hollenweger, W.J., 252, 254, *308*
Hook, S., 249, 251, *308*
Hoover, S., 241, 252, *306, 308*
Horn, B., 235, *308*
Horowitz, I., 90, *308*
Horsefield, P., 241, *308*
Horton, D., 20, 63, 67, 71, 238, 255, 261-262, 266-267, *308*
House Committee on Banking, 137, *308-309*
Huckshorn, K., 154, *308*

I

Iacocca, L., 138-139, 144-145, *308*
Ingoldsby, B., 34, *299-300*
Innis, H.A., 16, *308*
Irvine, J.R., 286, *308-309*

J

Jackson, D., 271, *320*
Jacobson, S., 229, *309*
James, E., 178-179, *309*
Jameson, F., 207, 209, *309*
Jassem, H.C., 90, *309*
Jeffries-Fox, S., 72, *306*
Jennings, D., 239, *309*
Jhally, S., 216, *309*
Jung, C.G., 173, *309*

K

Kael, P., 60, *309*
Kaplan, E.A., 207, 209-210, 212, *309*
Kaplan, J., 231-232, *309*
Keith, L., 230, *309*
Kelmenson, L.A., 136, 143-144, *309*
Kerényi, C., 1, *309*
Key, M.R., 25, *309*

King, A.A., 153, *309*
Kindred, D., 235, *309*
Kirkpatrick, W., 286, *308-309*
Klapp, O.E., 31, 35, 83, 170, 173, 222, 236, *310*
Koppett, L., 225, *310*
Kruse, N.W., 154, 164, 166, *310*
Krutch, J., 50-51, *310*
Kunhardt, P.B., Jr., 108, *310*
Kurnow, S., 124, *310*

L

Lafferty, E., 64, *319*
Lahr, J., 22, *310*
Land, S.J., 243-245, 252, 256, *310*
Langer, J., 45-46, 56, *310*
Langer, S.K., 297, *310*
Lee, R., 115, *310*
Leerhsen, C., 49, *310, 319*
Lehman, G., 84, *307*
Lewis, W.F., 244, *310*
Leonard, W.M., II., 222, *310-311*
Levy, M.R., 262, 264, 266, *311*
Lipsky, R., 84, *311*
Littlejohn, S.W., 194-195, 198, *305*
Littwin, M., 230-232, *311*
Lowenthal, L., 263, *311*
Lull, J., 216, *318*

M

Mackey-Kallis, S.294-295, *311*
Maher, J.M., 284, *311*
Maier., F., 63, *311*
Makay, J.J., 153, 286, *306, 311*
Mankiewicz, F., 76, 261, *311*
Marcus, G., 63, *311*
Marsh, D., 282, 287, 291, *311*
Martin, B., 89, *311*
Mathews, T., 63, 69, *311*
Matusow, B., 103, *311*
Mayer, A.J., 75-76, 78, *311*
Maynard, R.M., 237, *311*
McBee, S., 272, *311*
McCarver, T., 90-91, *311*

McDermott, I., 294-295, *311*
McGee, M.C., 173, *311*
McGinniss, J., 3-5, 84, 260, *311*
McGuire, M., 282, *312*
McLennan, D.B., 89, *312*
McLuhan, M., 16, 150, *312*
McQuail, D., 261, *312*
Mead, G.H., 71, *312*
Mechling, E.W., 153, *312*
Mernit, S., 60, *312*
Merton, R.K., 261, *312*
Meyer, M., 201, *312*
Meyrowitz, J., 7, 16, 54, 69, 73, 80, 84, 93, 267, *312-313*
Miller, C., 25-26, *312*
Miller, M.S., 34, *312*
Mills, N., 191, *312*
Mine, D.G., 77, *312*
Monaco, J., 7, 92, 260, 264, 268, *312*
Montana, J., 89, *312*
Moore, C., 8, 29, *312*
Morgan, M., 241, *306*
Morgan, R., 30, *312*
Moritz, M., 137-138, 145, *313*
Morris, H., 63, *311*
Morris, L., 178, *313*
Morrow, L., 105, *313*
Mosley, L., 172, *313*
Mullett, M.B., 179, *313*
Mulvey, L., 210, *313*

N

Navratilova, M., 89, *313*
Neumann, E., 155-157, 159, 173, *313*
Newhan, R., 226-229, *313*
Newman, B., 229, *313*
Newman, R.P., 153, *313*
Newsom, D., 135-136, *313*
Niebuhr, H.R., 242, 256, *313*
Nimmo, D., 112, *313*
Nixon, H.L., II., 222, *313*
Nolan, T., 87-88, *313*
Norman, D., 2, *313*
Novak, M., 222, *313*

O

Ong, W.J., 3, 6, 16-17, 56, 86, 253, *313-314*
Ostling, R., 251, *314*
Ostling, R.N., 241, *314*

P

Pagels, E., 25, *314*
Palmgreen, P., 261, *320*
Parks, R., 245-247, 249, 251, *314*
Parks, R.J., 153, *314*
Payne, D., 153, *314*
Pearson, C.S., 4, 32, *314*
Pepe, P., 89, *311*
Perse, E.M., 262, 264, 266, *316*
Perez, P.R., 272, *314*
Peters, A., 273, *304*
Phelan, J.M., 22, *314*
Phillips, K., 190, *314*
Poloma, M., 244, *314*
Postman, N., 16, *314*
Potok, C., 15, *314*
Powell, R.A., 262, 264, 266, *316*
Poyton, C., 25, *314*
Pullum, S.J., 241-242, *314*

R

Rader, B.G., 238, *315*
Raglan, F., 2, 30, *315*
Raissman, B., 89, *312*
Rank, O., 173, 181, *315*
Rapoport, R., 229, *315*
Rather, D., 102, *315*
Reid, K., 257, *315*
Reeves, J., 233, *315*
Rickey, C., 34, *315*
Ricoeur, P., 257, *315*
Ringolsby, T., 234-235, *315*
Riukas, S., 153, *315*
Robertson, J.O., 249, *315*
Rogers, P., 232-233, *315*
Rollin, R.R., 251, *315*
Rosengren, K.E., 65, 261-262, 267, *315*
Rovin, J., 248, *315*
Rowland, R.C., 244, *315*
Rubin, A.M., 261-262, 264, 266, *315-316*
Rubin, D.M., 68, *317*
Rubin, J., 112, *316*
Rudofsky, B., 6, *316*
Rushing, J.H., 2, 114, 153, 157, 237-238, *305, 316*
Ryan, N., 89, *316*
Rykwert, J., 6, 87, *316*

S

Sabatini, R., 30, *316*
Sachs, A., 64, *319*
Sachsman, D.B., 68, *316*
Sales, S., 53, *316*
Salisbury, H., 101, *316*
Sandman, P.M., 68, *316*
Sanger, D., 49, *316*
Schaap, D., 89, *317*
Schaumburg, R., 62, *316*
Schlafly, P., 150, 154, 157-162, 164-166, *316-317*
Schickel, R., 7, 44, 201, 268, 271, *317*
Schudson, M., 99, *317*
Scott, A., 135-136, *313*
Seaman, B., 137-138, 145, *312*
Seaver, T., 89, *317*
Sellnow, D.D., 282, *317*
Sellnow, T.L., 282, *317*
Sennett, R., 56, *317*
Sharrett, C., 141, *317*
Sidey, H., 109, *317*
Signorelli, N., 241, *306*
Simons, H., 223, *317*
Simounet-Geigel, A., 273-274, *304, 317*
Singer, M., 271, *317*
Sklar, R., 65, *317*
Smith, G., 222-224, *317*
Smith, K., 178, *313*
Solomon, M., 153-154, 156, 166, *317-318*

Sontag, S., 88, *318*
Spencer, S., 62, *318*
Springsteen, B., 283, 285, *318*
Stasio, M., 35, *318*
Stengel, R., 68, *318*
Stelzner, H., 237, *318*
Stone, G.P., 222, 239, *299, 318*
Strate, L., 2-3, 5-6, 82, 269, 284, *318*
Subjic, D., 212, *318*
Sun, S.W., 216, *318*
Swaggart, J., 247, *318*
Swerdlow, J., 76, 261, *311*
Swift, K., 25-26, *312*

T

Talese, G., 101, *318*
Tetzlaff, D., 210, 215-216, *318*
Thomas, E., 105, *319*
Tipton, S., 128, *319*
Tolley, J.L., 142, *319*
Toufexis, A., 64, *319*
Trujillo, N., 85, 93, 222, *319*
Trump, D.J., 189-193, 195-197, *319*
Tuccille, J., 192, *319*
Turk, J.V., 135-136, *313*
Turner, W., 106, *320*
Turpin, J., 283, *319*

U

Ulanov, A.B., 163, 165, *319*
United Press International, 75, 108, *319*

V

Vecsey, G., 89, *313*
Verna, T., 90-92, *319*

W

Wallace, R., 8, *319*
Waller, D., 69, *311*
Warhol, A., 216, *319*
Warner, M.G., 69, *311*
Warner, W.L., 44, *319*
Warren, A., 244, *320*
Warren, R.P., 84, *320*
Watzlawick, P., 271, *320*
Wecter, D., 2, 31-32, 246, 268, *320*
Wellek, R., 244, *320*
Welsh, D., 106, *320*
Wenner, L.A., 84-85, 238, 261, *320*
Weyrich, P., 159, *317*
White, T.M., 105, *320*
Whitmont, E.C., 156, 164, *320*
Wicker, T., 101, 108, *320*
Wilkie, C., 172-173, *320*
Williams, J., 245, *320*
Wills, G., 100, 107, *320*
Windahl, S., 65, 261-262, 267, *315*
Wohl, R.R., 20, 63, 67, 71, 238, 255, 261-262, 266-267, *308*
Wolfe, T., 191, *320*
Wright, C.R., 261, *321*
Wright, L., 100, *321*
Wuthnow, R., 241, *306*
Wyllie, I.G., 189-190, *321*

Y

Young, J., 75-76, 78, *311*

Z

Zelizer, B., 98, 102, *321*

Subject Index

A

Achievement, 19-20, 30, 47, 84-85, 88, 189-191, 193, 222, 224, 231, 233-234
Achilles, 16, 18
Actors/Actresses
  Alda, Alan, 23
  Barrymore, John, 41
  Baseheart, Richard, 107
  Beatty, Warren, 58
  Bernhardt, Sarah, 262
  Bogart, Humphrey, 20, 43, 77
  Bono, Sonny, 71
  Brando, Marlon, 205-213
  Burr, Raymond, 23
  Busey, Gary, 79
  Chaplin, Charlie, 20, 275, 279
  Cooper, Gary, 43
  Dean, James, 49, 73, 205-206, 213
  Eastwood, Clint, 21, 71, 272
  Estrada. Erik, 21
  Fairbanks, Douglas, Sr., 41, 268
  Field, Sally, 21, 272
  Finney, Albert, 205
  Fonda, Jane, 21, 130, 272
  Ford, Harrison, 217
  Forsythe, John, 21
  Foster, Jodie, 64
  Fox, Michael J. 64, 275
  Garbo, Greta, 275, 279
  Gilbert, John, 262
  Goldberg, Whoppi, 275
  Holbrook, Hal, 107
  Houseman, John, 139
  Keaton, Michael, 58
  Kilmer, Val, 79
  Landon, Michael, 77
  Lee, Bruce, 23
  MacLaine, Shirley, 113
  Martin, Steve, 21
  McCann, Larry, 107
  Monroe, Marilyn, 20, 77, 206
  Montalban, Ricardo, 139
  Murphy, Audie, 49
  Newman, Paul 205
  O'Conner, Carroll, 22
  Pickford, Mary, 43, 268
  Presley, Priscilla, 47
  Reynolds, Burt, 21
  Robertson, Cliff, 107
  Reeves, Christopher, 58
  Russell, Lillian, 262
  Schwarzenegger, Arnold, 275, 279
  Selleck, Tom, 275, 279
  Shatner, William, 22
  Stallone, Sylvester, 16, 21, 217
  Stewart, Jimmy, 21
  Taylor, Elizabeth, 66
  Wayne, John, 21
  West, Adam, 58
  Young, Robert, 23
Advertising, 9, 204-206, 208, 215-217
Age
  generational, 265, 267, 272, 274,

277
youth audience, 274
Akiyama, Toyohiro, 49, 52
Alexander the Great, 36, 38, 41, 49
Allende, Isabel, 277
American Dream, 120, 136, 153, 238, 295
Anthony, Susan B., 149
Anti-hero, 60-61
Archetype, 2, 4, 9, 113-114, 119, 123, 153, 155-156, 158-160, 163, 169, 180-181
Archbishop Romero, 74
Aristotle, 8, 54
   Aristotelian hero, 50, 61
   Poetics, 51
   view of tragedy, 8, 51
Armstrong, Louis, 20
Artists, 3, 6
   Michelangelo, 49
Assassination
   Bardo, Robert John, 64
   Chapman, Mark David, 20, 63-64, 71
   Hinckley, John, Jr., 20, 64
   Kennedy, John F., *see* Presidents
   Lennon, John, *see* Singers
   Oswald, Lee Harvey, 183
   Schaeffer, Rebecca, 64
Astronauts, 4, 48
   Armstrong, Neil, 139
   McAuliffe, Christa, 73-74
   Yeager, Chuck, 49
Athlete/Athletics, 83
   Olympians, 28, 86
   see also Sports
Autobiography, 9, 20, 89, 112-114, 132-133
Autographs, 86-87, 89
Authors
   Buckley, William F., 78
   Campbell, Joseph
      Hero With a Thousand Faces, 2, 30, 32, 169, 173

   Capote, Truman, 22
   Faulkner, William, 8
   Fitzgerald, F. Scott, 176
   Hemingway, Ernest, 8
   Kerouac, Jack, 121
   Kosinski, Jersy, 22
   Mailer, Norman, 22
   Miller, Henry, 8
   Vonnegut, Kurt, 22
   Wills, Gary, 107
   Wolfe, Tom, 111

B

Backstage, 69
   exposure, 263
Baseball, *see* Sports
Baudrillard, Jean, 141, 215-216
Baudrillard, Umberto, 141
Beatles, The, 70-72, 76, 78-79
   Epstein, Brian, 72, 76
   Lennon, John, *see* Singers
   McCartney, Paul, *see* Singers
   Ono, Yoko, 66, 71, 77, 79
Becket, Thomas a, 59
Behind the scenes, 8
Beowolf, 18
Berrgian, Daniel, 32
Berrios, Ruben, 274-277
Biography, 20, 89, 262
Blacklist, 74
Bolivar, 272
Bond, James, 59
Bormann, Frank, 197
   see fantasy theme analysis
Buddha, 250
Buffalo Bill Cody, 39-41
Bunyan, John, 39
Burke, Kenneth, 9, 121, 169-170, 176, 182-183
   theory of identification, 169-170, 174, 182-183

C

Camera angles, 67

SUBJECT INDEX

Campaign, 22, 112, 115, 122, 129, 133, 139, 142, 151, 163, 191, 194, 201
Campbell, Joseph, 2, 6, 9, 152-153, 156, 159, 169-170
  Hero With a Thousand Faces, see Authors
Caesar, 16
Camelot, 106, 109, 169, 180-181
Campos, Pedro Albizo, 275, 278
Capitalism, 143, 204-205, 210, 215-218
Cartoon, 58
  Simpson, Bart, 49
Catholic, 180, *see* Religion
Celebrity, 4-5, 7-8, 10-11, 48, 66, 93, 201, 224, 238-240, 260, 265-268
  definitions, 50, 85-86, 98, 189-190, 271, 280
  celebrification, 4, 10, 85, 92, 262
  fan relationship, 23, 64, 91-92, 261-267, 269
    fantasy distance, 265, 267
    heroic distance, 265, 267
    interpersonal distance, 265-267
    social distance, 265, 267
  journalistic, 98-105, 107-110
  mass-mediated, 67-68, 150-151, 172, 261, 268
  worship, 261
Challenger, The, 73-74
Close-ups, 43, 210
Charisma, 181, 204, 239
Chavez, Cesar, 272
Chicago Eight Trial, 126-127, 130
Church, *see* Religion
Churchill, Sir Winston, 144
Cleaver, Eldridge, 112
Colon, Rafael Hernandex, 275-277
Colson, Charles, 114
Columbus, Christopher, 19
Comedians
  Ball, Lucille, 49
  Barr, Rosanne, 66
  Belushi, John, 77

Benny, Jack, 44
Burns, George, 66
Cosby, Bill, 66
Hope, Bob, 44-45
Laurel and Hardy, 20
Lewis, Jerry, 21
Murphy, Eddie, 21, 272, 275, 279
Radner, Gilda, 77
Rivers, Joan, 67
Commemorative activity, 106-107, 109
Comics
  Books
    Marvel Comics, 52-53, 60
  Cartoonists
    Lee, Stan, 52
  Characters
    Dick Tracy, 53, 57-58
    Don Winslow of the Navy, 57
    Flash Gordon, 53-57
    Jack Armstrong, 57
    Little Orphan Annie, 57
    Tarzan, 53-57
    Terry and the Pirates, 53, 57
    Tom Mix, 57
    see also Superheroes
  Strips
    Alley Oop, 53
    Buck Rogers, 53
    Joe Palooka, 53
    Lone Ranger, 53, 57
Commercials, *see* advertising
Commodification, 206, 284
Community, 5-6, 84, 171
  interest-based, 84
Computer, 23
Confidence, 140, 143, 146
Copeland, Kenneth, 242
Corporations
  Chrysler
    advertising, 136, 139, 144
      Kenyon and Eckhardt ad agency, 139, 141
    television commercials, 136,

139, 141, 143
Chrysler Loan Guarantee Bill, 138
Chrysler, Walter P., 146
effect of recession, 136
government-backed loan, 136-138, 141-142, 145
Public Affairs Department, 142-143
Public Relations Department, 143
Corporate Leaders
Borman, Frank, 136
Jobs, Steven, 201-202
Perdue, Frank, 136
Sellinger, Frank 136
Corvetjer, Juan A, 275
Cousteau, Jacques, 21
Cowboy, 237
Credibility, 90, 136, 143, 145, 192, 200, 232
Cross-cultural, 280
Culture, 6-7, 216-217
Anglo, 272
electronic, 7, 9, 261
Hispanic, 272-273
literate, 17-19
oral, 6-7, 17, 19, 86-87

D

Davis, Rennie, 112, 130
de Burgos, Julia, 274-275, 277-279
de Hostos, Eugenio, 274, 278
de Tio, Lola Rodriguez, 274, 278
Death
purification, 182
symbolic, 126, 169, 176, 179-180, 182-183
Deeds, 264, 268-269, 271, 275, 280
Defeats, 33, 232
Demon, 123
Distance, *see* fan relationship
Drama

theory, 50-51, 114
Krutch, Joseph Wood, 50-51, 54
Dynamism, 132, 142, 146

E

Earhart, Amelia, 272
Edison, Thomas, 31
Editorials, 184, 186
Ego identity, 130
Einstein, Albert, 22
Emerson, Ralph Waldo, 4, 61
Endorsements, 234, 238-239
Entertainers, 4, 21-22, 262, 266
Entertainment Tonight, 66
Equal Rights Amendment (ERA), 150-151, 154, 157, 163, 166-167
Ethos, 140-141

F

Face-to-face communication, 6, 261-262, 265, 267, 269
Fame, 5, 8, 10, 16, 83, 189-190, 265
Fan, 20, 22, 64-65, 67-68, 71-72, 78-80, 86, 89, 91-93, 203, 261-263, 266-267
Fan Club, 266, 268
Fanatic, 262
Fantasy, 5
theme analysis, 189, 194-195, 198
Fashion model, 21
Fathers, 277
Fela, Dona, 274-276, 278
Female hero, 5, 24, 27, 33-35, 150, 277-278
Ferraro, Geraldine, 32
Ferre, Luis, 274, 276-277
Ferre, Sister Isolina, 274
Film, *see* Motion Picture
Ford, Henry, 31
Frank, Anne, 49
Franklin, Ben, 143
Frick, Henry Clay, 135
Froines, John, 131
Frontier thesis, 122, 237

G

Galileo, 16
Gandhi, Indira, 29
Gandhi, Mahatma, 49, 274-275, 278, 280
Gender, 277-278
  housewife, 158, 166
  and language, 24-27
  and military, 28
  and religion, 27
  male dominated, 28-29
  see also, female hero, heroine
Gender filter, 25
Gilgamesh, 17
Gitlin, Todd, 130
Glenn, John, 32
Gooddall, Jane, 49
Gorbachev, Mikhail, 274-276
Gotti, John, 48-49
Gospel, 28, 242, 247, 251-252
Great Mother, 151-160, 162-167
Grief, 75-78
Group, 271, 276, 280
  definition of, 273
Guilt, 121, 171, 184-188
Guns n' Roses, 208, 298

H

Hall of Fame, 82, 85
Hauptmann, Bruno Richard, 180
Hayden, Tom
  autobiography, 112, 115-121, 123, 125-128, 130-131
  campaign, 115, 129
  Kent State, 126
  marriage, 130
  protests, 122, 125-126
  trial, 126-127, 130
  Vietnam, 118-119, 124-126, 128-129
Hercules, 18, 21
Hero
  ageless, 232, 238
  alienated, 205
  American, 238-240, 249
  ancient, 36, 86
  anomic, 205
  archetype, 4, 153
  civic, 189-191, 201
  communication technologies, 10, 23, 37
  comic book, 52-53
  construction, 222
  contemporary, 7, 10, 47-50, 54, 193, 221-222, 236-237, 251, 266
  culture, 16-18, 155-156, 163, 166, 171, 280
  definitions, 1-3, 11, 24, 26-27, 30, 32-33, 36, 47-48, 50, 83, 86, 114, 140, 151, 158-157, 170, 180, 189-190, 221-222, 224, 247, 251, 271, 280, 283-284
  dramatic, 52
  divine, 248-251
  electronic, 19-21, 23, 263-268
  flaws, 7-8, 50, 54, 59-61
  folk, 274-275
  international, 274, 276, 278, 280
  interpersonal, 15-16
  lack of, 7, 20, 26, 35, 58, 114, 170
  political, 275, 277-278
  mass-mediated, 63, 140-141, 146, 171-172, 221-223, 236, 238-239
  monomythic, 186-187
  myth, 2, 6, 112-115
  mythic, 16, 18, 173, 181, 186
  organizational, 16
  political, 3
  rebel, 205-206
  redeemer, 183
  relationship to celebrity, 251
  rite of passage, 84, 113, 115, 119-121, 126, 131, 169-170, 173, 178, 180-181, 285
  scapegoat, 169-170, 180, 182, 186
  sports, 4, 83-84, 88, 90-91, 93,

    222-224, 238
  traditional, 3-5, 7-8, 22, 39, 46, 50, 54-55, 84, 93, 112, 265, 267, 269, 271, 280
  tragic, 50-52, 54
  unsung, 10, 16
  warriors, 3, 6, 29, 237
  working class, 40
  Western, 5, 58, 248-249
  worship, 6, 20, 186, 222, 248, 261-262
Heroic, 2, 5, 10, 24, 27, 31-33, 82, 92-93, 222, 248, 261
Heroine, 5-6, 24-27, 29-35
  see also female hero
Heroism, 5, 10, 83, 85, 92
Hierarchy, 182-183
Hitler, Adolf, 182
Hogan, Hulk, 91
Hollywood, 262
  gossip, 262
  motion picture industry, 262
  publicity, 8, 262
Homecoming, 230
Houdini, Harry, 49
Hype, 266
Hyperreality, 207

I

Iacocca, Lee, 22, 113-114, 136, 138-146
  see also Chrysler, corporations
Identification
  Kenneth Burke's theory, 169-170
Identity, 217-218
Image, 3, 8, 10, 20-22, 36-37, 45, 69, 112-114, 132-133, 156, 207-210, 214-216, 274
  commercialization, 37
  Mulvey's thesis of star image, 210-211
Independence, 140-141, 146
Industrial Revolution, 18, 37, 85
Intimacy, 20, 56, 64-65, 70-72, 75, 77, 80, 262, 266-268
Isabel of Spain, 29

J

Japan, 49, 143-144
Jews, 182
Jesus, 176, 182-183, 250, 274, 277
Joan of Arc, 16, 30-31, 49, 274, 277
Journalist(s), 38, 97-110
Journey, heroic, 32-33, 84-86, 116, 125, 245-246, 248-250
  initiation, 84, 113, 119, 123-124, 248
  separation, 84, 113, 119, 122-123, 132, 248
  return, 84, 113, 119, 125-127, 130-132, 248
Jovel, Carmen, 275, 279
Juarez, 272
Julia, Raul, 275, 278
Jung, Carl, 173
  archetype, 152-153
  collective unconscious, 152-153, 204
  personal unconscious, 152-153

K

Keller, Helen, 272
Kennedy, Edward, 32
Kennedy, John F., *see* Presidents
Kennedy, Robert, 126, 168
King, Martin Luther, Jr., 49, 79, 112, 168, 274-275, 278
Koop, Everett, 159
Ku Klux Klan (KKK), 133
  Duke, David, 133

L

Leadership, 3, 5, 29
Lincoln, Abraham, *see* Presidents
Lind, Angelita, 275, 278
Lindbergh, Charles, 31, 44, 169-170, 172-180, 185-187, 272
  Lone Eagle, 44
  Paris flight, 175

SUBJECT INDEX

Spirit of St. Louis, 44
Literate cultures/literacy, 22
Loman, Willie, 50
Loyalty, 79, 125, 150, 222

M

Machiavelli, 143
MacPherson, Elle, 69
Madison, Dolly, 272
Madonna
   Commercials
      Pepsi-Cola, 212-214
   Motion Pictures
      Desparately Seeking Susan, 212
      Truth or Dare, 211
   Music Videos, 213
   Songs, 212-217
   see also Singers
Magazines
   Fan, 45
      Good Housekeeping, 149
      People, 66
   News
      American Heritage Magazine, 108
      Editor and Publisher, 108
      Esquire, 108
      Newsweek, 103, 290
      The Saturday Review, 108
      Time, 23, 105, 290
      UPI Reporter, 108
      US News and World Report, 21
   Policy Review, 150, 167
   Psychology Today, 53
   Sports
      Sports Illustrated, 87, 229-231, 234
Male hero, 5, 24, 27, 34-35, 276-278
Mandela, Nelson, 48, 143, 274, 277
Marcuse, Herbert, 204-205
Marianismo, 277
Marín, Luis Muñoz, 274-275, 278
Marquez, Gabriel Garcia, 276-277
Marquez, Rene, 275

Maturation story, 115-117, 119-120, 123-124, 127-128, 130, 132-133
McCarthy, Eugene, 32
McLuhan, Marshall
   global village, 141, 150, 171
   The Guttenberg Galaxy, 150
   Understanding Media, 150
Media of communication, 57
Mediated interpersonal relationships, 56, 69, 74, 261-263
Media friends, 63-73, 75-81
Media packages, 266
Meir, Golda, 29
Methodology, 32, 140, 152, 154, 189, 194, 259
Michael, George, 204-205, 208, 211, 213-214, 217-218
   Bare, 218
   Commercials, 209, 213
      Diet Coke, 214
   Songs, 213-214
Milken, Michael, 50
Miller, C. William, 138
Modernism, 206-207
Monuments, 6
Morales, Jacabo, 277
Moses, 52
Mother Nature, 49, 175, 178
Mother Teresa, 21, 141, 274-276, 278, 280
Mothers, 277, 279
   motherhood, 166
Motion picture, 10, 20, 41-43, 55-56, 65, 68-69
   Characters
      Kruger, Freddy, 52
      Veder, Darth, 52, 60
   Makers
      Allen, Woody, 8, 66
      Coppola, Francis Ford, 72-73
      Spielberg, Steven, 8, 21, 272
      Stone, Oliver, 79
      Truffaut, Francois, 8
   theory, 204

Mourning, *see* grief
Moyers, Bill, 5
MTV, 203-204, 206-208, 210, 214-218
Muñoz, Victoria, 274-276, 278
Music
  influence on advertising, 204-206, 208, 217
  pop, 204
  rock (rock and roll), 66, 69, 73, 81, 282-284, 286, 290-294, 296-398
  stars, 204
  video, 208-211, 215-216
Mystique of faith, 153, 180, 244
Myths/mythology, 2-3, 86, 153, 180, 244
  myth-making, 8, 173
  monomyth, Joseph Campbell, 2, 5, 84, 114-115, 119, 133, 152-153, 156, 159, 169, 173, 176-178, 183
  mythic rhetoric, 154, 173, 179, 187
  mythic vision, 151-152, 154-155, 167
  rescuer myth, 248
  salvation myth, 158
  western, 237, 239

N

Napoleon, 7, 16, 19
Narratives, 86, 98, 100, 105, 109-110, 189, 194, 259
  narrative approach, 242
  narrative structure, 208, 211
National Organization for Women (NOW), 162
Native Americans
  Chief Red Cloud, 50
  Fools Crow, 50
Navratilova, Martina, 89
Needs, 10, 268-269
  psychological, 261
  social, 266-267
Negative elementary character, 160-162, 164-165

Negative transformative character, 162
Newscasters
  Brokaw, Tom, 70, 72
  Chancellor, John, 107
  Cronkite, Walter, 70, 72, 100, 103-107, 110
  Dickerson, Nancy, 107
  Jennings, Peter, 67, 70, 72
  Koppel, Ted, 72
  Murrow, Edward R., 44
  Newman, Edwin, 107
  Pettit, Tom, 106
  Pierpont, Robert, 105-106
  Rather, Dan, 70, 72, 97, 100, 102-103, 105, 109-110, 268
  Reyolds, Frank, 21
  Wallace, Mike, 72
  Walters, Barbara, 72
Newspapers, 38-39, 85, 262
  penny press, 38-39
  Reporters
    Aynesworth, Hugh, 106
    Bell, Steve, 109
    Broder, David, 99
    Daniel, Jean, 106
    Jones, Penn, 106
    Reston, James, 101
    Wicker, Tom, 100-103, 105-106, 108, 110
Neumann, Erich, 155-157, 159
Newton, Sir Isaac, 22
Nicaraguan contras, 158
Nightingale, Florence, 30
North, Oliver, 40
Notoriety, 106
Novello, Antonia Coello, 277

O

Oakley, Annie, 39
Odysseus, 16, 18-19
Ojeda, Luis Francisco, 275-277, 279
Ollier, Francisco, 275
Onassis, Jackie, 32, 79, 104-105, 108

SUBJECT INDEX

Oral cultures/traditions, 6-7, 10, 17-21, 23, 86-87, 252-254, 269

P

Painting, 16
Parasocial relationship, 238-239, 262-263, 266
Patriot, 158
Pentecostal
   community, 242-244, 254-256
   fusion, 256-257
   Pentecostalism, 242-244
   isolation, 243-244, 250, 252, 254-256, 258
   ministry, 242, 246-247, 255-259
   myth, 244-246, 248, 251
   narrative, 242-244, 248, 250-254, 256, 258-260
   style of worship, 243-244, 252
   and television, 251-254, 256-257
Personal style, 266
   clothing/dress, 274
Personality, 3, 21, 56, 71, 73, 266
Photography, 10, 20, 38, 55, 68, 87-88, 262
Plain speaking, 140, 143, 146
Plato, 16, 23
Playwrights
   Aeschylus, 50
   Euripides, 50
   Miller, Arthur, 50
   Shakespeare, William, 7, 16
   Sophocles, 50
Plutography, 191
Politics, 3
Politicians
   Agnew, Spiro, 120
   Aquino, Corazon, 69, 274
   Barry, Marion, 48-49
   Castro, Fidel, 277
   Cuomo, Mario, 199
   Dinkins, David, 49
   Gorbachev, Mikhail, 69, 280
   Hart, Gary, 112
   Humphrey, 126
   Jackson, Jesse, 71
   Kelly, Richard, 137-138
   Koch, Ed, 71, 197, 199
   Marcos, Ferdinand, 69
   O'Neill, Tip, 71
   Perot, Ross, 72
   Riegle, Donald, 139
   Thatcher, Margaret, 29, 48, 274 276
   Tunney, John, 129
   Walesa, Lech, 69
   Yeltsin, Boris, 69
Politics
   Consultants
      Weiner, Leo, 131
   Democratic National Convention, 125
   Protests, 122, 125-126
Pope John Paul I, 73
Pope John Paul II, 21, 73, 274-275, 280
Popieluszko, Jerzy, 74
Positive transformative character, 158-162, 164-165
Postmodernism, 204, 206-211, 214-218
Presidents, U.S.
   Bush, George, 69, 97, 112-113, 274-276, 280
   Carter, Jimmy, 69, 125, 138
   Ford, Gerald, 69
   Grant, Ulysses S., 49
   Harding, Warren G., 181
   Jefferson, Thomas, 79
   Johnson, Andrew, 181
   Kennedy, John F., 9, 20, 52, 64-66, 72, 75, 78-79, 81, 168-170, 180-185, 275, 278
      assassination of, 76, 98, 105, 107-110, 123, 181-184
   Lincoln, Abraham, 23, 38, 49, 52, 79, 181, 272
   Nixon, Richard, 69, 121, 126
   Reagan, Ronald, 21-22, 64, 69-71,

73, 116, 191, 201, 275, 277, 294
Roosevelt, Franklin, 31, 144, 181, 272
Roosevelt, Theodore, 143
Truman, Harry, 143
Washington, George, 7, 19, 38, 49, 70
Print(ing), 3, 6-7, 10, 17-19, 21-23
    moveable type, 19
    printing presses, 18
Prohibition, 174
Pseudo events, 19, 253, 267
public performance, 39
Public relations, 190
Puerto Rico
    culture, 272-280
    English, 272-273, 279
    gender, 277-278
    heroes, 34, 274-276
    media, 273
    politics, 276, 278
    religion, 277-278
    Spanish, 272-273, 277, 279
Purification, 185-186

Q

Qualities admired, 268, 274-275, 278
Queen Elizabeth I, 31

R

Radio, 10, 43-46, 55, 65, 76, 90
    personalities
        Cantor, Eddie, 45
        Crosby, Bing, 45
        Godfrey, Arthur, 44
        Pappas, Ike, 109
Reagan, Ronald, *see* Presidents
Rebirth, 126, 169, 176-179, 182-183
Recycling activity, 106-109
Redeemer, 182-183
Redemption, 121, 124, 177-178, 180, 182-183, 185-186
Religion
    Catholic, 27, 247
    priests, 18
    electronic church, 256-267
    ministers
        Bakker, Jim, 242
        Roberts, Oral, 24
        Robertson, Pat, 242
        Swaggart, Jimmy, *see* Swaggart
    New Testament, 250
    Old Testament, 250
    programming, 242
    saints, 27
Return motif, 116-119, 169
Rexach, Sylvia, 275
Rincón, Felisa, 274
Ritual, 88, 253
Rivera, Danny, 274
Rockefeller, J.D., 135-136
Rodriguez, Gladys, 275, 279
Rogers, Will, 45
Role models, 2, 15, 35, 50, 83, 171, 276, 280
Roosevelt, Eleanor, 275
Rosengren and Windahl
    typology, 261-262, 264
Rubin, Jerry, 112, 131

S

Sagon, Carl, 22
Sanchez, Luis Rafael, 277
Scapegoal, 169-170, 185-187
Schlafly, Phyllis, 149-150
    biography
        The Sweetheart of the Silent Majority, 151
    Books
        A Choice Not an Echo, 151
        Strike from Space, 151
        The Power of the Positive Woman, 154, 157, 159, 164-165
    Eagle Forum, 158, 160, 166-167
    Equal Rights Amendment, 150-151, 154, 157
    "Phyllis Schlafly Report", 154, 160

SUBJECT INDEX 339

and Great Mother archetype, 151-159, 162-165
and negative elementary character, 160-161, 164-165
and negative transformative character, 162
and positive transformative character, 158-162, 164
rhetoric, 152, 154-157, 166-167
Schwarzkopf, General Norman, 3, 112
Sculptures, 16
Seale, Bobby, 130-131
Self, 4, 6, 70-71, 83, 113, 264
   definition of, 270-271, 276, 279-280
Self-made hero, 189-190, 199, 206, 248
Self-reflexivity, 208, 215
Semiotics, 215
Schlesinger, Arthur M., Jr., 3
Sidey, Hugh, 100, 109
"Simulacra", 207, 211, 215
Singers
   Abdul, Paula, 208
   Baez, Joan, 32
   Blades, Ruben, 275, 279
   Bon Jovi, Jon, 211
   Bowie, David, 20, 66, 209
   Brown, Bobby, 211
   Browne, Jackson, 282
   Chayenne, 276-277, 280
   Cher, 66
   Cole, Nat King, 78
   Cole, Natalie, 77-78
   Collins, Phil, 208
   Cooper, Alice, 213
   Dylan, Bob, 70
   Franklin, Aretha, 208
   Gabriel, Peter, 282
   Hutchence, Michael, 211
   Iglesias, Julio, 272
   Jackson, Michael, 2, 11, 16, 21, 268
   Jagger, Mick, 213

Joplin, Janis, 32, 66
Lauper, Cyndi, 67
Lennon, John, 20, 63-64, 71, 75-79, 81
Lennon, Julian, 77
Lunna, 275, 279
Madonna, 16, 21, 58, 70, 72, 75, 81, 198-206, 209, 211-213, 217, 268, 275, 279, 282
Manilow, Barry, 66
McCartney, Paul, 66, 71
Miami Sound Machine, 275
Nazario, Ednita, 275
Nelson, Willie, 67
Newton-John, Olivia, 64
O'Conner, Sinead, 49, 66
Ochs, Phil, 70
Presley, Elvis, 21-22, 64, 70, 72-73, 78-79, 213, 268
Prince, 211
Public Enemy, 49
Rivera, Danny, 275
Simon, Paul, 67
Sinatra, Frank, 21, 139
Springsteen, Bruce, 21, 66, 214, 281
   career stages, 285-287
   songs, 283-295
Sting, 282
Turner, Tina, 21
Wynette, Tammy, 282
Signifiers, 210-211, 215-217
Sister Isolina, 276
Smith, Captain John, 31
Solitary identification, 93, 262, 263-265, 267
Songwriters,
   lyrics, 206, 212-213, 286-287, 289-290, 295-296
   Phil Ochs, 70
Space Travel, 48, *see also* Astronauts, The Challenger, 73
   NASA, 73-74
Spiritual, 30, 54, 73, 123, 131, 242,

244-249, 252, 256
transcendence, 242, 245, 257
Spock, Benjamin, 165
Sports,
    Baseball
        Players
            Boggs, Wade, 89
            Canseco, Jose, 89, 91
            Clemens, Roger, 89
            Clemente, Roberto, 275
            Cobb, Ty, 39
            Dykstra, Lenny, 92
            Gooden, Dwight, 89
            Gomez, Lefty, 89
            Hubble, Carl, 89
            Irvin, Monte, 89
            Jackson, Bo, 91
            Kiner, Ralph, 89
            Mantle, Mickey, 88
            Martin, Billy, 89
            Palmer, Jim, 91
            Rose, Pete, 89, 92, 112
            Ruth, Babe, 223, 268
            Ryan, Nolan, 89, 91, 224
                Endorsements, 228, 234, 238-239
                Fastball, 225, 227-228, 231
                Homecoming, 230, 236, 238
                Media coverage, 224-230, 233, 239
                Strikeouts, 228, 230
                Teams
                    California Angles, 225, 227-230
                    Houston, Astro, 225, 230-232
                    New York Mets, 225-227
                    Texas Rangers, 225, 232-235
                "The "Express", 229, 231
                Trades, 227
            Seaver, Tom, 82, 89
            Valenzuela, Fernando, 275, 279
            Winfield, David, 89
            Yaztremski, Carl, 89
    Basketball
        Players
            Bias, Len, 92
            Bird, Larry, 49
            Johnson, Magic, 66, 91
            Jordan, Michael, 49, 50, 59, 66, 89, 93, 268, 275, 277, 279
    Boxing
        Comacho, Hector, 275
        Commercialization, 91
        Tyson, Mike, 92, 275
    Endorsements, 91
    Football
        Players
            Garrison, Walt, 139
            Montana, Joe, 89, 91
            Nixon, Otis, 92
    Hockey, 89
    Olympics, 144
    reporters, *see* journalists
    Sportscasters, 89-90
        Garagiola, Joe, 139
        McCarver, Tim, 91
        Musburger, Brent, 90
    Sports magazine, 89, 229-230
    stadium as communication medium, 86-87
    Topps bubblegum cards, 88
    trading cards, 83, 87-89
Stanton, Elizabeth Cady, 149
Star
    and consumption, 204-205, 214, 217-218
    definition, 56, 204-205
    dichotonies, 205
    movie, 21, 56, 65, 204
    pop, 206, 217
    postmodern, 206

SUBJECT INDEX

and production, 204-205
rock, 21, 81, 206, 214
system, 262
theory, 204, 211, 217
Stardom, 266
Stewart, Justice Potter, 83
Storytellers, 2, 10, 105
storytelling, 6, 86, 97-99
Sullivan, John L. 39-40
Sunshine, 275
Superheroes, 53-54, 58-61
Batman, 57-59
Green Arrow, 53-54
Green Hornet, 57
Green Lantern, 53-54
Spiderman, 49, 52-53
Superman, 16, 53, 57-60
Wonderwoman, 57
Superstar, 46, 54, 228-230, 233
Swaggart, Jimmy,
Audience, 241-242, 247-249, 252-251, 255
Community, 240-244, 247-250, 254-256, 258-259
Confession, 246
Narrative, 245, 250-251, 253, 259
Rhetoric, 242, 246-248, 254
Sermons, 246-247
Stories, 246, 249-250, 252
Style of delivery, 252, 255
and television, 242, 245, 249, 251-254, 257-258
see also Pentecostal

T

Talent, 266
Telegraph, 10, 38, 40, 262
Telephone, 10
Sports-Phone, 82, 87, 91
Televangelists, 241-242, 247, 258
Television, 20-21, 45-46, 56, 58-59, 69, 91, 76, 90, 99, 101-103, 110, 252-253, 255-257, 266-267
CBS, 102, 104, 108

ESPN, 87
postmodern, 203
shows, 72
talk show hosts, 67, 81
Carson, Johnny, 67
Donahue, Phil, 67
Hall, Arsenio, 49, 67
Leno, Jay, 68
Letterman, David, 16, 21, 64, 67
Povich, Maury, 50
Rivera, Geraldo, 106, 109
Winfrey, Oprah, 66
theory of personality system, 56
usage, 143
Therapy, 85, 111-113, 127-130, 132
Tragic fallacy, 50, 52
Tribe, 250
Trump, Donald,
editorial, 50, 193, 195, 197
New York City, 191-192, 194-195, 197-199
on civil libertarians, 196-197
on criminals, 196-199
and media, 191
on police, 189, 196-198
open letter, 189, 193-195
The Art of the Deal, 191
transformatiuon, 193-194, 198, 201
Trump Princess, 191
Trump Shuttle, 191-192
Trump Tower, 191, 202
Wollman ice skating rink, 192, 199
Turner, Ted, 192
Tuto, Desmond, 141

U

U2, 208-209
Uses and gratifications, 261

V

Values
cultural, 35-36
Victim, 170, 176, 182-183

Victimage, 117, 121, 123, 170
Videotape, 206
Vietnam War, 3, 124-126, 128, 129
  Pentagon Papers, 128
  POW, 125, 128-129
Vigoreaux, Luis, 275
Villains, 8, 50, 185, 196-197
Voyeurism, 8, 212, 255

W

Wapner, Judge Joseph, 23
War, 3, 39, 80, 124-126, 128-129, 173, 178, 180, 184, 194, 231, 272
  Civil War
    Grant, Ulysses, *see* Presidents, 49
    Lee, Robert E. 49
Warhol, Andy, 20
Watergate, 3, 8, 97, 117-118, 126
Wealth, 39, 46, 181, 181-182, 189-193, 199-201
Wedgewood, Josiah, 37
Well-knowness, 92, 269
Western
  Characters
    Autry, Gene, 58
    Cassidy, Hopalong, 58
    Earp, Wyatt, 58
    Hickok, Wild Bill, 58
    Lone Ranger, 249
    Ritter, Tex, 58
    Rogers, Roy, 58
Weyrich, Paul, 159
White, Theodore, 100, 104-106, 108, 110
Whitman, Walt, 105
Winnie the Pooh, 49
Wrinkle theory, 58-59

Y

York, Sergeant, 49

Z

Zaiter, Sandra, 277
Zeitgeist, 206
Zeus, 28